Lecture Notes of the Institute for Computer Sciences, Social Informatics and Telecommunications Engineering 541

The LNICST series publishes ICST's conferences, symposia and workshops.

LNICST reports state-of-the-art results in areas related to the scope of the Institute.
The type of material published includes

- Proceedings (published in time for the respective event)
- Other edited monographs (such as project reports or invited volumes)

LNICST topics span the following areas:

- General Computer Science
- E-Economy
- E-Medicine
- Knowledge Management
- Multimedia
- Operations, Management and Policy
- Social Informatics
- Systems

Amar Seeam · Visham Ramsurrun ·
Suraj Juddoo · Amreesh Phokeer
Editors

Innovations and Interdisciplinary Solutions for Underserved Areas

6th EAI International Conference, InterSol 2023
Flic en Flac, Mauritius, September 16–17, 2023
Proceedings

 Springer

Editors
Amar Seeam (iD)
Middlesex University Mauritius
Flic en Flac, Mauritius

Visham Ramsurrun
Middlesex University Mauritius
Flic en Flac, Mauritius

Suraj Juddoo (iD)
Middlesex University Mauritius
Flic en Flac, Mauritius

Amreesh Phokeer (iD)
African Network Information Centre
Ebene, Mauritius

ISSN 1867-8211   ISSN 1867-822X (electronic)
Lecture Notes of the Institute for Computer Sciences, Social Informatics
and Telecommunications Engineering
ISBN 978-3-031-51848-5   ISBN 978-3-031-51849-2 (eBook)
https://doi.org/10.1007/978-3-031-51849-2

This Springer imprint is published by the registered company Springer Nature Switzerland AG
The registered company address is: Gewerbestrasse 11, 6330 Cham, Switzerland

Paper in this product is recyclable.

Preface

We are delighted to introduce the proceedings of this year's Interdisciplinary Solutions (InterSol) Conference, held in close collaboration with the European Alliance for Innovation (EAI). The sixth edition successfully brought together a diverse group of researchers, practitioners, and stakeholders from around the world. The focus was squarely on fostering interdisciplinary research that addresses pressing challenges in 'underserved areas,' particularly in Africa. The conference's core theme was "Fostering Interdisciplinary Research for Real-World Impact."

Over the course of two days—Saturday, 16th September, and Sunday, 17th September 2023—the conference showcased a compelling selection of 25 peer-reviewed papers. The first track, "Intelligent Systems and Security," featured six papers that explored innovative techniques for enhancing web security and real-time monitoring systems. The second track presented five papers that delved into "Blockchain and Machine Learning Algorithms," with a particular focus on applications in healthcare and economic prediction models. On the second day, the third track examined "Sustainable Technologies and Environmental Impact," sharing insights through five papers that covered topics from solar energy in Africa to advanced microbial eradication technologies. The fourth track, "Digital Learning and Social Adoption," consisted of four papers and dealt with the adoption of e-learning platforms and chatbots. The fifth and final track, "Networking Technology for Social Impact," featured five papers that covered topics from the technical limitations of Free-Space Optical Networks for rural communities to fog computing for maternal healthcare, emphasizing the diverse ways networking technology can benefit society.

Aside from these scholarly contributions, the technical program was enriched by inspiring keynote speeches. Xavier Bellekens, CEO of Lupovis and Chair of the Cyber-Security Group for IEEE UK and Ireland, illuminated the unique challenges and opportunities facing Africa, specifically Mauritius, in the digital landscape. Theophilus A. Benson, Professor of Electrical and Computer Engineering at Carnegie Mellon University, added another layer to the discourse, bringing forth his expertise in improving the performance and availability of computer networks.

Coordination with our esteemed organizing committee—Amar Seeam, Visham Ramsurrun, Suraj Juddoo, Aditya Santokhee, Girish Bekaroo, and Mrinal Sharma—was crucial for the conference's success. We also extend our gratitude to the Technical Program Committee for their diligent work in overseeing the peer-review process, whereby over 100 reviews were conducted (an average of 3 per paper), thereby ensuring a high-quality technical program.

We strongly believe that the conference served as a valuable forum for all researchers, developers, and practitioners, offering a unique platform to discuss a broad spectrum of interdisciplinary challenges and solutions. Based on the contributions and engagements at this year's event, we are confident that future editions of the InterSol conference will continue to be as impactful and thought-provoking.

September 2023

Amar Seeam
Visham Ramsurrun

Conference Organization

Steering Committee

Abdulhameed Danjuma Mambo	Nile University of Nigeria, Nigeria
Cheikh Mouhamed Fadel Kebe	Ecole Supérieure Polytechnique de Dakar, Senegal
Ababacar Ndiaye	Université Cheikh Anta Diop de Dakar, Senegal
Narcisse Talla Tankam	University of Dschang, Cameroon
Assane Gueye	Carnegie Mellon University Africa, Rwanda

Organizing Committee

General Chair

Amar Seeam	Middlesex University Mauritius, Mauritius

General Co-chair

Visham Ramsurrun	Middlesex University Mauritius, Mauritius

TPC Chairs and Co-chairs

Jeroen Steenbeek	Ecopath International Initiative, Spain
Suraj Juddoo	Middlesex University Mauritius, Mauritius
Assane Gueye	Carnegie Mellon University Africa, Rwanda

Sponsorship and Exhibit Chair

Zia Lallmohamed	Middlesex University Mauritius, Mauritius

Local Chair

Girish Bekaroo	Middlesex University Mauritius, Mauritius

Workshops Chair

Aditya Santokhee   Middlesex University Mauritius, Mauritius

Publicity and Social Media Chair

Denisha Seereekissoon   Middlesex University Mauritius, Mauritius

Publications Chair

Waseemah Moedeen   Middlesex University Mauritius, Mauritius

Web Chair

Mrinal Sharma   Middlesex University Mauritius, Mauritius

Panels Chair

Sanjay Matadeen   Middlesex University Mauritius, Mauritius

Technical Program Committee

Adeelah Kodabux   Middlesex University Mauritius, Mauritius
Emamdeen Fohim   University of Bern, Switzerland
Chukwudi Festus Uwasomba   Open University, UK
Preetila Seeam   University of Mauritius, Mauritius
Indeeren Vencatachellum   University of Mauritius, Mauritius
Viraiyan Teeroovengadum   University of Mauritius, Mauritius
Assane Gueye   CMU-Africa, Rwanda
Amreesh Phokheer   Internet Society, Mauritius
Cheikh Mouhamed Fadel Kebe   UCAD, Senegal
Ababacar Ndiaye   UCAD, Senegal
Abdulhameed Mambo   Nile University in Nigeria, Nigeria
Narcisse Talla   University of Dschang, Cameroon
Mouhamadou L. Ba   UADB, Senegal
Cheikh Ahmadou Bamba Gueye   UCAD, Senegal
Maissa Mbaye   UGB, Senegal
Jessica Thorn   University of York, UK
Ghada Bassioni   Ain Shams University, Egypt
Tembine Hamidou   New York University, USA

Charif Mahmoudi	Siemens, USA
Melissa Densmore	University of Cape Town, South Africa
Kieran Tierney	University of Glasgow, UK
Kamila Nieradzinska	University of Strathclyde, UK
Hanan Hindy	Ain Shams University, Egypt
Waseemah Moedeen	Middlesex University Mauritius, Mauritius
Parvesh Seeburrun	Middlesex University Mauritius, Mauritius
Nivede Issur	Middlesex University Mauritius, Mauritius
Karel Veerabudren	Middlesex University Mauritius, Mauritius
Ashley Hoolash	Middlesex University Mauritius, Mauritius
Zia Lallmahomed	Middlesex University Mauritius, Mauritius

Contents

Intelligent Systems and Security

An Analysis of Key Tools for Detecting Cross-Site Scripting Attacks
on Web-Based Systems 3
  Harshad Kissoon and Girish Bekaroo

Characterization of Malicious URLs Using Machine Learning and Feature
Engineering 15
  Sidwendluian Romaric Nana, Didier Bassolé,
  Jean Serge Dimitri Ouattara, and Oumarou Sié

Distracker: An Intelligent Assistant for Real-Time Distracted Driving
Detection and Mitigation 33
  Yash Krishna Sadien and Girish Bekaroo

InSightHub: Intelligent Notification and Status Indicator for Streamlined
Work-From-Home Environments 48
  Pierre Clarel Veerapen, Amar Seeam, and Visham Ramsurrun

Modern Detection Techniques of False Data Injection Attacks in V2X
Communication: A Critical Analysis 66
  Thejmeela Seetamonee and Girish Bekaroo

Enhancing Home Security with Pressure Mat Sensors: A Multi-modal IoT
Approach 81
  Karel Veerabudren, Visham Ramsurrun, Mrinal Sharma, and Amar Seeam

Blockchain and Machine Learning Algorithms

Blockchain Based Mobile-Patient Medical Records Management System 99
  Sarvesh Yugesh Soochit, Visham Ramsurrun, Mrinal Sharma,
  Karel Veerabudren, and Amar Seeam

A Mobile/Tablet App-Based Patient Records Management System Using
Blockchain 113
  Deepesh Rago, Visham Ramsurrun, Mrinal Sharma,
  Karel Veerabudren, and Amar Seeam

Comparative Performance Evaluation of Random Forest, Extreme
Gradient Boosting and Linear Regression Algorithms Using Nigeria's
Gross Domestic Products 131
    M. D. Adewale, D. U. Ebem, O. Awodele, A. Azeta, E. M. Aggrey,
    E. A. Okechalu, K. A. Olayanju, A. F. Owolabi, J. Oju, O. C. Ubadike,
    G. A. Otu, U. I. Muhammed, and O. P. Oluyide

XGBoost Algorithm to Predict a Patient's Risk of Stroke 151
    Sada Anne and Amadou Dahirou Gueye

On the Use of Machine Learning Technique to Appraise Thermal
Properties of Novel Earthen Composite for Sustainable Housing
in Sub-Saharan Africa 161
    Assia Aboubakar Mahamat and Moussa Mahamat Boukar

Sustainable Technologies and Environmental Impact

Solar Energy in Africa - An Overview, with a Focus on Egypt 173
    Manar Mostafa, Fathy El-Shahat, Moritz Riede, and Ghada Bassioni

Projected Hydroclimate Changes over Senegal (West Africa) 187
    Mamadou Lamine Mbaye, Babacar Faye, Bounama Dieye,
    and Amadou Thierno Gaye

Cotton Plant Pests and Phenology Knowledge Management in Côte
d'Ivoire Using Semantic Web Technologies 205
    Kouaho N'Guessan Narcisse Tehia, Sadouanouan Malo,
    Appoh Kouamé, Malanno Kouakou, Kouadio Kra Norbert Bini,
    and Ochou Germain Ochou

Microbial Fuel Cell for the Recovery of Sludge from the Treatment
of Effluents by Electrocoagulation 218
    Maryam Khadim Mbacké, Aby Sy, Cheikhou Kane, and Malick Mbengue

AMETHYST: Advanced Microbial Eradication Through High-Intensity
Yielding Sterilization Technology - A Multipurpose Decontamination
Chamber Using 405 nm HINS Light 233
    Amar Seeam

Digital Learning and Social Adoption

Covid-19 Contact Tracing Application Adoption: A Technology Readiness
Model Perspective 251
    Adesola Tolulope Olaegbe and Muhammad Z. I. Lallmahomed

Secondary School Teachers' Adoption of e-learning Platforms in Post Covid-19: A Unified Theory of Acceptance and Use of Technology (UTAUT) Perspective 264
Rakshay Verma Ramhith and Muhammad Z. I. Lallmahomed

Prof Pi: Using Whatsapp Bots and GPT-4 for Tutoring Mathematics in Underserved Areas 278
Laurie Butgereit and Herman Martinus

VITAL: Virtual Interactive Telegram Assisted Law Clinic 290
Preetila Seeam and Amar Seeam

Networking Technology for Social Impact

Assessing Data Protection Perspectives Among the Residents of Rumphi and Karonga in Northern Malawi Regarding the Use of Unmanned Aerial Vehicles (Drones) for Humanitarian Intervention 313
Rogers Alunge

Study of the Rewiring Factor in an Unstructured P2P 337
Aminata Bagre, Moustapha Bikienga, and Telesphore Tiendrebeogo

Networked Micro-services: Empowering Local Micro-enterprises in a South African Township Through Community Wireless Networks 355
Ndinelao Iitumba, Hafeni Mthoko, Keegan White, Mapule Madzena, Tristan Drummond, David Johnson, and Melissa Densmore

Fundamental Limitations in High Speed and Low Cost Architecture Free Space Optical (FSO) Networks for Rural Populations 379
Djibril Mbaye, Mamadou Diallo Diouf, Wilfried Albert Duniwangda Kiélem, and Omar Gueye

F4PW: Fog Computer for Pregnant Women 391
Amy Sene, Ibrahima Niang, Alassane Diop, and Assane Gueye

Author Index 403

Intelligent Systems and Security

An Analysis of Key Tools for Detecting Cross-Site Scripting Attacks on Web-Based Systems

Harshad Kissoon and Girish Bekaroo[✉] [ID]

Middlesex University Mauritius, Flic-en-Flac, Mauritius
HK759@live.mdx.ac.uk, g.bekaroo@mdx.ac.mu

Abstract. During the previous few years, there has been an escalating number of cyberattacks against web-based systems, that adversely resulted in significant data breaches, losses and reputational damages for businesses. Among these cyberattacks, cross-site scripting attacks, also known as XSS attacks, gained significant attention, which makes is imperative to explore detection methods. Taking cognizance of this issue, this paper reviews and analyses key XSS attack detection tools. To accomplish this objective, the study meticulously examines six distinct tools, notably, web application firewalls, intrusion detection systems, dedicated AI-driven tools, SIEM Systems, honeypots and browser extensions, and provides critical insights on their effectiveness. From our key findings, web application firewalls, AI-driven tools and browser extensions emerged as crucial components for detecting different kinds of XSS attacks, showcasing notable effectiveness. However, it is important to note that the efficacy of these tools may vary depending on factors such as application configurations and update frequency, among others.

Keywords: Cross-Site Scripting · XSS Attacks · Web Application Firewalls · Intrusion Detection Systems · Honeypots · SIEM · AI-Driven Tools · RAST · Browser Extensions

1 Introduction

During the previous years, web-based cyber-attacks have known a consequent increase, representing around 26% of all infractions in 2022 [1]. From 2004 to 2021, the web industry has lost around 9.9 billion records where only in 2019, during the outbreak of COVID 19, more than 1 billion records were lost from big enterprises such as Microsoft and Facebook [2]. Cyber-attacks are expected to increase and become worse throughout the coming years, with a variety of attacks facing web platforms including cross-site scripting, zero-day attack and distributed denial of service attacks, among others [3]. Among these attacks, cross-site scripting attacks, also known as XSS attacks, have gain significant attention recently, where around 40% of web attacks in 2019 involved the use of XSS attacks [4]. Cross-site scripting attacks involves the injection of malicious scripts

© ICST Institute for Computer Sciences, Social Informatics and Telecommunications Engineering 2024
Published by Springer Nature Switzerland AG 2024. All Rights Reserved
A. Seeam et al. (Eds.): InterSol 2023, LNICST 541, pp. 3–14, 2024.
https://doi.org/10.1007/978-3-031-51849-2_1

into the code of a trusted application or website. XSS has been a key security issue in web apps, which can also be executed by script kiddies as the attacks are almost the same and the scripts used during previous attacks can be slightly adapted and used during future attacks. In 2019, the popular game, Fortnite, was prey to the XSS attack combined with a single sign on issue which enabled attackers to steal the in-game currency, player's conversation as a reconnaissance through a fake dummy login page [5]. Consequently, the attacker had access to the player's account which contained personal information, game chats and friend lists. In addition, some users who have their credit cards linked to the game, saw that in-game currency was purchased and then sold for real cash. This attack damaged the reputation of the impacted company, thereby leading to a decrease in its number of users. As such, it is important to effectively detect XSS attacks in a timely manner so that consequences can be minimised. However, limited studies have been done to investigate and analyse between different XSS detection tools. Hence, to address the limitations in published literature, this paper compares and analyses different XSS detection tools. The insights derived as part of the study can be utilized by the web-community and researchers in the endeavour to further enhance web security against XSS attacks.

This paper is structured as follows: In the next two sections, a background on Cross-Site Scripting is provided followed by related works on the review and analysis of such tools in published literature. Then, the methodology used for achieving the purpose of this paper is discussed in Sect. 4. The review and analysis of the key tools for identifying cross-site scripting attacks are provided in Sects. 5 and 6. Conclusion of the paper is finally provided in Sect. 7.

2 Background: An Overview of XSS Attacks and Their Consequences

The term cross-site scripting was introduced by Microsoft security engineers in the year 2000 as hackers utilized JavaScript to run an invisible website within a frame of a legitimate website that would enable them to retrieve data entered on the legitimate website and execute malicious code. Thereafter, it became a popular web-application exploit. An illustration of the key steps involved in a typical XSS attack is provided in Fig. 1.

As depicted in Fig. 1, an intruder attempts to find and exploit a vulnerability within a targeted website that can potentially return malicious JavaScript to users. The attacker then writes (or uses) JavaScript-based malicious codes that can be injected in browsers to exploit the targeted vulnerability that would enable "keylogger with backdoor function-alities" to be installed without the targeted user notices. Eventually, the attacker will be able to gain access to the computer and capture cookies which is exchanged between the browser and server of data. As such, by exploiting XSS vulnerability, attackers are able to impersonate users, perform tasks through victim's account, gain access to sensitive data of a user (e.g., credentials, credit card details) or even deface websites. The key types of XSS attacks are described as follows and are summarised in Table 1:

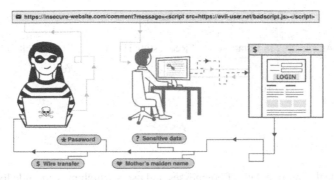

Fig. 1. Cross-Site Scripting Execution [6]

- *Reflected XSS*

    In reflected XSS, which is also known as non-persistent XSS, the code injected by the attacker does not reside on the web server. In reflected XSS, attackers send malicious links to targeted users using different medium such as email, messengers or by embedding the link on other websites, blogs, forums, etc. When a user clicks on the malicious link, the injected code goes to the attacker's web server, and the malicious script is sent back to the victim's browser. Eventually, the code is executed on the victim's browser and the attacker is able to fulfil the intended goal (e.g., stealing confidential information) [7].

- *Stored XSS*

    Stored XSS is also known as persistent XSS attacks and as compared to reflected XSS, the malicious code injected in stored XSS is permanently stored on the servers of targeted websites. Attackers use that method to inject harmful content also known as "payload" written in JavaScript into a vulnerable web app. The scripts inserted are stored permanently on the targeted server or memory. Once any user accesses the information via the web app by knowingly or unknowingly clicking some links, the malicious script is executed, and the attacker is able to access confidential information of the user [8].

- *DOM-based XSS*

    In the Document Object Model (DOM) based XSS, the attack is executed at the client side as compared to the two XSS attacks described above. In this type of XSS attack, the DOM environment in the targeted user's browser is modified so that it crashes or works differently [9]. As such, the page loaded does not change but the code on the client is executed differently due to the modifications within the DOM environment.

- *Induced XSS*

    Induced XSS is the least common type of XSS as compared to the others and is applicable to web applications where HTTP Response Splitting is vulnerability is present on web servers [7]. Attackers exploit this vulnerability by manipulating the HTTP header of the server's response in order to attempt to inject scripts and access confidential information of the victim.

XSS attacks pose various negative issues to both businesses and end users of IT systems [4]. Amongst, data theft is a key issue where successful XSS attacks can enable

Table 1. Summary of the types of XSS attacks.

Type of XSS Attack	In Database	Requesting HTTP	DOM Built in Browser
Reflected		Yes	Yes
Stored	Yes	Yes	Yes
DOM-based			Yes
Induced		Yes	Yes

attackers to steal sensitive data of businesses and users which may include login credentials, personal data and financial data, among others. In addition, XSS attacks can potentially enable attackers to run arbitrary and malicious codes within a victim's browser, leading to unauthorized actions on behalf of the user. Furthermore, XSS can be utilized by attackers to modify contents of legitimate websites whereby defacing them, thus adversely impacting trust and reputation.

3 Related Works

Although numerous studies have been conducted pertaining to detection of web-based attacks, limited work has been done pertaining to the comparisons of detection of Cross-Site Scripting. In a previous study [10], three types of detection to find weaknesses in XSS attacks in web browsers were discussed, namely, static analysis, dynamic analysis, and hybrid analysis. Static analysis involves finding vulnerabilities during the development and testing phases before the web application is deployed to live. Dynamic analysis is the process of checking for any vulnerabilities when the program has been deployed to the live environment and testing is done in a way to simulate attack processes same as an intruder would do. Hybrid analysis is a combination of both static and dynamic analysis to resolve issues found in the static analysis process and provide a better secured web app. Even though the work reviewed these three XSS attack detection types, no comparisons were made between these three approaches. In another paper [11], detection techniques and counter measures against XSS attacks were reviewed. However, reviews were brief, and no comparisons were made.

Another study [12] focused on the detection of SQL injection and XSS vulnerabilities in open-source JAVA web applications using static analysis. However, the approach used for mitigating XSS after the tests resulted in high false positive rate. Moreover, in another study [13], the dynamic analysis approach in JavaScript was used to detect XSS vulnerability in real time. The call graph method was used for finding issues and to derive outputs which were accurate overall. However, both studies focused only on certain XSS vulnerabilities and as such, the reliability of findings are questionable. Another study [14] used the hybrid analysis method to focus on XSS vulnerabilities. For the classification of nodes, static analysis was used and for targeting nodes which are at risk, dynamic analysis was approached. Tests were performed on six web applications built using PHP and the authors did come with proper results. However, the mixture of dynamic and static analysis was found to adversely impact reliability. As such, existing studies performed limited comparison of XSS detection approaches and hence, this study is relevant to undertake.

4 Methodology

The primary source of this paper has been carried out by filtering research databases like previous studies done in this field and some reports published by companies which faces such issues and their loss encountered [15]. The research databases filtered include IEEE Xplore Digital Library, ACM Digital Library, Research Gate, Google Scholar, Science Digest, and some websites such as OWASP and ENISA were explored. The key terms used in the searching process include "XSS detection tools" and "Cross-Site scripting attack detection tools" and "injection detection tools". Following a pool of 54 results, filtering was conducted to assess relevance and meant the context of Cross-Site Scripting. The selected tools are discussed in the next sections.

5 Cross-Site Scripting Detection Tools

Using the methodology described in the previous section, the selected key vulnerability detection tools are discussed as follows:

5.1 Web Application Firewalls (WAFs)

WAFs can be in the forms of hardware or software, and are typically positioned between a web application and the client to filter and monitor incoming and outgoing HTTP traffic [16]. Such tools utilize different approaches in their endeavour to detect XSS attacks. A key approach involves the use of pattern matching algorithms to analyse the content of HTTP requests and responses to look for specific patterns, keywords, or HTML tags commonly associated with XSS attacks. If a request or response contains suspicious patterns, the WAF can block or sanitize the content. Similarly, web application firewalls can also perform contextual analysis, to analyse the context of web requests and responses in order to detect anomalies and suspicious behaviour. For example, WAFs can check if user-supplied data is used inappropriately within HTML tags or if client-side scripts are modified or injected. By understanding the expected behaviour of web applications, WAFs can identify deviations that indicate XSS attacks.

5.2 Intrusion Detection Systems

Another tool used to detect XSS attacks is intrusion detection systems (IDS) [17, 18]. This approach involves capturing network packets that are in movement and then relevant TCP packets that are filtered and selected to detect irregularities. In other words, IDS can help to detect XSS attacks by analysing network traffic and identifying patterns that match known attack signatures to eventually alert system administrators when it detects suspicious activity that may indicate an XSS attack is in progress. To detect XSS attacks specifically, IDS can monitor for suspicious behaviour, such as unexpected input, HTML tags, and JavaScript code. IDS can also analyse HTTP headers and cookies for signs of tampering or injection of malicious code. A previous study [17] applied signature-based detection method on the packets to detect XSS attacks. As part of the same study, SNORT IDS, a tool from Cisco, has been used to monitor incoming and outgoing packet on the network with some additional rules configured so that when an intrusion is detected, an entry alert is written in a snort alert file. When an attacker is attacking a web-based system, the SNORT application analyses the application layer from OSI model to detect if the attacker is modifying the tags of the html and the implementing some malicious scripts in the browser to gain access. Thus, the rules defined in SNORT can detect the attacks and add them in a log file. This detection technique can detect all types of XSS attacks categories. For each rule added in the application, the attacks will be intercepted and logged, however, this method works only on the application layer and in case if no rule has been added for an attack technique, the attacker will be able to cause high damage. Similarly, behaviour-based or anomaly-based detection can also be used, or even integration of hybrid approaches.

5.3 Dedicated AI-Driven Tools

Many recent studies focused on the detection of XSS attacks involving the application of artificial intelligence (AI), machine learning and deep learning techniques to create a range of customised tools. These AI-driven tools can be stand-alone ones that are dedicated to detect XSS attacks in real-time or can be integrated within Runtime Application Security Testing (RAST) tools, that integrate with the application during runtime and monitor its behaviour. These tools can detect and even prevent XSS attacks by analysing the actual execution flow and identifying potential vulnerabilities. Such approaches target accurate real-time detection and isolation of attacks without any adverse effect on the running web app. As part of this endeavour, various studies involved the use of genetic algorithms, hybrid approaches, neural network models and dynamic analysis-based approaches, among others, to enhance the detection accuracy of XSS attacks [19]. For instance, a previous study [20] applied Convolutional Neural Network (CNN) to detect XSS attacks using a typical architecture provided in Fig. 2. The process involved removal of letters from characters in order to produce a new matrix and execute the CNN model process.

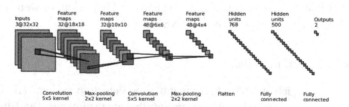

Fig. 2. Architecture of CNN model

The accuracy of different algorithms to detect XSS attacks were also compared as shown in Table 2 where all three algorithms achieved pretty good scores, where the CNN method got above 95% of accuracy and false alarms were minimum.

Table 2. Accuracy of Machine Learning Algorithms.

Algorithm	Score (% Accuracy)
CNN	98.59
RNN	90.25
Logistic Regression	82.12

5.4 Security Information and Event Management (SIEM) Systems

As compared to the AI-driven detection tools discussed above, Security Information and Event Management (SIEM) are more comprehensive security solutions that integrate security information management (SIM) and security event management (SEM) features. These solutions collect, analyse, and correlate security events and logs from various sources across an organization's IT infrastructure, with the goal to provide real-time visibility into security events, facilitate threat detection and response, and support compliance with security regulations. The key features of SIEM include log collection and management, event correlation, threat detection, real-time monitoring, incident response and compliance management, among others. In order to detect XSS attacks, SIEM systems can be configured to analyse logs and network traffic for suspicious patterns and indicators of XSS activity [21]. In addition, SIEM rules and alerts can be set up to trigger notifications or take automated actions when XSS attacks are detected.

5.5 Honeypots

Honeypots, which are tools designed to trap attackers during cyberattacks, can also be utilized in the detection of XSS attacks [22]. For instance, a honeypot can be set up as a web application that contains intentionally vulnerable code, which is designed to be exploited by attackers attempting to inject malicious scripts. The honeypot is then monitored for any suspicious activity, such as unexpected script injections or attempts to access sensitive information. By deploying honeypots on different systems and networks, security professionals can build a comprehensive picture of the XSS threat landscape and develop more effective countermeasures to protect against these attacks. This information can be used to improve the security of real web applications and to develop more effective intrusion detection and prevention mechanisms. A previous study [4] discussed the use of such tools to learn about the pattern and behaviour of attackers during XSS attacks. As part of the study, a low-interaction honeypot was utilized that emulates vulnerabilities that can be exploited through XSS. The key benefit of using this approach is that activities of an attacker can be logged, while also potentially exposing his identity. Nevertheless, this approach also faces the challenges for effectively detecting attackers if they are not successfully lured into the trap or if they hide their identities.

5.6 Browser Extensions

A browser extension is a small program that adds additional features to the browser and these tools can be downloaded from browser stores. Even though there have been various extensions reported for triggering XSS attacks, such tools can also be utilized to detect such attacks and alert the user in a timely manner. These browser extensions attempt to detect XSS attacks by analysing the content of web pages for potential XSS vulnerabilities and in the process, different approaches are used [23]. For instance, some extensions work by injecting a script into the page, which can then monitor user input and outgoing requests for suspicious activity. Some extensions may also use heuristics or pattern matching algorithms to identify potential XSS payloads in the page's HTML, JavaScript, or other embedded content. If a vulnerability is detected, the extension may alert the user and block the malicious script from executing. One such example of an extension is Counter XSS extension for Google Chrome, which enables users to scan web pages for potential XSS vulnerabilities and displays a warning if it finds any suspicious code. Similarly, the "NoScript" extension for Firefox, blocks JavaScript, Java, Flash, and other active content from running on web pages unless the user specifically allows it. This helps prevent XSS attacks by blocking the execution of malicious scripts that could be injected into web pages.

6 Analysis of XSS Attack Detection Tools

The detection tools were critically analysed on how they effectively detect the several types of XSS attacks. Effectiveness was evaluated based on criteria, such as its ability to detect diverse types of XSS attacks, its accuracy in distinguishing between malicious and benign code, its coverage of different types of XSS attacks, such as stored XSS, reflected XSS, or DOM-based XSS, as discussed earlier in this paper. In order to compare and analyse the XSS attack detection tools based on the two criteria above, published papers and literature was thoroughly reviewed and analysed. Results are summarised in Table 3 and findings are discussed in the next sections:

Table 3. Effectiveness of Detection Tools

XSS Detection Tool	Reflected	Stored	DOM-based	Induced
Web Application Firewalls	High	High	Medium	Medium
Intrusion Detection Systems	Medium	Medium	Low	Low
Dedicated AI-Driven Tools	High	High	High	Medium
SIEM Systems	Medium	Medium	Low	Low
Honeypots	Low	Low	Low	Low
Browser Extensions	High	Medium	High	Medium

6.1 Effectiveness of Detection Tools

Among the tools reviewed, WAFs and dedicated AI-tools were found to have relatively high effectiveness in detecting XSS attacks [16]. WAFs are particularly designed to protect web applications from attacks, including XSS. These tools provide a dedicated defense layer and offer comprehensive features like signature-based detection, pattern matching, content inspection, and behaviour monitoring. Even though WAFs are typically used on the server side of web applications, they can directly or indirectly detect stored, reflected, DOM-based and induced XSS attacks. Stored XSS attacks can be detected by analysing the content submitted to the web application and the subsequent delivery of that content to other users and reflected XSS can be detected by inspecting HTTP request parameters and the corresponding server responses to identify malicious input that may be reflected back to the user's browser. In addition, WAFs can also detect induced XSS attacks by identifying and blocking suspicious patterns or content that may attempt to deceive users into executing malicious JavaScript code. Furthermore, even though it is more challenging for WAFs to directly detect DOM-based XSS attacks which requires analysis of JavaScript code execution flow and dynamic manipulation of the DOM, the use of advanced techniques such as heuristics, static analysis, and runtime monitoring can help to identify malicious JavaScript behaviours and block them. As such, WAFs can effectively detect and prevent a range of XSS attacks, thus making them highly effective tools for XSS detection. Similarly, AI-driven tools have similar coverage as WAFs, although there are varying approaches and algorithms used in the process of identifying XSS attacks. Dedicated AI-Driven tools and RAST tools are specifically implemented with the aim analyse runtime behaviour of web applications in order to identify security issues, including XSS and are as such highly effective tools [20]. In addition, a range of algorithms and techniques can be employed to also strengthen detection against a range of XSS attacks. As compared to WAFs, machine learning techniques can also be integrated on the client-side within browser extensions to more effectively detect DOM-based or induced XSS attacks. Nevertheless, data is required to be able to train models and improve accuracy of detection.

Furthermore, browser extensions have the ability to effectively detect the key types of XSS attacks but run on client-side. In other words, browser extensions are generally more focused on user-side protection rather than comprehensive server-side XSS detection. For instance, these tools can analyse the content and source codes of web pages (HTML tags or JavaScript) in real-time and detect instances where user-supplied data is directly inserted into the HTML response without proper sanitization or encoding, to eventually flag such incidents and raise alerts. Moreover, browser extensions can monitor user interactions with web applications and identify instances where user-generated content is stored and displayed on subsequent visits [23]. By scanning the stored content and detecting any suspicious or untrusted script injections, extensions can block the execution of malicious code. Furthermore, these tools can analyse and keep track of changes to the DOM in real-time, detecting any unauthorized modifications or dynamic script insertions that could lead to XSS vulnerabilities. Finally, whilst browser extensions may not directly detect induced XSS attacks, they may warn users about potentially malicious links or suspicious website behaviour, to indirectly detect induced XSS attacks.

On the other hand, IDS and SIEM systems were found to have medium effectiveness to low effectiveness in the detection of different types of XSS attacks. IDS and SIEM systems work by identifying certain indicators or patterns related to XSS attacks whereby assisting in detecting XSS attacks either by analysing logs, network traffic, or event data for suspicious or anomalous behaviour that may indicate an XSS attack. Also, distinguishing between the several types of XSS attacks may not be the focus of IDS and SIEM systems. For instance, although intrusion detection systems can identify certain patterns and anomalies indicative of XSS attempts, they may have limitations in detecting sophisticated or context-specific XSS attacks as compared to dedicated web application security solutions such as WAFs and AI-driven tools. As such, reflected, DOM-based and induced XSS attacks are relatively more challenging to detect using such tools. Similarly, SIEM are more suitable for centralized monitoring and correlation of security events rather than real-time XSS detection. These tools rely on the availability of relevant data and proper configuration to be able to effectively detect XSS attacks and similar to IDS, directly detecting reflected, DOM-based and induced XSS attacks are more challenging.

Finally, honeypots were found to have relatively lower effectiveness as compared to others because of their core focus. The key purpose of honeypots is to lure attackers and gather intelligence on attackers rather than serving as a dedicated XSS detection tool to identify a broad range of XSS attacks. In addition to findings highlighted, it is also important to note that effectiveness of the tools may vary depending on various factors such as the specific tool being used, their configurations, implementations, and update frequency, among others. As such, it is recommended to use a combination of tools and techniques in order to further improve the effectiveness to detect XSS attacks in real-time.

6.2   General Discussions

Overall, analysis showed that AI-driven tools, WAFs and browser extensions are key tools involved in the detection of XSS attacks with relatively higher effectiveness as these tools directly focus on detection of such kinds of attacks. Also, browser extensions are useful tools in the detection of XSS attacks running on the client side as these tools are also easy to install and can potentially detect a range of XSS attacks. Among the various types of XSS attacks, tools have been focusing on directly detecting stored and reflected XSS since these can particularly cause most damages, especially stored XSS attacks. On the other hand, detection tools seem to focus less on induced XSS attacks as these are the least common ones, although the tools attempt to indirectly identify such attacks.

Nevertheless, it is important to note that effectiveness is expected to vary from tool to tool. For instance, there are WAFs available on the market that are expected to be more effective and having more user-friendly interfaces as compared to other WAFs and studying the different tools in practice was beyond the scope of this study. As such, a key limitation of this study is that findings were based on published papers and could be extended by practically using and assessing key tools available on the market in order to derive more critical insights. In addition, more quantitative approaches could be adopted to measure effectiveness. This would help to derive further insights and even better help in decision making related to selection of XSS tools for adoption in practice.

7 Conclusion

This paper reviewed and analysed the effectiveness of six tools to detect different types of XSS attacks on web-based systems. The tools studied are web application firewalls, intrusion detection systems, dedicated AI-driven tools, SIEM systems, honeypots and browser extensions. Among these tools, web application firewalls, dedicated AI-driven tools and browser extensions were found to have a relatively high effectiveness, with the ability to directly or indirectly the different types of XSS attacks studied in this paper, notably stored, reflected, DOM-based and induced XSS attacks. IDS and SIEM systems were found to be relative less effectiveness as these tools work by identifying certain indicators or patterns related to XSS attacks whereby assisting in detecting XSS attacks either by analysing logs, network traffic, or event data for suspicious or anomalous behaviour that may indicate an XSS attack. Finally, honeypots were identified as the least effective tool where their primary focus involves luring and gathering details about the attacker, rather than differentiating between the different kinds of XSS attacks. In addition, it is important to highlight that the effectiveness of XSS attack tools may vary depending on various factors such as the specific applications being used, application configurations, update frequency, and design principles employed. As such, in order to more effectively detect XSS attacks a combination of tools and techniques are recommended. As such, in terms of future works, limitations of this study could be addressed whereby investigating a range of XSS attack detection tools while practically using them in order to quantitatively analyse effectiveness of the tools whereby deriving more critical insights.

References

1. Caitlin, J.: 50 web security stats you should know in 2022. Expert Insights **24** (2022). https://expertinsights.com/insights/50-web-security-stats-you-should-know/. Accessed 12 Nov 2022
2. Brooks, C.: Alarming cyber statistics for mid-year 2022 that you need to know. Forbes (2022). https://www.forbes.com/sites/chuckbrooks/2022/06/03/alarming-cyber-statistics-for-mid-year-2022-that-you-need-to-know/?sh=1f079b247864. Accessed 13 Nov 2022
3. Singh, A., Sharma, A., Sharma, N., Kaushik, I., Bhushan, B.: Taxonomy of attacks on web based applications. In: 2019 2nd International Conference on Intelligent Computing, Instrumentation and Control Technologies (ICICICT) (2019)
4. Rodríguez, G., Torres, J., Flores, P., Benavides, D.: Cross-site scripting (XSS) attacks and mitigation: a survey. Comput. Netw. **166**, 106960 (2020)
5. Dizdar, A.: What is XSS? Impact, types, and prevention. Bright Security (2022). https://brightsec.com/blog/xss/. Accessed 11 Nov 2022
6. PortSwigger. Cross-site scripting. PortSwigger (2022). https://portswigger.net/web-security/cross-site-scripting. Accessed 10 Jan 2023
7. Malviya, V., Saurav, S., Gupta, A.: On security issues in web applications through cross site scripting (XSS). In: 2013 20th Asia-Pacific Software Engineering Conference (APSEC) (2013)
8. Abazi, B., Hajrizi, E.: Practical analysis on the algorithm of the cross-site scripting attacks. In: 2022 29th International Conference on Systems, Signals and Image Processing (IWSSIP) (2022)

9. OWASP. DOM Based XSS. OWASP (2022). https://owasp.org/www-community/attacks/DOM_Based_XSS. Accessed 28 Nov 2022
10. Marashdih, A., Zaaba, Z.: Cross site scripting: detection approaches in web application. Int. J. Adv. Comput. Sci. Appl. **7**(10) (2016)
11. Madhusudhan, R.: Cross channel scripting (XCS) attacks in web applications: detection and mitigation approaches. In: 2018 2nd Cyber Security in Networking Conference (CSNet) (2018)
12. Shar, L., Tan, H.: Automated removal of cross site scripting vulnerabilities in web applications. Inf. Softw. Technol. **54**(5), 467–478 (2012)
13. Toma, T., Islam, M.: An efficient mechanism of generating call graph for JavaScript using dynamic analysis in web application. In: 2014 International Conference on Informatics, Electronics & Vision (ICIEV) (2014)
14. Shar, L., Tan, H., Briand, L.: Mining SQL injection and cross site scripting vulnerabilities using hybrid program analysis. In: 2013 35th International Conference on Software Engineering (ICSE) (2013)
15. Veerabudren, K., Bekaroo, G.: Security in web applications: a comparative analysis of key SQL injection detection techniques. In: 2022 4th International Conference on Emerging Trends in Electrical, Electronic and Communications Engineering (ELECOM) (2022)
16. Garn, B., Lang, D., Leithner, M., Kuhn, D., Kacker, R., Simos, D.: Combinatorially xssing web application firewalls. In: 2021 IEEE International Conference on Software Testing, Verification and Validation Workshops (ICSTW) (2021)
17. Gupta, K., Singh, R., Dixit, M.: Cross site scripting (XSS) attack detection using intrustion detection system. In: 2017 International Conference on Intelligent Computing and Control Systems (ICICCS) (2017)
18. Frenz, C., Yoon, J.: XSSmon: a perl based IDS for the detection of potential XSS attacks. In: 2012 IEEE Long Island Systems, Applications and Technology Conference (LISAT) (2012)
19. Kaur, J., Garg, U., Bathla, G.: Detection of cross-site scripting (XSS) attacks using machine learning techniques: a review. Artif. Intell. Rev. 1–45 (2023)
20. Bhardwaj, A., Chandok, S., Bagnawar, A., Mishra, S., Uplaonkar, D.: Detection of cyber attacks: XSS, SQLI, phishing attacks and detecting intrusion using machine learning algorithms. In: 2022 IEEE Global Conference on Computing, Power and Communication Technologies (GlobConPT) (2022)
21. Kim, J., Kwon, H.: Threat classification model for security information event management focusing on model efficiency. Comput. Secur. **120**, 102789 (2022)
22. Rahul, S., Vajrala, C., Thangaraju, B.: A novel method of honeypot inclusive WAF to protect from SQL injection and XSS. In: 2021 International Conference on Disruptive Technologies for Multi-disciplinary Research and Applications (CENTCON) (2021)
23. Gupta, S., Gupta, B.: XSS-immune: a Google chrome extension-based XSS defensive framework for contemporary platforms of web applications. Secur. Commun. Netw. **9**(17), 3966–3986 (2016)

Characterization of Malicious URLs Using Machine Learning and Feature Engineering

Sidwendluian Romaric Nana(✉), Didier Bassolé, Jean Serge Dimitri Ouattara, and Oumarou Sié

Laboratoire de Mathématiques et d'Informatique, Université Joseph KI-ZERBO, Ouagadougou, Burkina Faso
sidnanaroma@gmail.com
https://www.ujkz.bf

Abstract. In this paper, we use Machine Learning models for malicious URL detection and classification by Feature Engineering techniques. These models were implemented with scikit-learn using Random Forest, Support Vector Machine and XGBoost classifier algorithms. Our models were trained, tested, and then optimized with a dataset of 641,125 URLs (benign, defacement, malware, and phishing) from several sources including ISCX-URL2016 from the University of New Brunswick. Through iterative learning, we have shown that the combination of certain hyperparameters and features reduces the false positive rate. The results obtained are interesting with scores close to 100% and zero false positive rates for some types of URLs. We then evaluated the performance of the models against other related works models.

Keywords: Malicious URL · Characterization · Feature Engineering · Detection · Classification

1 Introduction

Development of the web has been accompanied by new practices and new uses, among which we can note the multiplication of websites as well as a diversification of contents. Web sites handle sensitive data (passwords, credit card identifiers, banking transaction information, etc.), making them a prime target for hackers and malicious users. The latter multiply initiatives to steal sensitive information, usurp the identity of internet users or cause an interruption of services, thus discrediting the company that owns the website and damaging its brand image.

There are a wide variety of threats on the web and the techniques used to implement these threats are also diverse. Among the techniques, we can mention website defacement, SQL injections, DDoS attacks, ransomware, formjacking, spamming, use of phishing Uniform Resource Locator (URL), other malicious links, etc. According to the Internet Security Threat Report in 2019, attacks

© ICST Institute for Computer Sciences, Social Informatics and Telecommunications Engineering 2024
Published by Springer Nature Switzerland AG 2024. All Rights Reserved
A. Seeam et al. (Eds.): InterSol 2023, LNICST 541, pp. 15–32, 2024.
https://doi.org/10.1007/978-3-031-51849-2_2

using URL propagation techniques are increasing in number of attacks as well as in level of dangerousness [1].

An URL is an address that identifies a resource on the World Wide Web. An URL has two main components [2]:

- protocol identifier (indicates the protocol to be used);
- resource name (specifies the IP address with port or domain name where the resource is located)

The protocol identifier and resource name are separated by a *colon* (:) and *two slashes* (//), as in the Fig. 1 (inspired by [2]).

Malicious URLs lead users to unsolicited resources, phishing sites or web pages from which attackers can execute malicious code on their victims' computers or install malware. It is therefore imperative to detect these malicious URLs before internet users use them, which can compromise resources. Several approaches have been encountered in the literature for the detection of malicious URLs, notably methods based on signatures [2,3]. These methods have proven ineffective in recognising new malicious URLs in view of the increasing number of attacks and web pages consulted daily in the world[1].

Face of this new reality of massive data and widespread web attacks, methods for detecting malicious URLs have improved through analysis of URL behaviour and attributes. These new methods leverage the performance of Machine Learning (ML) and Deep Learning (DL) algorithms to detect and classify URLs [2,4,5]; but the challenges of false positives and false negatives remain.

The main purpose of this work is to improve the performance of ML models in the detection of malicious URLs and their classification (benign, defacement, phishing, malware). This includes reducing the False Positive Rate (FPR) and detecting new malicious URLs whose dangerousness has not yet been proven.

The rest of this paper is organised as follows: Sect. 2 deals with related works. Section 3 presents our methodological approach. Section 4 shows our implementation environment and the results obtained. We conclude this work in Sect. 5.

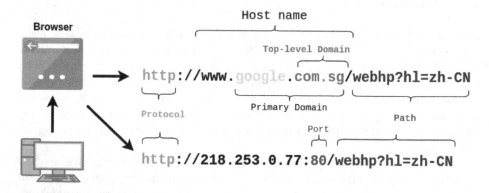

Fig. 1. Example of a URL

---

[1] https://www.akamai.com/fr.

2   Related Works

The web is one of the largest sources of information and knowledge sharing in the world. Unfortunately, attacks on the web are diverse. We can cite among others: formjacking, phishing, SQL Injection, ransomwares, File inclusion, DDoS attacks. In view of the enormous political, economic and social stakes of the web, content security has always been at the heart of the preoccupations of governments and the research world. Several approaches have been experimented in the literature to protect internet users against malicious URLs, some more effective than others, using different techniques. In this section, we will review what is known about detecting malicious URLs.

2.1   Malicious URL Detection by Signature Based Approach

Malicious URLs are a common and serious threat to cyber security. Malicious URLs lead to websites that host unsolicited content (spam, phishing, drive-by downloads, etc.) and lure unsuspecting users into becoming victims of scams (financial losses, theft of private information and installation of malware), which account for billions of dollars in losses each year [2].

For the detection of malicious URLs, the most intuitive method is blacklisting. This method has been explored in the literature for many years [6–8]. URL blacklists are databases of all known malicious URLs. However, the blacklisting method has significant shortcomings. Indeed, it is very difficult to keep the list of malicious URLs up to date. This method is therefore ineffective in detecting new URLs. Furthermore, cybercriminals use URL reduction services to hide their malicious URLs [9], thus bypassing blacklisting checks.

Signature based approach is a variant of the blacklisting method. A signature is assigned to the most common attacks. Some intrusion detection systems use this type of approach. They have the ability to scan web pages for suspicious signatures. Search for malicious signatures could also be done by analysing the dynamic execution of web pages [3]. For example the creation of an unusual process, a multiple redirection. This type of manipulation must be done in a controlled environment in order to limit the risks in case of an attack during the execution of web pages. On the other hand, if an attack is not launched automatically during the execution of the page, we could be faced with a case of false negative.

2.2   Malicious URL Detection by Behaviour Based Approach

Method of detecting malicious URLs based on behavioural analysis techniques adopts machine or deep learning algorithms to classify URLs according to their behaviour [5].

The behaviour and characteristics of URLs can be divided into two main groups: static and dynamic. In their studies [10,11], authors presented methods for analysing and extracting the static behaviour of URLs, including lexical features [2,12]; content based features [13–15]; host based features [16]. The machine learning algorithms used in these studies are online learning algorithms and SVMs. Malicious URLs detection using dynamic actions of URLs is presented in [17,18].

Gerardo Canfora et al. [18] proposed a method to count system calls (write, send, mkdir, open, etc.) when a web page is executed. The study of these system calls showed that malicious web pages execute system calls more frequently than others; then SVM was used to classify malicious and benign web pages. Maheshwari, Shantanu et al. [19] conducted a comparative study of Machine Learning algorithms in detecting malicious URLs. This study which consisted of a binary classification (malicious and benign URLs) revealed good performance for the Random Forest.

Nguyet Quang Do et al. [4] analysed the performance of various DL algorithms in detecting phishing activities. Four DL algorithms were involved in this empirical study: Deep Neural Network (DNN), Convolutional Neural Network (CNN), Long Short-Term Memory (LSTM), and Gated Recurrent Unit (GRU).

Clayton Johnson et al. [20] conducted a performance comparison between ML aglorithms (Random Forest, Classification and Regression Tree, k-Nearest Neighbor, Support Vector Machine, Logistic Regression, Linear Discriminant Analysis, AdaBoost, and Naive Bayes) and DL models (Fast.ai, Keras-TensorFlow across CPU, GPU, and TPU architectures).

Experimentation with RF, Fast.ai, Keras-TensorFlow proved more successful for binary classification (benign and malicious URLs) and mutiple classification (benign URLs, spam, defacement, phishing, malware) [20].

2.3   URL Feature Representation Methods

Doyen Sahoo et al. [2] have listed some key attribute groups for malicious URL detection. Their paper is a review of the literature on malicious URL detection techniques using ML. However, particular emphasis is placed on URL feature representation approaches. There are three types of URL feature found in previous works: lexical features, host-based features and content-based features.

Lexical features are obtained from the properties of string URL. The main idea is that the constitution of string URL could tell us more about its malicious nature. This idea is further supported as cyber-criminals attempt to circumvent blacklisting through URL obfuscation techniques [2]. The most common lexical features include the statistical properties of the string URL such as the length of the URL, the length of each URL component (Hostname, Top Level Domain, Primary Domain, etc.), the number of special characters, etc.

Host-based features describe the properties of the website host as identified by the hostname part of the URL. They enable us to determine approximately "where" malicious sites are hosted, "who" owns them and "how" they are managed. The use of host-based features is based on the assumption that malicious web sites may be hosted in less reputable hosting centers, on machines that are not those of conventional hosting providers, or via disreputable registrars [16]. The following properties can be considered when building host-based features: WHOIS information, Host location, connection speed, presence of URL on a blacklist.

Content-based features determine whether a URL is malicious by analyzing the content of the corresponding web page and the events (or actions generated) after a URL has been visited. The workload for these features is quite heavy, as a lot of information needs to be extracted, and access to this URL may pose security problems. Features based on the content of a website can be extracted mainly from its HTML content and the use of JavaScript [13–15]. Hyunsang Choi et al. [14] identify some native JavaScript functions that are often used in XSS (cross-site scripting) attacks and others web malware. These functions are escape(), eval(), link(), unescape(), exec() and search(). More recently, Yao Wang et al. [15] have applied deep learning techniques to build feature representations from JavaScript code.

A more complete survey of URL representation methods can be found in reference [2]. overall, we can see from this literature review that detection and classification of malicious URLs have been the subject of research for several years. The techniques used are constantly evolving, leading to improved results. Unfortunately, very few studies use False Positive Rate (FPR) as a metric for evaluating the approaches they propose. However FPR is a very important criterion for assessing the quality of an anomaly or hazard detection system. Furthermore, the absence of a study on the importance score of features makes it impossible to understand the contribution of each feature to the overall performance of models. Our detection approach, based on Feature Engineering with lexical features as representation method, aims to overcome the shortcomings identified in the related works.

3 Methodological Approach

In this section, we present our approach for detecting and classifying malicious URLs. We will first present the feature extraction technique (Feature Engineering), the dataset, and finally our learning models.

3.1 Feature Engineering

Feature Engineering is the process of transforming raw data into features that better represent the underlying problem for predictive models, thereby improving the accuracy of the model on data that it has not yet been subjected to.

In other words, feature engineering is the process of creating new features from existing data for machine learning models. These features are extracted from the accumulated raw data and then transformed into formats suitable for the machine learning process. For this purpose, knowledge of the data domain is essential, as well as programming and mathematical skills are also mandatory to apply feature engineering methods.

Performing feature engineering involves the following steps for machine learning algorithms:

- data preparation;
- exploratory analysis;
- Benchmarking.

3.2   Presentation of the Dataset and Exploratory Analysis

Our dataset contains 651,191 URLs divided into four (04) categories:

- 428,103 benign URLs;
- 96,457 website defacement URLs;
- 94,111 phishing URLs;
- 32,520 other malicious URLs.

Benign URLs: benign URLs are legitimate URLs that do not lead to any infectious websites and do not attempt to inject any harmful malware into the user's computer.

Defacement URLs: defacement of a website usually means changing some aspect of the site, such as its visual appearance and some of its content. The hacker takes advantage of a security hole and manages to change the content of a web page without the permission of the original 'owner' of the site [21].

Malware URLs: malware URLs lead the user to a malicious website that usually installs malware on the user's device, which can be used for identity theft, file corruption and even keystroke logging, etc.

Phishing URLs: phishing URLs usually entice the user to visit a fake website (with a URL that looks like the real one) and try to steal as much information as possible. Sometimes a simple typo in a URL can easily lead a user to a phishing site. Phishing can be defined as the hacker's intention to steal private information such as credit card numbers and other digital identities using social engineering techniques [22].

URLs of our dataset come from various sources[2,3,4] including [23] [URL dataset (ISCX-URL2016) of the University of New Brunswick]. The dataset is presented as a table with 651,191 rows and 2 columns. Table 1 presents the first three (03) rows of the dataset. A summary analysis of the dataset allows us to observe the proportion of URLs according to the type of threat: benign, defacement, phishing, malware (Table 2).

Table 1. Dataset overview

URLs	TYPE
br-icloud.com.br	phishing
mp3raid.com/music/krizz_kaliko.html	benign
bopsecrets.org/rexroth/cr/1.htm	benign

Table 2. Distribution of URLs

URLs	Number of Urls	Percentage
benign	428,103	65.74%
defacement	96,457	14.81%
phishing	94,111	14.45%
malware	32,520	5.00%
TOTAL	**651,191**	**100%**

In accordance with the Feature Engineering techniques outlined above, pre-processing and exploratory analysis of the data are important steps. The preprocessing on our dataset allowed us to detect duplicates (duplicated lines). The removal of these duplicates reduced our dataset to 641,125 rows distributed as shown in the Table 3.

Table 3. Distribution of URLs after preprocessing

URLs	Number of Urls	Percentage
benign	428,080	66.77%
defacement	95,308	14.86%
phishing	94,092	14.68%
malware	23,645	3.69%
TOTAL	**641,125**	**100%**

For a binary analysis of URLs (benign/malicious), we can group URLs of type (phishing, defacement, malware) under the common denomination "malicious URLs". Table 4 shows us the results of this binary division.

---

[2] https://www.phishtank.com/developer_info.php.

[3] https://github.com/faizann24/Using-machine-learning-to-detect-malicious-URLs/tree/master/data.

[4] https://research.aalto.fi/en/datasets/phishstorm-phishing-legitimate-url-dataset.

Table 4. Benign/malicious URLs

URLs	Number of Urls	Percentage
benign	428,080	66.77%
malicious	213,045	33.23%
TOTAL	**641,125**	**100%**

The knowledge of the field of study (URLs) led us to take an interest in certain elements of the URLs. Thus, we were interested in the domain extensions (Top-Level Domain) most represented in the URLs of our dataset according to the type of threat (phishing, malware, defacement). The extensions encountered are among others the most popular domain extensions such as: .com, .net, .org, .info. However, there are country domain extensions such as: .jp, .uk, .ru, .br, .de, .it, etc.

The rest of the exploratory analysis of our dataset was based on the practices of malicious users. Thus we were interested in the presence in our dataset of:

- the use of IP addresses in URLs;
- the length of URLs;
- the use of URL shortening services;
- the use of the "@" character in URLs;
- hidden redirects using "//" symbols;
- the use of dashes (-) in the domain name;
- use of the https protocol;
- use of the term "https" in the domain name;
- the use of suspicious words such as: *banking, secure, login, account, bank, confirm, paypal, update, hacking, hacker*, etc.

By applying the different steps of Feature Engineering as described above, we have extracted features from our dataset that we believe are relevant for our models. These features are summarised in the Table 5.

Table 5. List of features

FEATURES	TYPE	DESCRIPTION
1. length_url	Integer	Number of characters in the URL
2. number_letter	Integer	Number of alphabetical characters
3. numeric_character	Integer	Number of numeric characters
4. number_dot_com	Integer	Number of ".com"
5. number_dot_co	Integer	Number of ".co"
6. number_dot_net	Integer	Number of ".net"
7. number_of_slash	Integer	Number of "/" in the URL
8. number_of_uppercase	Integer	Number of uppercase characters in the URL
9. number_of_lowercase	Integer	Number of lowercase characters in the URL
10. number_dot_info	Integer	Number of ".info"
11. number_of_https	Integer	Number of "https" in the URL
12. number_of_http	Integer	Number of "http" in the URL
13. num_of_www_point	Integer	Number of "www."
14. special_characters	Integer	Number of special characters as &, _, #, ;…
15. num_of_percentage	Integer	Number of character "%" in the URL
16. question_mark	Integer	Number of "?" in the URL
17. number_of_dash	Integer	Number of "-" in the URL
18. dash_in_domain	Integer	Use of "-" dashes in the domain name
19. num_equal_symbol	Integer	Number of "=" in the URL
20. percentage_character	Real	Ratio of "%" in the URL
21. space_in_url	Boolean	Use of "%20" in the URL path
22. suspicious_words	Boolean	Presence of sensitive words in the URL
23. ip_adress	Boolean	Presence of the IP address in the URL instead of the domain name
24. protocol_https	Boolean	Use of the https protocol
25. https_domaine	Boolean	Use of the term "https" in the domain name
26. number_sub_domain	Integer	Number of subdomain in the URL
27. short_link	Boolean	Use of short links in the URL
28. number_at	Integer	Number of symbol "@" in the URL
29. num_double_slash	Integer	Hidden redirection by using the // symbol in the URL
30. hostname_length	Integer	Hostname length
31. path_length	Integer	Path length in the URL
32. first_directory_length	Integer	First directory length in the URL
33. tld_length	Integer	Length of the Top Level Domain in the URL

3.3 Implementation Scenario

Authors of the ISCX-URL2016 dataset propose 79 features that can be extracted from the URLs [24]. Contrary to other works in the literature [5, 20], our hypothesis is that the plethora of features does not necessarily contribute to the performance of models. Thus the reduction of features could improve the performances. Using Feature Engineering techniques, we have defined 33 features (see Table 5) that are essential for the detection and classification tasks which is a contribution of this research paper.

For this study, three (03) scenarios were implemented:

- detection of malicious URLs in general;
- detection of malicious URLs specifically (defacement, phishing, malware);
- classification of malicious URLs.

The detection of malicious URLs consisted of a binary classification. Using the dataset presented in Table 4, a model was trained to predict whether a URL is benign or not. For the second scenario, the aim was to create datasets by contrasting benign URLs with other types of URLs. Thus, three (03) datasets were created with the following pairs: (benign - malware), (benign - defacement), (benign - phishing). These datasets were trained to recognise one type of URL (phishing, defacement, malware). For the third scenario, we used the dataset presented in Table 3 and trained the model to recognize the four (04) classes of URLs (benign, phishing, defacement, malware). Figure 2 illustrates the description of scenarios.

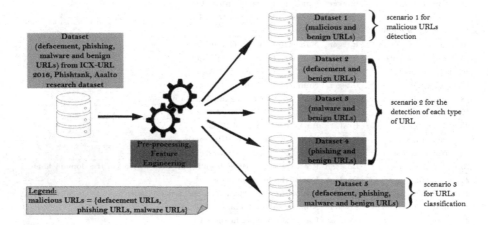

Fig. 2. Scenarios description

4   Implementation and Results

4.1   Execution Environment and Tools Used

We carried out this work using *open source* tools. The programming language used to write the scripts is Python with the Jupyter Notebook editor. Our work environment is a laptop computer with the Ubuntu 20.04 LTS operating system and the following characteristics:

- Processor: Intel® Core™ i7-4810MQ CPU @ 2.80 GHz × 8 threads
- RAM: 16 Gb
- Graphics: NVE6/Intel® HD Graphics 4600 (HSW GT2)

From our dataset, we performed data processing, feature extraction and model implementation tasks. To do so, we wrote python scripts with a set of libraries such as Pandas[5], Numpy[6], Matplotlib[7], Scikit-learn[8], xgboost[9], Seaborn[10], Pickle[11].

4.2 Models Implementation

Before submitting our datasets to the different learning models: Random Forest Classifier (RF), Support Vector Classification (SVC), XGBoost Classifier (XGB) (see table 6), we subdivided them into two parts: training data (train set) and test data (test set) with *train_test_split* function in scikit-learn. This data subdivision principle, which we describe below, has been respected for all types of experimentation (binary and multi-label classification). These are:

- spliting: Train set 80%, Test set 20%, Shuffle = True, random_state = 5. **shuffle** is a boolean that indicates whether or not the data will be shuffled before it is subdivided. **random_state** is an integer that controls the level of mixing of the data.
- determination of features (X_train, X_test) and labels (y_train, y_test)
- saving variables in different files in csv format. This ensures the reusability of these variables for all training models

By doing this we ensure that the different models have been trained and tested on the same variables. The comparison of the results of these models was done on a fairness basis. By tuning the hyperparameters, we obtained the best performance of each model before comparing them on the basis of scores and metrics. Figure 3 presents model implementation process. Table 6 presents a summary of the comparative analysis of some ML models [26–32].

---

[5] https://pandas.pydata.org/.

[6] https://numpy.org/.

[7] https://matplotlib.org/.

[8] https://scikit-learn.org/stable/.

[9] https://xgboost.readthedocs.io/en/stable/.

[10] https://seaborn.pydata.org/.

[11] https://docs.python.org/3/library/pickle.html.

Table 6. Summary of the comparative analysis of some ML models

Model	Advantages	Disadvantages
RF	no overfitting	complex in the implementation
	requires less data pre-processing	requires more computing resources for optimal implementation
	supports large data volumes	longer processing time
	suitable for multi-label classification	less intuitive as the number of decision trees increases
XGB	regularization	a model with multiple hyperparameters
	parallel processing	a bad extrapolation tool
	supports large data volumes	
	handling of missing values	
	integrated crossvalidation	
SVM	SVM works best when the data are linear	choosing the right kernel is not easy
	SVM is more efficient in high dimensions	SVM does not perform well on a large dataset
	Complex problems can be solved by SVM	Hyperparameters are difficult to adjust
	SVM is not sensitive to outliers	It is difficult to visualise the impact of hyperparameters

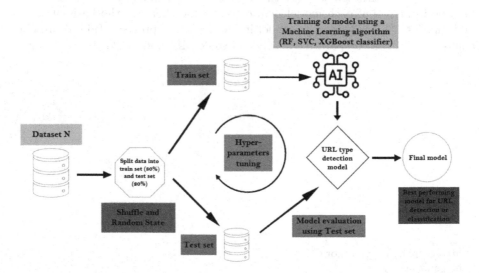

Fig. 3. Model implementation process

4.3   Scores and Metrics

To evaluate the models, we used the performance indicators of the algorithms. These indicators are based on the confusion matrix presented in Table 7. The confusion matrix is used to summarise and visualise the results of a classification problem.

Table 7. Confusion matrix

	Negative prediction	Positive prediction
Benign	TN (True Negative)	FP (False Positive)
Malicious	FN (False Negative)	TP (True Positive)

- TN: benign URLs are identified as benign
- FP: benign URLs are identified as malicious
- FN: malicious URLs are identified as benign
- TP: malicious URLs are identified as malicious

Among the performance indicators based on the confusion matrix, we have *Precision* (Pr), *Recall* (Re), *F1-score* (F1), *Accuracy* (Acc), *False Positive Rate* (FPR), *False Negative Rate* (FNR):

$$Pr = \frac{TP}{TP + FP} \tag{1}$$

$$Re = \frac{TP}{TP + FN} \tag{2}$$

$$F1 = 2 * \frac{Precision * Recall}{Precision + Recall} \tag{3}$$

$$Acc = \frac{TP + TN}{TP + FP + TN + FN} \tag{4}$$

$$FPR = \frac{FP}{FP + TN} \tag{5}$$

$$FNR = \frac{FN}{FN + TP} \tag{6}$$

FEATURE IMPORTANCE refers to a set of techniques for assigning scores to the features (input characteristics) of a predictive model that indicate the relative importance of each feature in the prediction. Feature importance scores can be calculated for regression problems as well as for classification problems. Thus in our study, the features with the highest importance scores for the detection of each type of URL are:

- **defacement URL**
    - number of times the term "http" appears in the URL;
    - number of times the term "www." appears in the URL;

- number of times the equal symbol "=" appears in the URL;
- length of the first directory of the URL;
- number of special characters in the URL.

– **malware URL**
  - number of times the term "http" appears in the URL;
  - path length of the URL;
  - URL length;
  - presence of the IP address in the URL instead of the domain name;
  - whether or not the https protocol is used;
  - number of subdomains in the URL.

– **phishing URL**
  - number of times the term "www." appears in the URL;
  - path length of the URL;
  - number of directories in the URL (Number of "/" in the URL);
  - presence of sensitive words in the URL (e.g. "secure", "account", "webscr", "login", "ebayisapi", "sign inv, "banking", "confirm", "hacker", "pirate", "paypal", ...);
  - length of the Top Level Domain in the URL.

Since we worked with unbalanced data (not all classes had the same number of examples), we will use the F1-score metric to compare the performance of different models. We will also compare the models on the basis of the FPR values. In Tables 8, 9, 10, 11, 12, we present results of our implementation.

Table 8. Malicious URLs detection

(a) Results of malicious URLs detection

	RF	SVC	XGB
Accuracy	97.8%	91.6%	97.1%
FPR	1.13%	2.15%	1.24%

(b) Comparaison of F1-score values

	RF	SVC	XGB
Benign	0.98	0.94	0.98
Malicious	0.97	0.86	0.95

Table 9. Defacement URLs detection

(a) Results of defacement URLs detection

	RF	SVC	XGB
Accuracy	100%	99.2%	99.9%
FPR	0.02%	0.24%	0.03%

(b) Comparaison of F1-score values

	RF	SVC	XGB
Benign	1.00	1.00	1.00
Defacement	1.00	0.98	1.00

Table 10. Malware URLs detection

(a) Results of malware URLs detection

	RF	SVC	XGB
Accuracy	99.9%	99.4%	99.9%
FPR	0.02%	0.01%	0.03%

(b) Comparaison of F1-score values

	RF	SVC	XGB
Benign	1.00	1.00	1.00
Malware	0.99	0.94	0.99

Table 11. Phishing URLs detection

(a) Results of phishing URLs detection

	RF	SVC	XGB
Accuracy	**97.2%**	90.4%	**96.6%**
FPR	**1.15%**	1.77%	**1.13%**

(b) Comparaison of F1-score values

	RF	SVC	XGB
Benign	**0.98**	0.94	**0.98**
Phishing	**0.92**	0.67	**0.90**

Table 12. Multi-label classification of URLs

(a) Results of multi-label classification URLs

	RF	SVC	XGB
Accuracy	**97.2%**	89.1%	**96.2%**

(b) Comparaison of F1-score values

	RF	SVC	XGB
Benign	**0.98**	0.94	**0.98**
Defacement	**0.99**	0.92	**0.98**
Malware	**0.95**	0.83	**0.92**
Phishing	**0.91**	0.58	**0.87**

4.4 Comparison with Related Works

As we can only compare elements with a common base, we present in the Tables 13, 14, 15 some of the results of our work in comparison with those of the state of the art on similar fields of study (detection of malicious URLs, phishing and multi-label classification of malicious URLs). Our results with Random Forest and XGBoost models are similar to those of [19] and [20]; they outperform some Deep Learning models [4] and [25] with very low false positive rates.

Table 13. Comparison of results with the state of the art - benign vs. malicious

Ref.	Dataset	Models	FPR
[5]	10 000 URLs	RF[tr. Acc: 99.77%]	12.037%
[5]	470 000 URLs	RF[tr. Acc: 96.28%]	–
[12]	–	RF [Acc: 95%]	8.15%
[19]	450 000 URLs	RF [F1: 99%]	–
[20]	19 072 URLs	RF [Acc: 98.68%]	–
Our model	**641 125 URLs**	**RF [Acc: 97.8%; F1: 98%]**	**1.13%**

Table 14. Comparison of results with the state of the art - benign vs. phishing

Ref.	Dataset	Models	FPR
[4]	–	DNN [Acc: 97.29%]	3.01%
[4]	–	CNN [Acc: 96.56%]	3.50%
[4]	–	LSTM [Acc: 97.2%]	1.80%
[4]	–	GRU [Acc: 96.7%]	2.48%
[25]	Phishtank	RNN-LSTM [Acc: 97.4%; F1: 96.4%]	–
[25]	web crawler	RNN-LSTM [Acc: 96.8%; F1: 96.2%]	–
Our model	**ISCX-URL2016**	**RF [Acc: 97.2%; F1: 97%]**	**1.15%**

Table 15. Comparison of results with the state of the art - multi-label classification

Ref.	Dataset	Models
[14]	–	KNN [Acc: 93.11%]
[20]	19 072 URLs	fast.ai [Acc: 96.77%]
Our model	**641 125 URLs**	**RF [Acc: 97.2%; F1: 97%]**

5   Conclusion

As a result of this work, we have shown that reducing the number of features (from 79 to 33) improves the performance of models (RF, SVC, XGBoost) in detecting and classifying malicious URLs. This confirms our hypothesis formulated in Sect. 3.3. Then, thanks to the feature importance scores, we observed the contribution of the features to the performance of the models. Three (03) features appear on all the experiments as having major contributions:

- number_of_http: number of times the term "http" appears in the URL;
- num_of_www_point: number of times the term "www." appears in the URL;
- path_length: path length of the URL.

Furthermore, the use of ML models to determine these criteria also contributes to the scientific debate on the explainability of artificial intelligence models. All of which reinforces our view that decision tree models such as RF and XGBoost, if well optimised with the different hyperparameters, perform well in detecting malicious URLs. Another lesson that we draw from this work is that despite the modest hardware resources (see Sect. 4.1), the performance of the models is satisfactory.

In terms of perspectives, we plan to train our models and to study their performance with URLs from the Burkinabe cyberspace. To do so, we will set up a strategy to collect URLs from websites hosted in Burkina Faso or dealing with Burkinabe content in order to constitute a dataset of URLs by type (benign, defacement, malware, phishing). Then, we will deepen the reflection on the detection of phishing attacks by proposing other models or by further refining the extraction of features on this type of URL. Finally, we will extend the study to other types of attacks, in particular SQL injections and cross-site scripting (XSS).

References

1. Internet Security Threat Report. https://docs.broadcom.com/doc/istr-24-2019-en. Accessed 13 June 2022
2. Sahoo, D., Liu, C., Hoi, S.C.H.: Malicious URL detection using machine learning: a survey (2017). https://doi.org/10.48550/arXiv.1701.07179

3. Moshchuk, A., Bragin, T., Deville, D., Gribble, S.D., Levy, H.M.: SpyProxy: execution-based detection of malicious web content. In: Proceedings of 16th USENIX Security Symposium on USENIX Security Symposium. USENIX Association, Boston (2007)

4. Do, Q.N., Selamat, A., Krejcar, O., Yokoi, T., Fujita, H.: Phishing webpage classification via deep learning-based algorithms: an empirical study. Appl. Sci. **11**(9210) (2021). https://doi.org/10.3390/app11199210

5. Xuan, C.D., Nguyen, H.D., Nikolaevich, T.V.: Malicious URL detection based on machine learning. Int. J. Adv. Comput. Sci. Appl. (IJACSA) **11**(1) (2020)

6. Seifert, C., Welch, I., Komisarczuk, P.: Identification of malicious web pages with static heuristics. In: 2008 Telecommunication Networks and Applications Conference, ATNAC 2008, Australasian, pp. 91–96. IEEE (2008)

7. Sinha, S., Bailey, M., Jahanian, F.: Shades of grey: on the effectiveness of reputation-based blacklists. In: 2008 3rd International Conference on Malicious and Unwanted Software, MALWARE 2008, pp. 57–64. IEEE (2008)

8. Sheng, S., Wardman, B., Warner, G., Cranor, L.F., Hong, J., Zhang, C.: An empirical analysis of phishing blacklists. In: Proceedings of Sixth Conference on Email and Anti-Spam (CEAS) (2009)

9. Chhabra, S., Aggarwal, A., Benevenuto, F.: The phishing landscape through short URLs. In: Proceedings of the 8th Annual Collaboration, Electronic messaging, Anti-Abuse and Spam Conference. ACM (2011)

10. Ma, J., Saul, L.K., Savage, S., Voelker, G.M.: Identifying suspicious URLs: an application of large-scale online learning. In: Proceedings of the 26th Annual International Conference on Machine Learning, pp. 681–688. ACM (2009)

11. Eshete, B., Villafiorita, A., Weldemariam, K.: BINSPECT: holistic analysis and detection of malicious web pages. In: Keromytis, A.D., Di Pietro, R. (eds.) SecureComm 2012. LNICST, vol. 106, pp. 149–166. Springer, Heidelberg (2013). https://doi.org/10.1007/978-3-642-36883-7_10

12. Joshi, A., Lloyd, L., Westin, P., Seethapathy, S.: Emphusing lexical Features for malicious URL detection - a machine learning approach. arXiv (2019). https://arxiv.org/abs/1910.06277

13. Hou, Y.-T., Chang, Y., Chen, T., Laih, C.-S., Chen, C.-M.: Malicious web content detection by machine learning. Expert Syst. Appl. **37**, 55–60 (2010)

14. Choi, H., Zhu, B.B., Lee, H.: Detecting malicious web links and identifying their attack types. In: Proceedings of of the 2nd USENIX Conference on Web Application Development (USENIX Association) (2011)

15. Wang, Y., Cai, W., Wei, P.: A deep learning approach for detecting malicious Javascript code. Secur. Commun. Netw. **9**(11), 1520–1534 (2016). https://doi.org/10.1002/sec.1441

16. Ma, J., Saul, L.K., Savage, S., Voelker, G.M.: Beyond blacklists: learning to detect malicious web sites from suspicious URLs, In: Proceedings of the 15th ACM SIGKDD International Conference on Knowledge Discovery and Data Mining. ACM (2009)

17. Tao, Y.: Suspicious URL and device detection by log mining. Master of science thesis, Applied Sciences, School of Computing Science, Simon Fraser University (2014)

18. Canfora, G., Medvet, E., Mercaldo, F., Visaggio, C.A.: Detection of malicious web pages using system calls sequences. In: Teufel, S., Min, T.A., You, I., Weippl, E. (eds.) CD-ARES 2014. LNCS, vol. 8708, pp. 226–238. Springer, Cham (2014). https://doi.org/10.1007/978-3-319-10975-6_17

19. Shantanu, Janet, B., Joshua Arul Kumar, R.: Malicious URL detection: a comparative study. In: International Conference on Artificial Intelligence and Smart Systems (ICAIS) (2021)
20. Johnson, C., Khadka, B., Basnet, R.B., Doleck, T.: Towards detecting and classifying malicious URLs using deep learning. J. Wirel. Mob. Netw. Ubiquit. Comput. Dependable Appl. JoWUA **11**, 31–48 (2020)
21. Romagna, M., van den Hout, N.: Hacktivism and website defacement: motivation, capabilities and potential threats. In: 27th Virus Bulletin International Conference, Madrid, Spain (2017)
22. Verma, R., Das, A.: What's in a URL: fast feature extraction and malicious URL detection. In: 3rd ACM on International Workshop on Security and Privacy Analytics (IWSPA 2017), Scottsdale, Arizona USA, pp. 55–63 (2017)
23. University of New Brunswick. https://www.unb.ca/cic/datasets/url-2016.html. Accessed 20 June 2022
24. Mamun, M.S.I., Rathore, M.A., Lashkari, A.H., Stakhanova, N., Ghorbani, A.A.: Detecting malicious URLs using lexical analysis. In: Chen, J., Piuri, V., Su, C., Yung, M. (eds.) NSS 2016. LNCS, vol. 9955, pp. 467–482. Springer, Cham (2016). https://doi.org/10.1007/978-3-319-46298-1_30
25. Dutta, A.K.: Detecting phishing websites using machine learning technique. PLOS One 1–17 (2021). https://doi.org/10.1371/journal.pone.0258361
26. https://www.upgrad.com/blog/random-forest-classifier/ . Accessed 18 Mar 2023
27. https://www.analyticsvidhya.com/blog/2021/06/understanding-random-forest/ . Accessed 18 Mar 2023
28. https://www.rebellionresearch.com/what-are-the-advantages-and-disadvantages-of-random-forest . Accessed 18 Mar 2023
29. https://www.simplilearn.com/what-is-xgboost-algorithm-in-machine-learning-article . Accessed 18 Mar 2023
30. http://theprofessionalspoint.blogspot.com/2019/03/advantages-and-disadvantages-of-svm.html . Accessed 18 Mar 2023
31. https://towardsdatascience.com/everything-about-svm-classification-above-and-beyond-cc665bfd993e . Accessed 18 Mar 2023
32. https://towardsdatascience.com/pros-and-cons-of-various-classification-ml-algorithms-3b5bfb3c87d6 . Accessed 18 Mar 2023

Distracker: An Intelligent Assistant for Real-Time Distracted Driving Detection and Mitigation

Yash Krishna Sadien and Girish Bekaroo[✉] [iD]

Middlesex University Mauritius, Flic-en-Flac, Mauritius
YS417@live.mdx.ac.uk, g.bekaroo@mdx.ac.mu

Abstract. Distracted driving is a significant issue that has sparked extensive research in detection and mitigation methods, with previous studies exploring physiological sensors but finding them intrusive, leading to the rise of computer vision techniques, particularly deep learning, for non-intrusive and real-time detection. While recent research has demonstrated the accuracy of MobileNetV2-tiny in detecting distracted driving using the State Farm Distracted Driver Detection Dataset, there remains a need to address real-time mitigation strategies and cognitive distractions. To bridge these gaps, this study developed the 'Distracker' prototype, an intelligent agent using deep learning and eye-tracking algorithms to detect and mitigate manual, visual, and cognitive distractions in real-time, incorporating multi-modal alerts to enhance road safety. Through real-life driving experiments, participants engaged in various distracted driving tasks, and the Distracker prototype demonstrated a remarkable overall classification accuracy of 93.63%. These findings highlight the potential practical implementation of the Distracker prototype in vehicles, making significant strides in detecting and mitigating distracted driving and contributing to the larger goal of accident reduction and promoting secure driving experiences for all.

Keywords: Distracker · Distracted Driving · Deep Learning · Confusion Matrix · In-Vehicle Intelligent Assistant

1 Introduction

Recently, distracted driving has raised significant safety concerns in the automotive industry, with increases of up to 22% in alarming road accidents, including both fatal crashes and near-crashes [1]. Recent statistics reveal a concerning surge of 8% in road accidents due to distracted driving over the course of five years, encompassing both fatal collisions and alarming near-crash scenarios [2]. This trend translates to an approximate average of 2,924 distraction-affected fatal traffic crashes per year [2]. This issue does not only affect road safety but also has economic implications, resulting in substantial losses in developing countries [3]. Moreover, distracted driving leads to higher rates of road fatalities, injuries, and emotional distress for individuals and their loved ones [4].

A. Seeam et al. (Eds.): InterSol 2023, LNICST 541, pp. 33–47, 2024.
https://doi.org/10.1007/978-3-031-51849-2_3

Despite the deployment of the Advanced Driver Assistance Systems (ADAS), distracted driving remains an ongoing challenge [5]. A recent study has shown that drivers engage in distracting activities, even with ADAS features, leading to near-crashes or crashes [6]. The study revealed that 68% of drivers using lane-keeping assistance were still prone to distractions like texting or adjusting the radio, resulting in near-crashes or crashes [6]. Similarly, another study identified that 45% of drivers involved in crashes with vehicles equipped with lane departure warning and forward collision warning systems were distracted by activities such as using a mobile phone or reaching for an object, leading to failures in responding to warnings [7].

Additionally, ADAS systems are often limited to premium vehicles, leaving a significant number of drivers without access to these safety features [8]. Even in vehicles equipped with high levels of driving autonomy, such as the autonomous Uber and Tesla Model S vehicles, human drivers are susceptible to distraction, resulting in accidents [9]. Therefore, there is a critical need to detect and mitigate driver distraction in real-time to ensure road safety. In order to address this overarching problem, a hybrid approach is adopted by integrating Convolutional Neural Networks (CNNs) and eye movement tracking. By leveraging these technologies, this study aims to detect and mitigate manual, visual, and cognitive distractions in real-time through a proposed prototype, while attempting to surpass limitations of previous approaches. As such, the outcome of this study is expected to advance driver safety, reduce the impact of distracted driving, and bring benefits to individuals, and societies.

This paper is structured as follows: In the next section, background on distracted driving is provided and prior research is critically reviewed. Subsequently, the implementation process of the proposed prototype is thoroughly explained in Sect. 3 prior to discussing the evaluation method used to rigorously assess the prototype's effectiveness. The paper then concludes with a concise summary of findings and discussions.

2   Background and Related Works

Distracted driving is a prevalent issue, with research indicating that a significant number of drivers engage in secondary tasks while driving [10]. There are different types of distraction, and these are:

- *Manual distraction*
   Drivers are manually distracted when they take their hands off the steering wheel to perform secondary tasks, such as using vehicle controls, drinking, eating, smoking, reaching for in-vehicle objects, or manipulating mobile phones while driving.
- *Visual distraction*
   Visual distraction occurs when a driver takes his eyes off the road, often due to the presence of attention-grabbing stimuli. For example, a study sponsored by the AAA Foundation which used in-vehicle video recordings of teen drivers found that glancing away from the forward roadway for more than 2 s increased the risk of a crash or near-crash to over two times that of normal driving [11].

- *Cognitive distraction*
  Cognitive distraction occurs when the focus required for safe driving is redirected toward other secondary tasks, resulting in divided attention [12]. An example of cognitive distraction during driving is when a driver's mind is preoccupied with thoughts, daydreaming, or engaging in complex mental tasks unrelated to driving. This can include being deep in thought about personal issues, work-related stress, planning future events, or even being engrossed in intense conversations or arguments with passengers. Cognitive distractions divert the driver's attention away from the road and can impair their ability to react to sudden changes or hazards, increasing the risk of accidents.

As related works, existing studies have utilized various physiological sensors to detect cognitive distractions while driving. For example, Electroencephalography (EEG) signals have been employed to measure brain activity [13], Electrocardiogram (ECG) signals have recorded heart activity [14], and physical eye-tracking sensors have monitored eye pupil diameter [15], providing valuable insights such readings fluctuations during the detection process. However, these sensors can be intrusive and potentially cause additional distractions for the driver [16]. In contrast, computer vision techniques, particularly deep learning, have gained popularity for non-invasive, accurate and faster real-time detection of distracted driving [17].

Recent research has focused on utilizing deep learning algorithms to detect driver distraction using the State Farm Distracted Driver Detection Dataset, a comprehensive and widely used dataset in the field [16, 18]. The dataset encompasses many driving scenarios, providing valuable insights into real-world distracted driving situations [19]. Among the tested models in existing literature, the MobileNetV2-tiny has demonstrated exceptional accuracy (99.88%) in detecting distracted driving [20].

This highlights the effectiveness of deep learning models in addressing the challenges of distracted driving detection. Although previous studies have primarily focused on detecting distracted driving, there exist gaps in simultaneously addressing mitigation strategies and exploring cognitive distraction detection. Additionally, the utilization of deep learning models to detect driver cognitive distractions using eye-tracking features requires further investigation [21].

3   Implementation of the Distracker

To address the gaps discussed in the previous section, this study aims to develop an in-vehicle smart agent prototype capable of accurately detecting and mitigating manual, visual, and cognitive distractions in real-time using deep learning and eye-tracking algorithms. By incorporating multimodal audio and visual alerts, the proposed system aims to effectively reduce distracted driving instances, thus enhancing road safety, reducing accidents, and improving driver focus and attention. By addressing these research gaps, the study intends to contribute to the advancement of techniques for detecting and mitigating distracted driving, ultimately making driving a safer and more secure experience for everyone on the road.

In order to fulfil the key objective of this paper, an in-vehicle assistant called 'Distracker' was designed and implemented. Distracker uses an eye-tracking algorithm and a deep learning model to detect distracted driving and issue real-time multi-modal warnings to the driver in order to encourage safe driving. The architecture of the system is depicted in Fig. 1. The Distracker utilizes a Raspberry Pi 3 B+ for data processing, with two webcams capturing driver images from the front and side views of the driver. The Driver Distraction Detection Algorithm analyses frames and triggers multi-modal warnings (audio and LED) for distractions. Components include Logitech cameras, speakers, a Max7219 LED matrix, and a Xiaomi power supply. The Distracker prototype was developed using Python programming language and various open-source libraries such as Dlib, OpenCV2, TensorFlow lite, Pygame, and Luma matrix library. Google Collab Pro and Google Drive were also used for training the model and storing the dataset respectively. The presentation of the two tables below provides a comprehensive insight into the development process of the Distracker prototype (Tables 1 and 2).

Table 1. Libraries used in the development of the Distracker prototype and their corresponding functions.

Libraries Used	Description/Purpose
Dlib	Employs precise machine learning techniques for accurate detection and mitigation of distractions, covering tasks like facial recognition for monitoring pupil movement and object detection
OpenCV2	Provides tools and algorithms for real-time vision tasks, aiding distraction identification
TensorFlow lite	Enables real-time execution of deep learning models for distraction detection on embedded devices
Pygame	Employs auditory alerts to engage users, enhancing the effectiveness of the Distracker through immersive audio feedback
Luma matrix library	Generates visual alert messages on LED matrices, translating distraction insights into immediate and comprehensible visual cues
Google Collab Pro	Enables model training and testing, enhancing the Distracker algorithm development
Google Drive	Facilitates secure storage for essential datasets and model checkpoints, supporting the iterative development of the Distracker solution

To assemble this setup, the Raspberry Pi 3b+ was utilized, accompanied by its luma LED matrix, power bank, speakers, and dual cameras. These elements were securely installed on the car's dashboard, as showcased in Fig. 2. The incorporation of flex tape ensured stable attachment, preventing any risk of components detaching. Notably, the two cameras were strategically positioned to effectively capture complete frames of the individual.

In terms of the underlying mechanism to detect distractions, a hybrid approach was adopted by integrating Convolutional Neural Networks (CNNs) and eye movement tracking. As part of the integrated approach, Distracker uses the State Farm Distracted Driver Detection (SFDDD) Dataset, which consists of 10 classes representing distracted

Table 2. Components used in the development of the Distracker prototype and their corresponding functions.

Hardware Components Used	Description/Purpose
Dual Logitech webcams	Capture real-world video frames for processing, aiding in detecting driver distractions
Logitech audio speaker	Generate audio alerts for timely and effective driver warnings
Max7219 LED matrix	Produce visual alerts, enhancing driver awareness
Raspberry Pi 3 B+ circuit board	Process camera frames, facilitating distraction detection and output provision
Xiaomi Power source	Supply power to the Distracker, ensuring continuous functionality

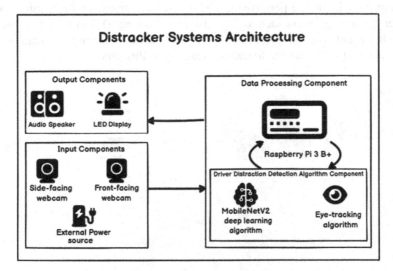

Fig. 1. Architecture of Distracker system.

driving scenarios [19]. The dataset includes 22,424 labelled training photos and 79,726 unlabelled test images. After the dataset was downloaded from Kaggle, pre-processing was done. Images were horizontally flipped to the right-hand side for testing in Mauritius, where vehicles are driven on the right-hand side. The labelled train dataset was used and split into 70% for training, 30% for validation, and 30% for testing. The resulting train, validation, and test folders split consisted of 15,696, 3,363, and 3,363 images respectively.

In addition, Distracker implements the MobileNetV2 architecture which is a deep-learning model used to process images of specific dimensions. A representation of the architecture is illustrated in Fig. 3 and it was applied to the State Farm Distracted Driver Detection (SFDDD) dataset by resizing the images to meet the required dimensions.

Fig. 2. Illustrates the positioning of various components within the setup.

The architecture includes bottleneck layers and an output dense activation layer. Transfer learning was employed by training the MobileNetV2 model with the dataset and modifying it for improved performance. This involved removing the original model's last layer and adding layers such as GlobalAveragePooling2D, Dense Activation Relu, Dropout layer, and Softmax layer. The modified architecture had ten classification nodes, which was found to be suitable to transfer learning in this study.

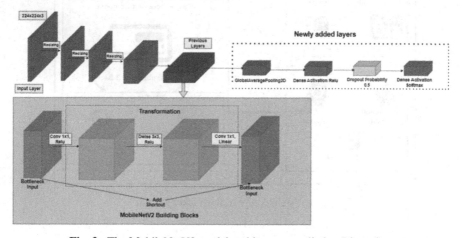

Fig. 3. The MobileNetV2 model architecture applied to Distracker.

After preprocessing, the model was trained using high-performance serverless GPU units on Google Collab Pro. Transfer learning and similar metrics from recent existing research were employed to train additional layers integrated into the MobileNetV2 pretrained model [20]. Categorical cross-entropy was chosen as the loss function, and model checkpointing was utilized to save the best model based on validation loss. During the training process, there was a notable improvement in accuracy. By the 30th epoch, the model's accuracy showed a substantial increase from 78.70% to 99.66%. The validation accuracy began at a high level of 92.47% and reached 98.12% in the final epoch. Both training and validation losses consistently decreased, with the validation loss reducing from 0.2344 to 0.0521. Overall, the model demonstrated exceptional performance in effectively generalizing distracted driving scenarios (Fig. 4).

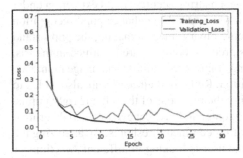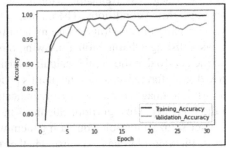

Fig. 4. a) Shows the training and validation loss curves for the trained MobileNetV2 model b) Shows the training and validation accuracy curves for the trained MobileNetV2 model.

To further enhance the model's performance, the last 8 layers of the pre-trained model were unfrozen and fine-tuned using the validation dataset for 20 epochs. The fine-tuned model achieved high accuracy values on both the training set 99.77% and the validation set 99.45%, accompanied by low losses (0.0092 and 0.0244, respectively) (Fig. 5).

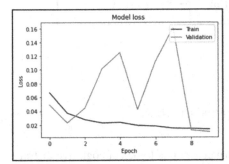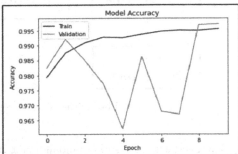

Fig. 5. a) Shows the training and validation loss curves for the fine-tuned MobileNetV2 model b) Shows the training and validation accuracy curves for the fine-tuned MobileNetV2 model.

The fine-tuned model was converted to a TensorFlow lite format to enable deployment on the Raspberry Pi 3B+. During the conversion process, a technique called quantization was applied. This involved removing unnecessary layers and optimizing the model to achieve a favorable balance between accuracy and speed. The quantization process ensured that the model maintained an average appropriate frame rate of 3.78 fps and a memory size 13.819 megabytes (MB), making it well-suited for deployment on the Raspberry Pi 3B+.

In the integrated approach utilized by Distracker, an eye-tracking algorithm is also involved, and the schema is depicted in Fig. 6. In terms of the process involved, the algorithm analyses the input image frames to identify faces and eyes using a face detector and facial landmarks shape predictor. The algorithm then converts the frames to grayscale, focuses on a single face, and extracts the eye region by identifying specific points within the facial landmarks. A calibration process determines the optimal threshold for converting the extracted eye frame into a binary image, ensuring accurate pupil extraction under varying lighting conditions. Then, binarization is applied to enhance pupil recognition by converting the eye frames into monochrome binary images, making the pupil stand out as a distinguishable blob. Following this process, contours are identified in the iris, and the centroid of the pupil is calculated using contour recognition and image moments, providing information about the pupil's position. Red crosshair marks are also added to the original image frame, accurately indicating the positions of the left and right pupils. In the final step, the algorithm calculates horizontal and vertical eye ratios to determine the user's gaze direction, comparing them with predefined thresholds. By analyzing the ratios, the algorithm can establish whether the user is looking in different directions or at the centre, ensuring reliable and precise gaze direction determination.

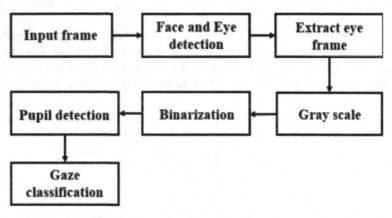

Fig. 6. The eye-tracking algorithm schema

The eye-tracking algorithm monitors the driver's pupils to detect cognitive distractions by analysing eye fixations. A continuous fixation duration exceeding 300 ms indicates cognitive distraction [21]. The algorithm tracks the position of the driver's pupils using red crosshair marks, enabling the analysis of pupil metrics for the detection of cognitive distraction as shown in the Fig. 7a) and b) below.

The Distracker underwent hardware integration to seamlessly fit into the car and was tested for its ability to generate real-time multimodal warnings, addressing functional requirements. For non-functional requirements, the prototype was optimized for portability, real-time response, lightweightness, and accuracy. Accuracy and responsiveness of distraction detection were quantitatively assessed and compared with ground truth data to validate distracted driving detection. Moreover, the model's accuracy and generalization capabilities were rigorously tested against an independent validation dataset.

Fig. 7. a) Shows user looking at centre b) Shows user cognitively distracted in eye fixations.

4 Evaluation Method

As part of evaluation, the accuracy of the Distracker prototype in detecting and mitigating manual, visual, and cognitive distractions in real-time was evaluated. For this, an experiment was conducted whereby involving participants who had to perform distracted driving tasks on a straight rural road and then data on true/false positives/negatives were collected based on the warnings produced by Distracker in order to derive the confusion matrix. For the experiment, ethical clearance was obtained from the Mauritius IT REC of Middlesex University Mauritius campus to prioritize safety of the participants involved. To conduct this assessment, an experiment was setup involving participants who were recruited via email. These participants were then asked to complete a consent form, signifying their interest in participating. Subsequently, they were provided with a health screening form, and a driving license form. This comprehensive approach ensured that participants met the necessary criteria for involvement.

A total of 20 participants, including 10 members of the public and 10 students from Middlesex University Mauritius Campus, took part in the prototype evaluation to meet the number requirements as past study [22]. The evaluation experiment was conducted in Flic-en-Flac, Mauritius, specifically at Morcellement Ramiah, The Waterway Residence, and Jardin d'Anna on straight road. Health screenings were conducted to ensure participants' suitability for the study and their driving licenses were checked to ensure their eligibility to participate in the experiment.

As key procedures of the experiment, participants received detailed information about the experiment entailing driving a passenger car equipped with the Distracker prototype on an actual road. Each participant then performed a series of distracted driving tasks while following clear instructions. These tasks are listed as follows:

- C0: Safe Driving
- C1: Texting Right
- C2: Talking on the phone right
- C3: Texting left
- C4: Talking on the phone left
- C5: Operating radio

- C6: Drinking
- C7: Reaching behind
- C8: Hair and Makeup
- C9: Talking to a passenger
- Cognitive distraction

The set of tasks underwent a repetition process twice, resulting in a total of 20 tasks performed (10 tasks for evaluating advisory multimodal warnings and 10 tasks for assessing cautionary multimodal warnings). When assessing advisory multimodal warnings, successful task completion necessitated participants to engage the brakes after the initial multimodal alert. If braking took place before the alert, it was considered a failure, requiring the task to be performed again.

Regarding the evaluation of cautionary multimodal warnings, accomplishing tasks successfully required participants to apply the brakes after the intensified multimodal alert. Conversely, if braking occurred before this heightened alert, it constituted a failure, leading to the task being repeated. During the evaluation, the prototype's performance in deep learning, and the warnings it generated across different modes were captured. The collected questionnaire data underwent careful examination to ensure reliability and validity. The collected data were analysed using ANOVA in SPSS to compare the means of the measured dependent variables. The Bonferroni test was used to identify groups with significantly different means, guided by the ANOVA results. The p-value was employed to test the null hypothesis and determine if there were any significant differences between the means. Eventually, accuracy was determined using the following formula:

$$Accuracy = \frac{(True\ Positives + True\ Negatives)}{(True\ Positives + False\ Positives + True\ Negatives + False\ Negatives)}$$

5 Results and Discussions

5.1 Performance and Accuracy Assessment in Real-Life Context

The accuracy of the built-in distraction detection algorithm within Distracker was assessed by analyzing the warnings it produced during real-life experiments, using the evaluation method discussed in the previous section. A total of 20 distracted tasks were performed, with 10 tasks used to generate advisory multi-modal warnings and another 10 tasks for generating cautionary multi-modal warnings. Additionally, the eye-tracking algorithm's performance was evaluated using a cognitive distraction detection task called the N-back task, as described by a previous study by Biondi et al. (2017) [23]. In this evaluation, participants were required to memorize a sequence of digits presented audibly through a speaker and spell out the second-to-last digit while driving. The evaluation results were presented in a confusion matrix, which indicated the true positives and true negatives for various distracted activities. These findings offer valuable insights into the effectiveness of the integrated deep learning and eye-tracking algorithm for accurately classifying distracted driving tasks in real-life situations (Fig. 8).

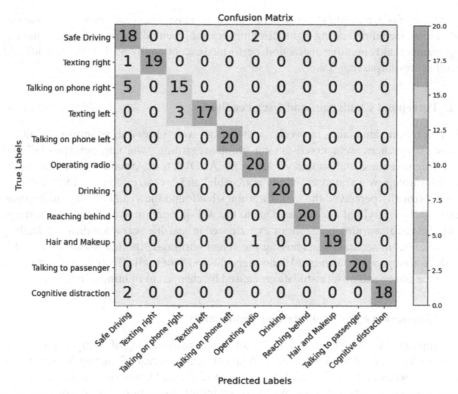

Fig. 8. The classification confusion matrix for all distracted driving tasks evaluated in the real-life experiment.

Table 3. F1 score, Recall and Precision Results following experiment.

Classes	Precision	Recall	F1 Score
C0: Safe Driving	0.6923	0.90	1
C1: Texting Right	1	0.9500	1
C2: Talking on the phone right	0.8333	0.75	1
C3: Texting left	1	0.85	1
C4: Talking on the phone left	1	1	1
C5: Operating radio	0.8695	1	1
C6: Drinking	1	1	1
C7: Reaching behind	1	1	1
C8: Hair and Makeup	1	0.95	1
C9: Talking to passenger	1	1	1
Cognitive distraction	**1.0**	**0.90**	**1.0**

The results in real-life scenario achieved an impressive accuracy of 93.63%. Various categories, including texting right, drinking, reaching behind, hair and makeup, talking to passenger, and cognitive distraction, performed exceptionally well, with precision and recall scores surpassing 0.9.

5.2 Perceptual Challenges and User Feedback

However, some anomalies in precision and recall were observed, as shown in Table 3 above. Differences were noted among groups regarding "warning perceptivity" and "warning timeliness and accuracy" during the ANOVA test. Around 3.4% of the multi-modal warnings were rated as "barely noticeable" and "not so effective". 15% of participants primarily perceived the audio warnings but found the visual display inadequate, particularly in daylight conditions. Due to the well-lit conditions in laboratory settings [24], the visual warning perceptions experienced in real-life scenarios differed, leading to challenges in accurately perceiving the visual warnings. Another 2.7% of the multi-modal warnings were considered "unnoticeable' and "not at all effective", primarily due to device issues and misclassifications caused by changes in lighting conditions.

5.3 Comparative Performance and Significance

In comparison to Biondi et al. (2017), this study achieved significantly higher mean ratings (20.35 vs. 14.58) for warnings being "highly noticeable" during N-back tasks. Similarly, when compared to Maltz and Shinar (2007) [25], this study achieved higher warnings perceptivity (95% vs. 66%) for cognitive distraction. The mean rating for multi-modal warnings perceptivity for cognitively distracted tasks were also higher by 10% as compared to the previous study by Roberts, Ghazizadeh and Lee (2012) [26]. Although this study's overall classification accuracy in real-life scenarios (93.63%) was lower than that of existing non-real-life experiments conducted by previous studies [16, 18, 20], it demonstrated high accuracy even in real-life situations.

5.4 Quantized MobileNetV2 Model Outperforms

Furthermore, in comparison to Li et al. (2022) [16], whose modified YOLOv5s model achieved a mean average precision of 95.60%, the quantized MobileNetV2 model in this study surpassed their performance with a mean average precision of 99.46%. Despite Li et al.'s higher frame rate of 70fps due to the use of a more powerful NVIDIA GEFORCE RTX 3080 GPU, this study aimed to balance accuracy, detection speed, and lightweight design. As a result, the quantized MobileNetV2 model was 13% lighter and more accurate in detection. Additionally, the quantized MobileNetV2 outperformed the unmodified MobileNetV2 used by Hossain et al. (2022) [18] on the SFDDD dataset, achieving an overall accuracy of 99.46% compared to their 98.12% for detecting distracted driving activities, surpassing it by 1.3%. Furthermore, the quantized MobileNetV2 model in this study outperformed the modified EfficientDet-D3 model developed by Sajid et al. (2021) [27] by 0.3% in mean average precision (mAP). The EfficientDet-D3 model achieved a high mAP of 99.16% for detecting distracted driving activities on the SFDDD dataset.

Nevertheless, it is worth noting that the modified MobileNetV2 model by Wang and Wu (2022) [20] achieved significantly higher accuracy of 99.88%, outperforming this present study by 0.46%. However, this difference can be attributed to limited implementation details and insufficient training of the MobileNetV2 model in this study. The model was trained for only 50 epochs due to resource constraints and limited GPU availability for intensive training. Nonetheless, the findings highlight the outstanding performance of the quantized MobileNetV2 model in accurately classifying distracted driving behaviors.

5.5 Challenges and Limitations

Nevertheless, a few challenges and limitations were also identified during the evaluation process. The current hardware utilized as part of the Distracker had relatively low performance and thus there were unexpected shutdowns during the experiment, particularly due to high temperatures. Moreover, 20% of participants found the warnings difficult to understand due to unfamiliarity with the audio alerts, where half of the same group claimed to have disliked the audio sound and also found it annoying. As such, further studying usability of the solution can help to derive further insights on the application of Distracker in practice.

6   Conclusion

To conclude, this study has developed an in-vehicle smart agent prototype that combines deep learning and eye movement tracking to detect and address manual, visual, and cognitive distractions in real-time. The analysis of distracted driving tasks showcased an overall classification accuracy of 93.63% in real-life scenarios, including the detection of cognitive distractions, which is a significant contribution of this research. Moreover, the Distracker prototype, equipped with non-intrusive multi-modal mitigation warnings aimed at enhancing its potential for practical implementation in vehicles.

Moving forward, future endeavours should prioritize addressing the identified limitations. This entails utilizing embedded devices with enhanced processing power, implementing advanced cooling systems, and exploring the possibility of powering the embedded device through the car's power supply to reduce reliance on external power sources. Involving end-users in the design process and improving the visibility of warnings through visual cues and adjustable audio volume are vital aspects to consider. Augmented datasets, deep learning techniques, and strategic device placement should be explored to optimize the performance of the eye-tracking algorithm. By pursuing these future improvements, the field of detecting and mitigating distracted driving can progress, ultimately ensuring a safer and more secure driving experience for all individuals on the road.

References

1. Li, W., Huang, J., Xie, G., Karray, F., Li, R.: A survey on vision-based driver distraction analysis. J. Syst. Architect. **121**, 102319 (2021)

2. National Center for Statistics and Analysis. Distracted Driving in 2021. National Highway Traffic Safety Administration (2023)
3. García-Herrero, S., Febres, J., Boulagouas, W., Gutiérrez, J., Mariscal Saldaña, M.: Assessment of the influence of technology-based distracted driving on drivers' infractions and their subsequent impact on traffic accidents severity. Int. J. Environ. Res. Public Health **18**(13), 7155 (2021)
4. Masilkova, M.: Health and social consequences of road traffic accidents. Kontakt **19**(1), e43–e47 (2017)
5. Parnell, K., Stanton, N., Plant, K.: What's the law got to do with it? Legislation regarding in-vehicle technology use and its impact on driver distraction. Accid. Anal. Prev. **100**, 1–14 (2017)
6. Dunn, N., Dingus, T., Soccolich, S.: Understanding the impact of technology: do advanced driver assistance and semi-automated vehicle systems lead to improper driving behavior. Virginia Tech Transportation Institute, American Automobile Association, Washington, DC (2019)
7. Ponte, G., Edwards, S., Wundersitz, L.: The prevalence of in-vehicle driver distraction in moving traffic. Transport. Res. F: Traffic Psychol. Behav. **83**, 33–41 (2021)
8. Darapaneni, N., et al.: Distracted driver monitoring system using AI. In: 2022 Interdisciplinary Research in Technology and Management (IRTM) (2022)
9. Chen, J., et al.: Fine-grained detection of driver distraction based on neural architecture search. IEEE Trans. Intell. Transp. Syst. **22**(9), 5783–5801 (2021)
10. Noble, A., Miles, M., Perez, M., Guo, F., Klauer, S.: Evaluating driver eye glance behavior and secondary task engagement while using driving automation systems. Accid. Anal. Prev. **151**, 105959 (2021)
11. Hamilton, B., Grabowski, J.: Cognitive distraction: something to think about: lessons learned from recent studies (2013)
12. Strayer, D., Drews, F.: Multi-tasking in the automobile. In: Attention: From Theory to Practice, pp. 121–133 (2007)
13. Wang, S., Zhang, Y., Wu, C., Darvas, F., Chaovalitwongse, W.: Online prediction of driver distraction based on brain activity patterns. IEEE Trans. Intell. Transp. Syst. **16**(1), 136–150 (2014)
14. Heine, T., Lenis, G., Reichensperger, P., Beran, T., Doessel, O., Deml, B.: Electrocardiographic features for the measurement of drivers' mental workload. Appl. Ergon. **61**, 31–43 (2017)
15. Miyaji, M., Kawanaka, H., Oguri, K.: Effect of pattern recognition features on detection for driver's cognitive distraction. In: 13th International IEEE Conference on Intelligent Transportation Systems (2010)
16. Li, T., Zhang, Y., Li, Q., Zhang, T.: AB-DLM: an improved deep learning model based on attention mechanism and BiFPN for driver distraction behavior detection. IEEE Access **10**, 83138–83151 (2022)
17. Alam, L., Hoque, M.: Real-time distraction detection based on driver's visual features. In: 2019 International Conference on Electrical, Computer and Communication Engineering (ECCE) (2019)
18. Hossain, M., Rahman, M., Islam, M., Akhter, A., Uddin, M., Paul, B.: Automatic driver distraction detection using deep convolutional neural networks. Intell. Syst. Appl. **14**, 200075 (2022)
19. Montoya, A., Holman, D., Smith, T., Kan, W.: State farm distracted driver detection. Kaggle (2016). https://kaggle.com/competitions/state-farm-distracted-driver-detection
20. Wang, J., Wu, Z.: Model lightweighting for real-time distraction detection on resource-limited devices. Comput. Intell. Neurosci. (2022)

21. Misra, A., Samuel, S., Cao, S., Shariatmadari, K.: Detection of driver cognitive distraction using machine learning methods. IEEE Access **11**, 18000–18012 (2023)
22. Horberry, T., et al.: Human-centered design for an in-vehicle truck driver fatigue and distraction warning system. IEEE Trans. Intell. Transp. Syst. **23**, 5350–5359 (2021)
23. Biondi, F., Leo, M., Gastaldi, M., Rossi, R., Mulatti, C.: How to drive drivers nuts: effect of auditory, vibrotactile, and multimodal warnings on perceived urgency, annoyance, and acceptability. Transp. Res. Rec. **2663**(1), 34–39 (2017)
24. Lylykangas, J., Surakka, V., Salminen, K., Farooq, A., Raisamo, R.: Responses to visual, tactile and visual–tactile forward collision warnings while gaze on and off the road. Transp. Res. Part F: Traffic Psychol. Behav. **40**, 68–77 (2016)
25. Maltz, M., Shinar, D.: Imperfect in-vehicle collision avoidance warning systems can aid distracted drivers. Transport. Res. F: Traffic Psychol. Behav. **10**(4), 345–357 (2007)
26. Roberts, S., Ghazizadeh, M., Lee, J.: Warn me now or inform me later: drivers' acceptance of real-time and post-drive distraction mitigation systems. Int. J. Hum. Comput. Stud. **70**(12), 967–979 (2012)
27. Sajid, F., Javed, A., Basharat, A., Kryvinska, N., Afzal, A., Rizwan, M.: An efficient deep learning framework for distracted driver detection. IEEE Access **9**, 169270–169280 (2021)

InSightHub: Intelligent Notification and Status Indicator for Streamlined Work-From-Home Environments

Pierre Clarel Veerapen[1], Amar Seeam[2(✉)], and Visham Ramsurrun[2]

[1] Medine, Flic en Flac, Mauritius
[2] Middlesex University Mauritius, Flic en Flac, Mauritius
a.seeam@mdx.ac.mu

Abstract. The rise in remote work has created a demand for innovative tools to assist telecommuters in managing their workflow and communications. This paper introduces the Smart Notification Bar, a device affixed atop computer monitors that employs IoT technology, facilitated by Raspberry Pi, to provide real-time visual and sound notifications from various platforms, including Gmail, Twitter, and Zoom. The system is designed to be reliable, easy-to-use, secure, and available 24/7. Utilizing LEDs and a buzzer, the device offers immediate visual and auditory cues for unread Gmail messages, pre-programmed Twitter notifications, and Zoom meeting statuses. Beyond enhancing personal productivity by consolidating notifications and reducing distractions, the Smart Notification Bar serves as a non-intrusive indicator for household members to know when the user is engaged in a video conference and should not be disturbed. This is particularly useful for remote workers with hearing challenges or sound phobias.

Keywords: Raspberry Pi · LED · Smart Notification System · API · Work from Home Employee

1 Introduction

The mobile phone is a significant source of distractions for work-from-home (WFH) employees [1]. The advent of the internet and advancements in communication technology have transformed the way people work. Over recent years, there has been a significant increase in the number of people working remotely. This trend was further accelerated by the COVID-19 pandemic, which forced companies and individuals to rapidly adapt to WFH arrangements. While WFH offers numerous benefits such as flexibility and reduced commute times, it also presents unique challenges in terms of managing communication and maintaining productivity in a domestic environment.

One of the common challenges faced by remote workers is the management of notifications from various communication platforms. The constant influx of emails, messages, and social media updates can become a source of distraction and reduce productivity. Moreover, when engaged in virtual meetings or calls, it is essential for remote workers to communicate their availability to others sharing the living space, so as to minimize interruptions. People working remotely frequently receive notifications from email and social media applications from their smartphones, interrupting their workflow and diverting their attention from essential tasks during working hours [2, 3]. Although mobile phones help WFH employees to collaborate with co-workers remotely [4], they contribute to notification overload and allow employees working remotely to engage in multitasking activities, such as chatting with their friends while participating in Zoom meetings [3]. This multitasking can disrupt concentration and decrease productivity [5]. In Westermann et al. [6], users were advised to use sophisticated notification settings on their mobile phones to manage app alerts. This recommendation, however, may only be useful to remote workers who are savvy with phone settings. A better solution to the productivity or distraction issues associated with frequent mobile phone notifications is smart notification systems.

Technology advancements have contributed to the significant development of intelligent notification systems [7]. Today's smart alert systems leverage information technology not only to communicate with mobile devices and home appliances but also to provide timely alerts to users [8]. They can support multiple communication channels, including email, SMS, video calls, and in-app alerts. Smartphone notification systems are designed to collect and process data from various sensors, such as location, motion, light levels, air quality, humidity, or temperature data [7]. Depending on users' preferences, the processed data are then used to send specific notifications. Hence, smart notification systems are invaluable to WFH employees in reducing notification overload and enhancing employee engagement [8]. Like mobile phones, they can provide WFH staff with notifications on important meetings [9], natural disasters [10], product updates [11], and crucial deadlines [10]. Smart alert systems are more attractive to WFH employees because, unlike mobile phones, they do not send users unsolicited adverts or distracting messages. They can also be programmed to send automated alerts to remote workers based on their preferences [12]. Ultimately, smart notification systems have the potential to quickly identify and block disruptive notifications from mobile apps, ensuring that WFH workers' productivity is not compromised during working hours.

This paper addresses the distraction problems associated with mobile phones by designing a prototype smart notification system that can provide tailored visual or sound alerts for WFH employees. The prototype is designed with Raspberry Pi 3 Model B+ to allow WFH employees to receive email, Twitter, and Zoom alerts. This system aims to demonstrate the possibility of improving remote workers' productivity. By using this system, WFH staff members can receive a display of red, blue, green, or orange light-emitting diode (LED) signals depending on whether the notifications are from Gmail, Twitter, or Zoom. The Gmail LED lights up when a new email is received, the Twitter LED is activated when a tweet arrives, and the Zoom LED illuminates when the user is engaged in a Zoom call. The Zoom LED also serves a dual purpose, acting as a visual indicator for household members to know when the user is occupied and should not be interrupted. The proposed alert system can allow remote staff to receive various alerts associated with project deadlines, office meetings, potential environmental crises, and urgent tasks. Apart from WFH employees, companies can use the notification system to receive visual or sound notifications from their social media accounts.

In the subsequent sections, we will review the existing literature on notification management and remote work tools, detail the design and implementation of the Smart Notification Bar, present the findings of the implementation, and discuss the implications and future prospects of this innovative device.

2 Background

The work in [13] details a project from Instructables.com for the creation of a Work From Home Status Indicator using an ESP8266 and an LED strip. The author developed this system to help establish boundaries while working from home. The system uses different colors to indicate the user's availability status to family members. The implementation is quite simple, involving basic components like an LED strip, a 330 Ω resistor, a prototype board, and connector wire. The ESP8266 connects to the internet and waits for instructions, which are sent from a connected device. The status light can be activated through a web browser, with the choice of color signifying the user's current status. This project demonstrates a hands-on approach to managing work-life balance in a remote working context, and also shows how the ESP8266 can be used as a simple but effective tool for IoT applications in this space.

The authors in [14] discuss the integration of Augmented Reality (AR) and lighting systems in a WFH setting. It outlines eight use-cases, such as coloured lighting for status feedback, hot-desk personalisation, meeting room controls, teleconferencing lighting, energy management, gesture control, light tracking, and data-centre assistance. These features are achieved through a system comprising Raspberry Pi IoT control, Vuforia, Unity3D, Node-Red, Philips Hue Lightstrip, and Philips Bridge.

The literature is replete with numerous solutions aimed at managing smartphone interruptions. Much of the research effort to address digital disruption focuses on determining "when" smartphone users should receive notifications from mobile apps. Researchers have developed smart notification systems like Attelia [15], InterruptMe [16], and smartNoti [17] to predict opportune moments to send users phone notifications. While the solutions proposed in these studies are compelling, users cannot used them to receive email, tweet, or Zoom notifications.

Some scholars have extended their smartphone interruption solutions from phone calls to a wide variety of digital services. Context-aware notification management systems (CNMSs) have received significant research attention as they show promising results in determining (a) when users should receive incoming notifications, (b) the appropriate timing for sending notifications, and (c) which device(s) should receive incoming notifications [18]. For example, Roecker et al. [9] designed a context-dependent email notification system that allowed users to receive email messages relevant to them at a particular time. While this system is similar to the one proposed in this study, it cannot provide visual alerts of emails, tweets, or Zoom calls.

Furthermore, Leonidis et al. [19] presented AlertMe to provide customized notifications to graduate students. This semantics-based CNMS exploited semantic web technologies, helping users to receive reminders about canceled lectures, timetable changes, or campus-related events based on their preferences [20]. Although this software-based system could send SMS notifications, users could not use it to receive tailored notifications from social media apps, making it less useful for WFH workers who need to receive only important messages from various social networking platforms. Most of the solutions proposed in the literature or the marketplace depend on users being in proximity to their smartphones, laptops, or computers to receive personalized notifications. Hence, there is a necessity to enable users who wish to disconnect temporarily from mobile devices yet receive alerts on simplified hardware dedicated to providing visual or audio notifications of incoming emails, tweets, or Zoom calls.

The Smart Notification Bar, as described, is designed to be an unobtrusive device that uses LED indicators to inform users about the status of various communication platforms such as Gmail, Twitter, and Zoom. There are many ways in which this device can be particularly beneficial for underserved areas.

Enhanced Focus and Productivity: In underserved areas, individuals may not have the luxury of separate workspaces and may need to work in shared or crowded environments. The Smart Notification Bar helps in reducing distractions by consolidating notifications. The visual cues allow users to quickly glance at the status without having to sift through multiple applications. This can lead to enhanced focus and productivity, which is crucial for individuals in these areas who might already be dealing with resource constraints.

Improved Internet Bandwidth Utilization: In underserved areas, internet connectivity might be limited or unreliable. By using LED indicators instead of pushing notifications through the internet, the Smart Notification Bar might reduce the bandwidth used by non-essential notifications. This can be beneficial for keeping the internet connection more stable and reliable for critical tasks.

Non-verbal Communication with Household Members: The device serves as a non-intrusive indicator for others in the household, signaling when the user is engaged in a video conference and should not be disturbed. In underserved areas, where households may be smaller and more crowded, this feature is particularly useful. It allows for a respectful and efficient way to communicate availability without interrupting the workflow.

Accessibility for the Technologically Less Proficient: Individuals in underserved areas might not be as technologically proficient. The simplicity of the Smart Notification Bar makes it accessible to a wide range of users. The visual cues via LEDs can be easily understood even by those who are not comfortable with sophisticated technology.

Potential Cost Savings: Depending on the implementation, the Smart Notification Bar could be a low-cost alternative to more expensive productivity tools. This is particularly beneficial for underserved areas where financial resources might be limited.

Encouragement for Remote Work: By enhancing productivity and minimizing distractions, the Smart Notification Bar can make remote work more feasible and attractive. This is particularly important for underserved areas, which may not have as many local employment opportunities. Encouraging remote work can lead to economic empowerment and improved standards of living in these areas.

Potential for Community Collaboration: In underserved areas, community collaboration can be a powerful tool for development. The Smart Notification Bar could potentially be used in community centers or shared workspaces to facilitate collaborative efforts among community members.

3 System Architecture

The proposed InSightHub prototype is a WFH smart notification system that allows staff working remotely to receive personalized alerts from Gmail, Twitter, or Zoom, depending on their needs and priorities. The system comprises a Raspberry Pi 3 Model B+, a buzzer, 4 LEDs, resistors, jumper wires, and Gmail, Twitter, and Zoom application programming interfaces (APIs) (Fig. 1). The Raspberry Pi 3 Model B+ is connected to the LEDs and buzzer with the jumper wires, resistors, and a 3D container. The single-board computer is also connected through the internet to Gmail, Twitter, and Zoom APIs. These components work as a unit to help users receive timely visual or audio notifications of incoming emails, tweets, or Zoom calls.

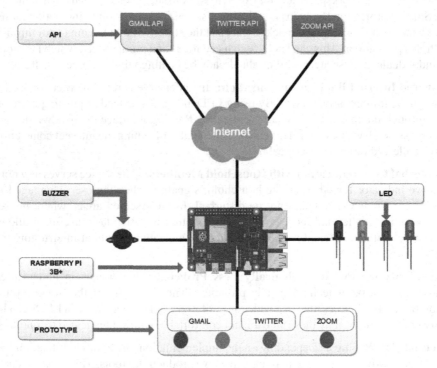

Fig. 1. System architecture of the proposed prototype

3.1 Raspberry Pi

Raspberry PI 3 Model B+ is an upgraded version of the Raspberry Pi 3 Model B. This single-board computer is used as the central unit for the WFH smart notification prototype in this project. It features 1 GB LPDDR2 RAM, built-in Bluetooth 4.2 and dual-band Wi-Fi, Bluetooth 4.2, a microSD card, an HDMI output, a 40-pin General Purpose Input/Output header, and Broadcom BCM2837B0 quad-core ARM Cortex-A53 processor running at 1.4GHz. Raspberry Pi 3 Model B+. Several programming languages can be used namely Python, Java, C, C++, HTML and others. These features make this single-board computer ideal for automating incoming notifications from Gmail, Zoom, or Twitter.

3.2 LED

Four LEDs are used in this project to provide lighting signals depending on the nature or source of the notifications. The colors of the LEDs include red, blue, green, and orange. Each LED emits one of these colors when currents flow through it. For instance, the green or orange LED is expected to switch on when users receive incoming emails. The blue and red LEDs should be switched on when users receive incoming tweets and Zoom calls, respectively. Compared to traditional bulbs, these LEDs are energy-efficient, environmentally friendly, durable, and easy to control. Hence, the four LEDs are expected to last tens of thousands of hours, providing timely alerts to users.

3.3 API

Three APIs are used in the proposed prototype. They include Gmail, Zoom, and Twitter APIs. Each API allow the Raspberry Pi 3 Model B+ to communicate and interact with the LEDs and buzzer through Python scripts.

4 System Design

The design of the proposed system aims to provide effective visual and sound notification alerts to employees working remotely. The activity diagrams show how the alert system works (Figs. 2, 3, and 4). Raspberry Pi 3 Model B+ access Gmail, Twitter, or Zoom via their respective APIs. The Gmail API scans unread emails from a user's Gmail account, while the Twitter API and Zoom API search for users' incoming tweets and Zoom calls. If there are unread emails, the orange LED is turned on. However, the green LED is switched on if there are no unread emails. The script pauses its activities for some seconds and then scans the Gmail inbox again for unread emails (Fig. 2).

Similarly, the Twitter API searches predefined keywords associated with personalized notifications. The result is saved in a CSV file, and the blue LED is switched on if a desired keyword is found (Fig. 3). The Zoom API also triggers Raspberry Pi 3 Model B+ to switch on the red LED when a user is in a Zoom meeting. Like the Gmail APIs, the Zoom and Twitter APIs stay idle for some seconds and continue with the search (Fig. 4).

The functional and non-functional requirements of the prototype are considered during the design stage. The functional requirements indicate the essential functions that the WFH notification systems must have. In contrast, the non-functional requirements indicate the qualities or attribute the prototype should possess, even though they are not directly related to its specific functionalities. Tables 1 and 2 indicate the functional and non-functional requirements of the proposed alert system for WFH employees.

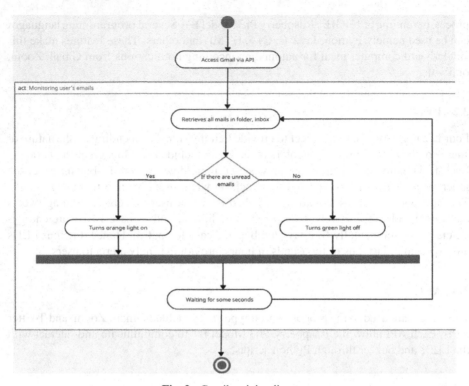

Fig. 2. Gmail activity diagram

Table 1. Functional requirements of the proposed WFH notification system

Applications	Functional Requirements
Gmail	• There must be light and sound alerts when there are unread emails
	• There must be light notification when all emails are read
	• The script should continue to scan the inbox for unread emails
Twitter	• There should be light alerts for incoming tweets
	• Users should be able to predefine keywords for search criteria
	• The number of adjusted search results should be displayed
	• All search results should be recorded
Zoom	• There should be LED notification when a user is in a meeting
	• The script should scan continuously to know if a user is in a meeting
	• The scan rate should be adjustable to check whether a user is in a meeting

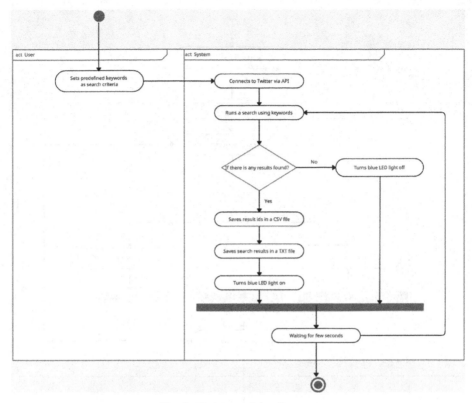

Fig. 3. Twitter activity diagram

Table 2. Non-functional requirements of the proposed WFH notification system

Features	Details
Reliability	• It must produce the same result every time
Usability	• It should be easy to use
Security	• It should protect users' personal data and prevent security breaches
Performance	• It should be able to provide notifications within a short time
Availability	• It should be able to run 24/7
Operation	• It should allow Twitter users to edit keywords for search criteria

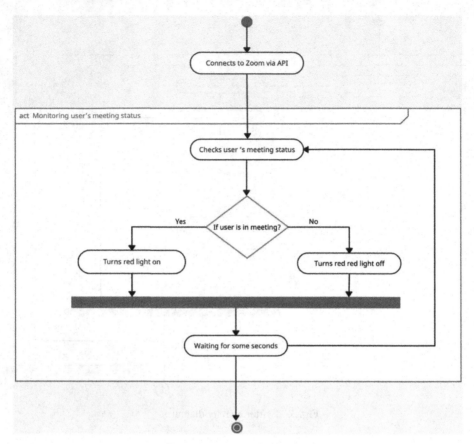

Fig. 4. Zoom activity diagram

5 Implemented System

Figure 5 illustrates the implemented WFH notification system and its components. The buzzer and the four LEDs are connected with jumper wires and enclosed in a container (Fig. 6).

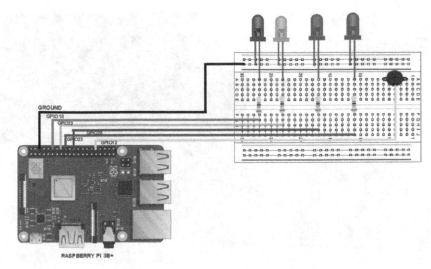

Fig. 5. System design of the prototype

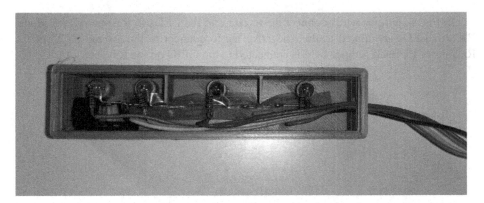

Fig. 6. A container with LEDs and a buzzer soldered with jumper wires

The outer part of the container is divided into three sections, and each section is labeled with Gmail, Twitter, and Zoom logos to enable users to recognize the meaning of the visual signal (Fig. 7).

Fig. 7. A container connected to Raspberry Pi with jumper wires

In Fig. 8, jumper wires connect the buzzer and the LEDs to Raspberry Pi 3 Model B+. All LEDs are linked to their negative leg to connect to the ground GPIO of the Raspberry Pi. Each jumper wire is connected to the GPIO on the Raspberry Pi.

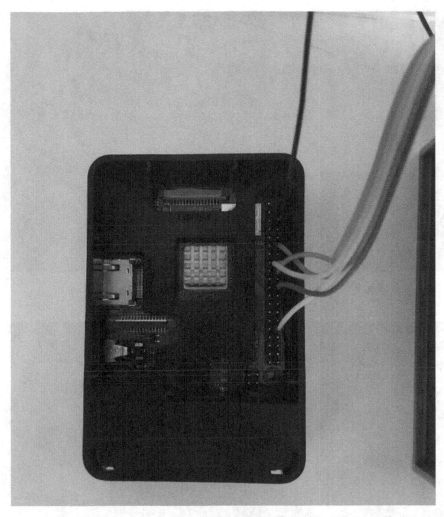

Fig. 8. Jumper wires connected to the GPIO pins on the Raspberry Pi

5.1 Gmail Testing

A new Gmail account is created to test the WFH notification system's ability to provide unread email alerts to users. As soon as the prototype is switched on, it checks the Gmail inbox and turns the green LED on if there are no unread emails (Fig. 9). However, if unread emails are in the inbox, the orange LED is switched on and the buzzer also is activated (Fig. 10).

Fig. 9. Green LED switches on when there are no unread emails

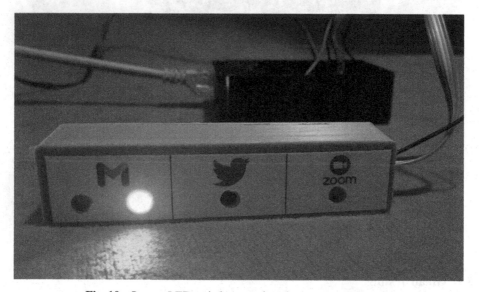

Fig. 10. Orange LED switches on when there are unread emails

5.2   Twitter Testing

A new Twitter account is created to test the prototype's effectiveness. A predefined keyword is entered into the keyword file, and the script can run. The prototype runs the script, searching for previous tweets with the targeted keyword. As shown in Fig. 11, the blue LED is switched on when the pre-programmed keyword is found.

Fig. 11. Blue LED switches on when a user receives tweet alerts

5.3 Zoom Testing

A new Zoom account is created to evaluate the performance of the proposed WFH alert system. As soon as the user joins a Zoom meeting, the red LED is switched on but turned off when the user leaves the meeting (Fig. 12).

Fig. 12. Red LED switches on when a user is in a meeting

6   Results

The results of each application and its functions are shown in Table 3. The Raspberry Pi 3 Model B+ triggered the LED bulbs to light up when users had unread emails (orange light) or all read emails (green light) in their inboxes. It also triggered the blue LED to switch on when users received incoming tweets, and the red LED turned on when users joined a Zoom meeting. As illustrated in Table 3, all the test results are positive.

LED bulbs to light up when users had unread emails (Orange light) or read emails (Green light) in their inbox. The blue LED bulb turned on when users received incoming tweets, while the red LED bulb turned on when they received incoming Zoom calls. Overall, all the test results are positive.

Table 3. Functional requirement results of the prototype

Applications	Functions	Actions	Results
Gmail	Unread emails	Trigger a LED to turn on	Yes
Gmail	Read emails	Trigger a LED to turn on	Yes
Gmail	Scan the email inbox	Adjust the refresh rate	Yes
Gmail	Scan the email inbox and adjust features	Do not trigger any LED to turn on	Yes
Twitter	No new tweets	Search for the pre-programed keyword	Yes
Twitter	Search functions	Modify the return of tweets from the search	Yes
Twitter	Return tweets from the search	Store all search results in a text file	Yes
Twitter	Record all search results	Do not trigger any LED to turn on	Yes
Zoom	In-meeting notifications	Trigger a LED to turn on	Yes
Zoom	Not in-meeting notifications	Do nothing, LED off	Yes
Zoom	Continuous scan	Continue to check users' meeting status	Yes
Zoom	Scan rate adjustments	Adjust the scan rate by seconds	Yes

Table 4 indicates the non-functional performance results of the proposed WFH notification system. The test findings indicate that the system can provide the same results at all times, that users need little programming knowledge to use the system, and that users' data are well-protected from cyber theft and threats. Overall, the prototype is reliable, easy to use, secure, and responsive 24/7.

Table 4. Non-functional requirements of the prototype

Functions	Actions	Test Result	Comments
Reliability	Must provide the same results every time	Yes	Users obtained the same results at all times
Usability	Should be easy to use and should power device and run script automatically	Yes	Users need little IT knowledge to use the system
Security	Should secure API scripts	Yes	Users' data cannot be easily compromised while using the system
Availability	Should be available 24/7	Yes	Users can run the notification system 24/7

7   Conclusion

This paper presents the design and implementation of a WFH smart notification system that provides remote workers visual and sound alerts of tweets, unread or read Gmail messages, and Zoom meeting status. The prototype exploits IoT technology to facilitate the communication between Raspberry Pi and notification indicators such as LEDs and the buzzer. The notification prototype is reliable, easy to use, secure, and responsive 24/7. It allows users to receive visual and sound notifications of unread and read messages from their Gmail inbox. Users can easily configure the WFH smart alert system to receive visual notifications of pre-programmed tweets. It is also possible for them to receive visual alerts when they join or leave a Zoom meeting. The apparent advantage of the alert-based system is its ability to help remote workers receive visual alerts without worrying about ads. Apart from this benefit, this alert prototype can be helpful to WFH employees with hearing challenges, including those with a phobia of sounds. Besides, remote workers can use this prototype to get warning alerts in real-time in the event of natural hazards. However, despite the numerous functionalities of the prototype, users cannot receive notifications from other social networking sites. Future research should demonstrate the feasibility of using this alert system to receive visual and sound alerts from Facebook, Instagram, YouTube, TikTok, and other social networking platforms. Furthermore, future studies should consider using other electronic boards with a simple microcontroller to explore this research topic, such as Arduino, Banana Pi, and Orange Pi. It would be interesting for future researchers to compare the performance of these microcontrollers in terms of their ability to provide users with visual and sound notifications.

References

1. Choy, M., et al.: Looking back on the current day: interruptibility prediction using daily behavioral features. In: Proceedings of the 2016 ACM International Joint Conference on Pervasive and Ubiquitous Computing (2016)

2. Gallud, J.A., Tesoriero, R.: Smartphone notifications: a study on the sound to soundless tendency. In: Proceedings of the 17th International Conference on Human-Computer Interaction with Mobile Devices and Services Adjunct (2015)

3. Pielot, M., Rello, L.: Productive, anxious, lonely: 24 hours without push notifications. In: Proceedings of the 19th International Conference on Human-Computer Interaction with Mobile Devices and Services (2017)

4. Sahami Shirazi, A., et al.: Large-scale assessment of mobile notifications. In: Proceedings of the SIGCHI Conference on Human Factors in Computing Systems (2014)

5. Exler, A., et al.: Preliminary investigations about interruptibility of smartphone users at specific place types. In: Proceedings of the 2016 ACM International Joint Conference on Pervasive and Ubiquitous Computing: Adjunct (2016)

6. Westermann, T., Möller, S., Wechsung, I.: Assessing the relationship between technical affinity, stress and notifications on smartphones. In: Proceedings of the 17th International Conference on Human-Computer Interaction with Mobile Devices and Services Adjunct (2015)

7. Jin, J., et al.: An information framework for creating a smart city through internet of things. IEEE Internet Things J. 1(2), 112–121 (2014)

8. Patel, S., et al.: A review of wearable sensors and systems with application in rehabilitation. J. Neuroeng. Rehabil. 9(1), 1–17 (2012)

9. Saravanan, M., Das, A.: Smart real-time meeting room. In: 2017 IEEE Region 10 Symposium (TENSYMP). IEEE (2017)

10. Sikder, M.F., et al.: Smart disaster notification system. In: 2017 4th International Conference on Advances in Electrical Engineering (ICAEE). IEEE (2017)

11. Halder, S., Ghosal, A., Conti, M.: Secure over-the-air software updates in connected vehicles: A survey. Comput. Netw. 178, 107343 (2020)

12. Mongiello, M., et al.: A complex event processing based smart aid system for fire and danger management. In: 2017 7th IEEE International Workshop on Advances in Sensors and Interfaces (IWASI). IEEE (2017)

13. Snorlaxprime. Work From Home Status Indicator. Instructables. https://www.instructables.com/Work-From-Home-Status-Indicator/. Accessed 30 June 2023

14. Purmaissur, J., Seeam, A., Guness, S., Bellekens, X.: Augmented reality intelligent lighting smart spaces. In: 2019 Conference on Next Generation Computing Applications (NextComp), pp. 1–5. IEEE (2019). IEEE Internet of Things J. 1(2), 112–121 (2014)

15. Okoshi, T., Ramos, J., Nozaki, H., Nakazawa, J., Dey, A.K., Tokuda, H.: Attelia: Reducing user's cognitive load due to interruptive notifications on smart phones. In: 2015 IEEE International Conference on Pervasive Computing and Communications (PerCom), 23–27 March 2015, pp. 96–104 (2015). https://doi.org/10.1109/PERCOM.2015.7146515

16. Pejovic, V., Musolesi, M.: InterruptMe: designing intelligent prompting mechanisms for pervasive applications. In ACM UbiComp, Seattle, WA, USA (2014). https://doi.org/10.1145/2632048.2632062

17. Hyungik, O., Jalali, L., Jain, R.: An intelligent notification system using context from real-time personal activity monitoring. In: 2015 IEEE International Conference on Multimedia and Expo (ICME), 29 June–3 July 2015, pp. 1–6 (2015). https://doi.org/10.1109/ICME.2015.7177508

18. Corno, F., Russis, L.D., Montanaro, T.: A context and user aware smart notification system. In: 2015 IEEE 2nd World Forum on Internet of Things (WF-IoT), 14–16 December 2015, pp. 645–651 (2015). https://doi.org/10.1109/WF-IoT.2015.7389130
19. Roecker, C., Bayon, V., Memisoglu, M., Streitz, N.: Context-dependent email notification using ambient displays and mobile devices. In: Proceedings of the 2005 International Conference on Active Media Technology (AMT 2005), 19–21 May 2005, pp. 137–138 (2005). https://doi.org/10.1109/AMT.2005.1505288
20. Leonidis, A., et al.: AlertMe: a semantics-based context-aware notification system. In: 2009 33rd Annual IEEE International Computer Software and Applications Conference, 20–24 July 2009, vol. 2, pp. 200–205 (2009). https://doi.org/10.1109/COMPSAC.2009.134

Modern Detection Techniques of False Data Injection Attacks in V2X Communication: A Critical Analysis

Thejmeela Seetamonee[✉] and Girish Bekaroo[iD]

Middlesex University Mauritius, Flic-en-Flac, Mauritius
`TS984@live.mdx.ac.uk`

Abstract. During the previous decade, renowned companies such as Tesla, Ford and Volkswagen have actively been researching and investing in the production of connected and automated vehicles (CAVs). The vehicle-to-everything (V2X) technology, which is used to operate CAVs, has recently gained considerable attention due to its various benefits such as improved road safety, energy efficiency and enhanced traffic efficiency on roads. A significant growth is expected in CAVs and V2X which will, however, be positively linked to an increase in the risk of cyber-attacks, notably, False Data Injection (FDI) attacks, due to their high connectivity. The aim of FDI in CAVs is to alter data and/or make CAVs unresponsive to the driver. The impact of these attacks is alarming due to the possibility of death, injury and major infrastructural damages. The ability of FDI attacks to modify or suppress data, such as speed, distance, acceleration and position of CAVs makes it even more critical to study FDI detection techniques. As such, this paper critically compares and analyses key techniques used to detect FDI attacks within V2X communication. As part of this study, five modern FDI detection techniques, notably, State Residuals-based detection, Data Fusion Algorithm, MFC-DI, History Trajectory Scheme and Machine Learning Approach were investigated in terms of their detection accuracy, time, reliability, adaptability to varying V2X environments and ability to detect new attacks.

Keywords: False data injection (FDI) · Vehicle-to-Everything (V2X) · Connected and Autonomous Vehicles (CAVs) · cyber-security · modern detection techniques

1 Introduction

In this age of intelligent mobility and automated vehicles, Vehicle-to-Everything (V2X) communication is increasingly gaining attention. The notion of "connected car", which is still at its early release stage, is enabled through wireless communication and has been designed to provide drivers with a panoply of services [1]. V2X is a wireless communication which enables vehicles to communicate with each other and with multiple components, such as physical infrastructures, road traffic signals, pedestrians and cloud computing infrastructures [2]. By allowing vehicles and infrastructures to communicate, V2X limits the risks of accidents and increases road traffic efficiency [3].

© ICST Institute for Computer Sciences, Social Informatics and Telecommunications Engineering 2024
Published by Springer Nature Switzerland AG 2024. All Rights Reserved
A. Seeam et al. (Eds.): InterSol 2023, LNICST 541, pp. 66–80, 2024.
https://doi.org/10.1007/978-3-031-51849-2_5

It is expected that the market for autonomous vehicle will be at a worldwide estimation of 400bn USD by 2025 and driver-free highways will be the norm in advanced countries by 2050 [4]. With the expected increase in intelligent mobility and automated vehicles, V2X communication will be used extensively as a wireless vehicular communication [5]. Consequently, V2X communication has resulted in expanded surface attacks and with its widespread use, novel security concerns arise. Attacks along the V2X communication channel are significantly more dangerous as it is challenging for the driver to circumvent the corrupted information or to fix a bug in the automated system [6]. Therefore, it is crucial to secure the line along the V2X communication to prevent injurious attacks that hinder road safety and put people at risks. There are multiple attacks to which the V2X channel can be subject to, such as denial-of-service (DOS) attacks or integrity attacks, replay attacks and false data injection (FDI) attacks [7].

Among these attacks, FDI is becoming increasingly significant, especially with the exponential increase in the use of internet and connected devices [8]. FDI is an attack that targets sensor communication network to alter and manipulate data packets, leading to a divergence in the expected result [9]. The aim of an FDI attack is to compromise the integrity of data. FDI attacks targeting the location and speed of the vehicle have drastic consequences for road safety [7]. Hence, the timely detection and prevention of security weaknesses which may lead to FDI attacks along the communication channel is a problem that should be researched upon [10]. Therefore, the purpose of this study is to critically compare and analyse the key techniques used to detect FDI attacks within V2X communication.

The research paper is structured as follows. The next section provides a background on the key topics investigated in this paper, notably, V2X communication and FDI. Then in Sect. 3, related research pertaining to detection of FDI are discussed. Section 4 then explores the methodology utilised in order to achieve the purpose of this research paper. Section 5 is the core of the research paper, whereby the modern techniques for FDI detection in V2X are elaborated and are then critically analysed in Sect. 6. Sect. 7 provides a final note on the research paper and explores possibilities for future research.

2   Background

2.1   An Overview of V2X Communication

Since its first release as 1G-V2X (Level 1 automation level for Society of Automotive Engineers (SAE) J3016), V2X has continuously evolved over the years and its conception propelled the manufacturing of CAVs. With advancement in V2X, the need for design of new or improved messages, communication protocols, and their standardisation are becoming prerequisites [11]. Vehicle-to-everything (V2X), which refers to vehicular applications and communications technologies, is divided into four categories: vehicle-to-vehicle (V2V), vehicle-to-infrastructure (V2I), vehicle-to-network (V2N), and vehicle-to-pedestrian (V2P) [12]. All the components of V2X are supported by Dedicated Short Range Communications (DSRC) which is being further designed with the help of standardisation bodies, such as IEEE, the European Telecommunication Standards Institute (ETSI) and the SAE International [13].

Figure 1 shows the interaction between various components of a V2X communication, namely V2N, V2I, V2V and V2P. Vehicle-to-self (V2S) and Vehicle-to-Roadside Unit (V2R) are sub-components within V2X.

1. V2N: V2N, or wide area cellular communication, is a cellular infrastructure that allows communication between vehicles to facilitate vehicular traffic operations [14]. The primary objective of V2N is to enable constant network coverage on the streets [15].
2. V2I: The term "vehicle-to-infrastructure" (V2I) refers to communication between a vehicle and the infrastructure, known as the Roadside Unit (RSU). They can share and transmit some delay-insensitive information, such as gathered traffic data for extensive traffic monitoring [3].
3. V2V: V2V communication is used among vehicles to send brief messages, mostly geared toward enhancing road safety [16]. V2V uses mainly ad hoc networks technology to allow vehicles to communicate over a short distance [17].
4. V2P: Vehicle to pedestrian (V2P) technology is designed to help pedestrians who have physical or visual challenges by sending appropriate alerts to oncoming automobiles [18].

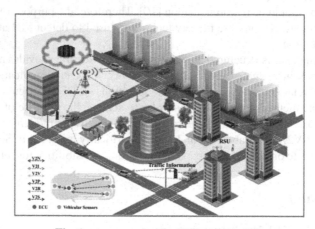

Fig. 1. An example of a V2X scenario [19]

A V2X communication system focuses on three key areas: energy efficiency, traffic efficiency, and road safety [19]. The inherent flexibility of V2X communication to adapt to any type of network, device, or data as well as to ensure the network's stability, resilience, and reliability are its most alluring advantages [20]. Additionally, V2X's role in enabling more effective vehicular transportation intervals from automated smart parking, to improved traffic flow through decreased vehicle-to-vehicle spacing on highways and coordinated intersections is crucial in today's overcrowded cities [21]. These are main reasons why V2X is becoming prevalent and is promoting autonomous driving.

However, with the extent of connectivity and autonomy provided by V2X, the need to address security and privacy concerns, including the potential identification and tracking of specific vehicles, the fabrication and jamming of real message traffic, the threat of vehicular malware, and the potential use of vehicular botnets are crucial [22].

2.2 An Overview of FDI and Its Impact on V2X Communication

An estimate of 400 crashes of vehicles operating with partially automated driver assist systems have been recorded from July 2021 to May 2022 [23]. Most automated vehicles require symmetrical sensors that constantly transmit information, such as location, speed and the state of surrounding over a channel (V2X) to understand the immediate environment [24]. Therefore, it is imperative to secure the communication line of automated vehicles to limit unauthorised interferences, such as FDI attacks, that may lead to severe crashes and even the possibility of death.

FDI is an attack scenario whereby a rogue vehicle, which acts as an authorised one, communicates with other legitimate vehicles and sends false data about its placement, celerity and acceleration (see Fig. 2) [25].

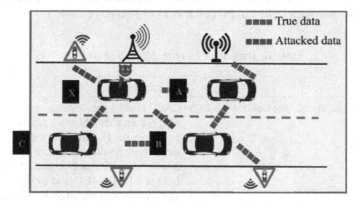

Fig. 2. FDI attacks launched by rogue vehicles [25]

In Fig. 2, there are four connected vehicles, namely A, B, C and X. Vehicles A, B and C are genuine connected cars and are transmitting true data within the environment. However, vehicle X is a malicious connected car and is transmitting distorted data, which is represented by the red dotted line. The aim of emitting distorted data is to tamper with the original state of the environment, specifically connected cars C and B and the traffic light. Therefore, FDI attacks within V2X, is simply the action of emitting distorted data to alter the original state of connected components. In the original state of the environment as depicted in Fig. 2, X is 20 m ahead of car C. However, X emits a distorted data, stating that it is 100 m behind C and can be overtaken. C would attempt to overtake and would eventually collide with X.

As further purported in a previous study, there is the possibility of collision between two connected and automated vehicles which are targeted by stealthy FDI attacks performed over V2V communication [26]. Ghost vehicles are injected into the network of connected vehicles as part of a smart FDI attack. Ghost vehicles have the ability to impair the system performance of authentic connected vehicles, resulting in fatal collisions and worsened traffic conditions [27]. Hence, FDI attacks have a high probability of causing considerable damage to road infrastructure and serious harm to pedestrians and drivers alike. Therefore, the purpose of this research paper, which is to critically analyse the techniques for the effective detection of FDI attacks over V2X network becomes pertinent.

3 Related Works

There have been various studies conducted on the security and challenges of V2X communication channel. The studies have focussed on either the detection and mitigation of cyber-attacks along V2X or the detection of FDI attacks over the whole Intelligent Transport System (ITS). However, limited studies have been done for the timely detection of FDI attacks along V2X. Among the related works, a previous study [2] discussed the security concerns related to V2X and classified as well as analysed the various security threats into active attacks, such as FDI attacks, and passive attacks. The study explored three key terminologies related to FDI attacks as explained in Table 1.

Table 1. Terminologies related to FDI attacks [2]

Terminology	Description
Cooperative Adaptive Cruise Control (CACC)	CACC enables cars to "cooperate" by talking with one another while in adaptive cruise control mode. For instance, with CACC, a car would keep a suitable distance by slowing down once it becomes too near of the car in front of it [28]. CACC is a key function in V2X and is oftentimes the target of FDI attacks
GPS Spoofing	It is a type of FDI attack during which an attacker would insert erroneous position data by targeting the GPS simulators of victim cars
Replay Attack	It is a type of FDI attack whereby the attacker would keep an event information and resend the same delayed information which is no longer valid. For instance, at 11pm, the speed of the car was 80 km/h, the attacker would send the same data at 12pm when the car is actually driving at 100 km/h

At the end of the same study, the authors emphasised on the need to investigate on innovative security techniques created for V2X for more safety-critical and cyber-physical domains. Another paper [29] developed and assessed the effectiveness of a new state residuals-based detection technique intended to address the issue of obsolete detection techniques. In addition to detecting FDI attacks, the proposed model also reduced the time taken to isolate the attacks. Similarly, another research proposed an attack detection decision scheme which relies on the results of the proposed data fusion algorithm applied to detect and confine the FDI attack in CAVs [30]. The proposed decision scheme was effective in identifying the rogue vehicle with a high true positive detection rate at 100% CAV penetration rate. In addition, a past study proposed a deep learning technique called Multivariate Fuzzy Clustering-based Data Imputation (MFC-DI) to identify if nodes have been compromised through FDI [31]. Another previous study proposed a scheme to detect complex attacks, such as FDI attacks, through the application of behavioural information [32]. The scheme was able to detect attacks with a probability of 97.56 in 80% of the simulated attacks. Likewise, a past research paper applied a machine learning approach, more specifically a neural network-based fault detection technique combined with a fuzzy decision system, to identify and trace FDI attacks targeting CACC [33].

Based on the previous studies, there exists several detection techniques to identify FDI attacks along V2X communication, be it for CAV or ITS. Nevertheless, limited studies have been undertaken to critically analyse existing detection approaches. Therefore, this research paper addresses this research gap to critically analyse the various modern detection techniques, as described in the following sections.

4 Methodology

The main sources of information for this research paper were research databases, such as Google Scholar, ResearchGate and IEEE Xplore. As per the title of this research paper, jargons such as "V2X", "FDI", "DSRC" and "Detection techniques" were searched among others to enhance the searches in accordance with the purpose of this research study. The most relevant and research papers published in the year 2015 and above were chosen to critically analyse the effectiveness of the selected modern proposed techniques used to detect FDI attacks along V2X. 12 applicable research papers were read and assessed to further shortlist most relevant papers based on the detection techniques applied for FDI detection. The 5 most recent research papers were shortlisted, and their proposed FDI detection techniques were thoroughly examined to perform a critical comparison of the proposed techniques. The proposed detection techniques were eventually elaborated and critically analysed through an adapted version of the criteria proposed in a previous research paper, meant for comparing attack detection mechanisms [34].

5 Techniques for the Detection of FDI Attacks in V2X Communications

Using the methodology described in the previous section, the following detection techniques are reviewed and analysed:

5.1 State Residuals-Based Detection

According to a previous study [29], State Residuals-based detection was proposed as a modern security measure to identify and confine FDI attacks. The study proposed an attack detection logic in the form of an equation designed from multiple logical equations. The equation is as follows:

$$\begin{cases} ||R(t)|| \leq Jth \, \text{Normal} \\ ||R(t)|| > Jth \, \text{Attack} \end{cases} \tag{1}$$

In the above equation, R (t) refers to the norm of state estimation error and the norm of disturbance error. If the estimation error is equal to or less than the adaptive detection threshold, then the data is deemed to be a proper estimate of the transmitted data. However, if the estimation error is higher than the adaptive detection threshold, then the transmitted data is detected as an attack. Figure 3 enumerates the steps to detect the FDI attack.

Algorithm 1: State residuals-based detection of FDI attacks in vehicle networking system.

1. Input: Establish the vehicle networking model in Equations (1)–(3);
2. Design the corresponding robust state observer in Equation (9);
3. Compute the adaptive threshold in Equation (24) and residual in Equation (25);
4. for All the intelligent vehicles
   if $||R(t)|| \leq J_{th}$ then
      No FDI attacks;
   else
      There exists the injected FDI attacks;
   end if
5. end for
6. Output: The vehicle networking system is attacked.

Fig. 3. Steps for State Residuals-based detection [29]

According to the same study [29], once the FDI attack has been detected, it should be isolated within the shortest possible timeframe. Iteratively repeating the detection algorithm for each half of the subset results in the isolation of the attacked vehicle networking sensor nodes. Therefore, the isolation range is immediately cut in half if the attack is discovered in the first subset. The suggested isolation method can hasten the separation of attacked vehicle networking sensor nodes through continual dichotomous iteration.

5.2 Data Fusion Algorithm

In another previous study [30], a data fusion algorithm has been derived from the Monte Carlo Localisation (MCL) algorithm, which consists of a collection of weighted samples (particles), each representing the position, speed and yaw angle of the vehicle. Particles alienated from the most likely state gradually dissipate while particles closer to the state combine to form an average. This principle is known as the particle filter (PF). The data fusion applies the modified version of the PF principle as shown in Fig. 4. In the same figure, the neighbouring vehicles are the samples used to provide an estimate of particle states of the ego vehicle. The neighbouring vehicles' estimation of the states of the ego vehicle are treated as further measurements since regular particles are assigned to them using stratified sampling based on their weights calculated in the first stage. This increases the reliability of the state estimation generated by the neighbouring vehicle.

Therefore, it is easier to detect an FDI attack launched by a neighbouring vehicle based on if the estimated state exceeds the threshold. The threshold is determined through statistical hypothesis testing. Based on the estimation and results of the study, the proposed data fusion algorithm was deemed to be scalable and was able to detect attacks within an average of 0.2 s with an average false alarm rate of 0.0156 over multiple CAV penetration rates.

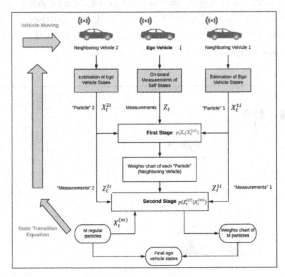

Fig. 4. Presentation of the data fusion algorithm in a two-stage architecture [30].

5.3 MFC-DI

The Multivariate Fuzzy Clustering-based Data Imputation (MFC-DI) technique was proposed by a previous study [31]. In this technique, the collected data from the ITS goes through the processes of normalisation, standardisation and imputation. First, the data is collected from neighbouring vehicles within the environment which is later used for estimation of missing values during imputation. Then data normalisation is applied based on the Min-Max formula in Eq. 2 below.

$$\overline{X} = \frac{X - Xmin}{Xmax - Xmin} \tag{2}$$

In Eq. 2, if $X = Xmin$, then the value is 0 while if $X = Xmax$, the value is 1. This allows for scaling between 0 and 1 only, whereby each attribute, such as speed, acceleration and distance are treated fairly. The data obtained during the initial stages are approximated by the MFC-DI to estimate missing data. The latter is the result of an FDI attack. This technique of imputation is used to address the possibility of missing data injection among connected vehicles. The results of the previous research work proved more effective than a mere Pearson-based missing data imputation.

5.4 History Trajectory Scheme

A previous study [32] proposed a scheme known as History Trajectory. The scheme adopts a two-step procedural security technique to identify FDI attacks. The first step is to detect normal and abnormal behavioural information. Through this first step, collisions are prevented as the autonomous vehicle is stopped when abnormal behaviour has been detected. In the second step, the attacked network communication is identified for further analysis. Current detection systems like Secure and Efficient Ad hoc Distance Vector (SEAD) and Cumulative Sum Control Chart (CUSUM) are used to identify a single assault. However, high performance computation is required as this approach calls for a thorough investigation (Fig. 5).

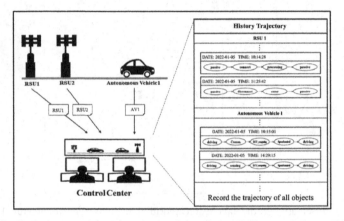

Fig. 5. Structure of the second step of the History Trajectory Scheme [32]

5.5 Machine Learning Approach (NN-Based)

According to a previous study, a neural network-based (NN-based) fault detection technique combined with a fuzzy decision system is proposed to identify and trace FDI attacks targeting CACC [33]. The proposed technique includes a bi-objective controller, a decision-making unit and a discrete controller. The bi-objective controller is in charge of adjusting vehicle speed and separation. Speed and distance errors are the controller's inputs, and its output is the braking or acceleration actuation. For the decision-making unit, a NN-based algorithm has been constructed to identify and estimate FDI attacks. The attack is identified in real time and the decision-making unit calculates a recommended safe distance (Fig. 6).

The speed of the following vehicle and the speed error—the difference between the leading vehicle's real and anticipated speed—are inputs to the proposed fuzzy system. The result is a recommended safe distance that is added to the present gap to prevent mishaps while alerts are delivered to the advisory system and the system waits for the user to take the proper action. The experiment resulted in accurate detection of the FDI attack and correction of the estimated false data transmitted.

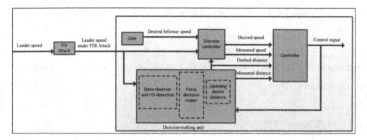

Fig. 6. Structure of the Machine Learning Approach [33]

6 Critical Analysis

The five selected modern detection techniques, explained in the previous section, are critically analysed and compared based on an adapted version of the comparison criteria used in a previous research paper [34]. This method of comparison was chosen due to its relevance in comparing attack detection techniques. As such, the following five criteria were selected to critically analyse the five modern FDI attack detection techniques, namely (Table 2):

Table 2. Criteria for Comparative Analysis

No.	Criteria	Description
C1	Detection Accuracy	The ability for the detection technique to correctly and precisely detect FDI attacks
C2	Detection Time	The time frame through which FDI attacks are detected
C3	Detection Reliability	The ability for the detection technique to detect a broad range of FDI attacks with varying parameters
C4	Adaptability to varying V2X environments	The ability of the detection technique to adapt to different V2X environments (e.g., small, and larger scales)
C5	Ability to Detect new attacks	The ability for the detection method to be adapted in order to detect new and more sophisticated types of FDI attacks targeting V2X

The selected criteria were applied to the five FDI attack detection mechanisms using the Low-Medium-High scale following review and critical analysis of published literature that refer each attack detection technique. Findings are summarised in Table 3.

As per Table 3, each detection technique was found to have its own strengths and limitations. Firstly, the State Residuals-based detection was able to effectively detect different simulated FDI attacks and showed high accuracy and reliability in detecting

Table 3. Analysis of modern FDI detection techniques

Technique	C1	C2	C3	C4	C5
State Residuals-based Detection [29]	High	Low	High	Med	Med
Data Fusion Algorithm [30]	High	High	Med	Med	Low
MFC-DI [31]	High	N/A	High	Low	Med
History Trajectory Scheme [32]	Med	Med	Low	High	High
Machine Learning Approach [33]	High	High	High	Low	High

such attacks. In addition to detecting the attack, the model was able to determine the impact of the attack on the vehicle's state. The model further developed the algorithm to also remediate attacks through isolation. Hence, algorithm 1 was applied to successfully detect the attack and algorithm 2 was applied to isolate the attack. However, the technique is not scalable and is incredibly difficult to implement in large-scale urban traffic networks, thus depicting low adaptability to varying V2X environments. The model is unreliable due to the high dispersion and hysteresis linked to a heavy-traffic network. The detection time of the model has been estimated at 58.7 s, which is higher than the other detection techniques. Finally, the detection technique also demonstrated a high ability to detect new and more sophisticated types of FDI attacks targeting V2X [29].

The Data Fusion Algorithm was tested under varying scale of attack. Results revealed that the algorithm was highly accurate based on the true positive rate and false alarm rate collected during the attack simulation. The Data Fusion Algorithm had a relatively low detection time of 0.2 s and a detection rate of 1.00 at 100% CAV penetration rate. The combination of the detection algorithm and decision-making scheme allowed the proposed technique to isolate the attacker. However, the proposed technique considered only position and velocity data as targets in the attack which were applied in the simulation of the FDI attack. The compromise of data such as relative distance and acceleration which may be compromised in some forms of FDI attacks were not considered during the simulation. Hence, its ability to detect new attacks was deemed as being low [30].

The MFC-DI involves the calculation of the missing values in addition to the values of the same attribute, unlike existing imputation methods that only consider the values of the same attributes. As a result, the MFC-DI guesses the missing values using both data from the associated attributes and data from the same attribute. This makes the MFC-DI reliable as it relies on varying parameters to detect FDI attacks. The simulation exercises for the MFC-DI did not consider the time taken to detect the attack and was thus deemed not applicable as illustrated in Table 3. While the MFC-DI can handle a V2X environment with a significant amount of adjacent missing data and surpassed results achieved using traditional Pearson correlation, the computational overhead of the multivariate approach is a potential drawback, particularly for online models that adjust to topological and environmental changes within the vehicular environment. Hence, its adaptability to varying V2X environments was deemed low [31].

During the simulation for the History Trajectory Scheme, a compound attack could be identified with an accuracy probability of 83.10% which is quite low compared to the other four detection methods. As all the history trajectories are stored in the control centre, historical behaviour can be examined to identify sophisticated attacks. Additionally, the first procedure of the method was found to be efficient in detecting and responding to the simulated FDI attack. The proposed approach, however, struggles to handle a significant amount of security knowledge; whereby, as security knowledge grows, the detection time increases since multiple situations must be identified. Furthermore, high-performance computer is necessary since this detection approach necessitates considerable analysis [32].

The Machine Learning approach and neural networks (NN) are effective for defect detection within the data collected, which facilitates function categorisation and approximation, as well as handling non-linearity and uncertainty. The NN-based method, hence, aids in not only the precise detection of FDI attack but also its high reliability. Additionally, under the ML approach, the attack is detected in real-time; hence the NN-based algorithm is able to detect the FDI attack as soon as it is occurring. The proposed method also changes based on the car's speed in accordance with the degree of errors in the distance estimations and the braking of the leading vehicle. In the NN-based algorithm, the ML can detect various types of FDI attacks which the targeted vehicle is subjected to as it relies on the nonlinear system. However, the attack was simulated within only a platoon of vehicles which normally has a leading vehicle and follower vehicle(s). The proposed method has yet to be tested within an environment where the CAVs do not operate in a platoon system [33].

All the studied FDI attack detection mechanisms were found to have respective limitations as illustrated in Table 3 and as discussed above. For instance, although the State Residuals-based Detection method was found to have medium-high scores in most criteria studied, it was rated low for "Detection Time" as the latter was higher than what was recorded for the other four detection techniques. Similarly, the Data Fusion Algorithm was deemed low for the ability to detect new attacks as not all data related to the vehicle, such as relative distance and acceleration, were considered as main points of FDI attacks. Overall, the ML approach has a higher combined results as compared to the other four detection techniques. However, this approach has not yet been applied within other large-scale V2X environments. It has yet to be fully relied upon for implementation within a real-world scenario. To overcome this limitation, the ML approach could be further developed and tested within several V2X environments, although more data will be required to further train and enhance existing detection models built within.

Even though the analysis revealed insightful findings as discussed above, this study is still undermined by a few limitations. Firstly, the comparative analysis was performed using literature analysis where simulation of the different detection techniques could yield varying results. Moreover, other aspects such as performance, efficiency, and data quality attributes, among other parameters could have been investigated in order to broaden the analysis and gather more critical insights.

7 Conclusion

V2X communication is increasingly gaining attention in this era of intelligent mobility and automated vehicles. Although V2X communication has significantly improved since its conception, there are still further research works being done on how to make V2X more scalable and stable, especially with the expected rise in CAV in the coming years. As any advancements in the IT industry, V2X and CAV are not without vulnerabilities and are often exploited by attackers. CAV are specifically vulnerable to FDI attacks. FDI attacks have a high likelihood of seriously harming both drivers and pedestrians while also causing significant damage to road infrastructure and the surrounding environment. Due to the alarming consequences of FDI attacks in V2X communication, this research study critically analysed the modern techniques used to detect FDI attacks, notably, State Residuals-based Detection, Data Fusion Algorithm, MFC-DI, History Trajectory Scheme and Machine Learning Approach. These detection mechanisms were analysed in terms of their detection accuracy, time, reliability, adaptability to varying V2X environments and ability to detect new attacks. It was found that all detection mechanisms have their own limitations pertaining to the criteria studied as none of them were able to achieve the highest scores in all the criteria. Among the approaches studied, machine learning scored the highest, although it showed low adaptability to varying V2X environments. Since this study did not perform a practical quantitative comparison of the five modern detection techniques, this limitation could be further explored in future research works.

References

1. Seo, H., Lee, K.D., Yasukawa, S., Peng, Y., Sartori, P.: LTE evolution for vehicle-to-everything services. IEEE Commun. Mag. **54**, 22–28 (2016)
2. Hasan, M., Mohan, S., Shimizu, T., Lu, H.: Securing vehicle-to-everything (V2X) communication platforms. IEEE Trans. Intell. Veh. **5**(4), 693–713 (2020)
3. Saulaiman, M.N.E., Kozlovszky, M., Csilling, A.: A survey on vulnerabilities and classification of cyber-attacks on 5G-V2X. In: IEEE 21st International Symposium on Computational Intelligence and Informatics, Budapest (2021)
4. Statista. Projected autonomous vehicle market size worldwide between 2021 and 2025. Statista (2020). https://www.statista.com/statistics/1224515/av-market-size-worldwide-for ecast/. Accessed 07 Nov 2022
5. Lozano Domínguez, J.M., Mateo Sanguino, T.D.J.: Review on V2X, I2X, and P2X communications and their applications: a comprehensive analysis over time. Sensors **19**(12), 2756 (2019)
6. Petit, J., Shladover, S.E.: Potential cyberattacks on automated vehicles. IEEE Trans. Intell. Transp. Syst. **16**(2), 546–556 (2015)
7. Chattopadhyay, A., Mitra, U., Ström, E.G.: Secure estimation in V2X networks with injection and packet drop attacks. In: 2018 15th International Symposium on Wireless Communication Systems (ISWCS), pp. 1–6 (2018)
8. Ahmed, M., Pathan, A.-S.K.: False data injection attack (FDIA): an overview and new metrics for fair evaluation of its countermeasure. Complex Adapt. Syst. Model. **8**(4), 2–14 (2020)
9. Mode, G.R., Calyam, P., Hoque, K.A.: False data injection attacks in internet of things and deep learning enabled predictive analytics. In: 32nd IEEE/IFIP Network Operations and Management Symposium (NOMS 2020), Hugary (2019)
10. Ullah, H., Nair, N.G., Moore, A., Nugent, C., Muschamp, P., Cuevas, M.: 5G communication: an overview of vehicle-to-everything, drones, and healthcare use-cases. IEEE Access **7**, 37251–37268 (2019)
11. Hobert, L., Festag, A., Llatser, I., Altomare, L., Visintainer, F., Kovacs, A.: Enhancements of V2X communication in support of cooperative autonomous driving. IEEE Commun. Mag. (ComMag) **53**(12), 64–70 (2015)

12. Sun, S.H., Hu, J.L., Peng, Y., Pan, X.M., Zhao, L., Fang, J.Y.: Support for vehicle-to-everything services based on LTE. IEEE Wirel. Commun. **23**(3), 4–8 (2016)
13. Chen, S., Hu, J., Shi, Y., Peng, Y., Fang, J., Zhao, R., Zhao, L.: Vehicle-to-everything (V2X) services supported by LTE-based systems and 5G. IEEE Commun. Stand. Mag. **1**, 70–76 (2017)
14. Tahir, M., Leviäkangas, P., Katz, M.: Connected vehicles: V2V and V2I road weather and traffic communication using cellular technologies. Sens. (Basel) **22**(3), 1142 (2022)
15. Saeed, U., Hämäläinen, J., Mutafungwa, E., Wichman, R., González, D., Garcia-Lozano, M.: Route-based radio coverage analysis of cellular network deployments for V2N communication. In: International Conference on Wireless and Mobile Computing, Networking and Communications (WiMob), Barcelona (2019)
16. Sanguesa, J., et al.: Sensing traffic density combining V2V and V2I wireless communications. Sens. (Basel) **15**(12), 31794–31810 (2015)
17. Santa, J., Gómez-Skarmeta, A.F., Sánchez-Artigas, M.: Architecture and evaluation of a unified V2V and V2I communication system based on cellular networks. Comput. Commun. **31**(12), 2850–2861 (2008)
18. Gupta, M., Benson, J., Patwa, F., Sandhu, R.: Secure V2V and V2I communication in intelligent transportation using cloudlets. IEEE Trans. Serv. Comput. **15**, 1912–1925 (2020)
19. Tong, W., Hussain, A., Bo, W.X., Maharjan, S.: Artificial intelligence for vehicle-to-everything: a survey. IEEE Access **7**, 10823–10843 (2019)
20. Khan, M.A., et al.: Robust, resilient and reliable architecture for V2X communication. IEEE Trans. Intell. Transp. Syst. **22**(7), 1–18 (2021)
21. Boban, M., Kousaridas, A., Manolakis, K., Eichinger, J., Xu, W.: Use cases, requirements, and design considerations for 5G V2X. arXiv preprint arXiv (2017)
22. MacHardy, Z., Khan, A., Obana, K., Iwashina, S.: V2X access technologies: regulation, research, and remaining challenges. IEEE Commun. Surv. Tutor. **20**(3), 1858–1877 (2018)
23. The Associated Press. Nearly 400 car crashes in 11 months involved automated tech, companies tell regulators. NPR (2022). https://www.npr.org/2022/06/15/1105252793/nearly-400-car-crashes-in-11-months-involved-automated-tech-companies-tell-regul. Accessed 28 Nov 2022
24. Alsulami, A., Abu Al-Haija, Q., Alqahtani, A., Alsini, R.: Symmetrical simulation scheme for anomaly detection in autonomous vehicles based on LSTM model. Symmetry **14**(7), 1450 (2022)
25. Koley, I., Adhikary, S., Rohit, R., Dey, S.: A CAD framework for simulation of network level attack on platoons. arXiv (2022)
26. Yang, T., Murguia, C., Lv, C.: Risk assessment for connected vehicles under stealthy attacks on vehicle-to-vehicle networks. J. Latex Class Files **14**(8), 1–12 (2020)
27. Biroon, R.A., Biron, Z.A., Pisu, P.: False data injection attack in a platoon of CACC: real-time detection and isolation with a PDE approach. IEEE Trans. Intell. Transp. Syst. **23**(7), 8692–8703 (2022)
28. UC Berkeley. Cooperative Adaptive Cruise Control. UC Berkeley | Institute of Transportation Studies (2022). https://path.berkeley.edu/research/connected-and-automated-vehicles/cooperative-adaptive-cruise-control. Accessed 25 Dec 2022
29. Huang, X., Wang, X.: Detection and isolation of false data injection attack in intelligent transportation system via robust state observer. Processes **10**, 1–13 (2022)
30. Zhao, C., Gill, J.S., Pisu, P., Comert, G.: Detection of false data injection attack in connected and automated vehicles via cloud-based sandboxing. IEEE Trans. Intell. Transp. Syst. **23**(7), 9078–9088 (2022)
31. Almalki, S.A., Sheldon, F.T.: Deep learning to improve false data injection attack detection in cooperative intelligent transportation systems. In: 12th Annual Information Technology, Electronics and Mobile Communication Conference (IEMCON), Vancouver (2021)

32. Chung, W., Cho, T.: Complex attack detection scheme using history trajectory in internet of vehicles. Egypt. Inform. J. **23**, 499–510 (2022)
33. Sargolzaei, A., Crane, C., Abbaspour, A., Noei, S.: A machine learning approach for fault detection in vehicular cyber-physical systems. In: 15th IEEE International Conference on Machine Learning and Applications, Anaheim (2016)
34. Shurman, M.M., Khrais, R.M., Yateem, A.A.: IoT denial-of-service attack detection and prevention using hybrid IDS. In: 2019 International Arab Conference on Information Technology (ACIT), Al Ain (2019)

Enhancing Home Security with Pressure Mat Sensors: A Multi-modal IoT Approach

Karel Veerabudren(⊠) ⓘ, Visham Ramsurrun, Mrinal Sharma ⓘ, and Amar Seeam ⓘ

Middlesex University, Uniciti, Flic-en-Flac, Mauritius
{k.veerabudren,v.ramsurrun,m.sharma,a.seeam}@mdx.ac.mu

Abstract. Home security is a major concern worldwide, and there are various solutions available, but with limitations. This paper proposes a novel security system that overcomes the limitations of current systems by using piezoresistive sensors placed inside a mat to detect intruders with varying levels of pressure intensities. The proposed system incorporates a camera and a CNN algorithm with the EfficientNet model to detect whether the object is a human, and it is equipped with features like an email and SMS notification mechanism, backup battery, and a sophisticated tracking mechanism. The proposed system is highly resilient to tampering or circumvention and outperforms existing security systems in terms of being non-intrusive, providing tracking features for the intruder, and being resistant to blackouts. This paper documents the research, development, testing, evaluation process, and contributions made to address the security challenges by developing an affordable, easy-to-use, and effective home security system.

Keywords: IoT Home Security · Floor sensors · Intruder detection

1 Introduction

Smart home security refers to the use of IoT devices, which consist of a network of interconnected devices with technologies put in place [1] to enhance the security of a domicile. This includes using cameras, sensors, and notification alarms, with the key benefit of being remotely controllable and accessible [2]. These systems have been growing in popularity, and one reason is the increasing risks of home intrusions [3]. In 2020, burglary ranked the most frequent crime in the United States and is among the most common crimes committed globally. SafeHome [4] conducted a study that revealed nearly half of the American population has been a victim of burglary, with 47.64% of them being present during the crime. The high crime rates and risky nature not only result in financial loss but also inflict emotional trauma on victims, affecting communities and society. The widespread use of traditional security mechanisms combined with IoT systems in households highlights the clear necessity for home security. However, these systems are not always effective, as burglars can bypass them and go undetected. Additionally, some systems have a high rate of false positives. In her research the author Gonzalez [5], expounded on the issue of security system sensitivity, highlighting its

A. Seeam et al. (Eds.): InterSol 2023, LNICST 541, pp. 81–95, 2024.
https://doi.org/10.1007/978-3-031-51849-2_6

potential obsolescence. They also presented a staggering statistic, with false positives accounting for up to 95% of triggered alerts. The susceptibility of sensors to various environmental and lighting factors has contributed to this phenomenon, resulting in the wastage of valuable resources such as time and money.

In addition, the reliance on internet connectivity for all IoT security devices also presents a significant security concern [6]. As noted by Tholen [7], in the event of a power outage, the entire system becomes vulnerable and unable to monitor the home. This outage can make the system an ideal target for burglars, who can exploit the security gap to gain undetected access to the property. Even more concerning is that homeowners who are away during the blackout may not be aware of the outage until it is too late, leaving them vulnerable to thefts and property damage. Therefore, it is crucial for homeowners to have contingency plans in place in case of power outages to ensure the continued security of their homes.

This paper presents the results of developing a non-intrusive multi-modal home security system using a mat-based flooring detection system. The system detects intruders by ensuring they step on the floor, and a heatmap displays their live location. False positives have been reduced using machine learning algorithms to confirm the presence of humans. The system is also blackout-resistant, and the homeowner is notified through different channels. A web application displays the heatmap and provides camera access, with a database to store intrusion and blackout history. Overall evaluation is based on the success of the system's effectiveness, blackout resistance, and user-friendliness.

The paper is organized as follows: Sect. 2 reviews existing home security systems and their sensors. Section 3 describes the proposed design and the development of its hardware and software to achieve the paper's aims and objectives. The testing of the system is detailed in Sect. 4, followed by an evaluation in Sect. 5. Finally, Sect. 6 concludes the paper with potential future pathway considerations.

2   Literature Review

2.1   Background

Technological advancements on the Internet of Things (IoT) have expanded the capabilities of home security systems. These systems now integrate with traditional security measures to provide enhanced protection against intruders. A modern home security system comprises input devices, a processing unit, and output devices. The input devices include sensors that monitor the home environment, and the data collected is transmitted to the processing unit, which is typically a microcontroller. The microcontroller analyses the data received and sends a signal to the output device, usually an alarm if any abnormalities are detected.

This concept has proven to give homeowners greater security and peace of mind. Various input sensors can further improve the accuracy and precision of the security system, providing even greater reassurance to homeowners—for example, the ability to detect fire/smoke and alert the homeowner via an application. Additionally, the system can detect intrusion using motion, door sensors, and a security camera. When the sensors detect unusual activity, such as motion or a door opening, a signal is sent to the microcontroller. The microcontroller receives the data from the sensors, analyses the data based on predetermined thresholds, and decides whether to notify the homeowner. If necessary, the microcontroller sends a notification to the respective parties via a Wi-Fi module, which enables it to connect to the home router. If an alarm is present, it will automatically trigger when the notification is sent.

For instance, Desnanjaya and Arsana [8] discuss creating a home security monitoring system using Raspberry Pi as the control centre. The system includes various sensors such as PIR, raspicam, temperature and gas. Telegram is used to send notifications from the Raspberry Pi to users. The system can detect intruders, take pictures, monitor temperature, and detect gas or smoke. Sharma et al. [9] discuss an affordable and innovative smart home monitoring system called RaspiMonitor. The system aims to provide a comprehensive smart home architecture that ensures the safety and security of its environment using PIR and gas sensors while also reducing energy wastage. Users can then control their homes and monitor their usage through the web application. In addition, there is also the Ring Alarm Pro [10], which is a commercial product. The system features an integrated router that allows the different sensors, such as motion and door sensors, to be easily connected. Other devices, such as smart bulbs or door cameras, can be paired easily. The whole system can be controlled through its mobile application.

The following section reviews some key literature to provide an overview of existing home security systems, their sensors, and technologies. A comparative analysis is also carried out to identify gaps in current research and highlight areas with potential for further investigation, including improvements in home security systems.

2.2 Related Works

Due to the extensive scope of IoT research, various studies have addressed gaps yielding varying levels of success in this field. To contextualize authors Taiwo and Ezugwu [11] proposed the iHOCS system, an intelligent home control and security system that provides a convenient and remote way for owners to control and supervise their electrical appliances using a mobile app. The system also includes a security monitoring component that uses a PIR sensor and camera to detect motion and take pictures. The authors proposed using a support vector machine learning algorithm to prevent false positives by recognizing the occupants in the snapshot taken by the camera. The system has several advantages, such as significantly reducing false positives and notifying the owner through an application and email. However, there are several limitations to the system, including the potential for random triggering of the PIR due to temperature changes, the need for adequate training of the machine learning algorithm, and the absence of a redundancy plan in the event of a power outage. Therefore, while the iHOCS system offers several benefits, areas still require improvement and careful consideration.

The proposed system by Taryudi et al. [12] for safety monitoring and home security has several advantages and limitations. One of the system's main advantages is its ability to detect and monitor various environmental factors, such as temperature, humidity, rain, and flames, which can help prevent potential hazards. The two-layer identification system, which includes an RFID card and numerical PIN code on the front door, adds an extra security layer to identify genuine users. Furthermore, the non-intrusive nature of the system means that the owner will not be disturbed while at home, and the system is activated. However, there are also some limitations to the proposed approach. For instance, the system cannot differentiate between pets and intruders, which may lead to false alarms. Additionally, the inability to track intruders' movements may make it challenging to monitor or locate an intruder in case of a security breach. Finally, the lack of a redundancy plan in case of a power outage may affect the system's reliability and pose a potential safety risk. Therefore, it is crucial to address these limitations to ensure the effectiveness and reliability of the proposed method.

Ramli et al. [13] propose a novel security system that avoids the limitations of the PIR sensor by utilizing load cells to detect the weight of an intruder. The load cells are placed behind tiles; the sensor can determine their weight if a person steps onto them. The weight threshold of 30 kg is set to avoid detecting animals and trigger alerts in real-time. The system allows tracking of the intruder's movement and is non-intrusive. However, the system requires many load cells, and an object falling on the tile may trigger a false alarm. Additionally, there is no way to ensure the detected entity is genuinely human. Furthermore, the load cell system's complexity and the need for a cable connection to an Arduino connected to the Wi-Fi network may increase the system's cost and installation complexity. Therefore, while the load cell system presents a promising alternative to the PIR sensor, further research is needed to improve its accuracy, reliability, and practicality for home security applications.

Das and Neelanarayan [14] proposed an anti-theft system for shops using a PIR sensor and camera. The system is manually activated when the shop is empty. The PIR sensor detects infrared radiation and triggers the camera to take a picture for face recognition. If the face is unrecognized, an alarm is triggered, and the owner is notified. One of the advantages is that the system provides a backup plan in case of a blackout, ensuring that the system can continue to operate uninterrupted. Additionally, the system can distinguish between employees and intruders using facial recognition technology, which enhances security. However, there are also some drawbacks to the approach. For example, false positives may occur if the camera fails to capture the intruder's face accurately. Furthermore, passers-by may trigger the PIR sensor unnecessarily, leading to false alarms. Finally, although the paper claims an accuracy rate of 75%, the system was tested on image datasets and not real-life footage, which raises questions about its real-world performance.

Dorothy et al. [15] present a unique approach to home security by using a reed switch and a camera to detect and capture images of intruders. The system's ability to minimize power consumption by sending complex processing to the fog and taking fewer images is commendable. However, the system's cost is a significant disadvantage, as a reed switch and camera are required for each door, and there is no solution for blackouts. Furthermore, the system's sole method of alerting the owner when there is an intruder may not be sufficient, as it may be easy to miss the alert. Overall, the proposed security system presents a promising solution to home security, but improvements are needed to address the system's limitations.

The proposed security system by Sivarathinabala et al. [16] is based solely on cameras, which can identify an occupant based on their face and gait. It continuously records video footage from two cameras installed at specific locations, which are then processed by a computer algorithm to identify occupants. An alarm is triggered if an intruder is detected. The system is advantageous because it can recognize occupants, and alarms are only activated for humans, not pets. Additionally, the intruder can be tracked as there are cameras in opposite directions, and when the alarm is triggered, it is almost sure that there is a person. However, the system has several disadvantages, including high power consumption due to continuous monitoring and processing and the requirement of high resources for processing. Furthermore, the approach is not practical if there is a power cut. Additionally, it is intrusive, and the owner can feel like they are losing their privacy. Finally, the positioning of the cameras is critical for system efficiency, which can be challenging to achieve.

The above studies have proposed different approaches for IoT-based home security systems, each with advantages and limitations. Taiwo and Ezugwu [11] proposed the iHOCS system, which uses a support vector machine learning algorithm to prevent false positives and includes a security monitoring component. Taryudi et al. [12] proposed a safety monitoring and home security system that can detect various environmental factors but cannot differentiate between pets and intruders. Ramli et al. [13] proposed a security system that uses load cells to detect the weight of an intruder but requires many load cells and has installation complexities. Das and Neelanarayan [14] proposed an anti-theft system for shops using a PIR sensor and camera, but real-life footage testing limitations exist. Dorothy et al. [15] proposed a home security system using a reed switch and a camera, which minimizes power consumption but has a high cost and no solution for blackouts. Sivarathinabala et al. [16] proposed a camera-based security system that can recognize occupants and track intruders but has limited coverage and requires a clear view of the cameras.

2.3 Comparative Analysis

The related works discussed have been compiled in Table 1. Each paper presents a distinct approach to securing homes from intruders using various sensors, algorithms, and technologies. The papers have been categorized based on their detection mechanisms, such as image processing, sound, and weight detection. A comparative analysis of the different approaches has been provided by summarising each paper's proposed system, advantages, and limitations.

3 Design and Development

This study aims to design a home security surveillance system with a floor detection mechanism to prevent unauthorized access. The floor mat will consist of a sensor array configured in a matrix to detect varying degrees of pressure. When the mat detects pressure, a camera will initiate recording to identify human presence. A Convolutional Neural Network (CNN) model will be employed to optimize accuracy and functionality on low-resource devices. This section provides a walkthrough of the various steps that entailed the development of the proposed system.

Table 1. Taxonomy of the Related Work

Security System	Identification Method	Sensors Used	Advantages	Disadvantages
Taiwo and Ezugwu, 2021	Machine learning algorithm to differentiate between occupants and intruders	PIR sensor, camera	Significantly reduces false positives, remote control, notifications via app and email	PIR may be triggered randomly, training the machine learning algorithm is time-consuming, no redundancy plan
Taryudi et al., 2018	RFID card and numerical PIN code on the front door	PIR sensor, flame, rain, temperature, humidity	Flame detection, two layers of identification, non-intrusive	Cannot differentiate between pets and intruders, no tracking or monitoring of intruders, no redundancy plan
Das and Neelanarayan, 2020	Face detection	PIR sensor, camera	Provides backup in case of power cut, can recognize employees from intruders	Positioning of camera is critical, PIR may be triggered unnecessarily, and accuracy not tested on real-life footage
Dorothy et al., 2017	Image processing to detect intruders	Reed switch, camera	Complex processing done in fog, fewer images taken than with PIR	Expensive, no solution for power cut, and only one method to alert the owner
Sivarathinabala et al., 2019	Face and gait recognition	Two cameras	Can recognize occupants, alarms triggered only for humans	Requires two cameras, may not work well in low light conditions
Ramli et al., 2021	Floor detection	Load cells	Intruders cannot bypass the system easily, and it allows tracking	Requires many load cells and risk of false alarm if an object falls on tile. Cannot be sure if detection is from a human

3.1 Methodology

The development of the security system utilized a prototyping methodology, where an initial prototype was constructed and tested against the initial requirements. Through the testing process, design issues were promptly detected and resolved, allowing for the continuous refinement of the prototype until a final design was achieved that met all requirements. This methodology detected and resolved issues early in the development process, saving time and resources while delivering a high-quality security system. The mat algorithm was also refined and adjusted based on the test results to optimize the detection.

3.2 Design

To create the monitoring device, it is necessary to assemble various hardware components, including sensors, and connect and program them to meet the system requirements. The design architecture of the system is shown in Fig. 1.

The sensor used to build the mat is a piezoresistive sensor. This type of sensor is affordable, widely available on the market and can be integrated easily into an electronic circuit. The sensors will be arranged in an $n \times n$ matrix to enable tracking features. Each cell in the matrix will correspond to a location on the carpet, and the pressure applied to adjacent cells will reveal the intruder's position. An Arduino will be connected to the mat and will continuously send the pressure values of each sensor wirelessly to a Raspberry Pi for monitoring. The design is represented in Fig. 2 (a).

The Raspberry Pi will collect the sensor data and then process them using standard deviation statistical analysis to determine if an object is on it. A signal is transmitted to activate the camera to ascertain whether the object is human. The camera captures five image frames of the surroundings for one second, and a trained CNN algorithm processes each image to detect human presence. If most of the frames indicate the presence of an intruder, the picture is saved, and bounding boxes are added around the burglar. Then, it is sent to the owner by email. The latter is also notified of the intrusion by SMS using the GSM network. The pressure values are also sent to a web application where the intruder's location on the mat can be observed.

To ensure uninterrupted operation, the Raspberry Pi will be equipped with a battery to sustain the system during blackouts. In the event of a power cut, the controller will take note of the internet connection loss and store the time and date in a log file. Once the internet connection is restored, the system will notify the owner of the power outage and upload information on the duration of the blackout to the online database. As long as there is enough battery power, the device will continue monitoring. However, without an internet connection, the owner will receive SMS notifications. Nevertheless, the system will record incidents locally and upload them to the online database once the internet connection is re-established. The design of the Raspberry Pi is represented in Fig. 2 (b).

3.3 Development

The material used to develop the mat is the Velostat. Velostat is an electrically conductive plastic film with piezoresistive properties, changing its electrical resistance in

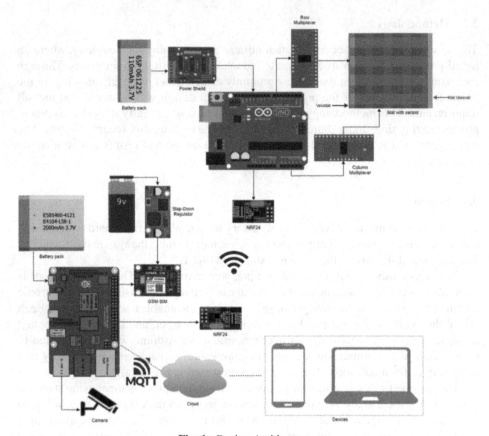

Fig. 1. Design Architecture

response to pressure or deformation. Hopkins et al. [17] briefly discussed the different applications for using this material, such as in human movement monitoring and finger gesture recognition.

The mat was built with a similar design as in the study of [18]. To achieve this, two 16-channel analogue multiplexers were implemented, with one managing signal transmission to the columns on the mat while the other was responsible for reading values from the rows. For the rows and columns, copper tape and aluminium were utilized as conductive materials. However, the copper tape was only available in a 5 mm width, and to increase this to 20 mm, it was paired with aluminium tape. Copper tape was preferred over aluminium tape for attaching ribbon cables, as it was easier to solder onto. Figure 3 shows the layout of the mat used for construction. The other materials used can be found in Table 2.

The pressure data collected from the mat was transmitted wirelessly to the Raspberry Pi via the Nrf24L01 operating on the 2.4 GHz frequency band. Subsequently, several analyses were conducted on the data to determine the presence of an individual on the mat. Statistical analysis, singular value decomposition, and eigenvalues were computed from the pressure values. The investigation results indicated that the standard deviation

(a). Arduino connected to Mat Sensor   (b). Connection of Raspberry Pi

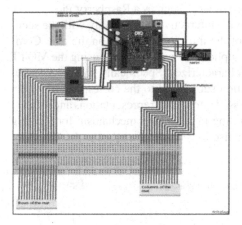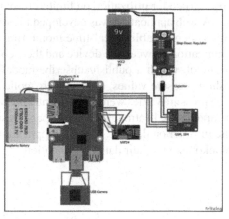

Fig. 2. Connections of the Arduino to the mat sensor

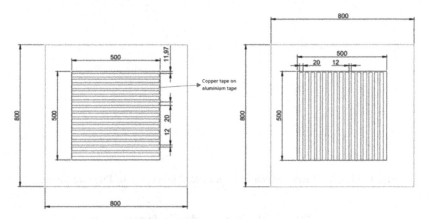

Fig. 3. Construction of the Mat

method produced more satisfactory outcomes when compared to other techniques. Thus, it was selected as the preferred approach and calculated using Eq. (1). The results of the standard deviation method, when an individual walked on the mat, were graphically represented and presented in Fig. 4.

$$\sigma = \sqrt{\frac{\sum_i \sum_j (x_{ij} - \mu)^2)}{nm}} \qquad (1)$$

The CNN algorithm employed in this study utilized Tensorflow Lite in conjunction with the EfficientNet model. This particular model was selected based on research conducted by Isuyama and Albertini [12], who demonstrated its superior accuracy in object classification, achieving an impressive 94% while exhibiting reduced memory usage and size compared to other models. Consequently, the EfficientNet model is the most appropriate for utilization on limited-resource devices such as a Raspberry Pi.

A web application was developed to provide interactive functionality with the security system, enabling real-time monitoring of the intruder's location on the mat. Communication between the device and the web application was facilitated using the MQTT protocol, which a publish/subscribe model characterizes. Specifically, the device published pressure values, and the web application subscribed to the corresponding topic. The pressure values were subsequently processed into colour representations and utilized to update the heatmap on the webpage, resulting in a tracking mechanism for locating the intruder on the mat. The web application also logs past intrusions and the history of blackouts with their dates and duration.

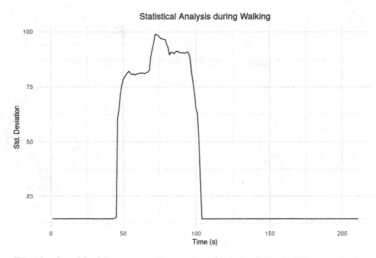

Fig. 4. Graphical Representation of Standard Deviation of Pressure Values

Table 2. Hardware Used in the System

Device	Model	Use
Raspberry Pi	Pi 4 Model B	The brain of the system. It processes the data received from the mat and activates the camera when needed. It also sends notifications to the user
Arduino Uno	ATmega328P 16 MHz	Reads pressure values from the mat and sends them to the Raspberry Pi
Uninterrupted Power Supply	PiJuice with 1820 mAh battery	Provide backup when there is no electricity to keep the system running
Radio Transceiver	Nrf24L01	Transmits & receives pressure values
Camera	C922 Pro	Takes pictures, which will be processed
Cellular Module	SIM800L Version 2	Sends SMS via the GSM network

4 Testing

An appropriate testing environment was established to validate the monitoring device's efficacy. The camera was strategically positioned to cover a significant portion of the room, with a clear line of sight to the intruder as they traversed the mat. Multiple test cases were conducted to evaluate the performance of the detection system, ensuring that it functioned under the anticipated specifications. The test cases are elaborated on in Table 3.

Table 3. Test Cases Performed on the System

ID	Test Cases	Description	Expected Behaviour	Pass
01	Human on the mat and in camera's vision	Humans of weights from 40 kg to 75 kg walked normally on the mat	The system should activate, detect the intruder, and alert the owner	Y
02	Human on the mat but only half body in camera's vision	Humans walk on the mat and activate the system, but only half of the body is in the camera's vision	The system should activate, detect the intruder, and alert the owner	Y
03	A non-human object on the mat	An arbitrary object of 2 kg is placed on the mat to activate the system	The system should activate but not alert the owner	Y
04	Both human and non-human objects on the mat	An arbitrary object is already on the mat. Then a human walked on it	The system should detect changes in pressure when an intruder walks on the mat and alert the owner, even if other objects are already on it	Y
05	A second mat is added to the system	Since pressure values are sent wirelessly to the Raspberry Pi, a second mat should be easily added, and the system should be able to process the values between the two mats	The system should be able to differentiate between the pressure values of the two mats and alert the owner of the exact location	Y

The system's responsiveness has also been assessed by measuring the duration between a human's detection and the owner's notification. Specifically, the instances when an object is initially detected when the system confirms the object as a human and when all the alerts are sent, and the database is updated have been recorded across fifteen trials. Table 4 presents the collected data on detection and notification times in seconds. Results show that the system exhibits an average detection time of 2.3 s and an average notification time of 12.8 s, encompassing SMS and email alerts and intrusion logging into the database.

Table 4. Responsiveness of the System

Tests	Detection Time (s)	Notification Time (s)
1	2.495529175	11.88773441
2	2.20410347	12.83382773
3	2.167779207	13.64314818
4	2.358976134	12.99078451
5	2.100421437	13.28403222
6	2.425074197	12.22190557
7	2.288811947	13.1683855
8	2.048316234	12.42726934
9	2.175364766	13.00719492
10	2.352291611	12.49614017
11	2.195211182	12.33180342
12	2.109123326	13.2607751
13	2.484581985	12.54253524
14	2.379875462	13.49991129
15	2.527416902	11.99954764
Average	**2.289137284**	**12.78823678**

Based on the results of 15 tests conducted, the system demonstrated a 100% detection rate and a 0% false positive rate in detecting intruders. The system's low false positive rate can only be attributed to its activation when pressure is applied to the mat, followed by confirmation via the CNN EfficientNet model. However, according to Liu [19], the EfficientNet model has an accuracy of 80.4%. Therefore, the system's overall accuracy is also 80.4%, as the detection depends on the vision model's performance.

5 Evaluation and Results

The developed home monitoring system was evaluated in terms of meeting the initially defined requirements. A comparative analysis has also been conducted with major related works to assess the uniqueness and distinctiveness of the system. Furthermore, the system's strengths and limitations are analyzed to evaluate the security system comprehensively.

5.1 Functional Requirements

(See Table 5).

Table 5. Fulfilment of the Requirement

Functional Requirement	Fulfilled?	Remarks
Correct identification of a human intruder	Yes	The system utilizes the TensorFlow framework with the EfficientNet model to detect human presence on the images captured by the camera when an intruder steps on the mat
Immediate owner notification	Yes	The system employs two notification channels to alert the owner of an intrusion. The average time taken to notify the owner is 13 s
Blackout resistance	Yes	The device is equipped with a battery that provides power during a power outage, enabling the device to function continuously during a blackout. The current battery capacity permits the device to operate for up to one hour
Intrusion and blackout logging	Yes	The device records the date and time of each intrusion and power outage in an online database accessible through the web application. When an intrusion occurs, the image of the intruder is uploaded to the database. The blackout duration is calculated and logged when there is a power cut

5.2 Comparative Analysis with Related Works

(See Tables 6 and 7).

Table 6. Comparative Analysis of Existing Research

Characteristics	Developed Security System	Taiwo and Ezugwu, 2021	Taryudi et al., 2018	Das and Neelanaray an, 2020	Dorothy et al., 2017	Sivarathi-nabala et al., 2019	Ramli et al., 2021
Non-avoidable	Yes	No	No	No	Partially	Yes	Yes
Human detection	Yes	Yes	Yes	Partially	Yes	Yes	No
Non-intrusive	Yes	Yes	Yes	Yes	Yes	No	Yes
Tracking	Yes	Partially	No	Partially	Partially	Yes	Yes
Redundant Notification	Yes	No	No	Yes	No	No	No
Powercut- resistant	Yes	No	No	Yes	No	No	No

5.3   Analysis of Developed System

Table 7. Analysis of the Developed System

Strengths	Limitations
Remote activation and deactivation	No notification in areas without mobile network
Accurate detection of human intruders	Ghost values may appear on the heatmap
Dual notification channels	Occasional disconnection from the mat sensor after intrusion
Unintrusive and real-time monitoring	No preventive action is taken against burglars
Scalability	The web application does not know when the device is offline
Blackout resistance	Latency issue on the heatmap during the human detection process
Log of intrusion and blackout history	Due to the complexity entangled with other parts of the system, the mat hardware alone could not be further tested

6   Conclusion and Future Works

The project has successfully developed a home security monitoring system that utilizes a flooring detection mechanism sensor. The system addresses the limitations of traditional security systems that rely on passive infrared sensors, which can be easily bypassed. The proposed method uses a low-cost piezoresistive material, Velostat, to create a matrix of 225 sensors that can track an intruder's location on the floor and determine whether it is a human. The system also incorporates a camera and a CNN algorithm using the EfficientNet model to confirm the presence of a human intruder. Furthermore, the system provides redundancy and is blackout-resistant, making it a reliable security solution for homeowners.

Future research can focus on developing more sophisticated algorithms that can detect and classify multiple intruders and homeowners to prevent false alarms. Other suggestions for future works include creating a separate thread for sending pressures to the web app to prevent latency during an intrusion, developing a mobile application to complement the web app, enhancing communication protocols between the RPi and Arduino to reduce packet loss, and researching the simultaneous increase of inter-distance on both top and bottom layers for better results. Overall, the developed prototype can serve as a foundation for further research and development of advanced home security monitoring systems.

References

1. Hoque, M.A., Davidson, C.: Design and implementation of an IoT-based smart home security system. IJNDC **7**(2), 85 (2019). https://doi.org/10.2991/ijndc.k.190326.004

2. Surantha, N., Wicaksono, W.R.: Design of smart home security system using object recognition and PIR sensor. Procedia Comput. Sci. **135**, 465–472 (2018). https://doi.org/10.1016/j.procs.2018.08.198

3. Rock, L.Y., Tajudeen, F.P., Chung, Y.W.: Usage and impact of the internet-of-things-based smart home technology: a quality-of-life perspective. Univ. Access Inf. Soc. (2022). https://doi.org/10.1007/s10209-022-00937-0

4. SafeHome.org Research, "Home Security Statistics in 2021," SafeHome.org (2021). https://www.safehome.org/data/home-security-statistics/. Accessed 21 Sep 2022

5. Gonzalez, M.: Reducing false alarms with AI and deep learning (2022). https://www.security101.com/blog/reducing-false-alarms-with-ai-and-deep-learning. Accessed 21 Sep 2022

6. Doan, T.T., Safavi-Naini, R., Li, S., Avizheh, S.K.M.V., Fong, P.W.:Towards a resilient smart home. In: Proceedings of the 2018 Workshop on IoT Security and Privacy, pp. 15–21. ACM, Budapest Hungary, August 2018. https://doi.org/10.1145/3229565.3229570

7. Tholen, C.: If the Power Goes Out, Does My Security System Still Work? SafeWise, 12 April 2021. https://www.safewise.com/home-security-faq/do-security-systems-work-power-out/. Accessed 21 Sep 2022

8. Desnanjaya, I.G.M.N., Arsana, I.N.A.: Home security monitoring system with IoT-based raspberry Pi. IJEECS **22**(3), 1295 (2021). https://doi.org/10.11591/ijeecs.v22.i3.pp1295-1302

9. Sharma, M., Assotally, A., Bekaroo, G.: RaspiMonitor: a raspberry pi based smart home monitoring system. In: 2022 3rd International Conference on Next Generation Computing Applications (NextComp), pp. 1–6. IEEE, Flic-en-Flac, Mauritius, October 2022. https://doi.org/10.1109/NextComp55567.2022.9932198

10. Ring, "Ring Alarm Pro," Ring. https://ring.com/products/alarm-pro-base-station. Accessed 19 Mar 2023

11. Taiwo, O., Ezugwu, A.E.: Internet of things-based intelligent smart home control system. Secur. Commun. Netw. **2021**, 1–17 (2021). https://doi.org/10.1155/2021/9928254

12. Adriano, D.B., Budi, W.A.C.: IoT-based integrated home security and monitoring system. J. Phys. Conf. Ser. **1140**, 012006 (2018). https://doi.org/10.1088/1742-6596/1140/1/012006

13. Binti Ramli, R., Binti Nazri, N.D.A., Al-Sanjary, O.I., Rozzani, N.: The development of weight detection system using IOT flooring. In: 2021 IEEE 11th IEEE Symposium on Computer Applications & Industrial Electronics (ISCAIE), pp. 250–255. IEEE, Penang, Malaysia, April 2021. https://doi.org/10.1109/ISCAIE51753.2021.9431787

14. Das, S., Neelanarayan, V.: IoT Based Anti-Theft Flooring System, p. 4 (2020)

15. Dorothy, A.B., Kumar, S.B.R., Sharmila, J.J.: IoT based home security through digital image processing algorithms. In: 2017 World Congress on Computing and Communication Technologies (WCCCT), pp. 20–23. IEEE, Tiruchirappalli, Tamil Nadu, India, Feburary 2017. https://doi.org/10.1109/WCCCT.2016.15

16. Sivarathinabala, M., Abirami, S., Deivamani, M., Sudharsan, M.: A smart security system using multi-modal features from videos. Pattern Recognit Image Anal. **29**(1), 89–98 (2019). https://doi.org/10.1134/S1054661819010218

17. Hopkins, M., Vaidyanathan, R., Mcgregor, A.H.: Examination of the performance characteristics of velostat as an in-socket pressure sensor. IEEE Sens. J. **20**(13), 6992–7000 (2020). https://doi.org/10.1109/JSEN.2020.2978431

18. Kumar, V., Yeo, B.-C., Lim, W.-S., Ra, J.E., Koh, K.-B.: Development of electronic floor mat for fall detection and elderly care. Asian J. Sci. Res. **11**(3), 344–356 (2018). https://doi.org/10.3923/ajsr.2018.344.356

19. Liu, R.: Higher accuracy on vision models with EfficientNet-Lite (2020). https://blog.tensorflow.org/2020/03/higher-accuracy-on-vision-models-with-efficientnet-lite.html. Accessed 30 Sep 2022

Blockchain and Machine Learning Algorithms

Blockchain Based Mobile-Patient Medical Records Management System

Sarvesh Yugesh Soochit, Visham Ramsurrun, Mrinal Sharma[✉] ⓘ,
Karel Veerabudren ⓘ, and Amar Seeam ⓘ

Middlesex University, Uniciti, Flic-en-Flac, Mauritius
SS4341@live.mdx.ac.uk, {v.ramsurrun,m.sharma,k.veerabudren,
a.seeam}@mdx.ac.mu

Abstract. The study outlines a blockchain-based mobile app-based patient records management system that aims to store and exchange all data in a more safe and open manner. The system was developed using Android Studio based on flutter SDK. Since flutter is a free and open-source software development kit that facilitates the creation of mobile apps that run on several platform, technological study based on flutter programming language has been chosen to be utilized for the implementation. The extendable, scalable, and adaptive nature of the language is more effective. Safekeeping and updating of medical records on paper is a major challenge. Additionally, these can be easily lost and swapped. Other existing electronic record systems lack robust security and in cases of emergencies can pose a delay. Thereby, this project proposes leveraging features of the blockchain technology by developing an easy-to-use mobile app, so that healthcare establishments can overcome the limitations identified in current systems while revolutionizing the healthcare system. To ascertain the issue's scalability, rigorous testing was carried out. The system architecture, user requirements, interface designs, necessary sequential patterns and the development process have been documented in this paper.

Keywords: DApp · Mobile-EHR · IPFS · Ethereum · Blockchain

1 Introduction

The latest advancement in technology influences every aspect of human existence and alters the way we previously used and perceived things. As with other areas of life, the healthcare industry is benefiting from the innovations brought about by technological advancements. Improvements in security, user experience, and other areas of the healthcare industry are the primary outcomes of technological progress. Electronic health records (EHRs) and electronic medical records (EMRs) provided these advantages. They do, however, have problems with data integrity, user ownership of data, and other similar concerns. The utilization of cutting-edge technology, such as Blockchain, may be the key to solving these problems. This technology has the potential to create a safe, tamper-proof environment for keeping sensitive healthcare data such as patient records.

Medical records have been traditionally kept in a paper-based system or otherwise manually until the widespread use of electronic storage media. This paper-based system for keeping track of patients' medical histories was not only slow and prone to errors, but also lacked security, proper organization, and was easily subject to alterations. Another challenge faced was that patient's medical records could be duplicated throughout several facilities they attend. Thereby, blockchain might be seen as a public record that can be seen by anybody due to the inherent openness of the technology [1].

In recent years, the public health sector has been one of the industries that has made significant progress toward digitization. The worldwide public health system, which is still plagued by inefficiency and deficiencies, has been brought to the attention of the by public opinion, which has underlined the need for a drastic reform in the workings of the system. These vary from the outdated handling of patients' healthcare records to the frequent mismanagement of such records to the seemingly endless wait times for medical visits. The administration of medical records is gradually transitioning away from the use of paper files and toward the use of digital records that contain the same information as their paper counterparts. These digital records are made possible by advancements in technology. It typically takes between 7 and 15 working days to satisfy requests for clinical records in Mauritius, which is plainly unacceptable when dealing with something as essential and priceless as a patient's health.

After identifying these gaps in the Mauritian context, this paper discusses the proposition, design, development, and evaluation of a system that addresses the outlined issues with EHRs whilst also catering for productivity, boosting decision making, and improving efficiency of resources available.

Therefore, the central aim of this project is to boost health care worker productivity by digitizing patient health data while guaranteeing security. Furthermore, EHRs provide more complete patient information, enabling practitioners to make well-informed care decisions more quickly, aiding in treatment improvement and reducing safety issues. This approach allows for more efficient use of resources.

Although, the use of blockchain technology in the healthcare industry faces major challenges, including technical obstacles and questions pertaining to ownership. As time passes, technical challenges like slow processing speed and the need to duplicate enormous amounts of data will be conquered. However, the key impediments to the use of blockchain technology in healthcare will be ownership issues, namely public vs private. A recommendation could be the blockchain initiative that is being supported by the Estonian government. This project makes it possible for businesses to develop their own blockchain solutions and establish a whole new environment for medical innovation. Nevertheless, the existence of a public blockchain does not guarantee that information will be accessible to each and everyone.

Another significant technical challenge for blockchain's distributed ledger solutions is meeting the requirements of the existing HIPAA privacy regulations while simultaneously keeping data that has been spread over the network. The distributed ledger infrastructure has to be built in a manner that prevents it from being broken into using cryptographic techniques. Only in January 2018, 433,192 people were affected by data breaches that occurred as a result of traditional systems. These breaches may have been averted by using solutions that are based on blockchain technology.

Adopting the blockchain technology for the storage of electronic health records would offer a wide range of benefits, including enhanced health data security, efficient management of information, smooth interoperability between relevant organizations, reliability/integrity of information, and transparency. By leveraging the features of blockchain, hospitals can overcome the limitations of paper-based systems while revolutionizing the current healthcare system. The proposed technology has many desirable characteristics that will significantly enhance EHR systems, namely: interoperability through version control, security via file-level permissions, and immutability via versioning where all participants contribute to a system that is immutable and becomes growingly secure.

The paper is structured as follows, Sect. 2 discusses some key literature in the blockchain and EHR domain. Section 3 provides a detailed outlook of the overall project design and development process. Section 4 demonstrates the application with few key screens, and Sect. 5 ends the paper with a conclusion.

2 Relevant Literature

2.1 Background of Blockchain

A proposal published by scientists [2] in 1990, defined the term digital timestamping which today is known as the distributed ledger. Years later this model was implemented and introduced by Nakamoto [3] as blockchain which became a very popular technology. As a Distributed Ledger Technology (DLT), blockchain is often referred to as a next-generation database architecture that allows information to be accessed, recorded, and shared with several copies of the same ledger [4]. Some of the major advantages of the blockchain technology is that it is decentralized, immutable, traceable, and most importantly provides a framework to achieve transparency all while keeping the data's integrity intact. These advantages can be leveraged for a proper EHR and m-health platform which has been proposed in this paper.

The blockchain technology has the potential to define the next generation of applications and solutions. However, there are some hurdles that have been limiting its progress and widespread adoption. Despite a couple of ground-breaking research areas such as healthcare, finance, insurance, or real-estate amongst others are yet to fully expand and adopt blockchain. A blockchain's data accessibility can either be permissioned or permissionless. The permissioned blockchain is a blockchain whose security, validity, and integrity is guaranteed by a trusted third party. No centralized entity may interfere with the implementation of the consensus rules in a permissionless blockchain, therefore the security and integrity of the blockchain can be trusted to the vast majority of its independent peers. Equally important, a majority vote from the peers is needed to alter the consensus rules [5]. Gaps identified for this issue are mainly due to lack of comprehensive and developer-friendly documentation. However, recently some scalable and innovative elements such as Ganache, Polygon, or Solana have been established. These help in building a community around and consequently more robust applications.

2.2 Blockchain for EHR

Amongst other domains where blockchain stands out the health care industry might be the one with great potential. There has been a recent surge of innovation in healthcare outcomes, thanks in large part to the fervor and financial backing of the industry. Authors [6] demonstrated that there are several barriers to the adoption of blockchain, such as security and accuracy concerns. The preservation and circulation of records involves institutional rules and technological problems. Therefore, most short-term suggestions centre on raising people's consciousness, encouraging critical thinking, and garnering support. An example of this is the collaboration between the government of Estonia and the Dutch IT firm Guard Time to implement a blockchain-based patient character validation system [7].

All inhabitants have a smart card that ties a blockchain-based identification to EHR information. All DSE refreshes are hashed on the Blockchain and are recorded. This technique implies that an unchangeable review trail is included in the EHR information, and that the library is not malevolently altered. Appointment preparation, time stamping, and encrypted and signed blocks are only some of the website modifications that will be recorded in immutable history logs that will be kept in current patient files and on the hospital's website.

MedRec, a collaboration between the MIT Media Lab and Beth Israel Deaconess Medical Center, was the EHR's second implementation. This stage offers a distributed method for keeping tabs on how rights, abilities, and specifics are shared throughout Wellness frameworks [8]. Patients will be able to control who has access to their health information and make the best-informed decisions possible with the use of Blockchain technology. Whether or not the actual health data is placed on the Blockchain, these rights may be exchanged to allow for a more automated approach to knowledge sharing for clinical and research reasons. While rights for external space and accounting paths may be kept on the Blockchain, all clinical data must still be stored in EHR frameworks, which necessitates extra programming components to enable true interoperability [8]. Because of its usefulness in verifying drug concepts, the engineers working on the MedRec project are currently attempting to bring it up to date by incorporating new data sources, information providers, and end users. This proof of concept demonstrates how blockchain technology might improve scientific research and the dissemination of discoveries by facilitating the easy and trustworthy sharing of data collected over time. When used to EHRs, blockchain technology improves the security of data storage, transfer, management, access control, and confidentiality. Rapid delivery of treatment to patients and assistance in navigating the complex health care system are both made possible by interoperability of clinical insurance. Therefore, it has been determined that blockchain technology may be used to address issues with EHR deployment. However, further study is needed to validate blockchain-based EHRs properly.

3 System Design and Development

After performing a thorough literature review analyzing the existing systems and identifying gaps to be resolved, the next step was to start development of a system that addressed the problems. This section mainly discusses the design and development of the system, where gathering of the system requirements was crucial so that the development of the application could start as per the specifications.

3.1 Development Methodology

For the implementation of the proposed system, most prominent development methodologies were explored and compared such that a basis on the better method could be employed. There is no generally applicable system development approach. Additionally, this consideration was useful since a number of alternate methodologies have emerged, each with their unique benefits but also drawbacks. After the comparison, the waterfall development methodology was preferred due to its simplicity, granularity, and firsthand experience. The main stages in development entailed: requirements gathering, designing the system, scripting, testing, and deployment of the DApp, with maintenance and documentation of the process involved. The diagram below shows the main stages of a development-based project that were practiced during this project (Fig. 1).

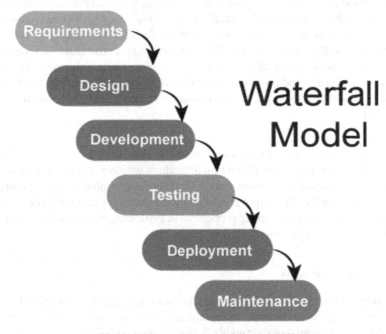

Fig. 1. Phases of the waterfall model [9]

Release Plan

A release plan plays a critical role in maintaining a structured and planned approach to development of software. Schedule and sequences of releases are outlined that define the delivery of features. The following are details of a release plan according to the waterfall model.

EHR System with Blockchain V1.0
For the first version of the system, the following features were focused on:

- Finalizing the blockchain type.
- Pick the best proceedings for development of the system.
- Creating a simple user interface.
- Login of the system.

EHR System with Blockchain V2.0
The following features were focused and delivered for the second version:

- Link the screens.
- Develop majority of the screens.
- Build test scripts and test users to vet the consensus mechanism.
- Implement the blockchain technology.
- Validations of input entries.

EHR System with Blockchain V3.0
The third version of the system released will be having all of the documented elements. Most prominent bugs found while initial testing of the app will be resolved with this release. In addition to a simplified user interface, features that change based on the user checking in will also be available. The system includes customizable features with the inclusion of blockchain technology. Moreover, imperative functionalities such as reading medical records and inputting prescriptions will be included. Finally, a separate set of unit tests will be carried out to ensure that the system is fully functional as per the standards set.

System Unit Tests
Unit testing will be employed to evaluate each functionality of the system. The tests are performed on every individual function to confirm whether it generates the required result as per the deliverables' requirements. This will be accomplished by providing input and determining whether the output produced by the system is genuine. After gathering the results, the features functioning properly will be documented and delivered as the final version of the DApp.

3.2 System Requirements

Prior to initiating the project, an initial concept encompassing the characteristics, functionalities, and behavior of the system was outlined. Moreover, before entering the development phase, it is essential to thoroughly document the system's behavior, features, and logic. Consequently, specific system requirements are collected using specialized tools, and methodologies. These requirements have a specific purpose of helping in understanding the intended performance and behavior of the technology. These are typically organized into groups such as model, service, task, or function. The comprehensive requirement tables, diagrams, and mock-ups demonstrated in this section depict the system's logic, decision-making processes, and design. This represents a fundamental step in the software development life cycle to be accomplished prior to designing, implementing, and testing the system.

Functional Requirements

Functional requirements outline functions or operations that the system is built to perform. In simpler terms, they represent the fundamental functionalities of the system which it should or should not do. The following table compiles the functional requirements of the proposed system (Table 1).

Table 1. Functional Requirements.

Functional Requirement	Description
1. User Registration	The system should allow users to create an account
2. Patient Health Records	Patients should be able to upload and view their previous health records
3. Patient Personal Details	Patients should be able to upload and view their personal details
4. Doctor Access	Doctors should be able to view: • health records and personal details of approved patients, • update and validate health records of patients
5. Hospital Staff Access	Hospital staff should be able to: • view health records of patients stored in the system, • modify personal details of patients, • grant access to doctors to view medical records of patients, • revoke access to medical records of patients

Non-Functional Requirements

Non-functional requirements refer to the characteristics or qualities that define the system's behavior and performance. These encompass aspects like security, performance, reliability, usability, efficiency, maintainability, and modifiability. They outline the specific attributes that the system should exhibit to meet user expectations and standards. These requirements go beyond the functional capabilities and focus on the system's overall effectiveness and user experience which are paramount in the acceptance of the system. The table provided below outlines the non-functional requirements for the system (Table 2).

3.3 System Architecture

Since the application is targeting both the healthcare industry and the general public, careful consideration of the features to be developed for the blockchain EHR system is essential. The system was developed while following best practices that ensured the quality of the user interface while also having a feature rich application. This was prioritized since the acceptance and comprehensibility were of the utmost importance for

Table 2. Non-Functional Requirements

Non-Functional Requirement	Description
1. Security	The system should ensure secure storage and transmission of sensitive patient data. Pre-defined set of protocols through consensus mechanism on the blockchain
2. Privacy	Give access to users with information only intended for their user role. Keep data to be collected minimal and private
3. Performance	System should be able to handle heavy loads with no drop in performance. Response time to actions to a minimal
4. Reliability	The system should be available with uninterrupted access to the users. Data integrity should remain intact with the decentralized network
5. Usability	The user interface of the system should be easy to use, user-friendly, and intuitive to use
6. Compliance	With the consensus algorithm, law, rules and regulations from the relevant respective parties international or local must be accommodated and respected
7. Efficiency	Pertaining to optimal utilization of system resources and the ability to perform tasks in a timely manner

such an app. The main considerations for implementing the features of the application were as follows:

- Understanding the health regulatory compliance (required for the security and privacy requirements),
- Thoughtfully comprehending the diverse roles, access and requirements based on users' roles and duties,
- Develop a robust consensus mechanism,
- Ensure data interoperability, and
- Implementation of proper logs and auditing (with integrated IPFS).

Incorporating the main findings from the literature review, the following steps were carried out to begin development of the mobile app and blockchain network:

- Instantiating digital wallets to carry out transactions,
- Using Ganache to host the blockchain,
- Implementing the app using Dart language, and
- Setting up an IPFS to store the data.

Overall, an effective blockchain EHR system would give patients and doctors access to their relevant medical data on the blockchain network, make transactions, and have the application efficiently interact with the IPFS system. The diagram below portrays the architecture diagram and overall logic of the system (Fig. 2).

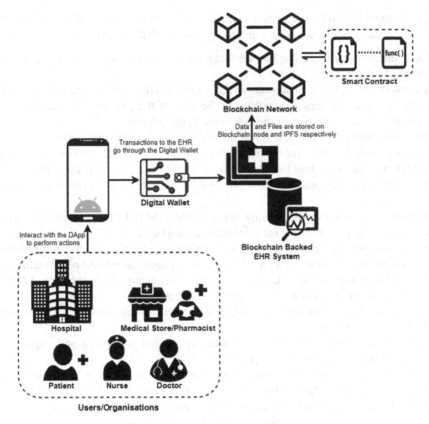

Fig. 2. Project Architecture Diagram

3.4 Implementation of System

The central aim for the project is to enhance healthcare worker productivity through the digitization of patient health data via the proposed EHR system. The system will leverage benefits from the blockchain technology whilst also ensuring transparency, security, and privacy for the healthcare industry. The goal of this project is to create an effective blockchain EHR system that provides patients and doctors with seamless access to their relevant medical data on the blockchain network. To initiate the development of the project the first steps include instantiating digital wallets for secure transactions, configuring Ganache and Truffle as the blockchain hosting platform, developing the app using the Dart programming language, and setting up an IPFS system to store and manage the data. While carefully considering the features to be developed, best practices were followed to ensure a high-quality and bug-free user interface in addition to a decentralized application that meets the needs of the diverse users.

Furthermore, the system will facilitate secure transactions and provide access to files through the IPFS system. By prioritizing user acceptance, and comprehensibility this project attempts to contribute towards the advancement of healthcare industry by introducing new technology through blockchain innovation.

The following is a list of features and advantage over other existing systems that provide beneficial outcomes supporting the proposed EHR system:

- Roles and access for users will be verified patient, verified doctor, pharmacy, hospital admin.
- Access to the patient's electronic health record (EHR) will be granted on a time-limited basis to all persons involved in the care of the patient. The smart contract facilitates the transmission of the electronic health record.
- All of the data is encrypted, and it is never distributed to any other entities.
- A zero-knowledge protocol is one in which the prover validates a statement for the verifier without providing the verifier with any information on the assertion that is being validated. The use of zero-knowledge evidence helps to improve users' levels of privacy.
- Because of the intrinsic adaptability of Blockchain, the EHR framework may be used by a broad range of different medical software applications.
- Interactions between a range of parties engaged in a patient's care may be carried out in a patient-friendly and confidential manner using zero-knowledge proof techniques.
- It ensures that the patient is in control of their own electronic health record (EHR), which speeds up the procedures of approval and consent.
- The whole chain of custody is made public to all parties involved thanks to the blockchain technology.
- Decrease the number of unfavorable occurrences that take place and improve the overall quality of the care that is provided.
- As a result of the network's interaction with the Central Drugs Standard Control Organization, both pharmacists and medical professionals get timely notifications about any newly approved or banned pharmaceuticals.

The main logic for implementing the logic of the organizations and overall users have been encompassed in the smart contracts written in the Solidity language. The central smart contracts that process the system's proceedings have been described briefly in the section below.

Smart Contracts
The sub-sections below briefly describe the smart contracts that form part of the EHR system. Overall there is a reliance on inheritance between multiple contracts as well for the smooth transfer of information.

Patient
The patient contract includes provisions for enrolling the patient with the network, update information, prescription and other records/uses. There is another built-in feature that retrieves the info for the patient individually as well.

Hospital and Pharmacy
These contracts processes registration of hospitals and pharmacies respectively on the network. There is also the patient agreement feature that performs the data retrieval process.

Doctor
The doctor contract serves several purposes, such as adding physicians to the network and providing payment for services. These screens are there in the registration process

for physicians, when information like doctors' names, hospitals' locations, and wallet addresses are transferred around through a number of different variables.

Healthcare

The healthcare contract accommodates functions for all entities in addition to performing general CRUD operations for all the users and organizations. Finally, the verification and grant mechanism for patients and doctors has also been devised.

DApp on Flutter

For each deployed smart contract, there is a specialized Dart script that handles ingression of information over the mobile app. For processing of files, the IPFS system has to be instantiated with a connection established between the system and Ganache. A wallet management module has also been developed which manages the retrieval of relevant or requested wallet addresses for the eventual transfer of gas fees.

4   EHR System with Blockchain

This section will demonstrate the overall user interface of the system and discuss the main sections with their features (Figs. 3, 4 and 5).

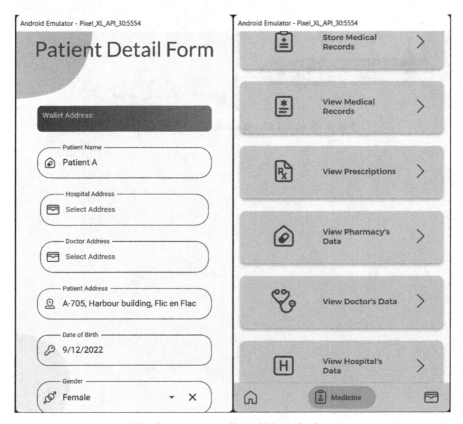

Fig. 3. Patient Details and Menu Options

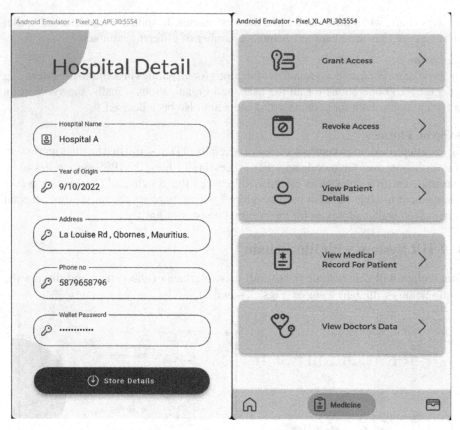

Fig. 4. Hospital Management and Menu Options

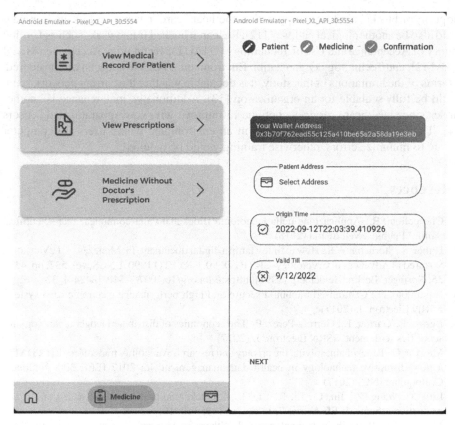

Fig. 5. General Patient Information

5 Conclusion and Future Works

Improvements in security, user experience, and other areas of the healthcare industry are the primary outcomes of technological progress. The digitization of health records means that cyber-security of medical records is becoming increasingly relevant. Thereby, the need for a blockchain based mobile EHR system is imperative. This project presented the development of a mobile-patient medical records management system using blockchain. The system was thoroughly tested through a series of unit tests. The smart contracts were also validated through tests using the truffle framework. As future considerations the application could be further tested in terms of performance, or usability. Concerning evaluation of the project, firstly the Mythril [10] framework could be used to assess its performance. Mythril has the capability to identify several security flaws, such as integer underflows, and other issues. Secondly, Hyperledger Caliper [11] benchmarking tool could also be used to measure and quantify the performance of the app in realistic environments. This platform helps in generating key references to reveal performance indicators. These details in return can be used to finetune the application. Furthermore, user acceptance testing could also be carried out in order to gather insights from the different user's perspective (Doctor, Nurse, Patient, Hospital). Alternatively, studying adoption of blockchain technology within the healthcare industry and its environment could also be another logical pathway [12]. Research backed frameworks such as Unified Theory of Acceptance and Use of Technology (UTAUT), Technology Acceptance Model 2 (TAM2), and Technology Organization Environment (TOE) Model can be considered. In terms of the limitations of this study, it is debatable whether the current network setup would be fully scalable for an organization [13]. Additionally, maintenance is another barrier since healthcare services continue to improve with new apparatus and sensors [14]. The system should be introduced in an environment where users are computer literate to minimize errors, otherwise training would be required.

References

1. Ciappelloni, R.: Applicazione della tecnologia Blockchain alla comunicazione scientifica. Sanita' Pubblica Veterinaria (2018)
2. Haber, S., Stornetta, W.S.: How to time-stamp a digital document. In: Menezes, A.J., Vanstone, S.A. (eds.) Advances in Cryptology-CRYPTO' 90. CRYPTO 1990. LNCS, vol. 537, pp. 437–55. Springer, Berlin, Heidelberg (1991). https://doi.org/10.1007/3-540-38424-3_32
3. Nakamoto, N.: Centralised bitcoin: a secure and high performance electronic cash system. SSRN Electron. J. (2017)
4. Benos, E., Garratt, R., Gurrola-Perez, P.: The economics of distributed ledger technology for securities settlement. SSRN Electron. J. (2017)
5. Magyar, G.: Blockchain: solving the privacy and research availability tradeoff for EHR DATA: a new disruptive technology in health data management. In: 2017 IEEE 30th Neumann Colloquium (NC) (2017)
6. Liu, X., Wang, Z., Jin, C., Li, F., Li, G.: A blockchain-based medical data sharing and protection scheme. IEEE Access **7**, 118943–118953 (2019)
7. Mettler, M.: Blockchain technology in healthcare: the revolution starts here. In: 2016 IEEE 18th International Conference on e-Health Networking, Applications and Services (Healthcom) (2016)
8. Azaria, A., Ekblaw, A., Vieira, T., Lippman, A.: MedRec: using blockchain for medical data access and permission management. In: 2016 2nd International Conference on Open and Big Data (OBD) (2016)
9. Bose, S.: Why automation testing is essential for Agile [Internet]. BrowserStack. 2016 [cited 2023 Jul 1]. https://www.browserstack.com/guide/automation-testing-in-agile
10. Mythril GitHub. https://github.com/ConsenSys/mythril. Accessed 01 July 2023
11. Hyperledger Caliper Homepage. https://hyperledger.github.io/caliper/. Accessed 01 July 2023
12. Liang, T.-P., Kohli, R., Huang, H.-C., Li, Z.-L.: What drives the adoption of the blockchain technology? A fit-viability perspective. J. Manag. Inf. Syst. **38**, 314–337 (2021)
13. Abu-elezz, I., Hassan, A., Nazeemudeen, A., Househ, M., Abd-alrazaq, A.: The benefits and threats of blockchain technology in healthcare: a scoping review. Int. J. Med. Inform. **142**, 104246 (2020)
14. Clim, A., Zota, R.D., Constantinescu, R.: Data exchanges based on blockchain in M-health applications. Procedia Comput. Sci. **160**, 281–288 (2019)

A Mobile/Tablet App-Based Patient Records Management System Using Blockchain

Deepesh Rago, Visham Ramsurrun[✉], Mrinal Sharma, Karel Veerabudren, and Amar Seeam

Middlesex University, Uniciti, Flic-en-Flac, Mauritius
DR661@live.mdx.ac.uk, {v.ramsurrun,m.sharma,k.veerabudren, a.seeam}@mdx.ac.mu

Abstract. As of 2022, the healthcare industry plays a crucial role in enhancing the quality of life as well as the overall well-being of individuals as it offers an extensive array of services across the globe. With the emergence of new technologies in the medical field, the healthcare universe is drastically evolving to provide better medical care, and such an example is the EHR systems. They changed the manner that patient medical health information is registered, stored, and shared. The traditional paper-based records systems have completely been replaced with its digital counterparts that offer superior benefits like better management of patients' medical records, raise in healthcare productivity, superior decision-making at managerial level and finally, a reduction in the overall healthcare expenditures. With the new EHR systems, patients can have access to their health records and take control over its management. However, the EHR systems are yet to be perfectionated and currently face numerous challenges like serious concerns related to data privacy, data interoperability, data ownership and date security, amongst others. Additionally, patient misidentification and misdiagnosis, are becoming a prevalent occurrence in medical care institutions that will have serious repercussions over patients' health or lives if this issue is not tackled at the earliest. Therefore, this project aims at developing the PatientCare Mauritius application. It is a mobile app-based patient records management system that makes use of blockchain technology with IPFS system to store and secure the patients' medical health records against cyber-attacks and other vulnerabilities as well as incorporating the NFC technology with patients' photo ID. The combination of NFC with photo ID contributes to accurately identifying patients at medical facilities to prevent patient misdiagnosis. To further uphold the acceptance and usability of the PatientCare Mauritius application, the Technology Acceptance Model (TAM) was adopted, and it made use of five constructs. The outcome was that the application obtained a TAM score of 4.33, implying that the PatientCare Mauritius application was valuable and user-friendly.

Keywords: EHR · Medical Health Records · Record Management · NFC · Blockchain · Ethereum · IPFS · Data Security · Smart Contract

A. Seeam et al. (Eds.): InterSol 2023, LNICST 541, pp. 113–130, 2024.
https://doi.org/10.1007/978-3-031-51849-2_8

1 Introduction

In the wake of the 2020 and ongoing outbreak of the COVID-19, the world has witnessed one of the most recent, disastrous pandemics which significantly affected all nations worldwide. Thereupon, mankind has unprecedented expectations from the healthcare industry to contain this disease which uncovered the underlying challenges currently present in this medical sector [1, 2]. One such shortcomings is the patient records management system presently in use in Mauritius. Indeed, most of the medical institutions are still making use of paper-based techniques to log patients' medical records that, inevitably, have considerable limitations. EHR is a key element in the medical industry [3–6]. This industry manages extremely sensitive information that ought to be handled very securely and EHR, too, is not an exception. EHR constitutes of private and confidential information about patients, such as, patients' identity, home address, contact details, health history and insurance details amongst others. This sensitive information is indispensable, not only for the patient but also for the medical institution as well as for the healthcare insurance firms. The medical and financial institutions, under any circumstances, cannot allow this crucial information to be leaked in the public, as it would enormously affect all the concerned parties.

1.1 Background

To have a robust and efficient healthcare system, it is mandatory that the past medical records of patients are promptly available and are accurate. Nonetheless, it is challenging and tedious to manage medical records over several hospitals [7]. Still, adopting a centralised solution for the storing of patients' medical data is not feasible as it leads to a single point of failure [8] and constitutes of various other constraints, namely, cyber-attacks, as well as wrongful handling of medical data [9]. Other critical concerns are recurrently, medical staff wrongly identify and incorrectly link patients to their respective medical records that, eventually, lead to the patients being receiving the wrong treatment or medications. As a matter of fact, the Institute of Medicine has set forth that around 26%–32% of adult patients have incorrectly been administered medication, while the accounted number for paediatric convalescents is approximately between 4% to 60% [10, 11]. Therefore, the need to have a convenient electronic patients records management system, along with appropriately identifying the in-patients, is of paramount importance. The number of phishing attacks in the healthcare sector has recently been escalating because of the high demand of personal information in the black market. Indeed, at the 2011 Digital Health Congress, a group of experts stated that a simple EHR data in the black market was worth 50 USD as compared to 0.25 USD for a bank credit card details [12, 13].

Therefore, it is crucial to come up with unique and advanced technologies to tackle these challenges in the healthcare industry. Blockchain technologies have been acknowledged to address those issues whilst making the patient records management system, better known as the Electronic Health Record (EHR), more efficient and safer since blockchain is decentralised [14]. Blockchain can help in safeguarding and providing logs for electronic health records for medical lawsuits or insurance claims [15]. Additionally, the need to have a convenient electronic patients records management system, along with appropriately identifying the patients, is integral. Adopting the Near Field Communication (NFC) technology in the healthcare sector, will surely minimise these blunders whereby the patients will be bonded to an NFC tag upon their visit at the hospital. Doctors and nurses will have to scan these NFC tags before diagnosing and inputting patients' vitals readings respectively [10].

1.2 Aims and Objectives

Thus, this work intends at developing a mobile application, entitled as PatientCare Mauritius (PCM), for managing and securing patients' medical health records by incorporating blockchain and NFC technologies in electronic health record system. These technologies will enormously reduce the current limitations of the paper-based health record system and the existing EHR systems as well as any cyber-attacks targeted at the existing EHR systems. The application will secure patients' personal information along with their medical data. Patients will have ownership of their medical health data as they can control whether to grant access to doctors to view their medical health history records. The mobile application will make use of NFC sensor, embedded in the mobile or tablet, to allow medical personnel to accurately identify patients in the medical facility. Hence, ensuring that patients are getting the right treatment, while all the medical information are correctly logged for that patient respective electronic health record. The application will also allow the patients to directly book or manage their medical appointments with their doctors on their mobile phones itself, saving time and no need for paperwork.

2 Literature Review

In the contemporary healthcare industry, security of data and its ownership are two significant concerns that should be addressed at the earliest. As patients' medical records presently do not feature a proper and reliable data structure, it induces to data breaches and other cyber-attacks, which have a devastating impact on the patients, medical institutions, and other implicated organisations. According to the Department of Health and Human Services' Office for Civil Rights, in 2018, they have been informed of multiple data breaches whereby more than 13 million of medical records were compromised [15, 16].

Over the last few years, IT experts have constantly been looking for proper and viable systems to retain patients' medical records. Most of the contemporary EHR systems are cloud-based solutions whereby they are fully depended on reliable and centralised third-party entities that have no concerns with data security and data privacy. They only provide the basic protection to secure the data [17–19]. These cloud environments are vulnerable to single point of failure, among other drawbacks like data privacy issues when transmitting data over public networks. Centralised cloud-based systems have a high running cost as well as occupy more storage space as the systems scale up.

2.1 Electronic Health Record System

The healthcare institutions produce considerable volume of medical data daily. It consists of patients' diagnostic reports and radiology reports like MRI scans and X-ray amongst others. EHR is better described as the patients' digital compilation of their medical dossier, consisting of their health medical history, their past treatments, their personal information, their allergies, laboratory test results, medications amongst others. Typically, each health facility maintains his own EHR system and does not involve any kind of interoperability. Hence, a particular patient could be having different medical records at different medical facilities [20].

Medical institutions, normally, do not share their patients' medical records with other health facilities. These medical records are stored physically on servers at their respective data centres or, simply, to cloud-based storage systems. It requires many skills as well as planning when managing and maintaining such crucial medical data storage on premise. Typically, it involves high costs and proper facilities to ensure data redundancy, in the event of a system crash, malfunction or data loss amongst others. To avoid such system failures, numerous medical institutions seek refuge in cloud storage. However, these cloud-based systems, too, have their constraints. Recently, there had been some ransomware attacks along with Distributed Denial-of-Service (DDoS) attacks that brought down the centralised EHR systems across various healthcare institutions. These institutions were unable to operate and provide the required health service to their patients [20]. Centralised EHR systems are also vulnerable to other cyber-attacks that could cause further damage to both patients and the healthcare providers by leaking patient-sensitive information to the public. In the end, such malicious attacks lead to the fact that the concerned healthcare institutions have their reputation tarnished whereby their share value drop drastically in the stock market.

Therefore, adopting a decentralised EHR system will, notably, revolutionise the way medical institutions store patients' medical records, especially, regarding the security aspect. With the new decentralised approach, the totality of the constraints of the centralised systems is dealt with and will further be secured through Blockchain and Inter Planetary File System (IPFS).

Embracing a decentralised approach for the EHR systems will minimise the shortcomings of centralised EHR systems; for instance; the new system will support interoperability by allowing both patients and medical personnels to gain access to electronic medical records, without compromising data security and privacy. The system will prevent any wrongful use of data by ensuring that the data remains undisclosed. Implementing the blockchain technology in conjunction with IPFS system will bring down the above-mentioned deficiencies of the centralised EHR systems. IPFS is a decentralised system whereby data is stored and shared using a distributed approach, that will help in managing privacy and availability of medical data. Indeed, IPFS operates by breaking down the data that needs to be stored into numerous fragments that will eventually be dispersed over the whole distributed network. This technique of scattering data over the decentralised network is highly effective, for instance, in a situation where a hacker takes over control of a server in the network, the latter cannot interpret or leak data from the compromised server. Additionally, distributed systems offer other practical benefits, like minimum downtime in situations where a server is offline, while data can still be retrieved from other online servers in the network. This feature of decentralised system is a boon for the medical industry as we cannot allow any downtime when retrieving or accessing patients' medical records, especially, in emergency circumstances where time is a critical factor in rescuing patients' lives [20].

2.2 NFC Technology in Healthcare

Near Field Communication, better known as, NFC is derivative of the RFID technology and is, today, incorporated in most, if not all, smart devices (smartphones, tablets, smartwatches) in the 2022 era. The initial incentive of embedding NFC sensors in these smart devices was to allow rapid and effective transmission of data throughout mobile applications [10]. As NFC makes use of lightweight sensors, and are already embedded in smartphones and tablets, it swiftly succeeded over the RFID in the healthcare industry. It was convenient as there was no need to get specialised readers to read the NFC tags that were allocated to patients, through silicone bracelets. Thus, patients could easily and accurately be identified at the tap of the smart device and the NFC-based silicone bracelet through a mobile application [10].

Other application of the NFC technology in the healthcare varies from medication administration to precisely linked patients to their respective medical records, reports, laboratory tests, amongst others. Using NFC technology and a specialised mobile application, partially sighted patients could use their smartphones to tap on the NFC tag affixed on medication bottles caps that would read aloud the medication name, instructions, and dosage for their medication consumption. NFC technology can, undoubtedly, be effective in other medical applications whereby it can work alongside with other medical sensors to help medical staffs in their daily medical tasks.

By automating these data captures, it will help in optimising the time taken to carry out these tedious and repetitive tasks which will eventually enable the medical staffs to boost their efficiency and work productivity. The goal behind incorporating NFC technology with electronic health record is to radically improve the current healthcare industry by simplifying the capture, storage, and exchange of medical data among patients, health care workers and the management. Ultimately, these changes will relieve the operational costs and will boost the overall quality of medical service [10, 21].

2.3 Security in Healthcare

In the contemporary, IT systems and other advanced technologies work closely together to offer the best of healthcare facilities. Most of these systems are online and are always connected with one and another, to seamlessly transmit and store data in view of reducing time and costs. Nowadays, the EHRs involve high-end medical equipment along with smart devices like wearables, embedded sensors, and micro-chips. These devices allow to continuously monitor patients' health and trigger alarms in case of emergencies or abnormal vital signs readings.

With these advents in the healthcare sector, it is of paramount importance to ensure that these technologies and systems are secured and work accurately, because they involve patients' medical records that are highly sensitive data. The developing EHR systems are capable of handling numerous tasks, namely, managing the whole patients' medical records; from scheduling the medical appointments, the proper diagnosis of patients' ailments, prescribing drugs, to storing all these medical records for future use or references. Therefore, security is a must in healthcare because medical data stored in these EHR systems, need to be assured and protected from any cyber-attacks, for the proper running of the medical institutions [22, 23].

The volume of medical data generated by big data is enormous across various systems and generally, these data are complexed and rarely optimised. Since the medical records need to be accessible across the various networks of the medical institutions, it is often the case that the medical data gets duplicated. This leads to data being inaccurate, as upon changes made to medical data, are not effected to all locations where these data are stored. It can have severe repercussion as medical records need to be error-free for doctors to make the correct diagnosis of their patients. Duplication of data also result in wastage of storage space on the system. Having a weak data management of sensitive medical records will, eventually, induce cyber-attacks and other data breaches. Other security measures involve that, only authorised personnels should have access to patients' sensitive information. The former should only be limited to restricted views depending on their nature of their jobs.

2.4 Blockchain Technology in Healthcare

Blockchain technology has constantly been in the spotlight following the inception of Bitcoin by Nakamoto back in 2008 [24, 25]. Blockchain can best be described as a Peer-to-Peer, better known as P2P, network that constitutes of computing nodes that interact with one another [3, 26]. P2P network signifies that the network is a decentralised one; which is one of the fundamental characteristics of the blockchain technology. Other attributes of this technology are distributed database, and to ensure tone,all P2P transactions are verified. In blockchain, data that needs to be stored, is maintained in a block whereby the blocks are connected to other blocks which, eventually, develop into a chain, known as, the blockchain. As a rule, the blocks are bound to the previous ones through a hash value as well as with a timestamp, implying that once a transaction has been generated in blockchain, it cannot be changed [3, 26]. Blockchain assigns this timestamp feature because it associates an identity to all the workflow before circulating the copies amid each node in the network, to ensure that integrity of data is maintained between the endpoints, while there is no human intervention implicated [3, 27]. Therefore, a typical block incorporates the previous hash of the block, the hash of the current block, a nonce and finally a digital signature. The position and the sequence of the block is determined by the stored hash numbers [1, 25]. Furthermore, blockchain technology is greatly resilient to cyber-attacks because the hacker needs to take over control of all the blocks of the blockchain at the same time, as each block are interlinked through the block's hash pointer. Therefore, it is practically impossible for the hacker to own the entire blockchain.

Blockchain has the potentiality to revolutionise the healthcare industry through the enhancement of patients' records privacy, security of data and interoperability. It is viewed as an optimistic and viable solution in the medical world [24, 28]. Given the numerous features of blockchain technology, it could be utilised in various applications in the healthcare sector, for instance, to enhance the various health monitoring devices with their health mobile applications, the management of patients' medical records in terms of their storage and sharing, the insurance and clinical trials and the management of supply chain, amongst others [15]. Blockchain will make a significant impact on EHR as it will allow to efficiently store patients' medical information which was once dispersed over numerous healthcare providers. Blockchain will allow the patients to have full and secured access to view their medical data and be able to manage who can access their medical history. This ability will significantly empower the patients to have better control over their personal data, which, in turn, will boost both privacy and confidentiality [9, 29]. EHR involves highly sensitive information about patients and their health status that must be always readily available, especially during emergency situations. Hence, blockchain is ideal for storing this category of data because blockchain employs a peer-to-peer network that can serve as a redundant resource, upon failure of any component of the system or, any other deficiencies. Therefore, using blockchain technology will eliminate the risk of any single point of failure (SPOF) of the system [1]. Additionally, blockchain strongly advocates to be a tamper-resistant technology that promotes non-repudiation, as any data stored in the blockchain network, is immutable.

Limitation of Blockchain Technology in Healthcare. One major drawback of Blockchain technology is the cost of running the blockchain system. Every transaction that occurs on the blockchain, the end user is required to remunerate for this data processing whereby in Ethereum network, this remuneration is established in 'gas', pay out in 'Ether'. Ether, better known as ETH, is the native cryptocurrency of the Ethereum Blockchain and as of April 2023, its value is 1,877 USD [15]. Therefore, even though blockchain is efficient against tampering of records, it is not convenient for maintaining a significant amount of data [17, 30]. Considering the amount of data and transactions that would be generated daily for the medical sector, especially when dealing with imaging laboratory reports like X-ray, CT scan and MRI, the cost would be exorbitant. Hence, it is impractical to store the whole EHR data on the blockchain itself, as the latter is a high-priced storage medium. Also, the block size in blockchain is very restricted and adding-on for new blocks, too, is expensive. Consequently, the feasible approach to use blockchain technology is to use it to protect the EHR data, rather than a storage tool for the medical records [1].

Therefore, the desirable solution is to store these medical records in an off-chain storage. IPFS, Interplanetary file system, is deemed to be the most feasible system to safeguard and store these highly sensitive data. IPFS constitutes of a Peer-to-Peer (P2P) protocol and a distributed storage technique that intends to connect every computing machine to a single file system, whereby making it possible to store enormous amounts of medical records [3]. IPFS involves making use of a cryptographic hash which serve as a distinctive fingerprint, that is, a unique key for every data within the IPFS. Since IPFS prohibits the data's hashing value to be altered, IPFS is said to be an immutable and permanent storage platform. With IPFS, only the hash address of the patients' medical records will be kept in the blockchain network, rather than the actual records themselves [3, 31], which will further secure the data stored since blockchain, too, is a distributed network.

2.5 Existing Systems

MediQuick. MediQuick is a patient management android application that was developed by [32]. It makes use of blockchain and Quick Response (QR) code technologies to provide a secured and efficient platform for storing and accessing highly sensitive data like patients' medical records. Within the application, the patients have access to book medical appointments with doctors as well as to view their medical data and their medications [32]. All the patients who visit the hospital or use its medical services, are allocated with a unique QR code which firstly, allow the medical staff to accurately identify the patients to prevent any kind of misidentification and secondly, the codes allow both the patient and medical personnels to access the former's medical records from the hospital protected database. The hospital database is secured using the blockchain technology.

The MediQuick application was developed to eliminate the traditional patient records management system which was paper-based, and all entries were being done manually by medical staffs. Hence, the existing system had various limitations, exposed to security threats and was tedious as well as time consuming. Consequently, MediQuick will store all the patients' medical records digitally and secured same in a database using the blockchain technology, which will speed up most of the hospital services, increasing its productivity.

MediQuick application bears a strong resemblance to PatientCare Mauritius application, which is also a patient records management system that will utilise blockchain technology to secure its sensitive information, but PatientCare Mauritius differs in the sense that it adopts NFC technology instead of QR code because NFC is more secured as it involves an authentication procedure when configuring the NFC tags and also, NFC is quicker as communication is established through a quick and simple tap. Patients' medical records are extensive in size, directly storing this data on blockchain will not only impair performance when retrieving data, but also, is extremely costly to sustain. Hence, PatientCare Mauritius shall use an off-chain storage like IPFS, a distributed storage platform, to store all its medical records. IPFS hashes all these information whereby these hash keys are finally stored on blockchain. This procedure not only relieves the load on the blockchain, but also, provides an additional security measure for the sensitive data. The PatientCare Mauritius application will also incorporate the patient's photo in its NFC tag, as a means for medical staffs to accurately identify patients.

NFC Tag-Based mHealth Patient Healthcare Tracking System. To tackle the problem of misidentification and misdiagnosis of patients on hospital premises, [10] built a patient healthcare management information system that will incorporate NFC technology to provide a better healthcare service [10]. Patient misidentification and misdiagnosis have been prevailing for quite some time and have been recurrent worldwide due to various reasons, namely, poor patient management by medical staffs, hospitals overcrowded with patients during peak time or medical staffs using less efficient patient management systems. Therefore, adopting the NFC technology, along with photo ID, to accurately identify patients using NFC silicone bracelets that are issued to the patients upon the registration at the hospital, will greatly minimise this delicate situation. It is a must to properly identify patients at hospitals because they need to be correctly linked to their respective medical records, especially, when it concerns with medical health test reports as doctors refer to these test reports to provide the appropriate treatment to their patients.

Although PatientCare Mauritius and NFC tag based Mhealth application both use NFC technology with Photo ID, they differ in the way they store patients' medical health records. [10]'s system makes use of centralised MySQL database that are prone to various cyber-attacks, performance limitations as well as no redundancy in case of failure of the system. Meanwhile, concerning PatientCare Mauritius, which shall use a distributed and tamper-proof storage mechanism, in terms of blockchain technology and IPFS system, to store patients' medical records. The system will also be resilient against single point-of-failure attacks.

3 Design and Development

The study intents to build a modern EHR system that will facilitate both the healthcare provider to better store and manage patients' medical records as well as the patients to benefit from better medical care services. The methodology, proposed system and list of tools that will be used to develop the system are listed out.

3.1 Research Methodology

As this project intents at determining a solution to a real-life issue, the type of research to be accomplished shall be an applied research. Consequently, a prototype application system was implemented. This methodology was beneficial as it helped enormously in detection of design faults and other shortcomings that were fixed accordingly during early development of the system.

3.2 Proposed System

The aim is to build a system that will incorporate a mobile based application that will manage patients' medical health records and secured them using blockchain technology and IPFS storage system. It will also make use of NFC technology to readily identify patients on the hospital premises, to avoid misidentification of patients. During the registration process, the hospital admin will issue the patient with a silicone bracelet fitted with an NFC tag that contains a unique code to identify the patient. Then, the admin will capture a live picture of the patient that will be used as a 'Photo ID'. A link to this Photo ID is stored in the same NFC tag of the patient. Nurses and doctors will have to scan the patient's NFC bracelet first to confirm the latter's identity before proceeding to upload the latter's vitals readings to the mobile application and carry out patient's diagnostics respectively. The doctor can then update and save the patient's medical information on the application. The patients will have control over their medical data and control access to this sensitive data. They can also schedule medical appointments with doctors based on their availability as well as make call to emergency services like fire station, hospital, police station amongst others.

3.3 Tools and Technology

PatientCare Mauritius Mobile App. The mobile application was developed in Visual Studio (VS) Code using Dart Programming Language as Dart natively supports asynchronous programming that help to develop apps that are more responsive and efficient. Also, VS Code allow app development for multi-platform, and it has strong debugging capabilities (Fig. 1).

Fig. 1. PatientCare Mauritius application screens

Blockchain Network Technology. Ethereum blockchain is used for the PatientCare Mauritius as it is an open-source, decentralised and public blockchain platform that provides a P2P network that is capable of securely run and validate application code, better known as smart contracts, that enable participants of the blockchain to perform transactions altogether without the need of a trusted central authority. It allows to simulate a blockchain environment in a virtual manner without the need to implement a real one, which is costly. Ganache is used to create dummy or mock Ethereum accounts which are loaded with free of charge test Ether (ETH) cryptocurrency. This ETH which is a virtual currency, is utilised for the transactions to pay for the miner nodes. A Metamask cryptocurrency wallet is used to manage the spending and use of the Ether coin to pay for the transactions. For the users to be able to use this wallet, their accounts should be linked to the Metamask wallet with the private key of their Ethereum account. Remix IDE is used for the development, testing and deployment of the smart contracts on the Ethereum network. It is a lightweight IDE as well as it is ideal for the rapid testing and deployment of smart contracts. As we shall be using Solidity programming language to explicitly build the smart contracts, Remix will be hugely beneficial as it features a Solidity compiler.

NFC Technology, NFC Tag and its Application Model. NFC technology is chosen over Bluetooth one as NFC is simple and can readily communicate. A simple touch of the NFC reader to the NFC tag, is all what is required for communication to occur [10]. NFC consumes less power, and it is already incorporated in most of the modern smart devices, therefore, no need of additional NFC reading equipment. For the PatientCare Mauritius project, we shall be using the NFC chip, NTAG216, as it can store much data like patient's identity information and is future proof whereby we can store additional information, should the need arise in the future. As for the NFC Tag Application Model, we shall use the silicone NFC bracelets as it is more practical since the NFC chips are embedded in wearables, and it is more comfortable for the patients as they can adjust the bracelets according to their wrist size. The silicone bracelets are non-irritation and unscented as well as waterproof and will not be affected by sweat, water or other liquid that may get into contact with the bracelets [10]. The NFC silicone bracelet is as follows in Fig. 2.

Fig. 2. NFC Chip embedded in Silicone Bracelet

3.4 System Architectural Diagram

The PatientCare Mauritius system architectural diagram is represented in Fig. 3.

The PatientCare Mauritius is a two-tier architecture, consisting of a client (mobile application) and datastore. We make use of Firebase and IPFS as storage. The mobile application authenticates its users using firebase authentication and data is stored on the firebase storage. However, patients' medical data records are stored in IPFS which is a decentralised storage and is widely known to be used as an off-chain storage solution when dealing with colossal files. For the Ethereum network, Ganache is used which comes with predefined accounts of 100 ethers. To transfer these ethers to the mobile application, metamask wallet is used. Thus, ethers from the Ganache account are transferred to the metamask wallet. Smart contracts are written in Solidity programming

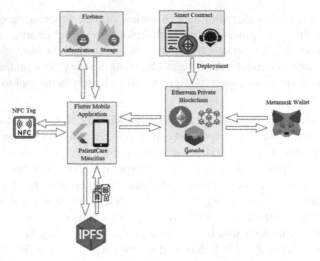

Fig. 3. PatientCare Mauritius System Architectural Diagram

language and deployed using Remix IDE. The flutter mobile application communicates with the Ethereum network such that whenever, a patient medical record is saved, the IPFS generates a CID hash, and that hash is saved on the blockchain. Therefore, whenever a patient wishes to retrieve his health medical records, the CID is retrieved from the blockchain and then passed to the IPFS URL gateway, and the file is retrieved.

4 Testing and Evaluation

To ensure that PatientCare Mauritius mobile application is indeed an efficient EHR system and is achieving all its intended objectives, various testing scenarios have been conducted. These testing varies from unit testing, integration testing, system testing, User Acceptance Testing (UAT) and Technology Acceptance Model (TAM).

With unit testing, the different functionalities of the system were tested independently of the other modules. The aim was to discover any shortcomings which may have occurred during the implementation of the new system. Integration testing was performed immediately after the unit testing of the different elements of the software, had been accomplished. These elements that were tested individually, now, needed to be put together to be tested as a whole component. Errors or any malfunctioning that went undetected in unit testing, were discovered in integration testing because the different components of the software behave differently when they work collectively. Following integration testing, system testing was carried out which main objective was to establish the new system reliability in various situations or surroundings, namely, accuracy tests or performance tests. We should determine whether the system produced the desired results under heavy load or factors affecting environmental conditions.

UAT and TAM are similar, and they were the most requisite type of testing when developing a new system because it required a real user to run and go through the new system. It was mandatory that this user did not have any implications or involvements in the creation of the new system, including from the early stages to the final implementation of the new system. The concept was that a real user who might or might not have a developer background, had more potential in identifying shortcomings or bugs of the new system, that the developer could have missed out. The user would go through the different functionalities of the app, and he was in a strong position to better assess the overall look and feel of the new system in terms of its user-interface. Also, he would be able to determine whether the application accomplished its purpose regarding its proposed requirements. To further confirm that the PatientCare Mauritius mobile application would be well adopted by end-users, the TAM was carried out as it is a prominent evaluation model and it would help to evaluate the level of user acceptability of the various features of the PatientCare Mauritius app. According to TAM, the factors that influenced an end-user to accept and use a technology are perceived usefulness (PU), perceived ease of use (PEOU), perceived convenience (PC), continuance intention to use (CIU) and attitude towards use (ATU). Therefore, these factors, also known as constructs, were listed in the TAM questionnaire to obtain a reliable technology acceptance level for the PatientCare Mauritius system. Other criteria of the TAM were that adequate number of participants, at least 45 participants, were required to participate in the testing of the system. They had various tasks to undertake which consisted of the different features of the mobile application like scanning patients' NFC bracelet, updating patients' vitals, requesting access to view patients' medical history, making diagnostics, scheduling, or cancelling medical appointments and calling the emergency services, amongst others. Those participants had to carry out these tasks and navigate through the application without any prior training on the system. The participants' interaction with the mobile app were captured for future analysis to determine the level of usability as well as to improve the application's user-interface if required. Afterwards, those participants had to fill in a predefined questionnaire consisting of the previously mentioned TAM constructs whereby these constructs were rated in a scale of '1' to '5'. '1' being Strongly Disagree and '5' being Strongly Agree. The participants could also make suggestions on the different sections of the questionnaire. Finally, following the completion of the data capture, a final check was done to ensure no data were unreliable or incoherent, and statistical analysis was carried out to finalise the testing and evaluation process (Table 1).

Table 1. TAM Constructs Definitions

TAM Constructs	Definition
Perceived Usefulness (PU)	It describes the extent a technology will contribute to facilitating a task
Perceived Ease of Use (PEOU)	It describes the point where end-users will feel that the technology is easy to use
Perceived Convenience (PC)	It describes the amount of convenience that the users will feel when executing an action of the technology
Continuance Intention to Use (CIU)	It describes how eager the users are to continue to use the new technology
Attitude Towards Use (ATU)	It describes the users' attitude towards using the technology in the near future

5 Results

Out of the 50 participants who agreed to go through that study, 20 were males and 30 were females. Their age group varied from 22 years old to 58 years old. The participants were all computer literate and familiar to use smartphones in their everyday life. Also, all the participants had a thorough medical knowledge.

Table 2. Results of the TAM Constructs

Constructs	Score					Avg. Score	Avg. Construct Score
	1	2	3	4	5		
PC1: PCM is similar to other existing mobile apps	0	0.02	0.1	0.68	0.2	4.06	4.3
PC2: Using PCM is engrossing	0	0	0.08	0.4	0.52	4.44	
PC3: Using PCM suits my occupation	0.04	0.04	0.14	0.3	0.48	4.14	
PC4: Using PCM is useful and diminish patient misdiagnosis	0	0	0.06	0.32	0.62	4.56	
PEOU1: Learning to use PCM was straightforward	0.02	0.04	0.12	0.36	0.46	4.2	4.23
PEOU2: Learning to operate PCM would be straightforward	0	0.02	0.06	0.5	0.42	4.32	
PEOU3: I think interacting with the PCM would be unambiguous	0	0.02	0.16	0.44	0.38	4.18	
PEOU4: I think going through where I want in PCM, would be easy	0.02	0.02	0.1	0.44	0.42	4.22	
PU1: With PCM, it would facilitate patient identification	0	0	0.06	0.5	0.44	4.38	4.26
PU2: With PCM, it would diminish patient misdiagnosis	0	0.02	0.08	0.48	0.42	4.3	
PU3: PCM would improve my efficacy on my job	0.02	0.06	0.06	0.4	0.46	4.22	
PU4: Using PCM is highly beneficial for my profession	0.02	0.02	0.1	0.48	0.38	4.18	
PU5: With PCM, I can better focus on other critical areas of my profession	0	0.04	0.14	0.4	0.42	4.2	

(*continued*)

Table 2. (*continued*)

Constructs	Score					Avg. Score	Avg. Construct Score
	1	2	3	4	5		
ATU1: PCM has a positive effect for me	0	0.02	0.06	0.46	0.46	4.36	4.43
ATU2: The development of PCM was an excellent initiative	0	0	0.12	0.4	0.48	4.36	
ATU3: PCM greatly reduces patient misidentification and misdiagnosis	0	0.04	0.04	0.3	0.62	4.5	
ATU4: I expect that PCM to be readily available at my workplace	0	0.02	0.02	0.4	0.56	4.5	
CIU1: Should I be granted access to PCM, I would be using it	0	0.02	0.04	0.46	0.48	4.4	4.45
CIU2: I would definitely be using PCM	0	0.02	0.04	0.46	0.48	4.4	
CIU3: I would like to have further understanding about EHR, Blockchain and NFC Technologies	0	0.02	0.02	0.36	0.6	4.54	
TAM AVERAGE SCORE							4.33

Following the overall TAM score of **4.33** as illustrated in Table 2, it can be deduced that implementing the PatientCare Mauritius system in real life, will definitely contribute to assisting medical care personnels as well as facilitating their daily tasks. It will also yield better productivity of the staffs. As the PCM system is convenient to use, it was well appreciated by the participants as the average score for PC was 4.3. Having a PEOU score of 4.23, signify that the overall user interface and UX of the application were well built and participants had no serious issues in going through the application. With the PU average score being 4.26, it implies that most of the participants found the new system to be effective and would help in improving their work. However, in the future, the system can further be improved as well as implementing new functionalities to better facilitate the medical staffs' daily tasks and improving the overall medical services of the healthcare institutions.

6   Conclusion and Future Works

In this paper, the traditional paper-based patient records system was critically contrasted to the EHR which is viewed as a viable system for the management of patient records. Yet, EHR systems are subjected to other significant challenges pertaining to data security, data privacy and data interoperability. As a patient records management system involves highly sensitive data, it is obligatory to defend the system through all possible ways. Also, common patient records management systems do not involve a special technological mechanism to accurately identify patients in hospital premises which may lead to wrongful diagnosis and treatment of the patients.

PatientCare Mauritius mobile application has successfully solved these shortcomings using Ethereum blockchain technology with IPFS system. Incorporating the blockchain technology in PatientCare Mauritius app, guarantees that patients' sensitive records are secured, immutable, tamper-proof, and resistant to cyber-attacks, while the mobile application itself, enables both the patients and medical staff members to access and share medical information in real-time. Moreover, since PatientCare Mauritius is a blockchain-based patient records management system, it eliminates Single Point of Failure in the EHR system, and it improves patient privacy as the latter is in total control of his medical health records. PatientCare Mauritius app also makes use of NFC technology with Photo ID feature to precisely identify patients throughout their entire visit at the hospital which contribute to patient safety, diminish medical errors, and boost the overall efficiency and productivity in healthcare delivery.

Finally, in view to ensure that the PatientCare Mauritius mobile application truly succeeded in achieving all its objectives, and is fully operational, various kinds of tests were carried out, namely, unit testing, system testing, user acceptance testing (UAT) and Technology Acceptance Model (TAM). Therefore, it can be deduced that the PatientCare Mauritius has been well developed and it is a promising tool that will surely contribute to enhancing healthcare services.

Nonetheless, the PatientCare Mauritius application can be improved by integrating an electronic prescription functionality that will allow the patients to instantly view their list of medication as well as their doses. Based upon the time interval set by doctors, it will automatically remind patients when it is due time to consume these medications. Also, smart medical sensors or wearables can be used to automatically read patients' vitals and upload same directly onto the mobile application, without any human intervention. This will allow the nurse personnels to carry out other crucial tasks as well as to increase hospital productivity. Additionally, the NFC-based bracelets can be used for other purposes, rather than patient identification. For instance, using the NFC bracelets to track patients' whereabouts as they move from one department to another.

References

1. Tan, T.L., Salam, I., Singh, M.: Blockchain-based healthcare management system with two-side verifiability. PLOS ONE 17(4) (2022). https://doi.org/10.1371/journal.pone.0266916
2. Herper, M.: The coronavirus exposes our health care system's weaknesses. We can be stronger (2020). https://www.statnews.com/2020/03/02/the-coronavirus-exposes-our-health-care-sys tems-weaknesses-we-can-be-stronger/
3. Sabu, S., Ramalingam, H.M., Vishaka, M., Swapna, H.R., Hegde, S.: Implementation of a secure and privacy-aware E-Health record and IoT data sharing using blockchain. Glob. Trans. Proc. 2, 429–433 (2021)
4. Reen, G.S., Mohandas, M., Venkatesan, S.: Decentralized patient centric e-health record management system using blockchain and IPFS. In: 2019 IEEE Conference on Information and Communication Technology (2019). https://doi.org/10.1109/CICT48419.2019.9066212
5. Le., T.G., Wang, J.W., Le, D.H., Wang, C-C., Nguyen, T.N.: Fingerprint enhancement based on tensor of wavelet subbands for classification. IEEE Access 8, 6602–6615 (2020). https://doi.org/10.1109/ACCESS.2020.2964035

6. Shivappriya, S.N., Karthikeyan, S., Prabu, S., Pérez de Prado, R.P., Parameshachari, B.D.: A modified ABC-SQP-based combined approach for the optimization of a parallel hybrid electric vehicle. Energies **13**(17), 4529 (2020). https://doi.org/10.3390/en13174529

7. Sethia., D., Gupta., D., Saran, H.: Smart health record management with secure NFC-enabled mobile devices. Smart Health **13**, 100063 (2019). https://doi.org/10.1016/j.smhl.2018.11.001

8. Chouhan, A.S., Qaseem, M.S., Basheer, Q.M.A., Mehdia, M.A.: Blockchain based EHR system architecture and the need of blockchain inhealthcare. Mater. Today Proc. **80**, 2064–2070 (2023).https://doi.org/10.1016/j.matpr.2021.06.114

9. Haleem, A., Javaid, M., Singh, R.P., Suman, R., Rab, S.: Blockchain technology applications in healthcare: an overview. Int. J. Intell. Netw. **2**, 130–139 (2021). https://doi.org/10.1016/j.ijin.2021.09.005

10. Ebere., O., et al.: NFC tag-based mHealth Patient Healthcare Tracking System. IEEE (2022)

11. Koppel, R., Wetterneck, T., Telles, J.L., Karsh. B.T.: Workarounds to barcode medication administration systems: their occurrences, causes, and threats to patient safety. J. Am. Med. Inform. Assoc. **15**(4), 408–23 (2008). https://doi.org/10.1197/jamia.M2616

12. Antwi, M., Adnane, A., Ahmad, F., Hussain, R., ur Rehman, M.H., Kerrache, C.A.: The case of HyperLedger Fabric as a blockchain solution for healthcare applications. Blockchain Res. Appl. **2**(1) (2021). https://doi.org/10.1016/j.bcra.2021.100012

13. Adefala, L.: Healthcare experiences twice the number of cyber attacks as other industries. IDG Communications, Inc. (2018). https://www.csoonline.com/article/3260191/healthcare-experiences-twice-the-number-of-cyber-attacks-as-other-industries.html

14. Huang, G.J., Foysal, A.A.: Blockchain in healthcare. Technol. Invest. **12**, 168–181 (2021). https://doi.org/10.4236/ti.2021.123010

15. Chen, H.S., Jarrell, J.T., Carpenter, K.A., Cohen, D.S., Huang, X.: Blockchain in healthcare: a patient-centered model. Biomed. J. Sci. Tech. Res. **20**(3), 15017–15022 (2019)

16. HIPAA Journal (2018) Largest Healthcare Data Breaches of 2018. https://www.hipaajournal.com/largest-healthcare-data-breaches-of-2018/

17. Costa, T.B.D.S., Shinoda, L., Moreno, R.A., Krieger, J.E., Gutierrez, M., Coração, I.D.: Blockchain-based architecture design for personal health record: development and usability study. J. Med. Internet Res. JMIR Publications Inc., Toronto, Canada (2022). https://www.jmir.org/2022/4/e35013. Accessed 17 Feb 2023

18. Zhang, A., Lin, X.: Towards secure and privacy-preserving data sharing in e-health systems via consortium blockchain. J. Med. Syst. **42**, 140 (2018). https://doi.org/10.1007/s10916-018-0995-5

19. Cao, S., Zhang, G., Liu, P., Zhang, X., Neri, F.: Cloud-assisted secure ehealth systems for tamper-proofing EHR via blockchain. Inf. Sci. **485** (2019). https://doi.org/10.1016/j.ins.2019.02.038

20. Khadse, D.B., Nikam, U., Mate, N.: DAPP to store electronic medical health records on ethereum blockchain and IPFS. Int. J. Adv. Res. Sci. Commun. Technol. (IJARSCT) **2**(2), 732–741 (2022)

21. Devendran, A., Bhuvaneswari, T.: Mobile healthcare -proposed NFC architecture. Int. J. Sci. Res. Publ. **2**(1), 1–3 (2012)

22. Godwin, P.C.: Design and Development of a Custom Blockchain-based Health Record System As an efficient management and tracking solution. Thesis (Masters), MiddleSex University London (2021)

23. Hathaliya, J., Tanwar, S., Tyagi, S., Kumar, N.: Securing electronics healthcare records in healthcare 4.0: a biometric-based approach. Comput. Electr. Eng. **76** (2019). https://doi.org/10.1016/j.compeleceng.2019.04.017

24. Meier., P., Beinke., J.H., Fitte., C., Brinke, J.S., Teuteberg., F.: Generating design knowledge for blockchain-based access control to personal health records. Inf. Syst. e-Bus.

Manag. Springer (2021). https://ideas.repec.org/a/spr/infsem/v19y2021i1d10.1007_s10257-020-00476-2.html

25. Nakamoto, S.: Bitcoin: A Peer-to-Peer Electronic Cash System. Cryptography Mailing list at (2009). https://metzdowd.com

26. Khan, F., Asif, M., Ahmad, A., Alharbi, M., Aljuaid, H.: Blockchain technology, improvement suggestions, security challenges on smart grid and its application in healthcare for sustainable development. Sustain. Cities Soc. **55**, 102018 (2020). https://doi.org/10.1016/j.scs.2020.102018

27. Onik, M.M.H., Aich, S., Yang, J., Kim, C.S. and Kim, H.C.: Chapter 8 - Blockchain in healthcare: challenges and Solutions. Advances in ubiquitous sensing applications for healthcare. Big Data Analytics for Intelligent Healthcare Management, pp. 197–226. Academic Press (2019)

28. Mettler, M.: Blockchain technology in healthcare: the revolution starts here, pp. 1–3 (2016). https://doi.org/10.1109/HealthCom.2016.7749510

29. Kumar, T., Ramani, V., Ahmad, I., Braeken, A., Harjula, E., Ylianttila, M.: Blockchain Utilization in Healthcare: Key Requirements and Challenges (2018). https://doi.org/10.1109/HealthCom.2018.8531136

30. BigchainDB 2.0 the blockchain database (no date). https://www.bigchaindb.com/whitepaper/bigchaindb-whitepaper.pdf. Accessed 22 Jan 2023

31. Kumar, R., Marchang, N., Tripathi, R.: Distributed off-chain storage of patient diagnostic reports in healthcare system using IPFS and blockchain. In: 2020 International Conference on COMmunication Systems & NETworkS (COMSNETS), Bengaluru, India, 2020, pp. 1–5 (2020). https://doi.org/10.1109/COMSNETS48256.2020.9027313

32. Solidity. (2021). https://docs.soliditylang.org/en/v0.8.15/

Comparative Performance Evaluation of Random Forest, Extreme Gradient Boosting and Linear Regression Algorithms Using Nigeria's Gross Domestic Products

M. D. Adewale[1]([✉]), D. U. Ebem[2], O. Awodele[3], A. Azeta[4], E. M. Aggrey[1],
E. A. Okechalu[1], K. A. Olayanju[1], A. F. Owolabi[1], J. Oju[1], O. C. Ubadike[1],
G. A. Otu[1], U. I. Muhammed[1], and O. P. Oluyide[1]

[1] African Centre of Excellence on Technology Enhanced Learning, National Open University of Nigeria, Abuja, Nigeria
ace22140007@noun.edu.ng
[2] Department of Computer Science, University of Nigeria, Nsukka, Nigeria
[3] Department of Computer Science, Babcock University, Ilishan-Remo, Ogun, Nigeria
[4] Department of Software Engineering, Namibia University of Science and Technology, Windhoek, Namibia

Abstract. Statistical methods like linear regression analysis are frequently used to create predictive analytic models. However, these methods have limitations that may affect the accuracy of the models. Using a typical dataset, this study seeks to accomplish two main goals. First, we fitted three predictive models, including linear regression analysis and two ensemble machine learning algorithms: Random Forest Regressor and Extreme Gradient Boosting Regressor. Secondly, we compared the performance of the models using a 5-fold cross-validation technique. The Random Forest Regressor outperformed the other models, with a Mean Absolute Error (MAE) of 10.138, Mean Square Error (MSE) of 139.729, Mean Absolute Percentage Error (MAPE) of 0.071, Root Mean Square Error (RMSE) of 11.821, and Normalised Mean Square Error (NMSE) of 13.782. These results suggest that the Random Forest Regressor is optimal for developing predictive models with similar datasets.

Keywords: Machine learning · Random Forest Regressor · XGboost Regressor · Linear Regression · Gross Domestic Product · 5-fold cross-validation

1 Introduction

In today's world, predictive modelling has taken the forefront in many industries, such as finance and healthcare. It is now a vital tool for companies to gain insights and make informed decisions. The advent of machine learning algorithms has played a significant role in this development, enabling organisations to handle vast volumes of data efficiently and precisely. According to Wang & Lee (2021), machine learning algorithms

© ICST Institute for Computer Sciences, Social Informatics and Telecommunications Engineering 2024
Published by Springer Nature Switzerland AG 2024. All Rights Reserved
A. Seeam et al. (Eds.): InterSol 2023, LNICST 541, pp. 131–150, 2024.
https://doi.org/10.1007/978-3-031-51849-2_9

have been widely adopted in various applications and have gained significant popularity. Among the machine learning algorithms, the Random Forest Regressor, Extreme Gradient Boosting (XGBoost) Regressor, and Linear Regression are some of the most commonly used algorithms. These algorithms have proven to be efficient and accurate in predicting outcomes. However, they have significant differences in predictive performance, computational efficiency, and interpretability. It is imperative to comprehend these differences to select the appropriate model for a given prediction problem. For instance, the Random Forest Regressor is a versatile algorithm that can handle a large number of variables and nonlinear relationships. On the other hand, the XGBoost Regressor is a gradient-boosted model that can provide superior predictive performance and scalability. Lastly, Linear Regression is a simple algorithm that is easy to interpret and is suitable for predicting outcomes when the relationships between variables are linear.

Machine learning algorithms have revolutionised the field of predictive modelling by enabling accurate predictions of outcomes in regression tasks such as predicting stock prices, house prices, or medical diagnoses (Kaliappan et al., 2021; Xu et al., 2022). However, selecting the best algorithm for a given problem can be challenging due to several factors, such as the data distribution, dataset size, and feature number (Raju et al., 1998). Thus, it is crucial to compare the relative performance of algorithms in terms of accuracy. The Random Forest Regressor is an ensemble learning technique that creates multiple decision trees and combines their predictions to generate a more precise forecast (Pandey et al., 2019; Garg & Poornalatha, 2019). It is a flexible algorithm that can handle numerous variables and nonlinear relationships, making various applications possible.

On the other hand, the XGBoost Regressor is a gradient-boosting algorithm (Li, 2021) that also uses decision trees to make predictions (Allawala et al., 2022). It has gained popularity due to its superior predictive performance and scalability. Lastly, Linear Regression is a simple but powerful algorithm widely used due to its ease of implementation and interpretation (Chien et al., 2023). It is suitable for predicting outcomes when the relationships between variables are linear.

This paper aims to present a comparative performance evaluation of the Random Forest Regressor, XGBoost Regressor, and Linear Regression algorithms based on metrics such as Mean Squared Error (MSE) and Root Mean Squared Error (RMSE) using a typical dataset. The objective is to conduct experiments on a given dataset and evaluate the performance of each algorithm using different metrics to provide insights into their relative performances and identify the most suitable algorithm for specific applications. By comparing the performance of these three algorithms, we hope to provide a comprehensive understanding of their strengths and limitations, aiding decision-makers in selecting the most appropriate algorithm for a given prediction problem.

The findings of our study are expected to be highly valuable to researchers and practitioners in machine learning and those who use regression analysis in their work. By providing a comprehensive comparative evaluation of the Random Forest Regressor, XGBoost Regressor, and Linear Regression algorithms, we aim to contribute to the growing body of knowledge on the performance of regression algorithms. The insights gained from our study will enable users to make enlightened choices when picking the most appropriate algorithm for their specific application, leading to more accurate and reliable predictions.

The paper is structured as follows to clearly and concisely present the evaluation and findings. The three algorithms and their properties are briefly described in Sect. 2, enabling readers to understand the underlying concepts and differences between them. Section 3 delves into the methodology used to evaluate the performance of the algorithms, including the dataset used, the evaluation metrics employed, and the experimental design. In Sect. 4, we present the results of the comparative evaluation, including the performance of each algorithm on various metrics, enabling readers to compare and contrast their relative strengths and weaknesses. Finally, in Sect. 5, we summarise our findings and conclusions, highlighting the most significant insights gained from our study and their implications for those working in the field of machine learning as researchers and practitioners.

2 Literature Review

According to Schonlau and Zou (2020), the question of whether linear regression should be considered a machine learning algorithm or just a statistical method for prediction has been a matter of debate. While some argue that it is a statistical method, others suggest it can also be classified as a machine learning algorithm. Regardless of the conflicting views, it is crucial to evaluate the effectiveness of linear regression and contrast it with that of other machine learning algorithms. This comparison can shed light on the strengths and limitations of each method, allowing us to choose the most appropriate approach for a given problem. Although linear regression is frequently considered a straightforward and simple technique, it has proven helpful in many applications, including forecasting stock prices, examining consumer behaviour, and predicting sales trends (Tan & Al-Barakati, 2022; Wang et al., 2022). The popularity of machine learning algorithms, on the other hand, is growing due to their capacity to learn from data and make precise predictions about challenging issues (Sandra et al., 2021). In order to select the approach that best meets the needs of the current problem, it is crucial to assess the effectiveness of both. Ultimately, the choice should be based on a thorough understanding of the strengths and weaknesses of each technique as well as the application's unique requirements.

Machine learning algorithms have gained popularity in recent years for their ability to predict future trends based on historical data. Regression analysis stands as a frequently employed technique in predictive analytics, and various algorithms have been developed to achieve accurate predictions. This section reviews the literature on three algorithms - Random Forest Regressor, XGBoost Regressor, and Linear Regression - and their performance evaluation in various applications.

Various applications, including economics, social sciences, and environmental studies, use linear regression, a straightforward but effective technique. It establishes a linear relationship between the dependent and independent variables and is widely used for predictive analytics (Mislick & Nussbaum, 2015). For instance, Li et al. (2013) used Linear Regression to predict the energy consumption of buildings, with the ventilation energy consumption predicted at high accuracies of over 99%. Similarly, Mirugwe (2021) used Linear Regression to predict the average dollar tip a waiter can expect from the restaurant given several predictor variables, achieving a minimum Root Mean Square Error

(RMSE) of 1.1815. While statistical methods like Linear Regression have been widely used in economics, they have been criticised for their inability to capture complex non-linear relationships between economic variables. Karen and Louise (2018) and Gareth et al. (2017) have highlighted these limitations and pointed out that relying solely on linear relationships can result in underestimating gross domestic product (GDP).

Moreover, several factors can affect the model's accuracy, such as multicollinearity, heteroscedasticity, and outliers. Therefore, researchers must adopt more advanced techniques to capture complex and dynamic relationships between economic variables. First, including irrelevant variables can reduce the effectiveness of the model. Second, a significantly higher or lower number of observations than predictors may cause the Linear Regression approach to produce inaccurate predictions. As a result, this issue can lead to overestimation or underestimation of the model, limiting its accuracy. Third, relying solely on R^2 statistics and correlation to measure the model's fitness may not be suitable for predicting future data. Finally, the lack of a support system for tuning parameters and cost function prevents applying a bias-variance trade-off to minimise the test Mean Square Error. Thus, alternative approaches, such as machine learning algorithms, may be better suited for accurately predicting economic variables (Agu et al., 2022).

An approach to ensemble learning is the Random Forest Regressor which constructs multiple decision trees and combines their predictions to improve accuracy. It has been used in various applications, including finance, healthcare, and marketing. For instance, Lawrence et al. (2021) used Random Forest Regressor to predict patient survival in healthcare, achieving an accuracy rate of 86.4%. Random Forest has been identified as the best technique for prediction for small data sets (Ameer et al., 2019).

XGBoost Regressor is another ensemble learning method that uses a gradient-boosting algorithm to improve accuracy (Sainikhileaswar & Parthasarathy, 2020). It has been used in various applications, including remote sensing (Öztürk & Colkesen, 2021), healthcare or medical informatics (Huang et al., 2022). A study by Raheja et al. (2021) used an XGBoost Regressor to evaluate groundwater indices over a Haryana state (India) study area. Similarly, Nguyen et al. (2021) used XGBoost Regressor to predict high-performance concrete's compressive and tensile strength. Extreme gradient boosting (XGBoost) is a powerful and efficient algorithm that can accurately handle large datasets (Xu et al., 2022).

In various applications, Random Forest Regressor, XGBoost Regressor, and Linear Regression are widely used algorithms that have proven effective. However, their performance varies depending on the application and dataset. Therefore, conducting a comparative performance evaluation of these algorithms is crucial to identify the most accurate and efficient algorithm for specific applications.

This study aims to overcome the shortcomings inherent in traditional statistical methods in predicting related projects by utilising two ensemble machine learning models, namely the Random Forest Regressor and XGBoost Regressor, along with a Linear Regression statistical model. Our objective is to determine the most effective approach for prediction and underscore the importance of integrating machine learning techniques in data science. While we recognise the limitations of machine learning, our approach aims to highlight its potential in prediction by demonstrating its superiority over traditional statistical methods. As interest in machine learning for prediction grows, our study contributes to the literature emphasising the necessity for data scientists to harness this technology while comprehending its limitations.

This study aims to develop precise predictive models for Nigeria's GDP by employing various relevant economic and non-economic indicators. The data set is carefully curated and refined to encompass healthcare spending, net migration, population, life expectancy, electricity access, and internet usage. In order to construct and compare predictive models, machine learning methods like Random Forest Regressor, XGboost Regressor, and statistical Linear Regression analysis are employed. The primary objective is to pinpoint the most efficient approach for forecasting Nigerian GDP, considering many factors that affect economic growth. Our research has significant implications for practitioners and scholars in selecting the most suitable algorithm for similar data sets.

3 Methods and Techniques

The relevant dataset consists of 22 instances from 2000 to 2021, has five attributes, and is focused on economic and non-economic parameters such as Nigeria's gross domestic product (gdp) in billions of dollars, healthcare spending (hs) in billions of dollars, population (p), life expectancy (le) in years, and index of economic freedom (ief). The research utilised a secondary dataset from the World Bank (World Bank, 2021) and Nigeria Corruption Perceptions Index, 2001–2022 - knoema.com, (2023). The experiment was carried out using the relevant Sklearn Python libraries at https://colab.research.goo gle.com/. Table 1 shows the first five rows of the sample dataset.

Table 1. First five rows of the sample dataset

Year	GDP	HS	P	LE	IEF
2021	440.78	11.13	213401323	55.12	58.70
2020	432.29	14.7	208327405	54.81	57.20
2019	448.12	13.58	203304492	54.49	57.30
2018	397.19	12.27	198387623	54.18	58.50
2017	375.75	14.09	193495907	53.73	57.10

Hotz (2023) highlighted the prevalence of the CRoss Industry Standard Process for Data Mining (CRISP-DM) adopted methodology in data science projects, as evidenced by Fig. 1. The CRISP-DM approach comprises six key phases, as shown in Fig. 2. The study followed the six stages of the CRISP-DM methodology, which are crucial in ensuring the success of any data mining project.

In the initial business understanding stage, our objective was aimed to contrast the efficacy of the Random Forest Regressor and XGBoost Regressor against Linear Regression Analysis. In the subsequent data understanding stage, we focused on deeply comprehending our data, including pinpointing any quality issues and recognising critical attributes valuable for the modelling process.

Our datasets were sourced from the World Bank (World Bank, 2021) and the Nigeria Corruption Perceptions Index, 2001–2022 - knoema.com, (2023) for the data preparation phase. These datasets encompassed variables such as healthcare spending (hs), population (p), life expectancy (le), and the index of economic freedom (ief), paired with GDP data. After consolidating this information, we identified no missing values, facilitating the designation of independent and dependent variables. A division into training and testing subsets followed this.

During the modelling stage, our dataset was trained, and the data was tailored to fit the three selected algorithms: Random Forest Regressor, XGBoost Regressor, and Linear Regression Analysis. The evaluation stage saw the application of a 5-fold Cross Validation method, aiding in determining key metrics like MAE, MAPE, MSE, RMSE, and NMSE across our modelling strategies. The final deployment phase, intrinsic to the CRISP-DM methodology, varied in its approach based on our set objectives. This ranged from a succinct report of findings to a comprehensive implementation of the developed models. It's paramount to note that our research's initial and final phases were oriented towards GDP prediction. Our exploration and evaluation of varied predictive models culminated in detailed findings in the final phase. Section 4 delves deeper into the nuances of the intermediary phases. Typically, a subset of the data, termed the training set, is utilised during modelling, while the residual dataset, the test set, is reserved for performance evaluation during the evaluation phase. A detailed breakdown of the algorithms employed in our analysis is provided in the following sections.

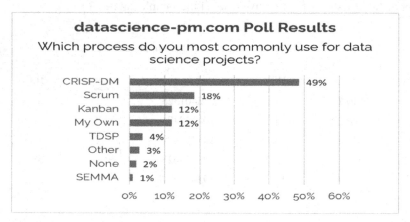

Fig. 1. Most commonly used process for data science projects. Source: Hotz (2023)

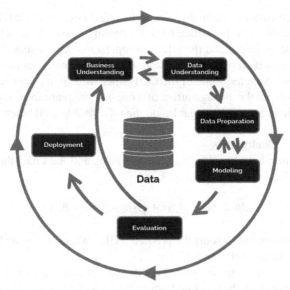

Fig. 2. The Six stages of the CRISP-DM methodology. Source: Hotz (2023)

3.1 Theory/Calculation

This study made use of five features, viz., gross domestic product (gdp), healthcare spending (hs), population (p), life expectancy (le), and Index of economic freedom (ief), that made up the study's conceptual model, with GDP standing in as the dependent variable as shown in Eq. 1 (Gareth et al., 2017). Here, we consider the GDP, which represents economic growth for this period, as a function of healthcare spending, population, life expectancy, and index of economic freedom. In this study, we analyse various machine learning models that take the following variables: healthcare spending, population, life expectancy, and index of economic freedom as the independent variables and gross domestic product (gdp) as the target variable. This is done to create accurate parameter estimates for the models. The research model employed can be described as follows:

$$gdp = f(hs, p, le, ief) + e \qquad (1)$$

where the random variable e stands for the error term, independent of the predictors and has a mean of zero, the fixed but unknown function f represents the information the predictors provide about the GDP.

3.2 The Linear Regression Model

The Linear Regression method assumes that the function f in Eq. 1 is linear in (*hs, p, le, ief*) as shown in Eq. 2.

$$gdp = \beta_0 + \beta_1 hs + \beta_2 p + \beta_3 le + \beta_4 ief \qquad (2)$$

The Linear Regression method assumes that only five coefficients $\beta_0, \beta_1, \beta_2, \beta_3, \beta_4$ need to be estimated, instead of having to estimate a completely arbitrary 5-dimensional function, making it easier to estimate f (hs, p, le, ief) (Gareth et al., 2017). These coefficients, represented by β_0 to β_4, define the relationships between the selected economic and non-economic variables and the GDP. β_0 represents the constant (intercept) of the equation, while β_1 to β_4 represent the coefficients of the macroeconomic variables. In particular, β_0 is the expected value of the GDP when all variables are zero. At the same time, β_1 to β_4 represent the average effect of a one-unit increase in each of the economic and non-economic independent variables on the GDP, holding all other predictors fixed.

Estimation of the Coefficients
To ascertain the link between the predictor variables and the GDP, the coefficients of Eq. 2 must be estimated, as seen in Eq. 3.

$$\widehat{gdp} = \hat{\beta}_0 + \hat{\beta}_1 hs + \hat{\beta}_2 p + \hat{\beta}_3 le + \hat{\beta}_4 ief \tag{3}$$

In this equation, $\widehat{gdp}$ represents the predicted GDP while $\hat{\beta}_0$, $\hat{\beta}_1$, and so on, up to $\hat{\beta}_4$, represent the estimated coefficients.

Least squares compute the estimated coefficients $\hat{\beta}_0$, $\hat{\beta}_1$ ..., $\hat{\beta}_4$ in Eq. 3 by utilising some calculus to diminish the residual Sum of Squares (RSS) given in Eq. 4 (Wikipedia, 2021).

$$RSS = \sum_{i=1}^{n} \left(gdp_i - \widehat{gdp}_i \right)^2$$

$$= \sum_{i=1}^{n} (gdp_i - \hat{\beta}_0 - \hat{\beta}_1 hs - \hat{\beta}_2 p - \hat{\beta}_3 le - \hat{\beta}_4 ief)^2 \tag{4}$$

where i denotes a single yearly observation and n denotes the total number of years.

3.3 The Random Forest Regressor Model

Random Forest Regression is a robust supervised learning algorithm that leverages the ensemble learning approach to perform regression tasks. Combining predictions from multiple machine learning algorithms can generate highly accurate predictions that outperform those from any individual model. The Random Forest model is structured as a collection of decision trees that operate in parallel, as illustrated in Fig. 3. Each tree is constructed independently during the training phase, and the predicted value from most trees is used as the final output (Chaya, 2022). This unique approach ensures that the model is highly robust, even when dealing with complex and noisy datasets, making it an excellent choice for various machine learning and data science applications.

The Random Forest Regressor generates predictions by averaging the forecasts made by the forest's trees. Averaging is a key factor in the superior performance of the random forest over a single decision tree. This increases its accuracy and prevents it from becoming overly effective at its job. The average of the forecasts made by the forest's trees is what the Random Forest Regressor produces (Mwiti, 2022).

Saabas (2014) explained that a decision tree consists of a series of paths from the tree's root to the leaf. Each path represents a series of decisions based on specific features contributing to the final prediction. To define the prediction function of a decision tree, the feature space is partitioned into *M* regions represented by the *M* leaves of the tree, denoted as *Rm* where *1 ≤ m ≤ M*. This partitioning is done through a series of decisions made at each internal node of the tree, based on specific features. According to Saabas (2014), the prediction function of a decision tree is defined based on the standard criteria presented in Eqs. 5, 6 and 7:

$$f(x) = \sum_{m=1}^{M} C_m I(x, R_m) \tag{5}$$

In a decision tree, the feature space is divided into *M* regions, where *M* is the number of leaves in the tree. Each region, denoted by *Rm, 1 ≤ m ≤ M*, is guarded by a specific feature. The prediction function of the tree is defined as follows: the value of *Cm* is established during the tree's training phase, which corresponds to the mean of the response variables for samples that fall under region *Rm* in the case of regression trees (or the ratio(s) for classification trees). The indicator function *I* returns *1 if x ∈ Rm and 0* otherwise. Although this definition provides a clear and concise understanding of a tree, it ignores the operational aspect of decision trees, including the informative decision nodes and the path through them. Predictions made by individual trees in a forest are averaged to form the forest's overall prediction.

$$F(x) = \frac{1}{J} \sum_{j=1}^{J} f_j(x), \tag{6}$$

The variable *J* represents the total number of trees included in the forest. It is clear from this that the predictions made by individual trees in a forest are averaged to form the forest's overall prediction:

$$\frac{1}{J} \sum_{j=1}^{J} c_{j\,full} + \sum_{k=1}^{K} \left(\frac{1}{J} \sum_{j=1}^{J} contrib_j(x, k) \right). \tag{7}$$

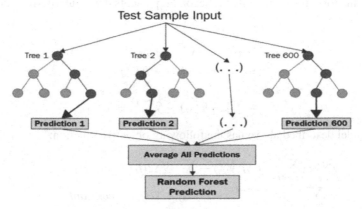

Fig. 3. Random Forest Tree Source: (Chaya, 2022)

3.4 The XGBoost Regressor Model

According to GeeksforGeeks (2023), XGBoost is an optimised distributed gradient boosting library designed for rapid and scalable machine learning model training. This ensemble learning technique combines the predictions from several weak models to produce a stronger prediction. Due to its capacity to manage massive datasets and produce ground-breaking results in numerous machine learning tasks like classification and Regression, XGBoost is one of the most well-known and popular machine learning algorithms. XGBoost is a Gradient Boosted decision tree implementation. XGBoost is a powerful machine-learning algorithm that generates decision trees in sequence while considering the importance of each independent variable. Each variable is assigned a weight, which is used to predict the output of the decision tree. If a variable is mispredicted, its weight is increased and used as input for the next decision tree. By combining multiple classifiers/predictors, XGBoost creates a more accurate and robust model that can handle various problems, including regression, classification, ranking, and user-defined prediction. For instance, let's consider a CART that predicts whether an individual would enjoy a hypothetical computer game X. The final prediction score is calculated by adding the prediction scores from each decision tree. The mathematical representation of the model is detailed in Eqs. 8–24, as cited by GeeksforGeeks (2023):

$$\hat{y}_i = \sum_{k=1}^{K} f_k(x_i), f_k \in \mathcal{F} \tag{8}$$

The model's objective function can be expressed mathematically as follows, where **K** represents the total number of trees in the model, f represents the functional space of the set **F**, and **F** represents the set of all possible decision trees:

$$obj(\theta) = \sum_{i}^{n} l(y_i, \hat{y}_i) + \sum_{k=1}^{K} \Omega(f_k) \tag{9}$$

Instead of attempting to optimise the learning of the tree all at once, which is a complicated process, an additive strategy is used, where the loss of what has been learned is minimised, and a new tree is added, as shown below. The first term in the equation represents the loss function, while the second represents the regularisation parameter.

$$\begin{aligned}
\hat{y}_i^{(0)} &= 0 \\
\hat{y}_i^{(1)} &= f_1(x_i) = \hat{y}_i^{(0)} + f_1(x_i) \\
\hat{y}_i^{(2)} &= f_1(x_i) = f_2(x_i) + f_2(x_i) \\
&\ldots \\
\hat{y}_i^{(t)} &= \sum_{k=1}^{t} f_k(x_i) = \hat{y}_i^{(t-1)} + f_t(x_i)
\end{aligned} \tag{10}$$

The model described above has the following objective function:

$$\begin{aligned}
obj^{(t)} &= \sum_{i=1}^{n} l(y_i, \hat{y}_i^{(t)}) + \sum_{i=1}^{t} \Omega(f_t) \\
&= \sum_{i=1}^{n} l(y_i, \hat{y}_i^{(t-1)}) + f_t(x_i)) + \Omega(f_t) + constant \\
obj^{(t)} &= \sum_{i=1}^{n} (y_i - (\hat{y}_i^{(t-1)} + f_t(x_i)))^2 + \sum_{i=1}^{t} \Omega(f_i)
\end{aligned}$$

$$= \sum_{i=1}^{n} [2(\hat{y}_i^{(t-1)} - y_i)f_t(x_i) + f_t(x_i)^2] + \Omega(f_t) + constant \tag{11}$$

Now, let's expand the Taylor series up to the second order:

$$obj^{(t)} = \sum_{i=1}^{n} [l(y_i, \hat{y}_i^{(t-1)}) + g_i f_t(x_i) + \frac{1}{2} h_i f_t^2(x_i)] + \Omega(f_t) + constant \tag{12}$$

With g_i and h_i defined as:

$$g_i = \partial_{\hat{y}_i^{(t-1)}} l(y_i, \hat{y}_i^{(t-1)}) \tag{13}$$

$$h_i = \partial_{\hat{y}_i^{(t-1)}}^2 l(y_i, \hat{y}_i^{(t-1)}) \tag{14}$$

Streamlining and getting rid of the constant:

$$\sum_{i=1}^{n} [g_i f_i(x_i) + \frac{1}{2} h_i f_t^2(x_i)] + \Omega(f_t) \tag{15}$$

The model must first be defined before we can determine the regularisation term:

$$f_t(x) = \omega_{q(x)}, \omega \in R^T, q : R^d \rightarrow \{1, 2, \ldots, T\} \tag{16}$$

In the XGBoost model, the regularisation term is determined by a combination of factors, including a function that maps each data point to the corresponding leaf *(q)*, a vector of scores on tree leaves *(w)*, and the total number of leaves *(T)*. The regularisation term can be expressed as a function of these components, which helps control the model's complexity and reduce the risk of overfitting. The regularisation term is then mathematically represented by:

$$\Omega(f) = \gamma T + \frac{1}{2} \lambda \sum_{j=1}^{T} \omega_j^2 \tag{17}$$

Our objective function is now:

$$obj^{(t)} \approx \sum_{i=1}^{n} \left[g_i w_{q(x_i)} + \frac{1}{2} h_i w_{q(x_i)}^2 \right] + \gamma T + \frac{\lambda}{2} \sum_{j=1}^{T} w_j^2$$

$$= \sum_{j=1}^{T} \left[(\sum_{i \in I_j} g_i) w_j + \frac{1}{2} (\sum_{i \in I_j} h_i + \lambda) w_j^2 \right] + \gamma T \tag{18}$$

The above expression is now simplified:

$$obj^{(t)} = \sum_{j=1}^{T} [G_j \omega_j + \frac{1}{2} (H_j + \lambda) \omega_j^2] + \gamma T \tag{19}$$

where,

$$G_j = \sum_{i \in I_j} g_i \tag{20}$$

$$H_j = \sum_{i \in I_j} h_i \qquad (21)$$

Given a particular structure of $q(x)$, the best w_j in this equation, which is independent of one another, is the greatest achievable objective reduction:

$$\omega_j^* = -\frac{G_j^2}{H_j + \lambda} \qquad (22)$$

$$obj^* = -\frac{1}{2} \sum_{j=1}^{T} \frac{G_j^2}{H_j + \lambda} + \gamma T \qquad (23)$$

This algorithm uses a pruning parameter γ, which determines the minimum information gain required to perform a split. To measure the effectiveness of the tree, we optimise one level at a time instead of optimising the entire tree. In this, a leaf is divided into two leaves, and the score it receives is calculated. The score is then used to determine if the split should be accepted. The score it gains is:

$$Gain = \frac{1}{2}\left[\frac{G_L^2}{H_L + \lambda} + \frac{G_R^2}{H_R + \lambda} - \frac{(G_L + G_R)^2}{H_L + H_R + \lambda}\right] - \gamma \qquad (24)$$

3.5 Error Costs and Estimation

The goal of the study is to compare the results obtained using each model and identify which is the most effective. Aftarczuk (2007) highlights several popular error metrics, as illustrated in Eqs. 25–29, which are frequently incorporated into various machine learning tools:

Mean Absolute Error (MAE): Eq. 25 is the average of individual errors while neglecting the signs to diminish the negative effects of outliers.

$$= \frac{1}{n} \sum_{i=1}^{n} |y_i - \hat{y}_i| \qquad (25)$$

$$\text{Mean Absolute Percentage Error (MAPE)} = \frac{1}{n} \sum_{t=1}^{n} \frac{|y_t - \hat{y}_t|}{y_t} \qquad (26)$$

$$\text{Mean Square Error(MSE)} = \frac{1}{n} \sum_{t=1}^{n} (y_t - \hat{y}_t)^2 \qquad (27)$$

$$\text{Root Mean Square Error(RMSE)} = \sqrt{\sum_{i=1}^{n} \frac{(y_t - \hat{y}_t)^2}{n}} \qquad (28)$$

$$\text{Normalised Mean Square Error (NMSE)} = \frac{\sum_{t=1}^{n} (y_t - \hat{y}_t)^2}{\sum_{t=1}^{n} (y_t - \bar{y}_t)^2} \qquad (29)$$

where y_t and $\hat{y}_t$ are the actual and predicted values $\bar{y}_t$ is the mean value of y_t. The smaller the error values, the nearer the estimated figures align with the true values.

3.6 5-fold Cross-Validation (5-fold CV) Technique

Since we are considering three prediction models: Random Forest Regressor, XGBoost Regressor, and Linear Regression, we compare the outcomes of their predictions and decide which model is more effective by comparing the results. The 5-fold cross-validation (5-fold CV) method is used for this. The data is split into five randomly chosen folds in this method, which is advantageous as it aids in preventing overfitting and provides a more precise estimation of the test error. Every iteration uses the remaining four folds as the model's training set while treating one-fold as a validation set. This procedure is repeated five times using a different fold as the validation set in each iteration. The MAE, MSE, MAPE, RMSE, and NMSE are computed for each fold. The final 5-fold CV estimate is obtained by averaging the MAEs, MSEs, MAPEs, RMSEs, and NMSEs. Each metric provides different insights into the model's performance and is helpful in different contexts. Thus, it is crucial to consider a diverse set of evaluation metrics to make informed decisions and comparisons when selecting models. Using the 5-fold cross-validation approach, we assess the performance of the models across various data subsets. This provides a more robust gauge of the model's generalisation capabilities. The equations for this validation, pertaining to each error metric, are presented in Eqs. 30–34, as adapted from Pandian (2023).

$$CV_{(5)mae} = \frac{1}{5} \sum_{i=1}^{5} MAE_i \tag{30}$$

$$CV_{(5)mse} = \frac{1}{5} \sum_{i=1}^{5} MSE_i \tag{31}$$

$$CV_{(5)mape} = \frac{1}{5} \sum_{i=1}^{5} MAPE_i \tag{32}$$

$$CV_{(5)rmse} = \frac{1}{5} \sum_{i=1}^{5} RMSE_i \tag{33}$$

$$CV_{(5)nmse} = \frac{1}{5} \sum_{i=1}^{5} NMSE_i \tag{34}$$

In addition to the benefits of evaluating MAE, MSE, MAPE, RMSE, and NMSE using a 5-fold CV, it also provides a way to balance between bias and variance in model selection by allowing us to choose the optimal cost function. Using a 5-fold CV; we can evaluate various models' efficacy and choose the most suitable one with the lowest test error. This helps to avoid overfitting, where a model adheres too tightly to the training data, compromising its ability to generalise well to new data. In this way, a 5-fold CV provides a way to optimise model performance and ensure accurate predictions.

4 Results and Discussion

4.1 Predictive Accuracy

Developing predictive accuracy models to aid data scientists in related research projects is critical. The study's contribution is to build predictive models using machine learning approaches. In this respect, Fig. 4, 5, 6, 7 and Fig. 8 present the 5-fold Cross-Validation of MAE, MSE, MAPE, RMSE, and NMSE of the 22 observations from Nigeria's dataset. The plotted small squares on the line correspond to the MSE values associated with each method on the x-axis. According to the plots, the Random Forest Regressor method resulted in the lowest MAE, MSE, MAPE, RMSE, and NMSE. The last square on the line indicates Var(e), the irreducible error corresponding to the minimum achievable MAE, MSE, MAPE, RMSE, and NMSE among all methods. Therefore, the values obtained from the Random Forest Regressor method are the closest to the optimal value and are recommended for developing a predictive model for Nigeria's GDP.

The study implies that a Random Forest Regressor approach to modelling decision-making in GDP behaviour in this context is more accurate than Linear Regression and XGboost regressor models. These findings are consistent with Giovanni et al. (2021) study, which shows that machine learning techniques perform better in predictive accuracy than conventional ordinary least squares (OLS). Achieving high accuracy and high explainability in forecasting is a critical best practice in developing trust between machine learning models and decision-makers, as Bellotti et al. (2021) highlighted. The concept is that decision-makers should embrace machine learning as a potent instrument and utilise it with mindfulness instead of treating it as an opaque "black box".

Numerous machine learning techniques exist, each with specific applications and inherent limitations, as noted by experts like Katrina (2021), Shaobo (2021), and Brownlee (2019). For this study, we selected algorithms designed for quantitative, continuous numerical data: Linear Regression, XGBoost Regressor, and Random Forest Regressor. In a comparative analysis of GDP prediction studies presented in Table 2, our research, employing the Random Forest Regressor, logged an MSE of 139.729. Agu et al. (2022), with the Principal Component Regression (PCR), reported an MSE of $-7.552007365635066e + 21$. Maccarrone et al. (2021) achieved an MSE of 173e-03 using the K-Nearest Neighbour (KNN), while Flannery (2020) documented an MSE of 2946980.9 using the Artificial Neural Network (specifically, the Multilayer Perceptron). Our model showcased robust performance. However, when interpreting these results, it's essential to account for potential dataset discrepancies and recognise that the selection of independent variables may vary across these research studies.

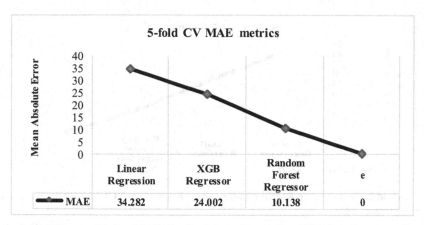

Fig. 4. 5-fold Cross validation MAE plot for Linear Regression, XGBoost Regressor, Random Forest Regressor and *e*

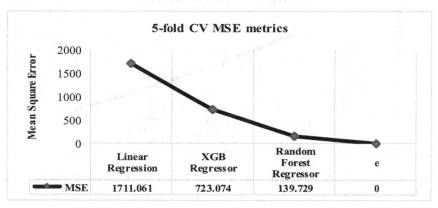

Fig. 5. 5-fold Cross validation MSE plot for Linear Regression, XGBoost Regressor, Random Forest Regressor and *e*

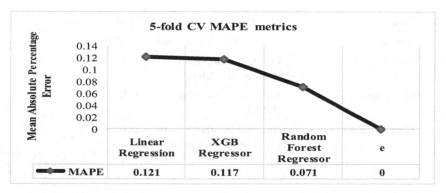

Fig. 6. 5-fold Cross validation MAPE plot for Linear Regression, XGBoost Regressor, Random Forest Regressor and *e*

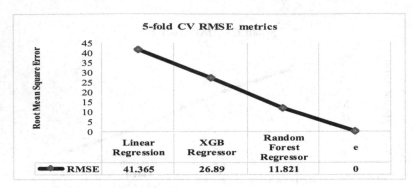

Fig. 7. 5-fold Cross validation RMSE plot for Linear Regression, XGBoost Regressor, Random Forest Regressor and *e*

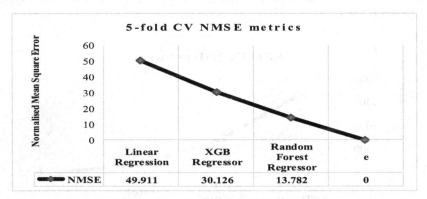

Fig. 8. 5-fold Cross validation NMSE plot for Linear Regression, XGBoost Regressor, Random Forest Regressor and *e*

Table 2. Comparing our best result with other models used to predict GDP

S/N	Study	Best Model	MSE
1	Our Research	Random Forest Regressor	139.729
2	Agu et al. (2022)	Principal Component Regression (PCR)	-7.552007365635066e + 21
3	Maccarrone et al. (2021)	K-Nearest Neighbour (KNN)	173e-03
3	Flannery (2020)	Artificial Neural Network (Multilayer Perceptron)	2946980.9

5   Conclusion

In this paper, we compared and evaluated the performance of three algorithms - Random Forest Regressor, XGBoost Regressor, and Linear Regression - in predicting the target variable. Our analysis was based on metrics, including MAE, MSE, MAPE, RMSE, and NMSE values. Our findings revealed that Random Forest Regressor outperformed the other two algorithms regarding accuracy. The results showed that Random Forest Regressor achieved the lowest MAE, MSE, MAPE, RMSE, and NMSE. On the other hand, Linear Regression was the most straightforward algorithm and performed reasonably well, while XGBoost showed high variability in performance. The rigid and high assumption of linear relationships between predictor variables and response variables, which are the limitations of the Linear Regression method, have prompted the adoption of ensemble machine learning techniques. Several models are trained using the Random Forest Regressor technique using various subsets of the training dataset. Predictions are made using an average of the predictions made by the forest's trees. Parameters must be tuned to achieve the best prediction accuracy when creating these models. Even when dealing with complex, high-dimensional data that defies linear relationships, more precise predictions can be made using this technique.

In our research, we explored the comparative performance of three algorithms: The Random Forest Regressor, XGBoost Regressor, and Linear Regression, especially in predicting GDP using notable variables like healthcare spending (hs), population (p), life expectancy (le), and the index of economic freedom (ief). Such a comprehensive approach offers policymakers detailed insight into societal and economic interrelations and bears profound practical significance. Through our analysis, we intended to guide practitioners and researchers in pinpointing the most suitable algorithm for their specific scenarios. Our findings were inclined favourably towards the Random Forest Regressor, which appeared to be especially adept for datasets characterised by complex inter-variable relationships and smaller sizes. Nonetheless, it's vital to underline the caveats in our study. Our conclusions were based on a single dataset, indicating that different datasets might yield different outcomes, especially with varied variables and aims.

Furthermore, our study was confined to these three algorithms, not accounting for potentially more apt algorithms for other unique applications. The apparent preeminence of the Random Forest Regressor within our studied dataset prompts the reference to the "No Free Lunch" theorem. This theorem emphasises that no singular algorithm is a definitive best across all conceivable contexts (Sterkenburg & Grünwald, 2021). As such, while our dataset-driven findings are significant, broad generalisations would be precipitant. It's always imperative to weigh various algorithms against distinct datasets to discern the optimal one, facilitating the creation of more nuanced and evidence-based economic policies.

Predictive models, especially those developed using statistical methods such as linear regression analysis, remain crucial in several fields. While the study presented here shows promising results for ensemble machine learning algorithms compared to linear regression analysis with a typical dataset and cross-validation technique, it is important to recognise their limitations. Traditional statistical models like linear regression analysis are often simpler and more interpretable while having fewer assumptions than some of these newer techniques.

In conclusion, our research offers insightful perspectives into the comparative performance evaluation of regression algorithms and demonstrates the importance of selecting the appropriate algorithm for specific applications. Future research can explore other algorithms and datasets to advance the field of comparative performance evaluation of algorithms in predictive analytics further.

5.1 Recommendations

To improve the accuracy of predictions, we suggest that future research explore additional non-parametric ensemble methods and Artificial Neural Networks (ANN) using related datasets and compare their predictive abilities to the methods utilised in this study. Furthermore, including more predictor variables and implementing feature selection techniques would be beneficial to determine which variables have the most significant effect on the target variable.

Disclosure of Potential Conflicts of Interest.   The authors have stated that any financial or other conflicts of interest did not influence the results and writing of the paper.

References

Aftarczuk, K.: Evaluation of selected data mining algorithms implemented in Medical Decision Support Systems, Blekinge Institute of Technology School of Engineering, Blekinge (2007)

Agu, S., Onu, F., Ezemagu, U., Oden, D.: Predicting gross domestic product to macroeconomic indicators. Intell. Syst. Appl. **14**, 200082 (2022). https://doi.org/10.1016/j.iswa.2022.200082

Allawala, A., Ramteke, A., Wadhwa, P.: Performance impact of minority class reweighting on XGBoost-based anomaly detection. Int. J. Mach. Learn. Comput. **12**(4) (2022). https://doi.org/10.18178/ijmlc.2022.12.4.1093

Ameer, S., et al.: Comparative analysis of machine learning techniques for predicting air quality in smart cities. IEEE Access **7**, 128325–128338 (2019). https://doi.org/10.1109/access.2019.2925082

Bellotti, A., Brigo, D., Gambetti, P., Vrins, F.: Forecasting recovery rates on non-performing loans with machine learning. Int. J. Forecast. **37**, 428–444 (2021). https://doi.org/10.1016/j.ijforecast.2020.06.009

Brownlee, J. (2019). Why One-Hot Encode Data in Machine Learning? https://machinelearningmastery.com/why-one-hot-encode-data-in-machine-learning/. Accessed 6 Feb 2020

Chaya. Random Forest Regression - Level Up Coding. Medium, 14 April 2022. https://levelup.gitconnected.com/random-forest-regression-209c0f354c84

Chien, Y., Zhou, H., Hanson, T., Lystig, T.: Informative g-priors for mixed models. Stats **6**(1), 169–191 (2023). https://doi.org/10.3390/stats6010011

Flannery, R.: A Machine Learning Approach to Predicting Gross Domestic Product. National College of Ireland College in Dublin, Ireland (2020). https://norma.ncirl.ie/4441/1/ronanflannery.pdf. Accessed 11 Aug 2023

Gareth, J., Daniela, W., Trevor, H., Robert, T.: An Introduction to Statistical Learning. Springer, New York (ISL) (2017). https://doi.org/10.1007/978-1-0716-1418-1

Garg, A., Poornalatha, G.: Online news feed data mining and prediction. Int. J. Innov. Technol. Explor. Eng. **8**(11), 409–414 (2019). https://doi.org/10.35940/ijitee.k1381.0981119

GeeksforGeeks. (2023). XGBOOST. https://www.geeksforgeeks.org/xgboost/

Giovanni, M., Giacomo, M., Sara, S.: GDP forecasting: machine learning, linear or autoregression? Front. Artif. Intell. (2021). https://doi.org/10.3389/frai.2021.757864

Hotz, N.: What is CRISP DM? Data Science Process Alliance (2023). https://www.datascience-pm.com/crisp-dm-2/. Accessed 2 Mar 2023

Huang, L., et al.: Comparing multiple linear regression and machine learning in predicting diabetic urine albumin-creatinine ratio in a 4-year follow-up study. J. Clin. Med. **11**(13), 3661 (2022). https://doi.org/10.3390/jcm11133661

Kaliappan, J., Srinivasan, K., Qaisar, S.M., Sundararajan, K., Chang, C.C.S.: Performance evaluation of regression models for the prediction of the COVID-19 reproduction Rate. Front. Public Health **9** (2021). https://doi.org/10.3389/fpubh.2021.729795

Karen, D., Louise, S.: GDP as a Measure of Economic Well-being (2018). https://www.brooki ngs.edu/research/gdp-as-a-measure-of-economic-well-being/. Accessed 6 Mar 2021

Katrina, W.: A Guide to the Types of Machine Learning Algorithms and their Applications (2021). https://www.sas.com/en_gb/insights/articles/analytics/machine-learning-algori thms.html. Accessed 29 Jan 2021

Lawrence, A., Sinha, R.A., Mitrasinovic, S., Price, S.J.: Clinical Features at Presentation for Glioblastoma Patients Impact Survival Predictions in a Machine Learning Model. Neuro-Oncology, 23(Supplement_4), iv18 (2021). https://doi.org/10.1093/neuonc/noab195.046

Li, H.: Responses to RC1, RC2 and RC3 – essd-2021-201. Earth System Science Data (2021). https://doi.org/10.5194/essd-2021-201-ac1

Li, N., Kwak, J., Becerik-Gerber, B., Tambe, M.: Predicting HVAC energy consumption in commercial buildings using multiagent systems. In: 30th International Symposium on Automation and Robotics in Construction and Mining; Held in Conjunction with the 23rd World Mining Congress (2013). https://doi.org/10.22260/isarc2013/0108

Maccarrone, G., Morelli, G., Spadaccini, S.: GDP Forecasting: machine learning, linear or autoregression? Front. Artif. Intell. **4** (2021).https://doi.org/10.3389/frai.2021.757864

Mirugwe, A.: Restaurant tip prediction using linear regression. Int. J. Data Sci. Big Data Anal. **1**(2), 31 (2021). https://doi.org/10.51483/ijdsbda.1.2.2021.31-38

Mislick, G.K., Nussbaum, D.P.: Linear regression analysis. J. Eval. Educ. (JEE) (2015).https://doi.org/10.1002/9781118802342.ch7

Mwiti, D.: Random Forest Regression: When Does It Fail and Why? neptune.ai, 14 November 2022. https://neptune.ai/blog/random-forest-regression-when-does-it-fail-and-why. Accessed 15 Jan 2023

Nigeria Corruption perceptions index, 2001–2022 - knoema.com. (2023). Knoema. https://kno ema.com/atlas/Nigeria/Corruption-perceptions-index. Accessed 9 Apr 2023

Nguyen, H., Vu, T.H., Vo, T.P., Thai, H.: Efficient machine learning models for prediction of concrete strengths. Constr. Build. Mater. **266**, 120950 (2021). https://doi.org/10.1016/j.conbui ldmat.2020.120950

Öztürk, M.Z., Colkesen, I.: Investigation of the effects of vegetation indices derived from UAV-based RGB imagery on land cover classification accuracy using advanced ensemble learning methods. Mersin Photogramm. J. (2021). https://doi.org/10.53093/mephoj.943347

Pandey, V.B., Choudhary, K., Murthy, C.S.R., Poddar, M.K.: Improved in-season crop classification performance using ensemble learning technique: a case study of lekoda insurance unit, ujjain, madhya pradesh. The International Archives of the Photogrammetry, Remote Sensing and Spatial Information Sciences, XLII-3/W6, pp. 477–481 (2019). https://doi.org/10.5194/isprs-archives-xlii-3-w6-477-2019

Pandian, S.: K-Fold Cross Validation Technique and its Essentials. Analytics Vidhya (2023). https://www.analyticsvidhya.com/blog/2022/02/k-fold-cross-validation-techni que-and-its-essentials/

Raheja, H., Goel, A., Pal, M.: Prediction of groundwater quality indices using machine learning algorithms. Water Pract. Technol. **17**(1), 336–351 (2021). https://doi.org/10.2166/wpt.202 1.120

Raju, K.A., Sikdar, P.K., Dhingra, S.L.: Micro-simulation of residential location choice and its variation. Comput. Environ. Urban Syst. **22**(3), 203–218 (1998). https://doi.org/10.1016/s0198-9715(98)00043-x

Saabas, A.: Interpreting random forests | Diving into data, 19 October 2014. https://blog.datadive.net/interpreting-random-forests/. Accessed 15 Feb 2023

Sainikhileaswar, S., Parthasarathy, G.: Early detection of breast cancer using ensemble machine learning algorithm. Adv. Parallel Comput. (2020).https://doi.org/10.3233/apc200204

Sandra, L., Lumbangaol, F., Matsuo, T.: Machine learning algorithm to predict student's performance: a systematic literature review. TEM J. 1919–1927 (2021). https://doi.org/10.18421/tem104-56

Schonlau, M., Zou, R.Y.: The random forest algorithm for statistical learning. Stata J. **20**(1), 3–29 (2020). https://doi.org/10.1177/1536867x20909688

Shaobo, L.: Research on GDP forecast analysis combining B.P. neural network and ARIMA model. Comput. Intell. Neurosci. **2021**(Article ID 1026978) (2021). https://doi.org/10.1155/2021/1026978

Sterkenburg, T.F., Grunwald, P.: The no-free-lunch theorems of super vised learning. Synthese, 4 June 2021. https://doi.org/10.1007/s11229-021-03233-1

Tan, Z., Al-Barakati, A.: Application of Sobolev-Volterra projection and finite element numerical analysis of integral differential equations in modern art design. Appl. Math. Nonlinear Sci. (2022). https://doi.org/10.2478/amns.2021.2.00054

Wang, F., Chen, W., Fakieh, B., Alhamami, M.A.: Stock price analysis based on the research of multiple linear regression macroeconomic variables. Appl. Math. Nonlinear Sci. **7**(1), 267–274 (2022). https://doi.org/10.2478/amns.2021.2.00097

Wang, J., Lee, R.Y.: Chaotic recurrent neural networks for financial forecast. Am. J. Neural Netw. Appl. (2021) https://doi.org/10.11648/j.ajnna.20210701.12

Wikipedia. (2021). Residual sum of squares. https://en.wikipedia.org/wiki/Residual_sum_of_squares. Accessed 11 Nov 2021

World Bank. (2021). Indicators. https://data.worldbank.org/indicator/. Accessed 26 Apr 2021

Xu, Y., Cao, Z., Wang, M.: Analysis of factors influencing regional economic expansion based on OOB coefficients under RF algorithm. BCP Bus. Manag. **33**, 242–249 (2022). https://doi.org/10.54691/bcpbm.v33i.2753

XGBoost Algorithm to Predict a Patient's Risk of Stroke

Sada Anne⬧ and Amadou Dahirou Gueye(✉)⬧

Alioune Diop University, Bambey, Senegal
{sada.anne,dahirou.gueye}@uadb.edu.sn

Abstract. The negative impact of stroke on society has led to a concerted effort to improve stroke management and diagnosis. As the synergy between technology and medical diagnostics grows, caregivers are creating opportunities for better patient care by systematically exploring and archiving patient records. The ubiquitous growth of artificial intelligence and its medical applications has improved the efficiency of healthcare systems for patients requiring long-term personal care. Today, chronic diseases such as stroke are the world's leading cause of death. Stroke can be caused by a number of factors. By measuring recorded values of patient characteristics such as heart rate, cholesterol levels, blood pressure, diabetes etc., this information can help doctors to make decisions about patient care, in order to predict a possible onset of the disease. Because most stroke diagnosis and prediction systems are image analysis tools such as CT or MRI, which are expensive and not available 24/7 in some African hospitals in general and Senegal in particular. We therefore use a dataset to predict stroke and compare its results with those of other models using the same data. We find that Xgboost, depending on the characteristics of the data, is the algorithm that can effectively predict stroke, and the results obtained are superior to those of other models.

Keywords: XGBoost (eXtreme Gradient Boosting) · Stroke Prediction · Machine Learning

1 Introduction

Artificial intelligence is revolutionizing the world, and its application in the medical field has increased the efficiency of medical care. With the help of technology, we have witnessed astonishing developments in the field of medicine [1]. Stroke, a cerebrovascular disease, is caused by damage to brain tissue due to abnormal blood supply to the brain as a result of cerebrovascular obstruction. Stroke is responsible for most deaths worldwide [2]. The mortality rate from stroke is very high. To be precise, between 2000 and 2019, stroke is responsible for around 11% of all deaths, making it the second leading cause of death [3]. The need for rapid diagnosis of stroke has become increasingly important and warrants great interest in both clinical and fundamental research, as this rapid management will enable adequate rehabilitation to minimize late sequelae and improve patients' quality of life. With this in mind, solutions are being considered, such

© ICST Institute for Computer Sciences, Social Informatics and Telecommunications Engineering 2024
Published by Springer Nature Switzerland AG 2024. All Rights Reserved
A. Seeam et al. (Eds.): InterSol 2023, LNICST 541, pp. 151–160, 2024.
https://doi.org/10.1007/978-3-031-51849-2_10

as the implementation of a stroke risk prediction system based on patient data, which would enable doctors to prescribe appropriate treatments and reduce the mortality rate. The use of artificial intelligence, and more specifically machine learning, will enable us to determine which characteristics have the greatest influence on stroke prediction. By identifying high-risk patients on the basis of these characteristics, doctors can prescribe preventive treatment to avoid stroke and save the patient's life. It is therefore important to collect sufficient data on patient characteristics to improve the accuracy of stroke prediction. The application of data mining techniques to medical records has had a considerable impact on the fields of healthcare and biomedicine [4, 5]. Several studies [6–9] have analyzed the importance of patients' lifestyle and medical records on their likelihood of suffering a stroke. In addition, machine learning models have also been used to predict stroke occurrence [10, 11]. Although the above models have achieved good results, the CNN, the K Neighbors Classifier, and SVMs, respectively, have drawbacks such as complexity, low accuracy, and difficulties in kernel selection. Xgboost itself is iterative learning, which means that the model will first predict something and then analyze its error on its own, giving more weight to the data point that made the wrong prediction in the next iteration. This process continues in a loop, so technically, if a prediction is made, it's at best certain that it didn't happen by chance, but was based on a thorough understanding of the data and models. In the present paper, we attempt to fill this gap by therefore using the Xgboost algorithm on various patient records with the aim of predicting stroke, the factors likely to cause stroke are identified, the stroke prediction model is established and the 3566 data set is used in the prediction. In the remainder of this paper, we organize ourselves as follows: in Sect. 2 we give an overview of related work, in Sect. 3 we focus on the methodology used. In Sect. 4, we highlight the results obtained. Section 5 concludes the paper.

2 Related Work

Existing work in the literature has focused on different aspects of prediction. Chidozie Shamrock Nwosu et al. [8] put together an article that addresses stroke prediction from electronic health record. Shi Y et al. [12] provide a study to understand the different risk factors of stroke probability. Multivariate logistic regression (MLR) analyses were performed. The analysis showed that risk factors for stroke included hypertension, diabetes mellitus, high low-density lipoprotein, hypertriglyceridemia, and smoking compared to the control group. The analysis also showed that the risk factors for SVD cerebral stroke were hypertension, diabetes mellitus, high cholesterol, hypertriglyceridemia, and smoking. Hanifa and Raja [13] improved the accuracy of stroke risk prediction by using radial basis functions and polynomial functions in nonlinear applications applied in a support vector classification model. The risk factors identified in this work divided into four groups: demographic, lifestyle, medical/clinical, and functional. Benjamin B. et al. [14] Shows evidence of a decrease in stroke incidence emerged from population-based studies a study to identify risk factors associated with specific outcomes after stroke hospitalization, relative to stroke-specific clinical factors, using machine learning techniques [15]. Work has been explored in [16–18] to build an intelligent system to predict stroke from patient records. In the study conducted by Hong et al. [19] a comparison is made between deep learning models and machine learning models for stroke prediction from the electronic health insurance database. Therefore, it is important for researchers to identify the different inputs. The factors in the electronic medical record are related to each other and how they are related to each other Impact on the accuracy of the final stroke prediction. Research in related areas [18] has shown that it is important to determine which features affect the final performance of a machine learning framework features affect the final performance of a machine learning framework. Thus, it is critical for practitioners of data mining in the healthcare field to determine how risk factors captured in electronic medical records relate to each other and how they affect patient health.

3 Methodology

This section presents the principle of XGBoost and its application to stroke prediction. We review the gradient tree reinforcement algorithm. We also highlight the mathematical foundations that govern it. We make minor improvements to the regularization objective, and explain how to move from the expression of a fairly generic objective function to the precise expression of the parameters required for the model.

3.1 The XGBoost Principle

XGBoost appeared in 2015 and quickly became one of the most efficient algorithms in machine learning. Its main functionalities: for regression tasks (prediction of continuous values) or classification/segmentation. It is a supervised learning algorithm that requires a set of training data to build a model that can be generalized, and is part of a so-called ensemble learning algorithm that involves the use of several decision trees to build predictions. It is particularly effective: in its ability to generalize, as it incorporates a very powerful and clever regularization mechanism into its construction, and the ability to handle missing data without degrading its performance, its speed of calculation on large volumes by making elegant approximations when constructing decision trees make XGBoost a very powerful tool. In this document, we will look at the principles that govern this algorithm and make it so powerful. It's called gradient boosting: the gradient boosting algorithmic model calls for multiple decision trees, to be used in a specific order. For an observation, each tree gives a result, and the final prediction is obtained by adding up each of the values obtained from the trees. Here's a diagram with N trees (Fig. 1).

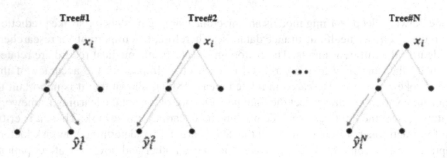

Fig. 1. Diagram with N trees in ullistration of the XGBoost function

3.2 Learning Phase and Objective Function

During the learning phase, XGBoost forces the global objective function to contain these two characteristics: a Loss function, measuring the deviation between predicted and target values, and a function to penalize model complexity, to avoid overfitting.

3.2.1 Loss Function

A Machine Learning classic for supervised learning.

The generic form is:

$$L = \sum_i^{\#instances} l(\hat{y}_i, y_i) \tag{1}$$

with $\hat{y}_i$: global prediction, y_i: target value and #instances: number of data used in the learning phase.

Classic example for regression - mean-square:

$$L = \frac{1}{2} \times \sum_i^{\#instances} (\hat{y}_i - y_i)^2 \tag{2}$$

Example for classification - Log loss (cross-entropy):

$$L = -\sum_i^{\#instances} (y_i \cdot \log(\hat{y}_i) + (1 - y_i) \cdot \log(1 - \hat{y}_i)) \text{ with } y_i = 0 \text{ or } 1 \tag{3}$$

3.2.2 Penalization (Regularization)

Without regularization, there is a high risk of overlearning. The model will then be perfect on the training data, but mediocre during the inference phase, when it will have to generalize on unknown data. In simple terms, this means that the model must perform well, and that the accuracy of the model in the training phase must not deviate significantly from the accuracy in the test phase. The risk is all the greater as decision trees have the ability to be perfect on training data, if we develop them until there is only one instance per leaf. Here, we define a function that expresses the overall complexity of the system. To do this, we sum up the complexity of each tree in the model.

$$\sum_k^{\#trees} \Omega(tree_{\#k}) \text{ or } \Omega(tree_{\#k}) = \gamma.T + \frac{1}{2}\lambda.\|w\|^2 \tag{4}$$

The complexity of each tree depends on two variables: T: number of leaves in the tree, $\|w\|^2$: L2 norm of the values of each tree leaf γ and λ are hyper-parameters of the global model. The larger they are, the less complexity the model will contain. Their influence on model construction will be seen later.

3.2.3 Objective Function: Loss + Penalization

As seen above:

$$L = \sum_i^{\#instances} l(\widehat{Yi}, Y_I) + \sum_k^{\#treess} \left(\gamma.T_K + \frac{1}{2}\lambda.\|w_k\|^2\right) \tag{5}$$

The shape of this function is what makes this algorithm mysterious to grasp. There are several things that prevent us from easily optimizing this function: The loss function involves the value: which is obtained by using all the trees. Indeed, classically, we try to calculate the gradient of the function to move the parameters towards its minimization. To do this, we will rewrite the objective function, using the first principle of this model's design: that of adding a new tree at each iteration, step by step, to get closer to the final prediction by adding up the values obtained. At the first iteration (t = 0), we choose a simple constant as the prediction value.

For example, take 0:

$$\hat{y}_i^{(0)} = 0 \tag{6}$$

At the next iteration, we add the result obtained from the first tree:

$$\hat{Y}_i^{(1)} = \hat{Y}_i^{(0)} + \varphi_i(x_i) \tag{7}$$

At iteration t we have:

$$\hat{y}_i^{(1)} = \sum_{k=1}^{t} \varphi_k(x_i) = \hat{y}_i^{(t-1)} + \varphi_t(x_i) \tag{8}$$

And the form of the objective function is then, at this iteration t:

$$L_t = \sum_i^{\#instances} l\left(\hat{y}_i^{(t-1)} + \varphi_t(x_i),\ y_i\right) + \Omega(tree_{\#t}) \tag{9}$$

So, if we want to minimize the objective function at iteration t, all we have to do is find $\varphi_t(x_i)$ that minimizes L_t. Here, we rely on reasoning by recurrence, which assumes that at iteration t, the model is already optimized for iteration t-1, so there's no need to come back to it.

In other words:

$$\varphi_t = \underset{\varphi_t}{\text{argmin}} \sum_i^{\#instances} l\left(\hat{Y}_i^{(t-1)} + \varphi_t(x_i),\ Y_i\right) + \Omega(tree_{\#t}) \tag{10}$$

This rewrite of the function will enable step-by-step optimization, which will be much simpler to implement.

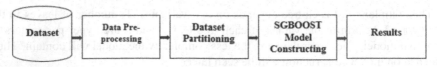

Fig. 2. Proposed methodology

3.3 The Application of XGBoost in Stroke Prediction

The first phase consists of acquiring the data to be used later. In phase 2, we pre-process the data, i.e. data cleansing, conversion of object-type data to float or int, feature selection and extraction, etc. In phase 3, the data set is divided in two respectively for training and testing. In phase 4, an XGBoost model is built. In this phase, we already have the pre-processed data, which enables us to build an XGBoost model. Here are the steps we follow: a) we start by importing the required libraries: from sklearn.model_selection import train_test_split, from sklearn.pipeline import Pipeline, from category_encoders.target_encoder import TargetEncoder, from xgboost import XGBClassifier. b) Installing the category_encoders library: this step is designed to perform the encoding, transforming the categorical data into a numerical form understood by the XGBoost algorithm. c) Definition of pipeline steps: We define the pipeline steps, creating a sequence of operations that will be applied sequentially during modeling. d) Optimizing the hyperparameters of the XGBoost model: we use a hyperparameter optimization process for an XGBoost model using the scikit-optimize library, as we explained mathematically the larger the hyperparameters, the less complexity the model will contain, so we need to find the best values for the hyperparameters to improve its predictive performance. To do this, we create a BayesSearchCV object that explores different combinations of hyperparameters to determine which give the best results according to the specified score metric. e) BayesSearchCV object fit: we fit the BayesSearchCV object to the training data (X_train and y_train) using the opt.fit(X_train, y_train) statement. Once optimization is complete, this attribute returns the best estimator (model) found by optimization, i.e. the model with the best hyperparameter values. You can obtain the best estimator using the opt.best_estimator_ statement. f) Model training: finally, we train the model using 50% of the randomly selected data to form the training set, with the remaining 50% of the data used as a verification set to adjust the model's prediction parameters. In phase 5, we obtain the results (prediction, most influential features in prediction (feature importance)) (Fig. 2).

3.4 Data Description

The dataset is available on Kaggle [20], a public data repository for datasets. The database contains the records of 5110 patients. It has a total of 11 input attributes and one output feature. The output response is a binary state indicating 1 if the patient has suffered a stroke and 0 means they have not. The other 11 input attributes are described in the table below (Table 1):

Table 1. Representative example of the dataset

Feature	Description
Id	the patient's identifier
Gender	The sex of the patient is indicated by "Male", "Female"
age	the patient's age
hypertension	the binary state (whether the patient has (1) or not (0) hypertension (HT)
heart_disease	Binary status (whether the patient has heart disease (1) or not (0))
ever_married	"No" to not get married and "Yes" to get married
work_type	"children" for the patient who has children, "Govt_job" for the patient who works in the administration the patient works in the administration, "Never_worked" for the patient has never worked, "Private" for the patient working in the private private work, or "Self-employed" for the patient who works for themselves
Residence_type	"Rural" if the patient lives in a rural area and "Urban" if the patient lives in an urban area
avg_glucose_level	the patient's average blood glucose level
bmi	the patient's BMI
smoking_status	"Formerly smoked" represents the patient who used to smoke, "never smoked" means the patient has never smoked, "smoked" represents the observer who currently smokes
stroke	1 or 0, i.e. 1 for a stroke, 0 for no stroke

4 Result

XGBoost can predict whether patients are having a stroke based on relevant information about them in the dataset. In this section, we perform a comparative analysis of three popular classification algorithms: CNN, SVM and XGBoost on our patient dataset. The accuracy rate is 0.83, which means that almost 8 out of 10 people can actually be predicted when they are sent to hospital and can be detected and receive the real treatment. We use classification accuracy as a measure of the performance of machine learning models. Table 2 presents the average classification for the three benchmark tests.

Table 2. Average binary classification accuracy of XGBoost, SVM and CNN over 3565 experiments on our dataset.

Approach	Average accuracy
XGBoost	82.8%
SVM	79.2%
CNN	72.16%

The following figures, Fig. 3 and Fig. 4, show the confusion matrix of our XGBoost model and the most important features in stroke prediction.

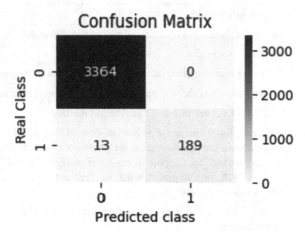

Fig. 3. Result measured by confusion matrix

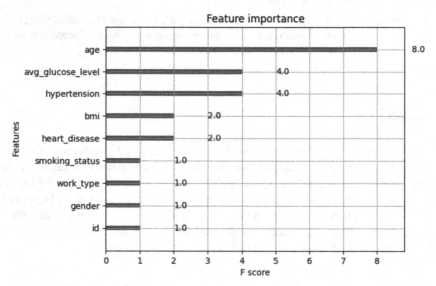

Fig. 4. Importance of patient attributes in predicting stroke occurrence using Xgboost

Figure 4 shows the importance of individual patient attributes in predicting stroke. The relative importance of a patient attribute is measured by the increase in the model's prediction error due to that attribute. We use the XGBoost estimator to calculate the relative importance of features. Patient age (A) is the most important feature for predicting stroke. Other very important characteristics are the patient's average blood sugar level and whether he or she suffers from high blood pressure.

5 Conclusion

Early detection and treatment of cerebrovascular disease is essential to reduce morbidity and mortality. Current applications of artificial intelligence in this field offer enormous potential for improving treatment choice and clinical outcomes at all stages of diagnosis and treatment, including outcome prediction. In this paper to solve the problem of stroke prediction, the XGBoost method is proposed. Two experiments are carried out in this paper to verify the above proposal: the first shows that, with regard to stroke prediction, the accuracy of XGBoost is 0.83, so we can conclude that XGBoost is capable of effectively predicting stroke, and that it performs very well and even better than other machine learning methods. The second is that there are a large number of characteristics, so in order to simplify the work of doctors and be efficient, we had to focus on those characteristics that had a strong impact on prediction. We found from Fig. 4 that characteristics such as age, hypertension, cholesterol level, body mass index and heart disease were more relevant, and in the same order, by way of verification, we created a new dataset considering only these 5 characteristics, and we obtained an accuracy with XGBoost of 0.825, roughly equal to that with all characteristics. This study has certain limitations in certain situations, as it is important to point out that other factors may be at the origin of a stroke; for example, many patients may even inherit from their parents. Furthermore, patients can only be correctly predicted if their health statistics are exactly the same as those of their parents. What's more, the data we've used comes from another part of the world, where certain characteristics differ from one place to another in Africa, for example, climate can influence hypertention, quality of life and lifestyle can influence stress, and so on. What's more, the majority of hospitals in Africa keep their data in physical rather than electronic form. Consequently, it will take some time to implement this predictive model in reality for some countries. However, although there are still limitations, stroke prediction remains very useful. In short, stroke prediction based on XGBoost can be applied to real-life problems. In future projects, the main contribution will be to be able to confirm the results of this article with local data from Senegal, which we have begun to collect from hospital facilities.

References

1. Sivapalan, G., Nundy, K., Dev, S., Cardiff, B., John, D.: ANNet: a lightweight neural network for ECG anomaly detection in IoT edge sensors. IEEE Trans. Biomed. Circ. Syst. **16**(1), 24–35 (2022)
2. Pastore, D., Pacifici, F., Capuani, B., et al.: Sex-genetic interaction in the risk for cerebrovascular disease. Curr. Med. Chem. **24**, 2687–2699 (2017)
3. The top 10 causes of death. https://www.who.int/news-room/factsheets/detail/the-top-10-causes-of-death. Accessed 22 June 2023
4. Koh, H.C., Tan, G.: Data mining applications in healthcare. J. Healthc. Inf. Manag. **19**(2), 64–72 (2011)
5. Yoo, I., et al.: Data mining in healthcare and biomedicine: a survey of the literature. J. Med. Syst. **36**(4), 2431–2448 (2012). https://doi.org/10.1007/s10916-011-9710-5
6. Meschia, J.F., et al.: Guidelines for the primary prevention of stroke: a statement for healthcare professionals from the American Heart Association/American Stroke Association. Stroke **45**(12), 3754–3832 (2014)

7. Harmsen, P., Lappas, G., Rosengren, A., Wilhelmsen, L.: Long-term risk factors for stroke: twenty-eight years of follow-up of 7457 middle-aged men in Goteborg, Sweden. Stroke 37(7), 1663–1667 (2006)
8. Nwosu, C.S., Dev, S., Bhardwaj, P., Veeravalli, B., John, D.: Predicting stroke from electronic health records. In: 2019 41st Annual International Conference of the IEEE Engineering in Medicine and Biology Society (EMBC), Berlin, pp. 5704–5707. IEEE (2019)
9. Pathan, M.S., Jianbiao, Z., John, D., Nag, A., Dev, S.: Identifying stroke indicators using rough sets. IEEE Access 8, 210318–210327 (2020)
10. Kim, J., Hong, D., Park, S.: A case-control study of risk factors for cerebrovascular disease. J. Prev. Med. 28, 473–486 (1995)
11. Park, J.K., Kang, M.G., Kim, C.-B., et al.: A meta-analysis on the risk factors of cerebrovascular disorders in Koreans. J. Prev. Med. Public Health 31, 27–48 (1998)
12. Shi, Y., et al.: Risk factors for ischemic stroke: differences between cerebral small vessel and large artery atherosclerosis aetiologies. Folia Neuropathol. 59(4), 378–385 (2021)
13. Hanifa, S.M., Raja-S, K.: Stroke risk prediction through nonlinear support vector classification models. Int. J. Adv. Res. Comput. Sci. 1, 4753 (2010)
14. Clissold, B.B., Sundararajan, V., Cameron, P., et al.: Stroke incidence in Victoria, Australia—emerging improvements. Front. Neurol. 8, 180 (2017)
15. Rana, S., et al.: Application of machine learning techniques to identify data reliability and factors affecting outcome after stroke using electronic administrative records. Front. Neurol. 12, 670379 (2021)
16. Khosla, A., Cao, Y., Lin, C.C.Y., Chiu, H.K., Hu, J., Lee, H.: An integrated machine learning approach to stroke prediction. In: Proceedings of the 16th ACM SIGKDD International Conference on Knowledge Discovery and Data Mining, pp. 183–192 (2010)
17. Hung, C.Y., Lin, C.H., Lan, T.H., Peng, G.S., Lee, C.C.: Development of an intelligent decision support system for ischemic stroke risk assessment in a population-based electronic health record database. PLoS ONE 14, e0213007 (2019)
18. Teoh, D.: Towards stroke prediction using electronic health records. BMC Med. Inform. Decis. Making 18(1), 1–11 (2018)
19. Hung, C.Y., Chen, W.C., Lai, P.T., Lin, C.H., Lee, C.C.: Comparing deep neural network and other machine learning algorithms for stroke prediction in a large-scale population-based electronic medical claims database. In: 2017 39th Annual International Conference of the IEEE Engineering in Medicine and Biology Society (EMBC), pp. 3110–3113. IEEE (2017)
20. Fed Soriano, Stroke Prediction Dataset. https://www.kaggle.com/datasets/fedesoriano/stroke-prediction-datase. Accessed 23 June 2023

On the Use of Machine Learning Technique to Appraise Thermal Properties of Novel Earthen Composite for Sustainable Housing in Sub-Saharan Africa

Assia Aboubakar Mahamat[1,2(✉)] and Moussa Mahamat Boukar[1]

[1] Nile University of Nigeria, Abuja, Federal Capital Territory, Nigeria
aassia@aust.edu.ng
[2] African University of Science and Technology (AUST), Abuja, Federal Capital Territory, Nigeria

Abstract. Earthen based bio-composite reinforced with agricultural waste represent a very important alternative for eco-friendly sustainable building materials. In addition, to the environmental-friendly aspect the use of agro-waste plays a major role in waste management primary by reducing the price related to the waste proper disposal. A novel bio-composite was modeled and tested for its thermal properties to enable the comfort to its habitant. The experimental results were used as primary data to test, train and validate two different machine learning algorithms. The two machine learning models used to predict the thermal conductivity are decision tree regressor (DTR) and random forest (RF). Various inputs were used based on their importance/relationship with the predicted output. The machine learning models were compared based on their efficiency/performance via the evaluation metrics R^2, RMSE, MSE and MAE. Decision tree displayed $R^2 = -0.26$, RMSE $= 0.077$, MSE $= 0.006$ and MAE $= 0.05$ while random forest displayed values $R^2 = -17.7$, RMSE $= 0.197$, MSE $= 0.039$ and MAE $= 0.119$. The results corroborate that both RFR and DTR performed poorly during the predictions, thus they are not suitable for similar composite with the selected input variables.

Keywords: decision tree · random forest · earthen composite · thermal conductivity

1 Introduction

Access to standard housing is an essential human right. This fundamental right must be fulfilled without destroying the nature. Therefore, the idea of learning from and emulating certain aspects of nature to solve human problems. This sustainability concept derives from the fact that nature has sustained itself for several million years unlike human-designed systems that fail to operate within a long period. To achieve standard housing, ordinary Portland cement (OPC) is the most used material. However, production and utilization of the OPC releases greenhouses gas (GHG) and significantly destabilizes the

© ICST Institute for Computer Sciences, Social Informatics and Telecommunications Engineering 2024
Published by Springer Nature Switzerland AG 2024. All Rights Reserved
A. Seeam et al. (Eds.): InterSol 2023, LNICST 541, pp. 161–170, 2024.
https://doi.org/10.1007/978-3-031-51849-2_11

environment. Alkali activated binders have gained a lot of attention as 'green' alternative to ordinary Portland cement (OPC). This technology is based on the dissolution of aluminosilicate in the presence of alkaline activator. The alkali activation process involves alkali solutions (two-part alkali activated binders) or solid alkali source (one-part alkali activated binders) [1]. The use of two-part alkali activation process is corrosive, difficult, and not user-friendly [2]. Meanwhile, one-part alkali activation process requires solid alkali source with the aluminosilicate precursor and water. During this process, the dry ingredients are mixed before addition of water. This is similar to the preparation of OPC, and it enables better cast-in-situ features which are among the main requirement in the construction field. During the mixture chemical reactions take place, among which the dissolution of the aluminosilicate precursor activated by the alkaline source (K_2CO_3) [3], followed by polycondensation and formation of amorphous network [4]. Artificial intelligence (AI) approaches are considered as an alternative or improvement of traditional statistical methods. They are used by many researchers, and they were found to be more efficient in prediction as compared to the empirical/traditional methods. Machine Learning (ML) is defined as a set of algorithmic structures enabling computer systems to learn and train their performances through established patterns [5]. Machine Learning is a subset of Artificial Intelligence (AI) that has been substantially used in different fields, especially in civil engineering to resolve complex problems related to materials science [6], structural engineering, geotechnical engineering etc. [7]. Machine Learning is a subgroup of AI that is divided into supervised and unsupervised techniques. Machine Learning application have gained a lot of interest in the medical field, engineering, etc. due to their high accuracy/efficiency in data processing. Machine Learning techniques are used in the construction field mainly to predict mechanical properties such as compressive and flexural strength [8]. They're used to save time of the experiments because many experiments require long curing period before getting the results and those experiment are costly due to their destructive nature. Thus, Machine Learning can be used because the algorithms require low/minimal human interference during the training and decision making. However, the selection of the appropriate features with the appropriate inputs is the bedrock for the predictions' efficiency. However, some of the ML models that are commonly used in the construction field are: Artificial Neural Network (ANN) [9], support vector machine (SVM) [10], decision trees (DT) [11]. This study intends to develop decision tree regression (DTR) and random forest (RF) models to predict the thermal capacity of an alkali-activated earthen composite.

Decision tree regression (DTR) model uses training data to create a model in the shape of a tree in which each internal node represents a test, the branches represent the outcome while the leaves represent the decisions during the training [12]. This kind of modeling involves two steps: The first step is the building tree step which entails dividing the training dataset into well-defined fragments. The second step is the tree pruning where branches from the built tree are selected to be removed to lower the dimension of the decision trees fragments that are non-critical or irrelevant [13].

Random Forest Regression (RFR) is a supervised ML algorithm that uses classification and regression trees (CART) for prediction. In RFR, inputs are randomly selected at each node to grow a tree. The accuracy of the individual classifiers and the dependence between them. Random Forest regression can handle large features with small samples, this characteristic makes RF a suitable option for this study where the primary data set are not large. Random Forest regression model is used to predict the compressive, splitting tensile and flexural strength of concrete incorporated with metakaolin. During their study, the evaluation metrics was the Coefficient of determination (R^2) and found to be 0.99, 0.98 and 0.99 for compressive strength, splitting tensile strength and flexural strength respectively [14]. For all the predicted properties the value of R^2 is all close to 1, that shows the efficiency of those models for this kind of prediction. The compiled data set consists of the measurements for the thermal conductivity which are obtained from experimental results thus primary data set. Due to the scarcity of existing literature on similar earthen composite the authors generated the primary data set. The use of the primary data set is also governed by the desire to avoid errors that would be generated from the mapping when using secondary data set.

The aim of the investigation is to explore ecofriendly alternative materials for sustainable construction in the sub-Saharan African region to ease the access and break down the prices of standard housing in that region. Henceforth the techniques used are green techniques with renewable materials and low energy requirement during manufacturing. Thus, the scaling up to industrial level wouldn't be challenging in that region and worldwide.

The oncoming sections of this investigation are organized as follows: Sect. 1 provides a brief literature review of the different ML algorithms used to predict the behavior of the novel earthen composite plus the contribution of this investigation to the knowledge gaps. In Sect. 2, the materials and methods used are presented with a brief description of the quality assessment used during this investigation. In Sect. 3, the results obtained from the training and testing of various models used are presented and discussed. In Sect. 4, important conclusions from this investigation are presented.

2 Materials and Methods

2.1 Experimental Part

a) **Bio-composite manufacture**
The materials used to fabricate the composite are excavated soil, Borassus fruit fiber and synthetic potash (KCO_3). The soil was obtained from an excavation in a construction field in the FCT, Nigeria. The soil was obtained at no cost and its use is intended to reduce waste placement. The soil was sieved to remove coarse particles. After sieving the size of the soil's particles retained for this investigation are within the range of 2 mm–2 μm. The chemical stabilisation technique used during this investigation is the alkali activation of the matrix. Therefore, synthetic potash (KCO_3) was used as activator with 99.8% purity. The activator content was fixed at 3wt% [1]. The fiber was manually extracted from the Borassus fruit and didn't undergo any chemical treatment. Fiber content of 0%, 0.5wt%, 0.75wt% and 1wt% were used during the samples fabrication [3].

In the manufacturing process the dry materials were mixed in a laboratory mixer before the addition of distilled water at room temperature (27 °C). The water's quantity used during manufacture was obtain from the optimum moisture content (OMC) of the soil which was equal to 18wt%. The paste was left on to cool for 5 min because of the exothermic reaction before being poured into mould and pressed with a hydraulic press prior to thermal conductivity testing. The samples were oven dried for 7-, 14- and 90 days at 60 °C. Each sample was replicated 5 times for each test for the various composition at different curing days. The overall manufacturing procedure is shown in Fig. 1.

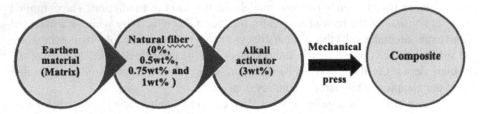

Fig. 1. Flowchart describing the production of the composite.

b) **Thermal capacity analysis**

For construction materials, thermal properties govern the thermal comfort of the building's habitant [15]. The thermal properties were assessed with the aid of the hot-disk technique (TPS hot disk equipment). Prior to the thermal properties experiments, the samples were enveloped in a polystyrene foil conserved in a closed environment to avoid contact with moisture. During the experiment the thermal conductivity (λ), and specific heat (Cp) were obtained in a single measurement meanwhile the density (ρ) was calculated, and the thermal diffusivity (α) was deduced from the Eq. (1):

$$\lambda = \alpha \, \rho \, Cp \tag{1}$$

To accurately predict the thermal conductivity (λ) or Y six independent variables were used as inputs X1, X2, X3, X4, X5 and X6 denoting the activator, fiber content, curing days, density, specific heat, and thermal diffusivity respectively (Table 1).

Table 1. Experimental data used as inputs for data training and validation of the ML models for the thermal conductivity's prediction.

Inputs	Output
X1 (activator), X2 (fiber content), X3 (curing days), X4 (density), X5 (specific heat) and X6 (thermal diffusivity)	Y (Thermal conductivity)

2.2 Machine Learning Models

The models used for the thermal conductivity's prediction are regression-based models namely the decision tree regressor and the random forest regression. They're used because of their efficiency to predict accurately outputs with limited dataset. Figure 2 shows the pseudocode of both models used during the prediction.

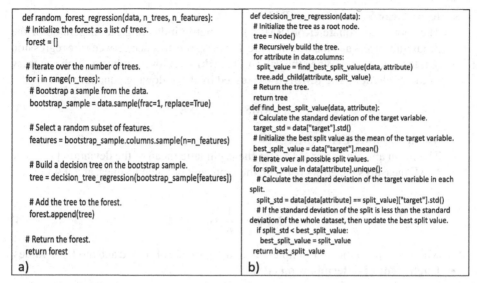

```
def random_forest_regression(data, n_trees, n_features):
  # Initialize the forest as a list of trees.
  forest = []

  # Iterate over the number of trees.
  for i in range(n_trees):
    # Bootstrap a sample from the data.
    bootstrap_sample = data.sample(frac=1, replace=True)

    # Select a random subset of features.
    features = bootstrap_sample.columns.sample(n=n_features)

    # Build a decision tree on the bootstrap sample.
    tree = decision_tree_regression(bootstrap_sample[features])

    # Add the tree to the forest.
    forest.append(tree)

  # Return the forest.
  return forest
```
a)

```
def decision_tree_regression(data):
  # Initialize the tree as a root node.
  tree = Node()
  # Recursively build the tree.
  for attribute in data.columns:
    split_value = find_best_split_value(data, attribute)
    tree.add_child(attribute, split_value)
  # Return the tree.
  return tree
def find_best_split_value(data, attribute):
  # Calculate the standard deviation of the target variable.
  target_std = data["target"].std()
  # Initialize the best split value as the mean of the target variable.
  best_split_value = data["target"].mean()
  # Iterate over all possible split values.
  for split_value in data[attribute].unique():
    # Calculate the standard deviation of the target variable in each split.
    split_std = data[data[attribute] == split_value]["target"].std()
    # If the standard deviation of the split is less than the standard
deviation of the whole dataset, then update the best split value.
    if split_std < best_split_value:
      best_split_value = split_value
  return best_split_value
```
b)

Fig. 2. Pseudocode of the used models: a) Random Forest regression and b) Decision Tree regression

a) **Decision Tree Regression (DTR)**

A decision tree regressor is a class of supervised machine learning technique that fulfills the task of both classification and regression. It's classification form is a tree-structure that displays the given dataset. The internal nodes of the tree represent the dataset [16].

b) **Random Forest Regressor (RFR)**

A random forest regressor is also a type of supervised machine learning technique that uses averaging to increase the accuracy of the prediction and control over-fitting. Numerous decision trees are generated from the data set to enable ensemble learning within the decision tree framework. It leads to excellent predictions due to the average of the results that are used to get a new result [13].

c) **Quality assessment of results**

To assess the efficiency of the developed machine learning models in this investigation, four performance indicators are used: Mean Square Error (MSE), Root Mean Square Error (RMSE), coefficient of determination (R^2) and Cross Validation Score (CV Score).

- **Mean Square Error (MSE)**

The mean square error (MSE) displays the quantity of error in the statistical models between the input variables and the predicted output. It calculates the average squared difference when the MSE is equal to 0 it means that the model is error-free. The MSE is obtained based on the following equation:

$$\text{MSE} = \frac{1}{n} \sum_{i=1}^{n} (\text{Tm} - \text{To})^2 \tag{2}$$

- **Root Mean Square Error (RMSE)**
  The root mean square error (RMSE) is a metric indicating the dispersion of the prediction errors and the way they are, meaning the distance between the regression and the data points. When the value of the RMSE is low it indicates high accuracy of the prediction. The RMSE is expressed by the following equation:

$$\text{RMSE} = \sqrt{MSE} \tag{3}$$

- **Mean Absolute Error (MAE)**
  The mean absolute error (MAE) is the arithmetic mean of the deviation [17]. The MAE measures the errors between the input and predicted values, and it is defined as:

$$\text{MAE} = \frac{1}{n}|\text{Tm} - \text{To}| \tag{4}$$

where n is the number of samples, T_o and T_m are the observed and modeled values.
- **Coefficient of determination (R^2)**
  The coefficient of determination (R^2) is a metric that evaluates the statistical relationship between the experimental and predicted values. Its value is comprised between 0 and 1, the higher its value means higher correlation. The equation to determine the R^2 is given in Assia et al. investigation [10].
- **Experimental framework**
  Intel Core (TM) i5-4790 CPU, 3.60 GHz and 4 GB RAM was the environment used for the execution and the experiments were carried out in Python 2.7.12 during this investigation. The summarized stages undertaken during this study is displayed in Fig. 3.

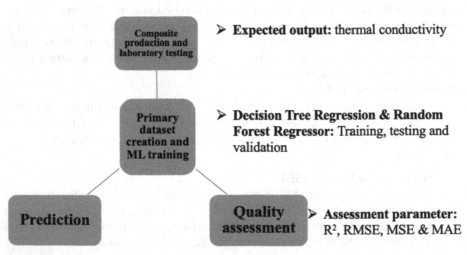

Fig. 3. Flow diagram representing the experimental scheme summarizing the various stages of this study.

3 Results and Discussions

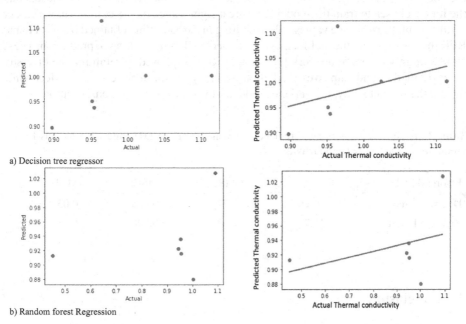

a) Decision tree regressor

b) Random forest Regression

Fig. 4. Predicted vs experimental values of the thermal conductivity via: a) decision tree regressor and b) random forest regressor.

The results of the developed models to predict the thermal conductivity of the novel earthen composite is shown in Fig. 4. These results validate the successful training, testing and validation of the RF and DTR during the prediction of the thermal conductivity.

The models' quality assessment showcased in Fig. 4 corroborates that the error values to assess the models exhibited $R^2 = -0.26$, RMSE = 0.077, MSE = 0.006 and MAE = 0.05 for the decision tree regressor (DTR) model and $R^2 = -17.7$, RMSE = 0.197, MSE = 0.039 and MAE = 0.119 for random forest regressor (RFR) model. The negative value obtained for the coefficient of determination from both models indicate the weak correlation between the chosen inputs and output during this prediction. However, the value obtained for the DTR was closer to 0 than the value obtained for the RF highlighting the inaccuracy level of both models for this prediction. Because for a higher accuracy the model's coefficient of determination should be closer to 1.

The negative error obtained from the thermal conductivity's prediction by the DTR and RFR may be because the DTR takes all possible consequences into account before the ultimate prediction based on a comprehensive analysis [18]. Those possible consequences can vary negatively with the variation of heat capacity and the thermal resistivity. However, RFR reinforces the diversity of the basic model and improve the prediction by variance reduction [19, 20].

The predictions results obtained from the DTR and RFR demonstrated negative values of R^2 which imply that the model has very high error level (Table 2). Because when the coefficient of determination (R^2) is higher than 0.5 and closer to 1, it indicates that the inputs chosen to train the model have great significance on the output. However, our results displayed negative values of R^2 resulting in the bad fitting obtained from DTR and RFR models showing the inefficiency of the used models in this kind of prediction. These results align with previous work [20], where RF is supposed to reinforce the diversity of basic models and improves prediction accuracy by variance reduction. Meanwhile during the present study, the variance reduction wasn't taken into consideration.

Table 2. Evaluation metrics and efficiency comparison of the DTR and RFR models for the prediction of the thermal conductivity

Errors/Models	R^2	RMSE	MSE	MAE
Decision Tree	−0.26	0.077	0.006	0.05
Random Forest	−17.7	0.197	0.004	0.119

4 Conclusion

Earthen materials constitute the best alternative in terms of eco-friendliness, durability and low-energy consumption during production and life service to conventional construction materials. Depending on the manufacturing process, the earthen material can be used partially or completely alone as a construction material. In this study, the application of ML models for the prediction of thermal conductivity was assessed. In the initial part of the study, the authors created a database from experimental results carried out on manufactured specimens. The specimens were produced from earthen matrix reinforced with natural Borassus as strengthening process and produced through one-part alkali activation. The manufactured specimens were cured for different periods. The primary database created by the authors consisted of thermal conductivity of unreinforced and reinforced composite obtained at different curing days. Generated inputs parameters by the authors varied based on their signification on the output parameter. Two (2) machine learning (ML) models: decision tree regression (DTR) and random forest regressor (RF) were used in this study to predict/evaluate the thermal conductivity of the manufactured composite. A comparison of the two models was carried out based on their efficiency and that was evaluated using four (4) evaluation metrics: coefficient of determination (R^2), mean square error (MSE) root mean square error (RMSE), and mean absolute error (MAE). The results obtained from the various metrics show that the inputs variable chosen to predict the thermal conductivity through those models are not significant or efficient. It shows that the models used are not very efficient in predicting similar property. This may be due to the limited dataset or from the correlation existing between the inputs and output. Thus, it can be concluded that DTR and RFR models are not efficient to predict the thermal conductivity of earthen composite with the inputs variables selected during this investigation. Therefore, for future work the exploration of different inputs can be taken into consideration, or the dataset size should be increased significantly. Also, the various properties of the novel composite can be assessed differently because the composite is made of novel materials however the testing procedure used are the standard used for conventional materials. Henceforth, by altering the testing standard different results can be obtained too.

In sum, this study demonstrates the capability of DTR and RFR models in the prediction of novel composite manufactured from earthen materials, reinforced with vegetal natural fiber, and produced through geo-polymerization technique. The results demonstrated the inefficiency of the models for such prediction. This inefficiency can be attributed to many factors such weak correlation between input-output, limited dataset or inappropriate testing standard used for such novel composite Therefore, for future prediction of similar composite other models can be used for better performance or the input parameters should be changed for a larger dataset. The main limitation of this study is the inexistant literature because significant research has not been carried out in the application of ML models for novel earthen composite reinforced with natural fiber. Also, the geo-polymerization is a technique that is not widely used the sub-Saharan Africa.

Acknowledgments. This investigation is funded by the L'Oréal-UNESCO *for women in science*, sub-Saharan Africa young talents postdoctoral fellowship 2022.

References

1. Mahamat, A., et al.: Alkali activation of compacted termite mound soil for eco-friendly construction materials. Heliyon **7**(3) (2021). https://doi.org/10.1016/j.heliyon.2021.e06597
2. Abdollahnejad, Z., Mastali, M., Luukkonen, T., Kinnunen, P., Illikainen, M.: Fiber-reinforced one-part alkali-activated slag/ceramic binders. Ceram. Int. **44**(8), 8963–8976 (2018). https://doi.org/10.1016/j.ceramint.2018.02.097
3. Mahamat, A., et al.: Assessment of hygrothermal and mechanical performance of alkali activated Borassus fiber reinforced earth-based bio-composite. J. Build. Eng. **62**, 105411 (2022). https://doi.org/10.1016/j.jobe.2022.105411
4. Barone, G., Mazzoleni, P., Finocchiaro, C.: FT-IR study of early stages of alkali activated materials based on pyroclastic deposits (Mt. Etna, Sicily, Italy) using two different alkaline solutions. Constr. Build. Mater. **262** (2020). https://doi.org/10.1016/j.conbuildmat.2020.120095
5. Shoar, S., Chileshe, N., Edwards, J.D.: Machine learning-aided engineering services' cost overruns prediction in high-rise residential building projects: application of random forest regression. J. Build. Eng. **50** (2022). https://doi.org/10.1016/j.jobe.2022.104102
6. Mahamat, A.A., Boukar, M.M.: Machine learning techniques versus classical statistics in strength predictions of eco-friendly masonry units. In: 16th International Conference on Electronics Computer and Computation (ICECCO 2021) (2021)
7. Xie, J., Huang, J., Zeng, C., Huang, S., Burton, G.J.: A generic framework for geotechnical subsurface modeling with machine learning. J. Rock Mech. Geotech. Eng. (2022). https://doi.org/10.1016/j.jrmge.2022.08.001

8. Ben Chaabene, W., Flah, M., Nehdi, M.L.: Machine learning prediction of mechanical properties of concrete: critical review. Constr. Build. Mater. **260**, 119889 (2020). https://doi.org/10.1016/j.conbuildmat.2020.119889

9. Tosee, S.V.R., et al.: Metaheuristic prediction of the compressive strength of environmentally friendly concrete modified with eggshell powder using the hybrid ANN-SFL optimization algorithm. Materials **14**(20) (2021). https://doi.org/10.3390/ma14206172

10. Mahamat, A., et al.: Machine learning approaches for prediction of the compressive strength of alkali activated termite mound soil. Appl. Sci. **11**(11), 4754 (2021). https://doi.org/10.3390/app11114754

11. Khan, K., Ahmad, W., Amin, M.N., Ahmad, A.: A systematic review of the research development on the application of machine learning for concrete. Materials **15**(13) (2022). https://doi.org/10.3390/ma15134512

12. Mangalathu, S., Jang, H., Hwang, S.H., Jeon, J.S.: Data-driven machine-learning-based seismic failure mode identification of reinforced concrete shear walls. Eng. Struct. **208** (2020). https://doi.org/10.1016/j.engstruct.2020.110331

13. Breiman, L.: Classification and Regression Trees, 1st edn. Routledge, New York (1984). https://doi.org/10.1201/9781315139470

14. Shah, H.A., et al.: Application of machine learning techniques for predicting compressive, splitting tensile, and flexural strengths of concrete with metakaolin. Materials **15**(15), 5435 (2022). https://doi.org/10.3390/ma15155435

15. Moussa, H.S., Nshimiyimana, P., Hema, C., Zoungrana, O., Messan, A., Courard, L.: Comparative study of thermal comfort induced from masonry made of stabilized compressed earth block vs conventional cementitious material. J. Miner. Mater. Charact. Eng. **07**(06), 385–403 (2019). https://doi.org/10.4236/jmmce.2019.76026

16. Anysz, H., Brzozowski, Ł., Kretowicz, W., Narloch, P.: Feature importance of stabilised rammed earth components affecting the compressive strength calculated with explainable artificial intelligence tools. Materials **13**(10) (2020). https://doi.org/10.3390/ma13102317

17. Kang, M.C., Yoo, D.Y., Gupta, R.: Machine learning-based prediction for compressive and flexural strengths of steel fiber-reinforced concrete. Constr. Build. Mater. **266** (2021). https://doi.org/10.1016/j.conbuildmat.2020.121117

18. Chen, L., Tran, H., Batra, R., Kim, C., Ramprasad, R.: Machine learning models for the lattice thermal conductivity prediction of inorganic materials. Comput. Mater. Sci. **170** (2019). https://doi.org/10.1016/j.commatsci.2019.109155

19. Bang, H.T., Yoon, S., Jeon, H.: Application of machine learning methods to predict a thermal conductivity model for compacted bentonite. Ann. Nucl. Energy **142** (2020). https://doi.org/10.1016/j.anucene.2020.107395

20. Li, K.Q., Liu, Y., Kang, Q.: Estimating the thermal conductivity of soils using six machine learning algorithms. Int. Commun. Heat Mass Transfer **136** (2022). https://doi.org/10.1016/j.icheatmasstransfer.2022.106139

Sustainable Technologies and Environmental Impact

Solar Energy in Africa - An Overview, with a Focus on Egypt

Manar Mostafa[1], Fathy El-Shahat[2], Moritz Riede[3], and Ghada Bassioni[1]([✉])

[1] Chemistry Division, Faculty of Engineering, Ain Shams University, Cairo, Egypt
ghada_bassioni@eng.asu.edu.eg
[2] Chemistry Department, Faculty of Science, Ain Shams University, Cairo, Egypt
[3] Department of Physics, University of Oxford, Oxford OX1 3PU, UK

Abstract. More than 85% of Africa's land area receives a high amount of solar energy, at least 2,000 kWh/m^2 per year, making it the most sunlit continent on the planet. Despite having the potential to produce 40% of the world's solar power, Africa currently contributes only 1.48% of the total global capacity for electricity production from solar energy. Many African counties currently focus on transforming their fossil-fuel powered electricity sector into a low-carbon system to reduce their CO_2 emissions and therefore solve the climate change problem. The aim of this paper is to present the current situation and future outlook of solar energy in Africa, focusing on Egypt. Egypt has a great opportunity for solar energy development, as it receives a high amount of solar radiation throughout the year, ranging from 9 to 11 h per day. It also hosts one of the largest solar energy projects in the world, the Benban Solar Park in Aswan.

Keywords: solar energy · renewable energy · Africa · Egypt

1 Introduction

Energy consumption affects our lives in many aspects such as industry, health, food production, security, and peace. Fossil fuels (such as coal, natural gas, and oil products) are the main sources of energy for most countries in the world. The percentage of electricity generated by renewable energy sources rose to nearly 13% in 2021, and they are likely to rise more in the future and take the place of the non-renewable ones [1, 2].

The increasing energy demands especially in times of the Ukraine-Russian war and increasing world population challenges abundance [3]. Moreover, the utilize of these fossil fuels as the main source of energy has also aggravated global warming [4].

The world population has grown by about 2,000 times since 12,000 years ago, as shown in Fig. 1, where the population since 1950 is displayed [5]. As the world population approaches 10.9 billion by 2100, with a yearly growth rate of less than 0.1% which cause a flattening in the world population in the next decades with increasing the world population and the rapid electrification of many processes, the global electricity demand is growing [6].

© ICST Institute for Computer Sciences, Social Informatics and Telecommunications Engineering 2024
Published by Springer Nature Switzerland AG 2024. All Rights Reserved
A. Seeam et al. (Eds.): InterSol 2023, LNICST 541, pp. 173–186, 2024.
https://doi.org/10.1007/978-3-031-51849-2_12

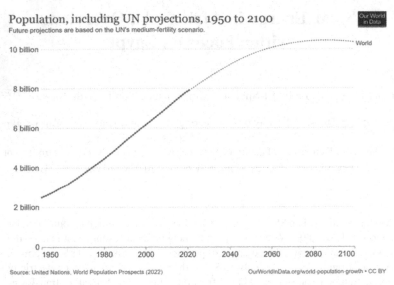

Fig. 1. The increasing number of people living on our planet since 1950 [7].

Leading researchers consider climate change as a major threat to the future of humanity [8, 9]. Since 2010, the world has experienced the ten hottest years on record, and 2022 ranked as the sixth highest in terms of global temperature since 1880, when the records began [10]. Climate change has resulted from the long-term use of fossil fuels as a primary energy source, and it will keep getting worse if we do not adopt alternative sources of energy. The environment and livelihoods are affected by the constant release of carbon dioxide (CO_2) and other greenhouse gases (GHG) such as Methane (CH_4), and Nitrous oxide (N_2O) [11]. Climate change, which is caused by the long-term use of fossil fuels as a main energy source, will alter the planet's geography, cause water scarcity, and accelerate the extinction of animals and the loss of biodiversity if we fail to slow down, control, and stop it. To solve these problems, we have to use low-carbon sources instead of fossil fuels [12].

The UN announced in 2015 a plan for Sustainable Development that consists of 17 objectives to be achieved by 2030. Goal 7 of the 17 goals that the UN set for the 2030 agenda for Sustainable Development is to "Ensure access to affordable, reliable, sustainable and modern energy for all". The aim of this goal is to increase the share of renewable energy and encourage investment in energy infrastructure and clean energy technology to create a green energy future (UN, 2015). The global CO_2 emissions from energy use dropped by 5.8% in 2020 due to COVID, according to the International Energy Agency's report in 2021. However, the global energy-related CO_2 emissions in the atmosphere did not change [13]. The global community has a long-term aim of reaching net zero CO_2 emissions by 2050, which requires various measures, such as changing from conventional fuels to low or zero carbon energy sources, as this is the most viable single way to stabilize the climate [14]. The report by IRENA in 2022 states that the percentage of renewable energy in electricity production needs to rise from 19% in 2019 to 79% by 2050 [15].

Renewable energy sources (such as wind, solar, hydro, tidal, biomass, geothermal, and wave) are gaining attention from many countries and international organizations. They think that these sources are vital for sustainable development, environmental protection, green gas emission reduction, and energy security [16–18]. Renewable energy technologies are becoming more common in both high-income and low-income countries as they are more affordable, dependable, and accessible [19]. Recently, more and more countries are getting interested in investing in renewable energy but developing countries start to show incredible attention toward investment in green energy sources (Fig. 2). Low-income countries surpassed high-income countries in renewable energy investment per capita in 2021, with 491 USD and 42 USD respectively [20].

Renewable energy systems are becoming more viable as the cost of renewable sources continues to decline. Solar energy is the most promising renewable energy source, as it can provide clean, dependable, and safe power. The solar energy that arrives the Earth's landmasses is over 27 times higher than the total annual commercial energy that humans use, making it a very attractive renewable resource [21, 22].

The amount of solar energy that the surface gets during a certain time period is related to solar radiation, which is the most important factor for scientists to decide where to install solar power farms [23, 24]. The total radiation that reaches the horizontal surface on the ground, called global horizontal irradiation GHI (kWh/m^2), is usually measured either daily or yearly. High GHI values indicate good locations for investing in photovoltaic (PV) farms [25–27].

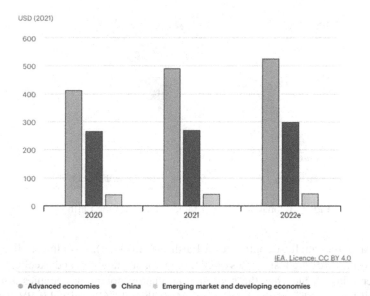

Fig. 2. Global New Investment in Renewable Energy per capita: advances and emerging economies [20].

2   A Quick Overview of Global Solar Energy

Figure 3 shows the GHI map for the Earth. To determine the best areas for PV farms investment, solar potential is classified according to GHI data into superb potential (annual GHI > 2221.8 KWh/m^2), outstanding (annual GHI from 2035.9 to 2221.8 KWh/m^2), excellent (annual GHI from 1843.8 to 2035.9 KWh/m^2), good (annual GHI from 1641.8 to 1843.8 KWh/m^2), fair (annual GHI from 1419.7 to 1641.8 KWh/m^2), marginal (annual GHI from 1191.8 to 1419.7 KWh/m^2), and poor (annual GHI < 1191.8 KWh/m^2) classes. From Fig. 3 we notice that almost 40% (60 mil km^2) of the land area on Earth has high solar resources with potential classes of superb, outstanding, and excellent (> 1800 kWh/m^2 per year) for GHI. The analysis reveals that there are six main regions in the world with high GHI (Australia, Arabian Peninsula, eastern, northern, and southwestern Africa, and the western coast of South America). The solar resources in Africa are the highest in the world (Fig. 3), with 90% of the continental area is in superb, outstanding, and excellent classes. Furthermore, one-third of Africa's area (almost 10 mil km^2) has the highest potential for solar energy, based on GHI (Fig. 4) so, Africa is the best continent location for large-scale PV systems [28].

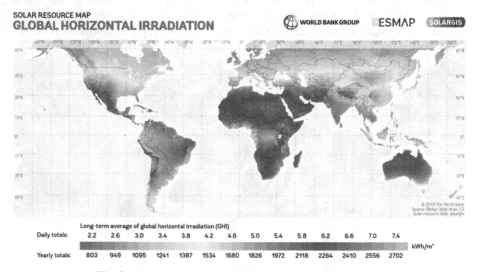

Fig. 3. Global horizontal irradiation map for the Earth [31].

Australia, the smallest continent on Earth (~8 mil km^2), has almost all of its area covered by the three highest classes of GHI (superb, outstanding, and excellent) (Fig. 4). The superb class, which has the highest solar energy potential, occupies a huge area of 2.4 mil km^2 (~30% of the total) [28]. More than 11 GW of solar PV capacity is installed on over 30% of Australian homes, which shows how Australians make use of the abundant solar energy available to them [29].

Asia has the biggest land area on Earth (~45 mil km^2), but only a small portion of it (almost 10 mil km^2, 22% of the continent's area) has high GHI resources compared to its size (excellent, outstanding, and superb GHI classes). However, it still produces a

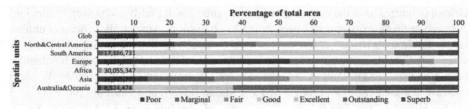

Fig. 4. Percentage classes' extent of GHI (kWh/m^2). Note: the absolute values on the left of the columns represent the total analyzed continental area (the global land area = 116,853,085 km^2, the land area of North & Central America = 16,842,830 Km^2, the land area of South America = 17,186,731 Km^2, the land area of Europe = 7,317,931 Km^2, the land area of Africa = 30,055,347 Km^2, the land area of Asia = 36,925,772 Km^2, and the land area of Australia & Oceania = 8,524,474 Km^2) [28].

lot of PV power [28]. Over the last ten years, Asia added 40 GWp of solar PV each year and almost 80 GWp in 2020. This annual addition is expected to increase to 210 GWp through 2030. This great expansion concentrated in India and China. Solar PV production in North America and Europe increased twofold in 2020, and they are projected to have 19% and 14%, respectively, of the global solar PV installations by 2030. Africa and the Middle East have abundant GHI resources, but they have not invested much in the PV sector so far. They should prioritize solar PV projects, as they will need 70 GWp of yearly installations in this decade (IRENA, 2022) [30].

3   Africa's Solar Energy Prospects

The whole world is looking to Africa and the future of solar energy in it for many reasons. First, Africa occupies about one-fifth of the total land area of the Earth (the land area of Africa is approximately 30,365,000 km^2) [32]. Second, high population in Africa where the current population of Africa is estimated by the United Nations to be about 1.4 billion people and is expected to grow more than twice by 2050 reaching about 2.4 billion in a world where population growth is decreasing [33]. This increasing population has the lowest degree of electrification in the world. One of the areas most affected by this low in electricity in Africa is sub-Saharan Africa where more than two-thirds of people without access to electricity in the world live in this area So, we need new sources of energy to compensate this deficiency [34]. Third, The United Nations has identified Africa as the continent that is most susceptible (although the least responsible) to the impacts of climate change due to human activities, population growth, impending water shortages, and low capacity to adapt [35–37]. For example, the current electricity production in Africa mostly relies on fossil fuels (30% Coal, 9% Oil, and 40% natural gas), and continuing at this percentage increases the risk of climate change. The final reason is that Africa is blessed with solar energy in most of their countries (Fig. 5) [34].

Africa is the continent that receives the most sunlight on Earth, with more than 85% of its land area getting at least 2,000 kWh/m^2 of solar radiation every year [38]. Africa has the highest potential for solar power in the world, with 40% of it, but it only contributes 1.48% of the total global capacity for electricity production from solar energy [39]. Many

African countries have the goal of transforming their fossil fuel-based power sectors into low-carbon energy systems to lower their CO_2 emission. Almost all African countries have suitable solar resources but there are only 9 countries that are actual GHI hotspots taking into consideration that at least 50% of the area of the country has superb potential, those countries are Djibouti (52%), Libya (56%), Eritrea (58%), Chad (69%), Western Sahara (72%), Egypt (77%), Niger (84%), Sudan (86%), and Namibia (96%) (Fig. 5 and 6). However, the first 9 hotspots in terms of absolute areas in Africa are Sudan (~1.6 mil km^2), Niger (~1 mil km^2), Chad (~900,000 km^2), Libya (~900,000 km^2), Egypt (~800,000 km^2), Namibia (~800,000 km^2), Algeria (~700,000 km^2), Mauritania (~400,000 km^2), and Mali (~400,000 km^2) (Fig. 6) [28].

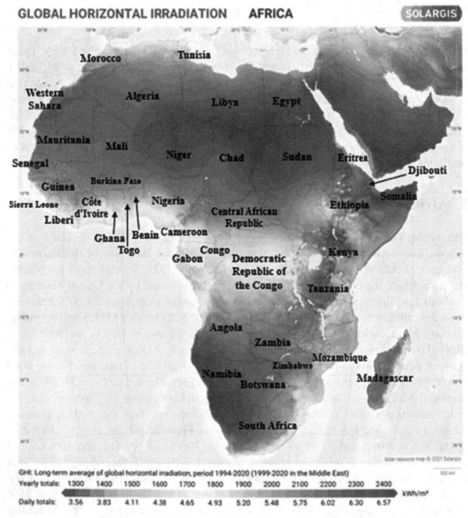

Fig. 5. Global horizontal irradiation map for Africa [40].

The continent's capacity for installing solar PV has grown from 8 GW in 2009 to 47 GWp in 2015 [41]. The Africa Solar Industry Association (AFSIA) reported that Africa's solar capacity increased by 989 MWp in 2022, a 14% growth compared to the previous year, and the continent's total solar capacity surpassed 10 GWp by the end of that year. However, The International Energy Agency predicts that Africa will need 497 GW of PV power by 2030 [42].

4 Solar Energy in Egypt

A region called the "Sun Belt" covers vast parts of the United States, North Africa, the Middle East, and the Mediterranean [43]. Egypt is part of this region, which belongs to the North Africa and Middle East area. The country gets direct solar radiation between 5.5 and more than 9.0 kWh/m^2 per day, and has a daily sunlight duration of 9 to 11 h [44]. According to IRENA, Egypt has one of the best conditions in the world for using solar energy for electricity and heating purposes [45]. The population of Egypt is 110 million and it is expected to grow to 160 million by 2050. The report by the Egyptian Electricity Holding Company in 2018 showed that only 10% of the total electricity generation capacity, which was around 54.5 GW, came from renewable energy sources [46]. By 2035, the Egyptian government has a plan to raise the percentage of electricity from renewable energy sources to 42%. Solar energy will provide 25% of this, wind energy will contribute 14%, and hydroelectricity will supply 2% (See Fig. 7) [47].

The highest potential locations in Egypt are Upper Egypt cities such as Asyut, Aswan, Luxor and around the Red Sea coast. According to Egypt-PV (2021), Egypt has over 125 solar PV power plants in operation, which can produce up to 9 GWp of electricity and decrease CO$_2$ emissions by about 9 t/y [48].

IRENA reports that solar energy projects have great economic importance [49]. Egypt's solar energy plan aims to achieve 3.5 GWp of installed capacity by 2027, with 2.8 GWp coming from photovoltaic and 700 MWp from concentrated solar power. This is much higher than the current electricity production in Egypt from solar energy [50, 51]. Under the supervision of the Ministry of Electricity and Renewable Energy, Egypt has launched several solar energy projects such as Benban, Zafarana, Siwa, Farafra, Darb El-Arbayeen, and Shalten (Fig. 8) [52].

Benban Solar Park (Fig. 9) is one of the largest solar PV stations in the world (The table 1 shows the world's top five solar parks by size). On average, Benban Solar Park produces about 18% of Egypt's total electricity generation [53, 54]. The total capacity of the Benban Solar Park is 1650 MW and it occupies 37.2 Km^2 of land near Benban village in the Aswan Governorate in Upper Egypt. NASA studies and reports were used to choose the project site, which was recognized by the World Bank as the best project of 2019. The Benban Solar Park is projected to generate 3.8 TWh of electricity annually, which is almost equal to 90% of the power output of the high dam in Aswan [55]. The Benban solar park is made up of 41 solar power plants, with different capacities depending on the shape of the land. Most of them (31) can produce 50 MW$_{AC}$ (64 MW$_{DC}$) each, while the rest (10) have varying capacities [56]. The project included 40 specialized companies, with 10 from global and Arab regions. It cost 3.4 billion euros, which is equivalent to 40 billion pounds. It generated 200 direct and indirect jobs and helped avoid 2 million tons of CO$_2$ emissions [57].

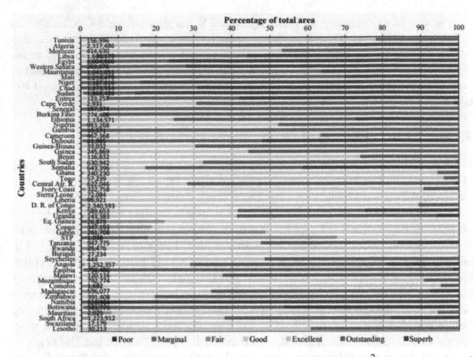

Fig. 6. Percentage classes' extent of global horizontal irradiation (kWh/m^2) in the countries of Africa. Note: the absolute values on the left of the columns represent the total national area (the land area of Tunisia = 156,996 km^2, the land area of Algeria = 2,317,486 Km^2, the land area of Morocco = 414,630 Km^2, the land area of Libya = 1,630,179 Km^2, the land area of Egypt = 1,004,866 Km^2, the land area of Western Sahara = 269,976 Km^2, the land area of Mauritania = 1,041,851 Km^2, the land area of Mali = 1,259,479 Km^2, the land area of Niger = 1,187,816 Km^2, the land area of Chad = 1,273,554 Km^2, the land area of Sudan = 1,868,489 Km^2, the land area of Eritrea = 123,257 Km^2, the land area of Cape Verde = 2,931 Km^2, the land area of Senegal = 197,374 Km^2, the land area of Burkina Faso = 274,406 Km^2, the land area of Ethiopia = 1,134,571 Km^2, the land area of Nigeria = 913,268 Km^2, the land area of Gambia = 10,571 Km^2, the land area of Cameroon = 467,368 Km^2, the land area of Djibouti = 21,985 Km^2, the land area of Guinea-Bissau = 33,032 Km^2, the land area of Guinea = 245,869 Km^2, the land area of Benin = 116,832 Km^2, the land area of South Sudan = 630,942 Km^2, the land area of Somalia = 643,396 Km^2, the land area of Ghana = 240,230 Km^2, the land area of Togo = 57,239 Km^2, the land area of Central African Republic = 622,046 Km^2, the land area of Ivory Coast = 322,758 Km^2, the land area of Sierra Leone = 72,084 Km^2, the land area of Liberia = 95,921 Km^2, the land area of Democratic Republic of the Congo = 2,340,593 Km^2, the land area of Kenya = 589,653 Km^2, the land area of Uganda = 243,383 Km^2, the land area of Equatorial Guinea = 26,879 Km^2, the land area of Congo = 347,193 Km^2, the land area of Gabon = 261,708 Km^2, the land area of São Tomé and Príncipe (STP) = 1,038 Km^2, the land area of Tanzania = 947,775 Km^2, the land area of Rwanda = 25,476 Km^2, the land area of Burundi = 27,234 Km^2, the land area of Seychelles = 444 Km^2, the land area of Angola = 1,252,357 Km^2, the land area of Zambia = 756,486 Km^2, the land area of Malawi = 120,116 Km^2, the land area of Mozambique = 792,774 Km^2, the land area of Comoros = 1,682 Km^2, the land area of Madagascar = 596,077 Km^2, the land area of Zimbabwe = 391,408 Km^2, the land area of Namibia = 826,564 Km^2, the land area of Botswana = 581,775 Km^2, the land area of Mauritius = 2,025 Km^2, the land area of South Africa = 1,223,912 Km^2, the land area of Swaziland = 17,179 Km^2, and the land area of Lesotho = 30,213 Km^2) [28].

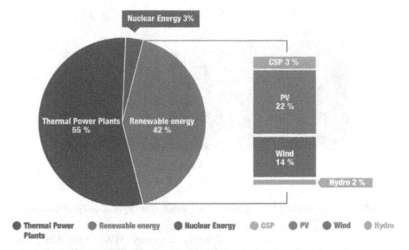

Fig. 7. Egyptian electricity target generation in 2035 [47].

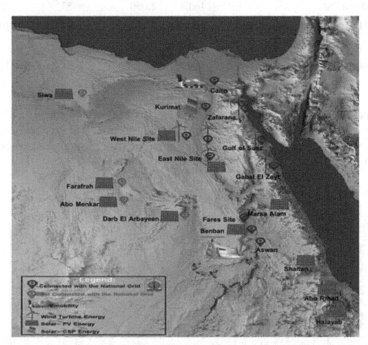

Fig. 8. Location of Benban Solar Park (We marked Benban with a red line, it is located 40 km northwest of Aswan city and has the coordinates 23.9786° N, 32.8739° E) [52].

The Web of Science database shows the trend of research articles on 6 renewable energy sources (i.e., wind, photovoltaic, concentrated solar, biomass, geothermal energies, and hydropower) in Egypt from 2010 to 2020 in Fig. 10. Researchers have shown great interest in renewable energy technologies in Egypt over the past decade. The

Fig. 9. Benban Solar Park [63].

Table 1. The world's five biggest solar parks, country, capacity, and area.

Name	Country	Capacity (MW)	Area (km^2)	Reference
Bhadla Solar Park	India	2,245	56	[58]
Pavagada Solar Park	India	2,050	53	[59]
Huanghe Hydropower Golmud Solar Park	China	2,200	42.5	[60]
Tengger Desert Solar Park	China	1,547	43	[61]
Benban Solar Park	Egypt	1,650	37.2	[62]

research papers on these technologies have a clear rising trend in Fig. 10, which indicates their importance for both the academic and industrial sectors. Another observation is that photovoltaic energy has received more attention than the other renewable energy sources in Egypt [64].

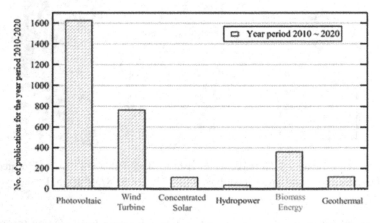

Fig. 10. The number of publications on renewable energy sources in the last 10 years [64].

5 Conclusion and Recommendations

This paper summarizes data of Africa's excellent solar resources, with a focus on Egypt. So far, these resources are not fully in use and its usage needs to get better. Egypt as example, has major GWp projects, yet not all possibilities of growth are explored. It is recommended that governments should integrate universities and research institutions beside industry to develop the renewable energy sector locally and regionally. This implies capacity building to make African researchers competitive on an international level and to increase the role universities play in technology development. Funds shall be more available for equipment and more recognition for research endeavors shall be anticipated. The future of research on this level in Africa and Egypt can be built through training, education, and increasing grant opportunities for researchers.

References

1. bp Statistical Review of World Energy 2022, 71st edn. https://www.bp.com/content/dam/bp/business-sites/en/global/corporate/pdfs/energy-economics/statistical-review/bp-stats-review-2022-full-report.pdf
2. IEA, World Energy Outlook 2022. https://iea.blob.core.windows.net/assets/830fe099-5530-48f2-a7c1-11f35d510983/WorldEnergyOutlook2022.pdf
3. Tollefson, J.: What the war in Ukraine means for energy, climate and food. Nature **604**, 1476–4687 (2022)
4. IPCC: Climate Change 2023: Synthesis Report (2023). https://www.ipcc.ch/report/ar6/syr/
5. www.ourworldindata.org
6. United Nations Department of Economic and Social Affairs, Population Division, "World Population Prospects 2019". https://population.un.org/wpp/Publications/Files/WPP2019_Highlights.pdf
7. Future Population Growth, Our World in Data (2013). https://ourworldindata.org/future-population-growth
8. Ripple, W.J., et al.: World scientists warning of climate emergency. Bioscience **71**, 894–898 (2021)
9. Ripple, W.J., et al.: World scientists' warning to humanity: a second notice. Bioscience **67**, 1026–1028 (2017)
10. NOAA National Centers for Environmental Information: Monthly Global Climate Report for Annual 2022 (2023). https://www.ncei.noaa.gov/access/monitoring/monthly-report/global/202213
11. Hassan, S.T., Batool, B., Sadiq, M., Zhu, B.: How do green energy investment, economic policy uncertainty, and natural resources affect greenhouse gas emissions? A Markov-switching equilibrium approach. Environ. Impact Assess. Rev. **97**, 106887–106897 (2022)
12. Sims, R.E.H.: Renewable energy: a response to climate change. Sol. Energy **76**, 9–17 (2004)
13. Global Energy Review 2021: Assessing the Effects of Economic Recoveries on Global Energy Demand and CO_2 Emissions in 2021, International Energy Agency, Paris, France (2021). https://www.iea.org/reports/global-energy-review-2021
14. IEA: Net Zero by 2050, IEA, Paris (2021). https://www.iea.org/reports/net-zero-by-2050
15. IRENA: Global Renewables Outlook: Energy transformation 2050 (Edition: 2020). International Renewable Energy Agency, Abu Dhabi (2020). /-/media/Files/IRENA/Agency/Publication/2020/Apr/IRENA_Global_Renewables_Outlook_2020.pdf?rev=1f416406e50d447cbb2247de30d1d1d0

16. Carley, S.: State renewable energy electricity policies: an empirical evaluation of effectiveness. Energy Policy **37**, 3071–3081 (2009)
17. Marques, A.C., Fuinhas, J.A., Pires Manso, J.R.: Motivations driving renewable energy in European countries: a panel data approach. Energy Policy **38**(11), 6877–6885 (2010)
18. Olanrewaju, B.T., Olubusoye, O.E., Adenikinju, A., Akintande, O.J.: A panel data analysis of renewable energy consumption in Africa. Renew. Energy **140**, 668–679 (2019)
19. International Energy Agency (IEA): Renewable Energy: Medium-Term Market Report (2015). https://www.iea.org/Textbase/npsum/MTrenew2015sum.pdf
20. IEA: World Energy Investment Report 2022, Overview and Key Findings. https://www.iea.org/reports/world-energy-investment-2022/overview-and-key-finding
21. Alrikabi, N.K.: Renewable energy types. J. Clean Energy Technol. **2**, 61–65 (2014)
22. Perez, M., Perez, R.: Update 2022 – a fundamental look at supply side energy reserves for the planet. Sol. Energy Adv. **2**, 100014–100021 (2022)
23. Sánchez-Lozano, J.M., García-Cascales, M.S., Lamata, M.T.: Comparative TOPSIS-ELECTRE TRI methods for optimal sites for photovoltaic solar farms. Case study in Spain. J. Clean. Prod. **127**, 387-398 (2016)
24. Azevêdo, V.W.B., Candeias, A.L.B., Tiba, C.: Location study of solar thermal power plant in the state of Pernambuco using geoprocessing technologies and multiple-criteria analysis. Energies **10**, 1042–1065 (2017)
25. Aly, A., Jensen, S.S., Pedersen, A.B.: Solar power potential of Tanzania: identifying CSP and PV hot spots through a GIS multicriteria decision making analysis. Renew. Energy **113**, 159–175 (2017)
26. Hafeznia, H., Yousefi, H., Astaraei, F.R.: A novel framework for the potential assessment of utility-scale photovoltaic solar energy, application to eastern Iran. Energy Convers. Manag. **151**, 240–258 (2017)
27. Tercan, E., Eymen, A., Urfalı, T., Saracoglu, B.O.: A sustainable framework for spatial planning of photovoltaic solar farms using GIS and multi-criteria assessment approach in Central Anatoliam, Turkey. Land Use Policy **102**, 105272–105286 (2021)
28. Pravalie, R., Patriche, C., Bandoc, G.: Spatial assessment of solar energy potential at global scale. A geographical approach. J. Clean. Prod. **209**, 692–721 (2019)
29. energy.gov.au is a Department of Climate Change, Energy, the Environment and Water website
30. IRENA: World Energy Transitions Outlook 2022: 1.5 °C Pathway. International Renewable Energy Agency, Abu Dhabi (2022). https://www.irena.org/publications/2022/mar/world-energy-transitions-outlook-2022
31. Global Solar Atlas. https://globalsolaratlas.info
32. Khapoya, V.: The African Experience, 4th edn. Routledge (2013). https://doi.org/10.4324/9781315662596
33. Yorke, H., Beard, J., Coughlin, C., Evans-Pritchard, C., Hymas, C.: Africa's population to double to 2.4 billion by 2050. https://www.telegraph.co.uk/news/worldnews/africaandindianocean/10305000/Africas-population-to-double-to-2.4-billion-by-2050.html
34. IEA. Africa energy outlook (2019). https://www.iea.org/reports/africa-energy-outlook-2019
35. De Vries, B.J.M., van Vuuren, D.B., Hoogwijk, M.M.: Renewable energy sources: their global potential for the first half of the 21st century at a global level: an integrated approach. Energy Policy **35**(4), 2590–2610 (2007)
36. Abbas, A.S., et al.: Optimal harmonic mitigation in distribution systems with inverter based distributed generation. Appl. Sci. **11**(2), 774–790 (2021)
37. Banks, D., Consulting, R., Schäffler, J., Energy, N.: The potential contribution of renewable energy in South Africa. Energize **1**, 37–41 (2005)
38. World_Bank: Global Solar Atlas (2017). https://globalsolaratlas.info
39. IRENA: Renewable Capacity Statistics 2021. International Renewable Energy Agency (IRENA), Abu Dhabi (2021)

40. Solar resource map © 2021 Solargis. https://solargis.com
41. Taylor, M., So, E.Y.: Solar PV in Africa: Costs and markets. IRENA (2016). https://www.afr ica50.com/fileadmin/uploads/africa50/Documents/Knowledge_Center/IRENA_Solar_PV_ Costs_Africa_2016.pdf
42. Joshi, A.: Africa's Solar Capacity Grew by 14% in 2022 to Nearly 1 GW (2022). https://www. mercomindia.com/africa-solar-capacity-grew-14-in-2022-to-nearly-1-gw
43. Islam, M.T., Huda, N., Abdullah, A., Saidur, R.: A comprehensive review of state-of-the-art concentrating solar power (CSP) technologies: current status and research trends. Renew. Sustain. Energy Rev. **91**, 987–1018 (2018)
44. Salah, S.I., Eltaweel, M., Abeykoon, C.: Towards a sustainable energy future for Egypt: a systematic review of renewable energy sources, technologies, challenges, and recommendations. Clean. Eng. Technol. **8**, 100497–100527 (2022)
45. IRENA, R.E.S.: Renewable Energy Outlook: Egypt. Technical report. International Renewable Energy Agency, Abu Dhabi (2018)
46. Egyptian Electricity Holding Company. Annual report (2016–2017)
47. New and Renewable Energy Egyptian Authority. Annual report (2018)
48. Egypt-PV, 2021. Egypt PV. https://egypt-pv.org
49. IRENA: The Socio-economic Benefits of Solar and Wind Energy (2014). https://www.irena. org/-/media/Files/IRENA/Agency/Publication/2014/Socioeconomic_benefits_solar_wind. pdf
50. Moharram, N.A., Bayoumi, S., Hanafy, A.A., El-Maghlany, W.M.: Hybrid desalination and power generation plant utilizing multi-stage flash and reverse osmosis driven by parabolic trough collectors. Case Stud. Therm. Eng. **23**, 100807–100820 (2021)
51. Elshafey, S., et al.: Solar thermal power in Egypt. In: 2018 IEEE Industry Applications Society Annual Meeting. IAS 2018. Institute of Electrical and Electronics Engineers Inc. (2018). https://doi.org/10.1109/IAS.2018.8544513
52. Mohamed, A.S.A., Maghrabie, H.M.: Techno-economic feasibility analysis of Benban solar Park. Alex. Eng. J. **61**, 12593–12607 (2022)
53. Steady state analysis and impact of Benban solar park on the Egyptian transmission system. Int. J. Adv. Trends Comput. Sci. Eng. (2021). https://doi.org/10.30534/IJATCSE/2021/641 022021
54. Benban solar park, Egypt, world's biggest solar photovoltaic (2014). Checked online 2022. https://www.nsenergybusiness.com/projects/benban-solar-park/
55. Metwally, M., Magdy, G., Elbaset, A.A., Zaki, E.: Carbon footprint study on renewable power plants: case study on Egypt's Benban solar park. Int. J. Appl. Energy Syst. **5**, 6–12 (2022)
56. New and Renewable Energy Authority (NREA): Benban 1.8 GW PV Solar Park, Egypt, Strategic environmental & social assessment-final report (2016). https://www.eib.org/attach ments/registers/65771943.pdf
57. Nordrum, A.: At last, a massive solar park for Egypt: a 1.8-GW, $4 billion solar power plant is coming online in the Sahara - [News]. IEEE Spectr. **56**(11), 8–9 (2019)
58. China completes world's second-largest solar power plant. Balkan Green Energy News. Accessed 03 May 2023
59. World's Largest Solar Park at Karnataka's Pavagada is Now Fully Operational (2019). Accessed 27 Dec 2019
60. The world's largest solar parks. Coo Solar Power. Accessed 08 Nov 2021
61. 10 really cool Solar Power installations in (and above) the world (2018). Accessed 30 Jan 2018
62. Benban, Africa's largest solar park, completed. www.ebrd.com. Accessed 29 Nov 2019

63. The 5 Largest Solar Power Plants in the World (2022). https://ornatesolar.com/blog/the-5-lar gest-solar-power-plants-in-the-world
64. Abubakr, H., Vasquez, J.C., Mahmoud, K., Darwish, M.M.F., Guerrero, J.M.: Comprehensive review on renewable energy sources in Egypt—current status, grid codes and future vision. IEEE Access **10**, 4081–4101 (2022)

Projected Hydroclimate Changes over Senegal (West Africa)

Mamadou Lamine Mbaye[1]([✉]), Babacar Faye[2], Bounama Dieye[3],
and Amadou Thierno Gaye[4]

[1] Laboratoire d'Océanographie, des Sciences de l'Environnement et du Climat (LOSEC),
Université Assane SECK de Ziguinchor, Ziguinchor, Senegal
mlmbaye@univ-zig.sn
[2] Département Environnement, Biodiversité et Développement Durable, Université du Sine
Saloum El Hadj Ibrahima NIASS, Kaolack, Senegal
[3] Ministère de l'Agriculture et de l'Equipement Rural, Dakar, Senegal
[4] Laboratoire de Physique de l'Atmosphère et de l'Océan Siméon Fongang (LPAO-SF),
Université Cheikh Anta Diop, Dakar, Senegal

Abstract. Understanding and assessing hydroclimate changes is essential to provide reliable information in developing countries such as Senegal in order to guide adaptation strategies. In this work, we have examined the projected changes in temperature and precipitation over the six eco-geographical zones in Senegal. Furthermore, we have assessed the river flow changes in the three major river basins (Casamance, Gambia, Senegal). Climate simulations from the Coupled Model Intercomparison Project Phase 6 (CMIP6) were analyzed. The ensemble mean of the climate models projects a continued increase in mean, minimum and maximum temperatures across Senegal (up to more than 4 °C in the long term under the SSP5-8.5 scenario). The projected warming is greater in eastern Senegal and the Sylvo-pastoral zone. As for rainfall, it is characterized by very high interannual variability; the projections show decreasing trend from 2015 to 2100. The groundnut basin is the most area affected by the decrease in rainfall (24%). However, slight humidity conditions are projected for the near future (2021–2040). The downward trend of rainfall is much more pronounced around 2045 to 2100. In addition, we found a slight increase in extreme wet events that are more marked in the near future. This could increase the risk of flooding in urban and peri-urban areas. Moreover, future flows are strongly impacted by climate change. Thus, the stations of Kolda (Casamance River), Gouloumbou (Gambia River) and Kidira (Senegal River) could experience a slight increase in flow rates (up to 20%) by 2030; while by 2060 and 2100, a decline of about 40% is projected. Our findings can help the water managers and decision-makers to better plan their adaptation measures.

Keywords: Climate change impacts · Senegal · rainfall · temperature · river flow

A. Seeam et al. (Eds.): InterSol 2023, LNICST 541, pp. 187–204, 2024.
https://doi.org/10.1007/978-3-031-51849-2_13

1 Introduction

Today, the issue of climate change in Sub-Saharan Africa (SSA) is no longer in doubt. Indeed, even if progress remains to be made both in terms of the production of knowledge and its availability, as well as the ability to implement it in order to reverse the current trend, efforts are being carried out for better consideration of the said changes with regard to their serious economic implications on the entire development process, but also on the daily lives of the populations. It is commonly accepted that, due to its low adaptive capacity, Africa remains very vulnerable to climate change (Nicholson 2013; Engelbrecht et al. 2015; Niang et al. 2014; IPCC 2014). Indeed, not only does it remain the continent whose warming is faster than average, but climate projections show a rise of 3 to 4 °C over the course of the century. This will necessarily lead to or even exacerbate existing challenges, whether economic and financial, scientific and technological, etc. Senegal is one of the most vulnerable countries to climate change. The State of Senegal is not only a signatory of international conventions in the field of environment and climate, but it is resolutely committed to taking better account of climate change in development policies and plans. Thus, this contributes to strengthening the country's adaptation and resilience capacities. It is in this context that the government of Senegal submitted its updated version of the NDC to the UNFCCC secretariat in December 2020, with a mitigation target of 36% (including an unconditional target of 7% and a conditional target of 29%) by 2030, relative to the reference scenario. In the same vein, Senegal has been engaged since 2015 in the process of carrying out its National Adaptation Plan (NAP). Today, studies are being carried out in certain agro-ecological zones or in progress. Thus, it is urgent that Senegal, like other signatory countries of the Paris Agreement (PA) on climate, be more ambitious by developing long-term strategies with an inclusive economy with low greenhouse gas emissions 2050 and beyond. The strategy carried by a visionary program, a political certainty, will be around the scaling up of agriculture that sustainably increases productivity and resilience (adaptation), reduces/eliminates GHGs (mitigation) in a possible way and enhances the achievement of food security and development goals for sustainable economic transformation. In all agro-ecological zones of the country, climate change is already dramatically affecting the natural ecosystems on which poor rural communities, and in particular women, depend to develop their production systems and, in short, their survival. In addition, major environmental problems are emerging and have repercussions both on animal and plant biodiversity, and both on agricultural production, water resources, economy and food security of populations are threatened, even weakened, and this situation continues to exacerbate. The overall objective of this work is to investigate the hydroclimate changes using the new SSP (Shared Socio economic Pathways) scenarios over the century.

2 Study Area

Six eco-geographical zones of Senegal, namely Niayes, Casamance, Ferlo (Sylvo-pastoral zone), River Valley, Groundnut Basin and Eastern Senegal are marked by specific pedo-climatic, human and agricultural conditions (Fig. 1). They hosted a high ecosystem diversity with the presence of forest ecosystems, agroforestry ecosystems, fluvio-lacustrine ecosystems and finally coastal marine ecosystems thanks to the existence of a coast of more than 700 km. The country is located in three climatic domains at the same time (Sahelian in the north, Sudanian in the center and sub-Guinean in the south).

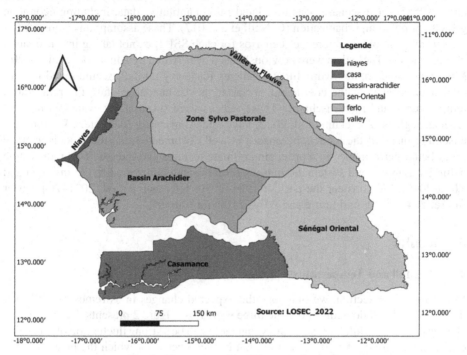

Fig. 1. Eco-geographical Zones in Senegal

3   Data and Methods

Climate change affects many climate variables including precipitation and temperature. At the international level, many countries have committed to the Paris Agreement to hold the global temperature increases to "well below 2 °C" and to pursue efforts to limit warming to 1.5 °C above pre-industrial levels. Meeting this target implies a drastic reduction in greenhouse gas (GHG) emissions and drastic social, political and economic transformations. The extent and exact nature of this transition to a low-carbon economy will depend on the actions that our societies will implement, and therefore cannot be perfectly known in advance. This transition induces risks and opportunities for economic actors that they must anticipate in order to build their strategy in a context of uncertainty. In this regards, the scientific community has developed scenarios called SSP (Shared Socio-Economic Pathways). These SSPs are narratives of socioeconomic development exploring plausible developments in the world in the absence of additional policies and measures to limit global warming (Riahi et al. 2017). These scenarios were defined by the scientific community to build a common framework and to facilitate analysis of climate change impacts, mitigation and adaptation options, and their costs. These five scenarios (SSP1, SSP2, SSP3, SSP4 and SSP5) describe the possible social, economic, political and technological evolutions by the end of the 21st century.

In this work, we will study three of the five scenarios, namely SSP126, SSP245 and SSP585. Each scenario was translated into quantitative data, including economic growth, population, urbanization (O'Neill et al. 2017). These assumptions were used as model inputs to obtain reference scenarios for each SSP (i.e., not taking into account a climate target). These data were previously used over Africa by Almazroui et al. (2020). Moreover, we compute hydroclimate changes for heavy rainfall, accumulated rainfall over 5 days interval, the coefficient of variation, the annual rainfall, the rainy days, temperatures, and river discharge. These indices were successfully evaluated in West African regions (Agyekum et al. 2022; Faye and Akinsanola 2022; etc.). We took the ensemble mean of the models because it is well documented that the models average gives better performance in reproducing climate features and indices. This reduces the natural variability and systematic biases present in individual models (Akinsanola and Zhou 2019). We consider the period: 1981–2010: reference period, 2021–2040: near future. 2041–2070: mid future and 2071–2100: far future.

4   Results

4.1   Rainfall and Temperature Changes

In the following section, we diagnose the expected changes in extremes rainfall over the six considered domains under the three scenarios. Figure 2 presents the interannual changes of heavy rainfall. Results show that there will be a strong fluctuation of this index during the future marked by an alternation between years for which the heavy rainfall will decrease or increase over the six areas of the country for all scenarios. This decrease of heavy precipitation will be more pronounced during the far future (2071–2100) for all SSPs in particular under the SSP585 scenario.

Furthermore, our results are in line with those of Saley and Salack 2023 who found showed significant changes toward higher values in the probability distribution function of the future heavy rainfall events in West Africa, which may likely trigger more floods in the region. Mbaye et al. (2019) have also found a slight increase in heavy rainfall over Senegal in the coming decades. Figure 3 present the changes in the interannual 5-days precipitation accumulations in the six zones of Senegal under the three scenarios. The 5-days rainfall cumulative are known to be favorable to flooding and therefore they are a major concern for local populations. During the future, there would be an alternation between years for which the 5-days cumulative rainfall will decrease or increase in the six areas of Senegal under the three scenarios. The magnitude of these changes will be much pronounced under the SSP585 scenario over the river valley, the Niayes area, the groundnut basin and the Sylvo-pastoral area compare to the SSP126 and SSP245 scenarios. Strong peaks of changes of the 5-days cumulative rainfall will be recorded in 2055 and 2075 in the groundnut basin and the Niayes area under the SSP585 scenario.

The interannual changes of the coefficient of variation of precipitation as well as the interannual changes of mean rainfall are presented respectively in Fig. 4 and 5.

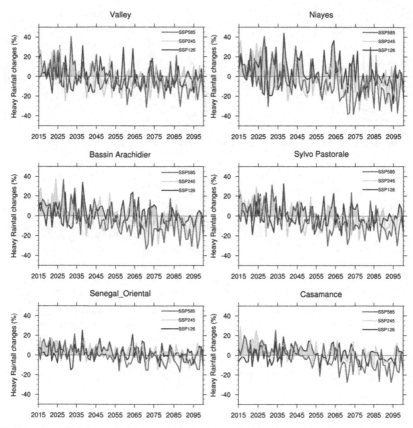

Fig. 2. Interannual changes in heavy precipitation under the three scenarios and the six areas of the country. Blue, green and red lines depict SSP126, SSP245 and SSP585, respectively. (Color figure online)

The coefficient of variation of precipitation will remain below 20% in the present-day and medium term (2015–2040) with a strong interannual fluctuation in the six zones of the country under the three scenarios (Fig. 4). This high variability could be explained by the changes in Sea Surface Temperature (SST) as stated by Mohino et al. (2011). From 2055 onwards, there will be many years for which the coefficient of variation of precipitation will be above 20% with weak interannual fluctuation. When considering the interannual changes of the mean rainfall (Fig. 5), there will be a strong interannual fluctuation marked by a succession of years for which the mean rainfall will decrease or increase in the six zones of the country in the present-day and medium term (2015–2050) under the three scenarios. From 2066 onwards, there will be a general decrease of the mean rainfall in the six zones of the country under the three scenarios. This decrease will be more pronounced under the SSP585 scenario and less under the SSP126.

Figure 6 presents the changes in the number of rainy days (in percentage) in the near, mid and far future over Senegal under three different scenarios. In the near future (2021–2040), the results project a slight increase in the number of rainy days in the northeast

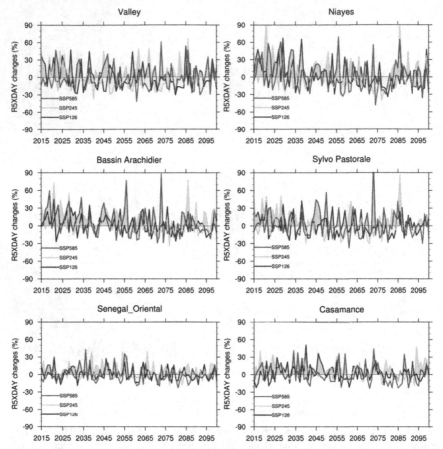

Fig. 3. Year-to-year changes in total 5-day rainfall under the three scenarios and the six areas of the country. Blue, green and red lines depict SSP126, SSP245 and SSP585, respectively. (Color figure online)

and southwest of the country under the scenarios SSP2-4.5 and SSP5.8.5. This slight increase of rainfall was also observed in previous study in the near future by Mbaye et al. (2020a). The results also show that the number of rainy days decreases over some regions l of Senegal during the near future (2021–2040) under the SSP1-2.6 scenario. In the medium (2041–2070) and the far future (2071–2100), there will be a decrease in the number of rainy days throughout Senegal under the scenarios SSP2-4.5 and SSP5.8.5.

This decline will be much greater in the centre and north of the country and will have negative consequences on pastoralism, which is one of the pillars of the country's economy.

These dry conditions in mid and far futures were also observed in the past by Mbaye et al. (2021) over Sub-Saharan countries.

Figure 7, shows the temporal variations of the mean temperature in the future with respect to the historical period. The results show that all six areas of the country have

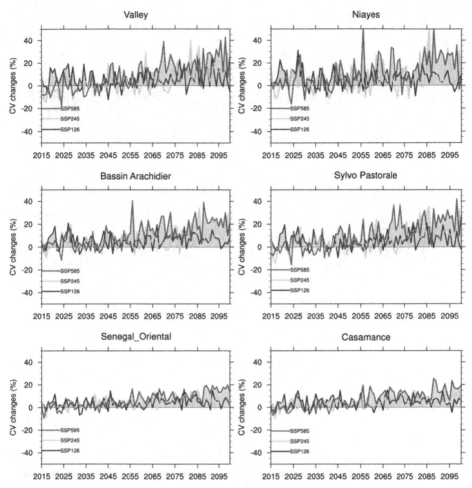

Fig. 4. Interannual changes in the coefficient of variation of precipitation and the six areas of the country. Blue, green and red lines depict SSP126, SSP245 and SSP585, respectively. (Color figure online)

experienced a weak warming during the historical period 2015–2020. The temperatures will increase in all six areas of the country under the three scenarios which highest magnitude for the SSP585. The warming trend will increase by 2050s under the SSP245 scenario (Fig. 8). In addition, agriculture, which is an important source of income for the country's farmers, is the most sensitive sector to temperature changes. Indeed, a strong increases of temperature could inhibit the growth of some plants (Salack et al. 2015; Basak et al. 2013) or reduce their growing cycle which could lead to yield losses. For example, some crops yields such as wheat, rice, maize, or peanuts could be significantly impacted by extremely high temperatures. These temperature increases can also have negative impacts on human health as shown by Hass et al. (2016) and Garland et al. (2015). This increase could be linked to some factors such as the warming of the Sahara,

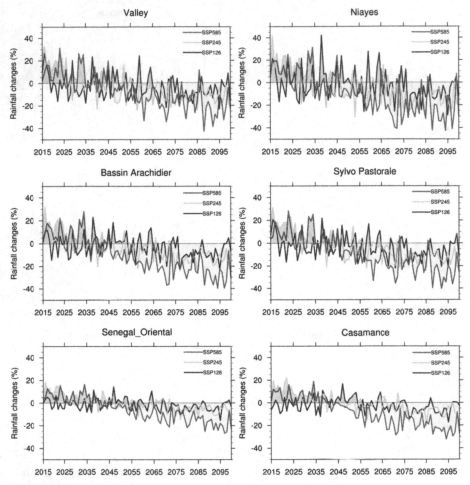

Fig. 5. Interannual changes in mean precipitation and the six areas of the country. Blue, green and red lines depict SSP126, SSP245 and SSP585, respectively. (Color figure online)

the increasing concentration of aerosols and greenhouse gases in the atmosphere (in Saley and Salack 2023).

Generally, temperatures could reach more than 3 °C under the scenario SSP245 at the end of the century. Eastern Senegal shows the highest warming while the river valley shows the lowest increase. The shift in warming between the different zones appears around 2050; this could be explained by the dominance of internal climate variability over projections at near horizons, while anthropogenic forcing have much more influence over the long term in climate simulations.

Figure 9 presents the spatial patterns of annual mean temperature change over Senegal during the future under the SSP126, SSP245 and SSP585. The results show that the whole country will undergo warming under the three scenarios during the near future (2021–2040), the medium (2041–2070) and the far future (2071–2100). This warming

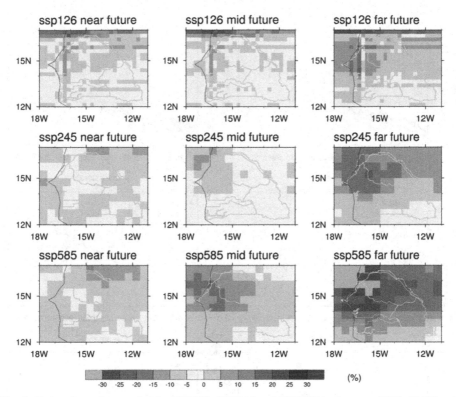

Fig. 6. Rainy days changes for the SSP126, SSP245 and SSP585 in the near (2021–2040), mid (2041–2070) and far future (2071–2100) over Senegal.

will increase at the end of the century under the three scenarios. During the near future (period 2021–2040), the warming will be more pronounced under the SSP126 scenario. There will be no large differences between the SSP245 and SSP585 scenarios during the near future. The warming will increase considerably in the eastern part of the country during the medium and far future under the SSP585 scenario. This area could face a situation of thermal discomfort of populations and livestock.

The increase of temperatures should lead to an intensification of the hydrological cycle. Todzo et al. (2020) have underlined that this intensification is expected to increase over the Sahel as a result of increasing rainfall intensity and lengthening of dry spells. Moreover, the increasing temperatures could favor an increase in the rainfall intensity through the the Clausius–Clapeyron (CC) relation. In addition, extreme rainfall are projected to intensify with increasing moisture under global warming following the Clausius-Clapeyron (CC) relationship (Martinez and Neelin 2023).

Figure 10 summarizes the changes in mean temperature and precipitation in each eco-geographic zone over the near, middle and far future. Thus, for the near future, the rates of change do not exceed 1.5 °C whatever the scenario considered. In generally, the warming is around 1 °C with small increases (>5%) in precipitation under the SSP245 and SSP585 scenarios. Relatively normal conditions for precipitation accompanied by

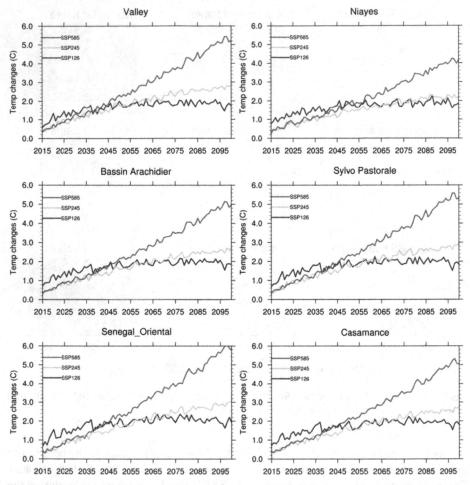

Fig. 7. Interannual changes in average temperatures for six different areas of the country. Blue, green and red lines show SSP126, SSP245 and SSP585, respectively. (Color figure online)

a warming of around 2 °C are found at medium term under the low scenario SSP126. In addition, the warming is accentuated with the highest scenario SSP585 (increase of 2 to 3 °C). The decrease in rainfall is much more marked in the groundnut basin, while for temperatures warming are more pronounced in eastern Senegal. At the end of century, the decrease in precipitation varies from −5% (eastern Senegal) to −25% (groundnut basin), while the increase in average temperature varies from 3.5 °C (in the Niayes area) to 4.85 °C (in eastern Senegal).

The decrease of rainfall is in line with the work of Cook et al. (2022) who fund a drier western Sahel. In general, the rates of change are greater under the SSP585 scenario for both temperature and precipitation in the far future. The increase in temperatures will lead to more water losses through evapotranspiration because the increases in PET (potential evapotranspiration) would have a larger drying effect on the surface layer (Zhao and

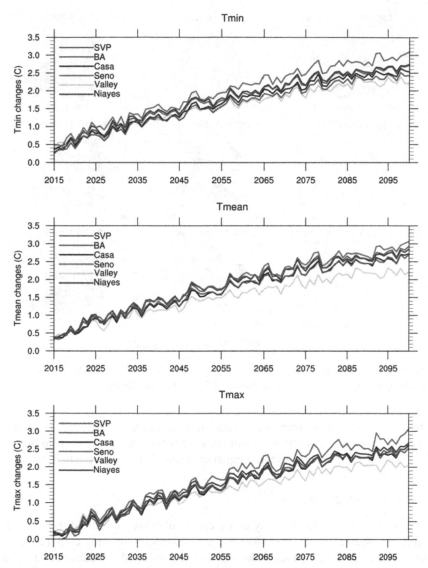

Fig. 8. Absolute change in temperature under the SSP 245 scenario. SVP: sylvopastoral, BA: groundnut basin, casa: Casamance, seno: eastern Senegal. The minimum temperature (top row), the mean temperature (medium row) and the maximum temperature (bottom row) were considered.

Dai 2022). In addition, this decrease of rainfall was revealed by Todzo et al. (2020) who found that mean precipitation decreases with the increase of temperature over the Sahel. The changes are more pronounced under the extreme scenario (SSP585); this means that more there will be warming, more the impacts will be great. Osima et al. (2018) have underlined the higher effect of global warming under 2 °C level compared to the 1.5 °C warming level over the Greater Horn of Africa. This warming will most likely

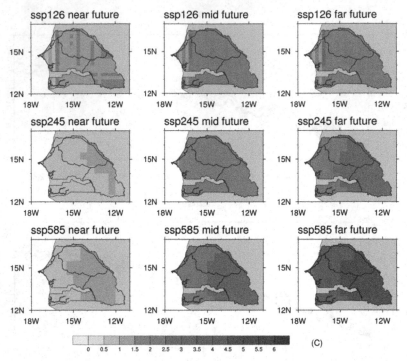

Fig. 9. Annual change in mean temperature for the SSP126, SSP245 and SSP585 in the near (2021–2040), mid (2041–2070) and far future (2071–2100) over Senegal.

lead to an increase in evapotranspiration and heat waves particularly in the eastern and south-eastern regions. Furthermore, Myhre et al. (2019) found that for a 2 K global mean surface warming, the extreme events frequency would double or triple in the future.

4.2   River Discharge Changes

In this section, we have used the hydrological simulations carried out in West Africa within the framework of the AMMA-2050 project by Rameshwaran et al. (2022). The analyses were carried out on three major watersheds, namely: the Casamance River basin (Fig. 11), the Gambia River (Fig. 12), and the Senegal River watershed (Fig. 13).

We considered only hydrometric stations located in Senegal for transboundary basins. The inter-annual change rates were calculated relative to the baseline period 1985–2014. Strong interannual variations are observed in all the stations studied in all the watersheds areas. From 2015 to 2045, the watersheds could experience slight increases in flows (20%) as shown in Figs. 11, 12 and 13. All the watersheds will face a considerable drop in flows up to 40% towards the end of the century with the SSP585 scenario. In the Casamance River basin, the Medina Namo station recorded the most significant changes of up to -50%. The stations of Simenti and Gouloumbou would be much more affected by the hygrometric deficit than those of Kédougou and Mako in the Gambia River basin.

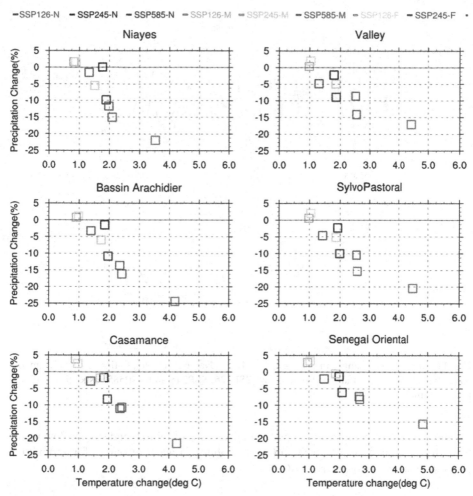

Fig. 10. Relation between absolute change in mean temperature and relative change in precipitation under the SSP126, SSP245 and SSP585 scenarios for the near, mid and far future. SVP: sylvopastoral, basin A: groundnut basin, Casa: Casamance, Seno: eastern Senegal).

For the watershed of the Senegal River, the stations of Podor, Matam and Bakel show similar trends; while the hydrometric station of Kidira would experience the most pronounced changes. This was revealed by Mbaye et al. (2020b) in the Faleme Basin where a downward trend in annual and monthly average flows is expected. These hydrological conditions could negatively impact water uses (human water consumption, agriculture, livestock, fishing, mines, industries, etc.). In addition to these, the salinization of soils, the degradation of vegetation, the disappearance of native animal and plant species, diseases over the Senegal River valley and the estuary (Taibi et al. 2023) may increase the vulnerability of the basin and the people.

This decline of river discharge was also suggested by Dembélé et al. (2022) in a West African basin (Volta River Basin) decrease under RCP2.6 and RCP4.5 scenarios. Hence,

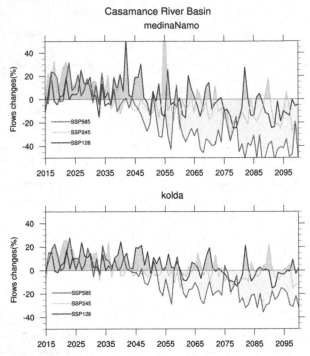

Fig. 11. Interannual changes in discharge for Médina Namo and Kolda stations in the Casamance River basin. Blue, green and red lines show SSP126, SSP245 and SSP585 respectively. (Color figure online)

the increase of temperature combined with decreased of rainfall and stream flow would have drastic consequences for the future availability of water resources for agricultural purposes and hydropower (NASAC 2015).

The Gambia River Basin

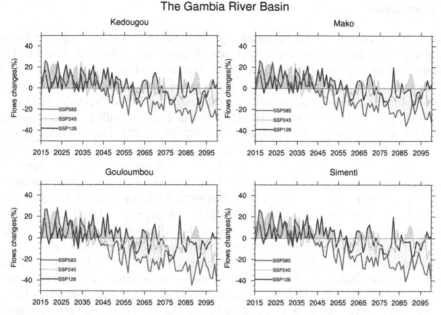

Fig. 12. Interannual changes in discharge for Kédougou, Mako, Simenti and Gouloumbou stations in the Gambia River basin. Blue, green and red lines show SSP126, SSP245 and SSP585 respectively. (Color figure online)

Senegal River Basin

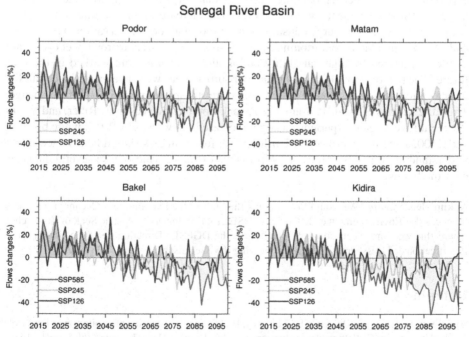

Fig. 13. Interannual changes in discharge for Podor, Matam, Kidira and Bakel stations in the Senegal River basin. Blue, green and red lines show SSP126, SSP245 and SSP585 respectively. (Color figure online)

5 Conclusion

This study assessed the hydroclimate changes over Senegal and its major river basins. The new climate change scenarios SSPs (Shared Socioeconomic Pathways) from CMIP6 models were used under different time slices. The first part of this work was focused to the changes in rainfall and temperatures over six eco-geographical zones in Senegal; the hydrological changes were assessed over the three major river basins in Senegal, in the second part. In the first part, the results show that Rainfall is likely to decrease over almost the whole Senegal in the far future under SSP126, SSP245 and SSP585 scenarios. The results also show that the number of rainy days decreases over almost all of Senegal during the near future (2021–2040) under the SSP1-2.6 scenario. In the medium term (2041–2070) and the far future (2071–2100), there will be a decrease in the number of rainy days throughout Senegal under the scenarios SSP2-4.5 and SSP5.8.5. This decline will be much greater in the center and north of the country and will have negative consequences on pastoralism, which is one of the pillars of the country's economy. Moreover, the decrease in heavy rainfall will be much more felt in the far future (2071–2100) over the six areas of the country under scenario SSP5.8.5. The decrease in rainfall is much more marked in the groundnut basin, while temperatures are warming up more in eastern Senegal. As for the far future, the decrease in precipitation varies from -5% (eastern Senegal) to -25% (groundnut basin). As for the average temperature, it will rise from 3.5 C (in the Niayes area) to 4.85 C (in eastern Senegal). This decrease in rainfall will have negative consequences on agriculture. In terms of temperature, a general increase is noted under these three scenarios. Much of the country could experience much larger temperature increases than the 1.5 °C and 2.0 °C levels set by the 2015 Paris Agreement for all scenarios. The increase in temperature in the future could lead to increased energy consumption for food and food preservation in rural areas and for cooling and air conditioning in urban areas. In addition, extreme wet events are also characterized by high variability and a slight increase more marked in the near future. The risk of flooding in urban and peri-urban areas would be exacerbate with the increase in extreme wet events. Future flows are strongly impacted by climate change. Thus, the stations of Kolda (Casamance River), Gouloumbou (Gambia River) and Kidira (Senegal River) could experience a slight increase in flow rates by 2030; while by 2060 and 2100, a decline is projected. Furthermore, future studies should be oriented in the understanding of the dynamics of hydrological extremes which cause several damages over the basins.

Acknowledgements. We would like to thank the Staff of the Laboratoire d'Océanographie, des Sciences de l'Environnement et du Climat (LOSEC) at the University Assane Seck of Ziguinchor where this work has been done. We thank also the DGPRE (Direction de la Gestion et de la Planification des Ressources en Eau) for proving the river discharge data.

References

Agyekum, J., Annor, T., Quansah, E., Lamptey, B., Okafor, G.: Extreme precipitation indices over the Volta Basin: CMIP6 model evaluation. Sci. Afr. **16**, e01181 (2022). https://doi.org/10.1016/j.sciaf.2022.e01181. ISSN 2468-2276

Akinsanola, A.A., Zhou, W.: Projections of West African summer monsoon rainfall extremes from two CORDEX models. Clim. Dyn. **52**, 2017–2028 (2019). https://doi.org/10.1007/s00 382-018-4238-8

Almazroui, M., Saeed, F., Saeed, S., et al.: Projected change in temperature and precipitation over Africa from CMIP6. Earth Syst. Environ. **4**, 455–475 (2020). https://doi.org/10.1007/s41748-020-00161-x

Basak, J.K., Titumir, R.A.M., Biswas, J.K., Mohinuzzaman, M.: Impacts of temperature and carbon dioxide on rice yield in Bangladesh. Bangladesh Rice J. **17**(1&2), 15–25 (2013)

Cook, P.A., Black, E.C.L., Verhoef, A., Macdonald, D.M.J., Sorensen, J.P.R.: Projected increases in potential groundwater recharge and reduced evapotranspiration under future climate conditions in West Africa. J. Hydrol. Reg. Stud. **41**, 101076 (2022). https://doi.org/10.1016/j.ejrh.2022.101076

Dembele, M., et al.: Contrasting changes in hydrological processes of the Volta River Basin under global warming. Hydrol. Earth Syst. Sci. **26**(5), 1481–1506 (2022). https://doi.org/10.5194/hess-26-1481-2022

Engelbrecht, F., Adegoke, J., et al.: Projections of rapidly rising surface temperatures over Africa under low mitigation. Environ. Res. Lett. **10**, 085004 (2015). https://doi.org/10.1088/1748-9326/10/8/085004

Faye, A., Akinsanola, A.A.: Evaluation of extreme precipitation indices over West Africa in CMIP6 models. Clim. Dyn. **58**, 925–939 (2022). https://doi.org/10.1007/s00382-021-05942-2

Garland, R.M., et al.: Regional projection of extreme apparent temperature days in Africa and the related potential risk to human health. Int. J. Environ. Res. Public Health **12**, 12577–12604 (2015). https://doi.org/10.3390/ijerph121012577

Hass, A.L., Ellis, K.N., Mason, L.R., Hathaway, J.M., Howe, D.A.: Heat and humidity in the city: neightborhood heat index variability in a mid-sized city in the Southeastern United States. Int. J. Environ. Res. Public Health **13**, 117 (2016). https://doi.org/10.3390/ijerph13010117

IPCC. Changements climatiques 2014: Rapport de synthèse. Contribution des Groupes de travail I, II et III au cinquième Rapport d'évaluation du Groupe d'experts intergouvernemental sur l'évolution du climat [Sous la direction de l'équipe de rédaction principale, R.K. Pachauri et L.A. Meyer]. GIEC, Genève, Suisse, p. 16 (2014)

Martinez-Villalobos, C., Neelin, J.D.: Regionally high risk increase for precipitation extreme events under global warming. Sci. Rep. **13**, 5579 (2023). https://doi.org/10.1038/s41598-023-32372-3

Mbaye, M.L., Sylla, M.B., Tall, M.: Impacts of 1.5 and 2.0 °C global warming on water balance components over Senegal in West Africa. Atmosphere **10**(11), 712 (2019). https://doi.org/10.3390/atmos10110712

Mbaye, M.L., Sy, K., Faty, B., Sall, S.M.: Hydroclimate analysis under 1.5 and 2 °C global warming in the Faleme river basin. In: Thorn, J.P.R., Gueye, A., Hejnowicz, A.P. (eds.) InterSol 2020. LNICSSITE, vol. 321, pp. 121–133. Springer, Cham (2020a). https://doi.org/10.1007/978-3-030-51051-0_9

Mbaye, M.L., Sy, K., Faty, B., Sall, S.M.: Modeling the impact of 15 and 20 °C global warming on the hydrology of the Faleme river basin (West Africa). J. Hydrol. Reg. Stud. **31**, 100719 (2020b). https://doi.org/10.1016/j.ejrh.2020.100719

Mbaye, M.L., Bodian, A., Kimambo, O.N., Rouamba, F.I., Gaveta, E.: Analyses of past extremes precipitation-evapotranspiration indices over Sub-Saharan countries. J. Extreme Events **08**(04), 2250002 (2021). https://doi.org/10.1142/S2345737622500026

Mohino, E., Rodríguez-Fonseca, B., Losada, T., et al.: Changes in the interannual SST-forced signals on West African rainfall. AGCM intercomparison. Clim. Dyn. **37**, 1707–1725 (2011). https://doi.org/10.1007/s00382-011-1093-2

Myhre, G., Alterskjær, K., Stjern, C.W., et al.: Frequency of extreme precipitation increases extensively with event rareness under global warming. Sci. Rep. **9**, 16063 (2019). https://doi.org/10.1038/s41598-019-52277-4

NASAC: Climate Change Adaptation and Resilience in Africa: Recommendations to Policymakers, Network of African Science Academies (2015). https://nasaconline.org/index.php/2016/09/12/climate-change-adaptation-and-resilience-in-africa-recommendations-to-policy makers-2

Niang, I., et al.: Africa. In: Barros, V.R., et al. (eds.) Impacts, Adaptation, and Vulnerability. Part B: Regional Aspects. Contribution of Working Group II to the Fifth Assessment Report of the Intergovernmental Panel on Climate Change, pp. 1199–1265. Cambridge University Press, Cambridge (2014). https://doi.org/10.2134/agronj2010.0303

Nicholson, S.E.: The West African Sahel – a review of recent studies on the rainfall regime and its interannual variability. ISRN Meteorol. **2013**, 1–32 (2013). https://doi.org/10.1155/2013/453521

O'Neill, B.C., et al.: The roads ahead: narratives for shared socioeconomic pathways describing world futures in the 21st century. Glob. Environ. Chang. **42**, 169–180 (2017). https://doi.org/10.1016/j.gloenvcha.2015.01.004

Osima, S., et al.: Environ. Res. Lett. **13**, 065004 (2018). https://doi.org/10.1088/1748-9326/aaba1b

Rameshwaran, P., Bell, V.A., Brown, M.J., Davies, H.N.: Historical (1950-2014) and projected (2015-2100) hydrological model (HMF-WA) estimates of monthly mean and annual maximum river flows across West Africa driven by CMIP6 projected climate data. NERC EDS Environmental Information Data Centre (Dataset) (2022). https://doi.org/10.5285/346124fd-a0c6-490f-b5af-eaccbb26ab6b

Riahi, K., et al.: The shared socioeconomic pathways and their energy, land use, and greenhouse gas emissions implications: an overview. Glob. Environ. Chang. **42**, 153–168 (2017). https://doi.org/10.1016/j.gloenvcha.2016.05.009

Salack, S., Sarr, B., Sangare, S.K., Ly, M., Sanda, I.S., Kunstmann, H.: Crop-climate ensemble scénarios to improve risk assessment and resilience in the semi-arid regions of West Africa. Clim. Res. **65**, 107–121 (2015)

Saley, I.A., Salack, S.: Present and future of heavy rain events in the Sahel and West Africa. Atmosphere **14**, 965 (2023). https://doi.org/10.3390/atmos14060965

Taïbi, A.N., Kane, A., Bourlet, M., Lorin, M., Ballouche, A.: The Senegal River, a disturbed lifeline in the Sahel. In: Wantzen, K.M. (ed.): River Culture – Life as a Dance to the Rhythm of the Waters, pp. 79–113. UNESCO Publishing, Paris (2023). https://doi.org/10.54677/YRPT3013

Todzo, S., Bichet, A., Diedhiou, A.: Intensification of the hydrological cycle expected in West Africa over the 21st century. Earth Syst. Dyn. **11**, 319–328 (2020). https://doi.org/10.5194/esd-11-319-2020

Zhao, T., Dai, A.: CMIP6 model-projected hydroclimatic and drought changes and their causes in the twenty-first century. J. Clim.Clim. **35**(3), 897–921 (2022)

Cotton Plant Pests and Phenology Knowledge Management in Côte d'Ivoire Using Semantic Web Technologies

Kouaho N'Guessan Narcisse Tehia[1,3]($\boxtimes$) , Sadouanouan Malo[1] ,
Appoh Kouamé[2] , Malanno Kouakou[3] , Kouadio Kra Norbert Bini[3],
and Ochou Germain Ochou[3]

[1] Université Nazi Boni, Bobo-Dioulasso, Burkina Faso
tehiako@gmail.com
[2] Institut National Polytechnique Félix Houphouët Boigny, Yamoussoukro, Côte d'Ivoire
[3] Centre National de Recherche Agronomique, Bouaké, Côte d'Ivoire

Abstract. In this paper, we are interested in the management of knowledge on the dynamics of pests and the phenology of cotton plant. This issue is a serious concern for the cotton sector in Côte d'Ivoire. Indeed, enormous parasitic pressures cause crop losses that vary between 30% and 100% of the production potential. A phytosanitary surveillance strategy for cotton has therefore been put in place. It is in this context that an ontologically based decision support system has been proposed. This system includes a mobile application for data collection and an ontology-based semantic wiki for knowledge management. The mobile application is deployed, and an ontology dedicated to the phytosanitary surveillance of cotton plant has been proposed. This ontology should be used as a knowledge base for the semantic wiki. We present in this paper the implementation of this semantic wiki that we call SYSPARCOT-CI WikiS. This platform is the first of its kind in cotton cultivation, mainly in phytosanitary surveillance. It is based on Semantic MediaWiki. The data from this semantic wiki as well as the data from the mobile application will be used to populate the ontology and to enrich it. The construction approach of our semantic wiki platform is based on *ontologies for wikis*. Using the ontology we built, we constructed a semantic web platform. Then, using a Python script, this ontology was imported into the semantic wiki.

Keywords: Knowledge management · Semantic MediaWiki · Ontology · Web platform · SPARQL · RDF

1 Introduction

Cotton is largely cultivated in the countries of the West African sub-region [1]. In Côte d'Ivoire, it is mainly cultivated in the central and northern regions. It allows the producers who cultivate it to prosper financially [2]. Unfortunately, cotton cultivation is confronted with enormous parasitic pressures. These pressures cause crop losses that vary between 30% and 100% of production potential [3, 4]. To reduce pest damage and limit crop losses, it is necessary to update knowledge on cotton plant pests and phenology. Indeed, this knowledge is influenced by climatic and environmental changes [5].

© ICST Institute for Computer Sciences, Social Informatics and Telecommunications Engineering 2024
Published by Springer Nature Switzerland AG 2024. All Rights Reserved
A. Seeam et al. (Eds.): InterSol 2023, LNICST 541, pp. 205–217, 2024.
https://doi.org/10.1007/978-3-031-51849-2_14

To update knowledge, a systematic surveillance was set up in the ivorian production zones. The implementation of this surveillance for more than forty years is not without difficulty. To overcome these problems, we proposed in [6] a solution to facilitate the collection and transfer of phytosanitary data in real time from cotton plant parcels. This surveillance is the main activity that allows us to update our knowledge of cotton plant pest population dynamics and phenology every year. To build a collaborative platform for the management of knowledge from cotton plant surveillance, we proposed in [7] a domain ontology, ontoSYSPARCOTCI. Based on this ontology, we propose in this paper a collaborative platform for homogeneous communication between cotton sector actors and management of knowledge on pests and phenology of cotton plant. Indeed, by this platform, actors will be able to share, reuse and capitalize on knowledge and experiences in the domain of cotton plant phytosanitary surveillance [19]. The implementation of this platform is done with MediaWiki which is a powerful and flexible web wiki platform for collaborative content creation and management. The integration of semantics MediaWiki, an extension of MediaWiki, allows for easier semantic search and exploration of the dataset contained in the platform, which we name SYSPARCOT-CI WikiS. The construction approach of our semantic wiki platform is based on ontologies for wikis.

Except introduction and conclusion, this paper is structured in three parts. The first part deals with the related works. The second part is devoted to the implementation of SYSPARCOT-CI WikiS. Finally, the third part presents the results and discussion of part two.

2 Related Works

2.1 Brief State of the Art on Semantic Wikis

The notion of a Wiki was first introduced by Ward Cunnigham in 1995 [8]. The term Wiki means "quickly" [9]. It is of Hawaiian origin and can be defined as a class of groupware that allows to co-construct a knowledge base in an agile way. It is presented in the form of a website that can be accessed, modified, or enriched according to the privileges defined for each user. There are several wikis platform, the most famous of which is Wikipedia[1]. In practice, Wikis are generally composed of a set of editable pages, organized in categories, and linked together by hypertext links. The content, structuring, layout, and organization of Wiki pages are the result of the collaboration of a community of users. The limitations of wikis have led to integration of semantics web [10]. Thus, Semantic Wikis were born. Contrary to traditional Wikis, Semantic Wiki considers the meaning of the terms. Indeed, Semantic Wikis characterize resources and the links between them by formalizing them in the form of triplets to make them exploitable by machines through artificial reasoning processes. The power of Semantic Wikis comes from the fact that they combine Wikis and Semantic Web technologies [11]. To build a semantic Wiki, two types of approaches exist namely ontologies for wiki (OFW) and wiki for ontologies (WFO) [10]. The first approach consists in building a Semantic Wiki from an ontology. The second approach consists in building a vocabulary and a knowledge base from a wiki, i.e., an ontology. There are several Wikis, the most popular of which is MediaWiki. This last is an open-source wiki engine, which is used by all projects of the WikiMedia Foundation [8]. It is constantly updated and is maintained by a strong community.

---

[1] https://www.wikipedia.org/ accessed in April 2023.

One of the additional reasons for choosing MediaWiki are its features. Indeed, MediaWiki facilitates a good co-elaboration of knowledge, thematic search, contributions, traceability of contributions, constitution of a knowledge base [8, 9]. The extension that transforms MediaWiki into a semantic web platform is Semantic MediaWiki. Thanks to the latter, the MediaWiki technology is able to facilitate the construction of a virtual community related to a domain for knowledge management with query and export capabilities. Semantic MediaWiki can implement both approaches. Given the existence of an ontology for cotton plant surveillance [7], we opted for the ontologies for Wiki approach in the construction of our Semantic Wiki. There are semantic Wikis based on the ontologies for wiki approach such as IKE WIKI[2], Kiwi[3]. Kiwi being the improved version of IKE WIKI. Unfortunately, they aren't maintained anymore.

2.2 Semantic Wikis as Platforms for Sharing and Co-constructing Knowledge

There are several projects in the literature relating to semantic web platforms. Based on knowledge graphs, these platforms enable multi-scale data to be integrated, as was the case in [12], whose objective was to build networks of molecular interactions from scattered data in order to identify key genes for plant improvement, specifically rice. Semantic web technologies enable content to be created, reused, linked and shared across the web [13]. In [14], Eric Leclerq et al. proposed an information system using the semantic wiki approach for knowledge production by developing WikiBridge. WikiBridge was developed by [14] from the MediaWiki wiki. It is of ontologies for wikis type. Papa F. Diallo in [9] has set up a virtual community made up of three layers, namely GUI, persistence, and semantics. This platform uses Semantic MediaWiki and Exhibit for the GUI layer, Jena, SPARQL engines and rules for the semantic layer and Virtuoso for persistence. To share endogenous knowledge for adaptation of cropping techniques in a context of climate change, Trawina [11] set up a virtual semantic web platform combining semantic Media Wiki, SweetWiki, Virtuoso and Jena EE, which enabled it to implement a Java API for management of its ontology. There is a plethora of methods in literature for building a semantic web platform. However, each author justifies his or her choices because there is no set construction methodology. Our field of study is the phytosanitary surveillance of cotton in Côte d'Ivoire. KOFIS (Knowledge for Organic Farming and Innovative System) is an ontology-based knowledge management system for agriculture [15]. It provides practical solutions to sharing and shortages of information in organic farming. Unfortunately, it does not deal specifically with plant health monitoring in cotonculture. Lack of farmer input into data collection and decision-making raises issues of trust between farmers and smart farming technologies, which led [16] to set up a platform for integrating textual data in agriculture to detect natural hazards. [17] has proposed a platform for integrating heterogeneous data into knowledge bases to support and inform farmers and researchers in their activities in real time using semantic technologies and linked data. To our knowledge, no work has been done on the construction of a semantic web platform in the domain of phytosanitary surveillance of cotton, particularly in Côte d'Ivoire. Having an ontology at our disposal, we plan to build a semantic web platform that will communicate with a FUSEKI server. Despite Virtuoso's storage capacity [9], our choice to use FUSEKI is explained by the fact that

---

[2] https://wiki.c2.com/?IkeWiki accessed in April 2023.

[3] https://wiki.c2.com/?KiWi accessed in April 2023.

initially, we have a PostgreSQL database of phytosanitary surveillance of cotton in Côte d'Ivoire, which is populated by a mobile application that we designed and developed. FUSEKI server also offers improved execution time for SPARQL queries [18]. FUSEKI server is dedicated to storing RDF triples, SPARQL query management and is able to function as a high-performance operating system service [11].

3   Implementation of SYSPARCOT-CI WikiS

The construction of our collaborative virtual community is based on the ontology proposed in [7], realized using Protégé (Fig. 1).

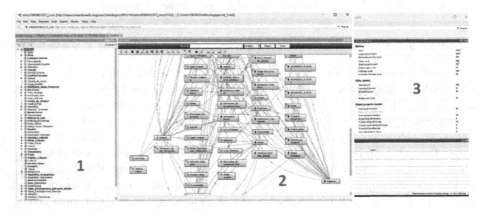

Fig. 1. Extract from ontology in Protégé (concepts (1) + knowledge graph (2)) and metrics (3)

Relative to competence questions, some evaluation results of this ontology are presented in Fig. 2, Fig. 3 and Fig. 4. Formulated in French and noted CQ1, CQ2 and CQ3, these questions have their English translation in titles of Fig. 2, Fig. 3 and Fig. 4 respectively.

CQ 1 : Quels sont les maladies du cotonnier en Côte d'Ivoire ?

Algorithme 1 : Requête SPARQL
PREFIX rdf: <http://www.w3.org/1999/02/22-rdf-syntax-ns#>
PREFIX owl: <http://www.w3.org/2002/07/owl#>
PREFIX rdfs: <http://www.w3.org/2000/01/rdf-schema#>
PREFIX xsd: <http://www.w3.org/2001/XMLSchema#>
PREFIX ontosys:<http://www.semanticweb.org/user/ontologies/2022/10/ontoSYPARCOTCI_core#>
SELECT ?maladie_cotonnier
WHERE { ?maladie_cotonnier rdf:type ?nuisible.
?maladie_cotonnier ontosys:est_nuisible_de ontosys:Cotonnier.
FILTER(?nuisible=ontosys:Maladie)
}

Résultat de CQ1

	maladie_cotonnier
Virescence florale	
Fusariose	

Fig. 2. SPARQL query and answer to the competency question "What are diseases of cotton plant in Côte d'Ivoire?"

CQ 2 : Quels sont les ravageurs du cotonnier en Côte d'Ivoire ?

Algorithme 2 : Requête SPARQL

```
PREFIX rdf: <http://www.w3.org/1999/02/22-rdf-syntax-ns#>
PREFIX owl: <http://www.w3.org/2002/07/owl#>
PREFIX rdfs: <http://www.w3.org/2000/01/rdf-schema#>
PREFIX xsd: <http://www.w3.org/2001/XMLSchema#>
PREFIX ontosys:<http://www.semanticweb.org/user/ontologies/2022/10/ontoSYPARCOTCI_core#>
SELECT ?ravageur_cotonnier
        WHERE {?ravageur_cotonnier rdf:type ?arthropode.
        ?ravageur_cotonnier ontosys:est_nuisible_de ontosys:Cotonnier.
        FILTER(?arthropode=ontosys:Arthropode_Nuisible)
}
```

Résultat de CQ2

	ravageur_cotonnier
Pectinophora gossypiella	
Haritalodes derogata	
Anomis flava	
Spodoptera littoralis	
Dysdercus voelkeri	
Diparopsis watersi	
Earias insulana	
Helicoverpa armigera	
Thaumatotibia leucotreta	
Polyphagotarsonemus latus	
Jacobiella fascialis	

Fig. 3. SPARQL query and answer to the skill question "What are arthropod pest of cotton plant in Côte d'Ivoire?"

CQ 3 : Quelles sont les variétés locales de coton cultivées en Côte d'Ivoire ?

Algorithme 3 : Requête SPARQL

```
PREFIX rdf: <http://www.w3.org/1999/02/22-rdf-syntax-ns#>
PREFIX owl: <http://www.w3.org/2002/07/owl#>
PREFIX rdfs: <http://www.w3.org/2000/01/rdf-schema#>
PREFIX xsd: <http://www.w3.org/2001/XMLSchema#>
PREFIX ontosys:<http://www.semanticweb.org/user/ontologies/2022/10/ontoSYPARCOTCI_core#>
SELECT (?subject as ?plante) (?object as ?variété)
        WHERE {?subject rdf:type ontosys:Plante.
        ?subject ontosys:a_pour_variete_locale ?object.
        FILTER(?subject = ontosys:Cotonnier)
}
```

Résultat de CQ3

plante	variété
Cotonnier	Y331_BLT/R2
Cotonnier	Y331_BLT/R3
Cotonnier	Y331_BLT/R1
Cotonnier	SICAMA_VIR1/R3
Cotonnier	SICAMA_VIR1/R1
Cotonnier	SICAMA_VIR1/R2
Cotonnier	GOUASSOU_FUS1/R3
Cotonnier	GOUASSOU_FUS1/R2
Cotonnier	GOUASSOU_FUS1/R1

Fig. 4. SPARQL query and answer to the skill question "What are local cotton plant varieties cultivated in Côte d'Ivoire?"

The evaluation allowed to verify that the ontology meets the specifications of the requirements defined from the exchanges with the domain experts. This evaluation consisted in formulating and executing SPARQL queries on the ontology in the Protégé software.

3.1   General System Architecture

In [6], we proposed an original global architecture of our system composed of three technological machines and tools. This general architecture of cotton plant phytosanitary surveillance system is here recalled (Fig. 5). The first part of our architecture allows domain experts to dispose of real-time plant health surveillance data during the cotton campaign. The second part gives back raw data from the data collection in time to domain experts. These two parts constitute a major innovation in the domain of phytosanitary surveillance of cotton in Côte d'Ivoire. Indeed, the acquisition of data in real time was an obstacle to regular monitoring of the phytosanitary situation of cotton plant in production zones. This work concerns the third and last part of this architecture (Fig. 5) which is represented by technology machine 3 (circled black).

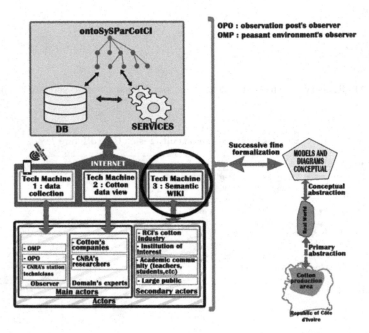

Fig. 5.   General architecture of the cotton plant phytosanitary surveillance system

Realization of the last part of our architecture consists in Semantic Wiki implementation for cotton plant pest and phenology management in Côte d'Ivoire.

3.2   SYSPARCOT-CI WikiS Use Cases

The main use cases of SYSPARCOT-CI WikiS are presented in Fig. 6. This Wiki is used to update knowledge on the spatiotemporal dynamics of pests and the phenology of cotton plant in Côte d'Ivoire. It is also used to know the spatiotemporal dynamics of pests and the phenology of cotton plant for those who are interested in them. No account creation is required for a visitor of SYSPARCOT-CI WikiS to get information.

However, any modification must be done in a secure access account that is managed by the agricultural research team in collaboration with ontologist. SYSPARCOT-CI WikiS is not closed, so it is possible to extend it by adding other use cases.

Contributions to wikis are mainly made by creating pages. In our case study, this creation has restrictions. Any visitor can create one or more pages. However, validation of these pages is reserved for experts (researchers and technicians) in the field. The creation of pages in our case study is guided by the ontology ontoSYSPARCOTCI [7]. This ontology is maintained by an ontology specialist assisted by domain experts. Administrators (domain experts and ontologists) maintain the platform and manage users. A visitor is any person in addition to administrators who visits our semantic web platform. A visitor can consult information on the wiki by browsing its various pages and create new pages.

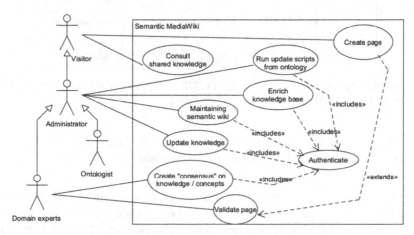

Fig. 6. Some use cases of SYSPARCOT-CI WikiS

3.3 Implementation Description

Figure 7 represents the third step in the implementation of our general architecture (Fig. 5). This third step concerns the implementation of a semantic web platform (red color). Figure 7 details connections and interactions that underlie Semantic MediaWiki implementation.

SYSPARCOT-CI WikiS is based on three main layers (Fig. 7), namely the user layer, the semantic layer, and the persistence layer. In this work, user layer is represented by Semantic MediaWiki (SMW). Semantic layer consists of the SPARQL query and Jena inference engines. Persistence layer is constituted by relational databases, an ontology, and RDF depot.

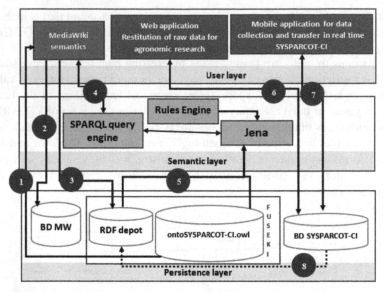

Fig. 7. Detailed internal architecture of SYSPARCOT-CI as presented in [6] according to 3 layers with focus on Semantic MediaWiki. (Color figure online)

To understand our approach, we proceed by steps. These steps show the composition of our persistence layer and how we build it. They also describe how we set up our semantic wiki.

- Step 1: It concerns the import of ontoSYSPARCOTCI into Semantic MediaWiki. The ontology was exported from Protégé in RDF format. Then, thanks to ontology2smw [10], from this RDF format, we imported it into the Semantic MediaWiki platform.
- Step 2: Semantic Platform textual data is saved directly in a database. This last created during installation and configuration of Semantic MediaWiki while the annotated data is saved in an RDF repository created in the FUSEKI server; this is Step 3.
- Step 4: From MediaWiki Semantics, SPARQL queries are performed on the FUSEKI server implementing Jena Apache. The latter exploits the RDF repositories available in the FUSEKI server (this is Step 5). SPARQL queries from SMW are possible using LinkedWiki, an extension of MW. To import ontoSYSPARCOTCI into the FUSEKI server, we exported it from Protégé in RDF format. An interface in the FUSEKI server allowed us to create an RDF repository and then import the exported ontology.
- Step 6: allows the team of the laboratory of agricultural entomology and cotton companies to extract the raw data from the relational database SYSPARCOTCI-BD. This database is fed during each cotton season by agents of cotton companies who carry out observations and measurements on the parcels via digital tablets [6] (this is Step 7).

– Step 8: Thanks to the D2RQ[4] platform, the main tool for generating RDF files from a relational database, the relational database of SYSPARCOT-CI (SYSPARCOTCI-BD) is transformed into an RDF file and then loaded as an RDF repository in the FUSEKI server by a script in an automatic way. The communication between the RDF repository from SYSPARCOTCI-BD and the ontology ontoSYSPARCOTCI is possible thanks to a mapping file that establishes the correspondences.

The import of the ontology into Semantics MediaWiki (see Step 1 of Fig. 7) allows to dispose of a vocabulary specific to the study domain to guide the administrators of the platform in the knowledge management. A series of transforms are observed during the ontology import as shown in Table 1.

Table 1. Matching the ontology syntax to the Semantic MediaWiki syntax

Ontology	OWL syntax	SMW	SMW syntax
Concept	owl: Class	Category	[[Category:Pest]]
Subconcept	rdfs:subClassOf	Subcategory	Subcategory of [[:Category: Observed Plant]] [[Category: Observed Plant]]
Instance	owl:NamedIndividual	Page	Individual Name + its category, relations, and attributes
Attribute	owl:DatatypeProperty	Attribute	[[Attribute:sowing date:: '2022–05-25']]
Relation	owl:ObjectProperty	Hyperlink	[[Attribute:is disease of::Cotton_Plant]]

Attribute is relationship between a page and a predefined type. Hyperlink is relationship between two pages.

4 Results and Discussion

Concepts or classes of the ontology have been transformed into categories (Fig. 8). One of these categories, namely Pest, is shown in Fig. 9.

---

[4] http://d2rq.org/ accessed in April 2023.

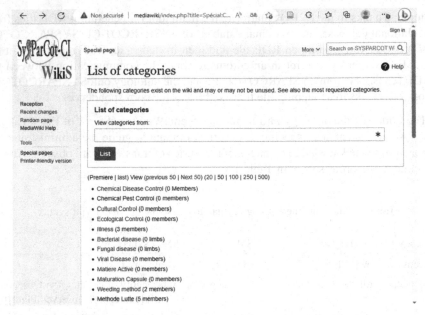

Fig. 8. Extract of the category list in SYSPARCOT-CI WikiS

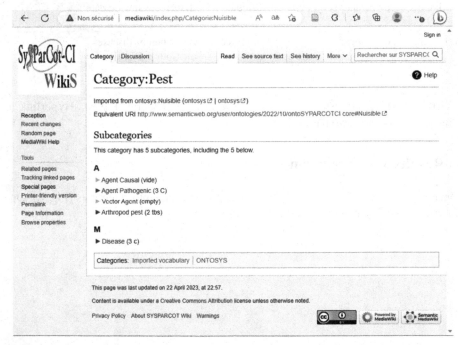

Fig. 9. Category Pests and its subcategories in SYSPARCOT-CI WikiS provided by ontoSYS-PARCOTCI (see Step 1 Fig. 7)

Detailed architecture presented and proposed approach to implement our MediaWiki semantics is one proposal among many others. We think it could be improved. However, there is no imposed methodology or tool to implement a Semantic Wiki. Respecting the ontology approach for wikis, our tests proved to be conclusive. Transforming relational DB into RDF and loading it into the FUSEKI server can be time consuming as the RDB becomes voluminous. Studies will be conducted in this direction to reduce the execution time.

Using a triple store in this case, FUSEKI server is justified by the fact that a relational database is not an ideal storage type for semantic data. However, Semantic MediaWiki uses a relational database. Also, a triple store that supports the SPARQL standard allows other applications to query it without going through the Semantic MediaWiki web frontend. This allows for independence from the semantic database for reuse. FUSEKI server allowed us also to create an endpoint to facilitate data exploitation.

Compared to traditional web, semantic web adds semantic information to web content and gives machines the ability to distinguish their meaning. In semantic web, data is linked together, and inferences are made automatically by the machine.

Currently, ontology and semantic wiki are accessible locally. Tests have been done locally as well.

5 Conclusion

A semantic wiki dedicated to knowledge resulting from cotton plant phytosanitary surveillance in Côte d'Ivoire exists. It allows to manage cotton plant pests and phenology knowledge in Côte d'Ivoire. To our knowledge, we believe that it is the first of its kind. It implements several technologies and tools that are not easy to use. These include the FUSEKI server, RDF repository, Ontology, MediaWiki and its extensions, especially Semantic MediaWiki. Finally, we were able to do it. This semantic web platform will allow to enrich the ontology that was the basis of its implementation and provided a domain vocabulary. The next part of our work will focus on three major points: wiki validation, considering user requests written in natural language and wiki improvement. Validating the wiki will involve conducting a survey to measure user satisfaction using a Likert scale. Likert is a psychometric tool used to measure attitudes in individuals. Given the inability of experts to perform SPARQL queries and master data graph schemas, we will develop an extension to take into account queries written in natural language.

References

1. Doffou, N.M.: Impact de la gestion de la résistance aux pyréthrinoïdes sur les popula-tions de cryp-tophlebia leucotreta (meyrick, 1913) (lepidoptera :tortricidae) et de pectinopho-ra gossypiella saunders, 1843 (lepidoptera : gelechiidae) en culture cotonnière en côte d'ivoire: de la sensibilité au mécanisme de résistance. UNIVERSITÉ FÉLIX HOU-PHOUËT-BOIGNY, Abidjan, Côte d'Ivoire (2013)
2. Koné, P.W.E.: Evolution spatiale et temporelle, diversité taxonomique et génétique, et mécan-isme de résistance aux insecticides chez les cicadelles du cotonnier en Côte d'Ivoire: approches de lutte intégrée. Université NANGUI ABROGOUA (2019)

3. Ochou, G.O., Matthews, G.A., Mumford, J.D.: Farmers' knowledge and perception of cotton insect pest problems in Cote d'Ivoire. Int. J. Pest Manag. **44**(1), 5–9 (1998). https://doi.org/10.1080/096708798228455

4. PR-PICA. Acte de la douzième réunion bilan du PR-PICA: restitution des résultats des activités de recherche-développement de la campagne 2018/2019 (2019)

5. Huffaker, C., Berryman, A., Turchin, P.: Dynamics and regulation of insect populations. Ecol. Entomol. **2**, 269–305 (1999)

6. Téhia, K.N.N., Malo, S., Kouamé, A., Kouakou, M., Bini, K.K.N., Ochou, O.G.: Towards an ontology-based cotton phytosanitary surveillance system: a case study in Côte d'Ivoire. In: Arai, K. (ed.) FTC 2021. LNNS, vol. 358, pp. 962–974. Springer, Cham (2022). https://doi.org/10.1007/978-3-030-89906-6_61

7. Téhia, K.N.N., Malo, S., Kouamé, A., Kouakou, M., Bini, K.K.N., Ochou, O.G.: Contribution to the construction of an ontology for the phytosanitary surveillance of cotton in Côte d'Ivoire. In: 2023 IEEE Multi-conference on Natural and Engineering Sciences for Sahel's Sustainable Development (MNE3SD), Bobo-Dioulasso, Burkina Faso, pp. 1–8. IEEE, févr (2023). https://doi.org/10.1109/MNE3SD57078.2023.10079897

8. Cunningham, W.: What is wiki. WikiWikiWeb Httpwww Wiki Orgwiki Cgi (2002)

9. Diallo, P.F.: Aspects socioculturels et temporels dans les ontologies pour les communautés virtuelles. phdthesis, COMUE Université Côte d'Azur (2015–2019); Université de Saint-Louis (Sénégal), 2016. Consulté le: 9 avril 2023. [En ligne]. Disponible sur: https://theses.hal.science/tel-01402394

10. Meilender, T.: Un wiki sémantique pour la gestion des connaissances décisionnelles - Application à la cancérologie. phdthesis, Université de Lorraine, 2013. Consulté le: 11 avril 2023. [En ligne]. Disponible sur: https://theses.hal.science/tel-00919997

11. Trawina, H.: Vers une plateforme web social et sémantique de partage de connaissances endogènes pour l'adaptation des techniques culturales dans un contexte de changement climatique. Université Nazi BONI, Bobo-Dioulasso, Burkina Faso (2022)

12. Larmande, P.: Intégration de données multi-échelles et extraction de connaissances en agronomie: exemples et perspectives. Ph.D. thesis, Montpellier II (2019)

13. Kinsella, S., Passant, A., Breslin, J.G., Decker, S., Jaokar, A.: The future of social web sites. In: Advances in Computers, pp. 121–175. Elsevier (2009). https://doi.org/10.1016/S0065-2458(09)01004-3

14. Leclercq, É., Savonnet, M.: Système d'information pour la production de connaissances. L'approche wiki sémantique. Rev. Sci. Technol. Inf.-Sér. ISI Ingénierie Systèmes Inf. **17**(3), 143–166 (2012)

15. Géraldine, A., Stephan, B., Daniel, B., Eva, L., Anais, W.: TR Irstea Motive, équipe COPAIN, Systèmes d'information communicants et agri-environnementaux. Assoc. Fr. Pour L'Intelligence Artif., p. 22 (2012)

16. Jiang, S.: Intégration de données textuelles pour la détection des risques naturels en agriculture. These de doctorat, Reims (2022). Consulté le: 13 août 2023. [En ligne]. Disponible sur: https://www.theses.fr/2022REIMS025

17. Jiang, S., Angarita, R., Chiky, R., Cormier, S., Rousseaux, F.: Towards the integration of agricultural data from heterogeneous sources: perspectives for the French agricultural context using semantic technologies. In: Dupuy-Chessa, S., Proper, H.A. (eds.) CAiSE 2020. LNBIP, vol. 382, pp. 89–94. Springer, Cham (2020). https://doi.org/10.1007/978-3-030-49165-9_8

18. Rivault, Y., Dameron, O., Le Meur, N.: Une infrastructure générique basée sur les apports du Web Sémantique pour l'analyse des bases médico-administratives. In: Plate-forme Intelligence Artificielle 2015, conférence Ingénierie des Connaissances, Rennes, France, juin 2015. Consulté le: 15 août 2023. [En ligne]. Disponible sur: https://hal.science/hal-01678828
19. Kouame, A., Brou, K.M., Lo, M., Lamy, J.B.: Vers un système iconique d'aide à la décision pour les praticiens de la médecine traditionnelle. In: Colloque Africain sur la Recherche en Informatique et en Mathématiques Appliquées (CARI 2016), Hammamet, Tunisia, oct. 2016. Consulté le: 17 août 2023. [En ligne]. Disponible sur: https://hal.science/hal-03491875

Microbial Fuel Cell for the Recovery of Sludge from the Treatment of Effluents by Electrocoagulation

Maryam Khadim Mbacké[1]([⊠]), Aby Sy[2], Cheikhou Kane[2], and Malick Mbengue[2]

[1] Laboratoire des Sciences, Technologies Avancées et Développement Durable, Université Amadou Mahtar Mbow, Dakar, Senegal
maryammbacke@gmail.com, maryam.mbacke@uam.edu.sn

[2] Laboratoire Eau Energie Environnement et Procédés Industriels (LE3PI); Equipe de recherche Procédés de Valorisation des Ressources Naturelles et Environnement (ProVaRNE), Université Cheikh Anta Diop, B.P. 5085, Dakar Fann, Senegal

Abstract. The micro-organisms present in the domestic effluents allowed the formation of an electroactive biofilm by oxidation of the organic matter on the surface of a carbon fabric anode, in a microbial fuel cell (MFC). Previous studies have demonstrated the effectiveness of the electrocoagulation process for the treatment of industrial effluents. During treatment, the metal hydroxide sludge formed adsorbs pollutants. These sludges could be recovered through their use as fuel in a microbial fuel cell. The cell was inoculated with sludge from tests on effluents taken from a wastewater treatment plant. The results showed a decrease in chemical oxygen demand by 90.27%, dissolved oxygen by 75% and turbidity by 72%. Analysis of the sludge from this treatment showed the presence of sulphite-reducing coliforms and clostridium which oxidize the organic matter contained in a substrate enriched with acetate or glucose.

The maximum power densities obtained are 41.29 mW/m^2 with acetate and 27.57 mW/m^2 with glucose respectively. The study was carried out on a microbial fuel cell with two compartments separated by an ion exchange membrane.

Keywords: Electrocoagulation · microorganism · fuel cell · biofilm

1 Introduction

Energy, like water, is one of the major contemporary issues of our time. Indeed, industrial development, population growth, agriculture and transport are, among others, sectors that contribute to the increase in energy demand and the scarcity of natural resources. The current global energy crisis has highlighted the urgency as well as the benefits of an accelerated transition to cheaper and cleaner energy sources. Microbial fuel cells (MFC) are an alternative for a double contribution: electricity production and effluent treatment.

The principle is based on the use of bacteria which convert part of the energy available in a biodegradable substrate into electricity. Indeed, microbial fuel cells are characterized

A. Seeam et al. (Eds.): InterSol 2023, LNICST 541, pp. 218–232, 2024.
https://doi.org/10.1007/978-3-031-51849-2_15

by "the use of microorganisms as catalysts" [1]. These are deposited on the exchange surfaces, at the anodes, and produce H$^+$ electrons and protons, by decomposing an organic substrate, derived from wastewater, recovered from a treatment plant. If the biological mechanisms of decomposition of the substrate are complex, we nevertheless know the corresponding reduction reaction at the cathode. MFCs can be fed with a variety of simple organic molecules (sugars, proteins, etc.) or directly with the effluents to be treated. The MFCs can be completely microbial when the catalysis of the reactions at the two electrodes is done thanks to microorganisms or semi-microbial in the case where the catalysis at the cathode is carried out by mineral catalysts [2].

The anodic oxidation reactions involved depend on the type of substrate used. In the case of acetate, the reaction is such that [3]:

$$CH_3COO^- + 4H_2O \rightarrow 2HCO_3^- + 9H^+ + 8e^- \tag{1}$$

Electrons are transferred from the biofilm to the anode by various mechanisms such as direct contact, nanowires or mediators [4]. Electrons migrate from the anode to the cathode through an external electrical circuit, while selected ions move through a separator membrane to complete the circuit.

At the cathode, oxygen is used as an oxidant in many cases, due to its availability and high reduction potential. Indeed, an ideal electron acceptor is necessary and must be durable, without interference or toxic effect on the microbial community or any other element of the system [5].

In the case of a proton exchange membrane, once the protons have diffused through the membrane, they can react with the oxygen present, leading to the generation of water according to the following reaction [3]:

$$O_2 + 4H^+ + 4e^- \rightarrow 2H_2O \tag{2}$$

The treatment of industrial effluents by electrocoagulation generates sludge composed of aluminum hydroxide and pollutants from the treated effluent. This sludge is considered as chemical waste and its recovery makes it possible to offer an integrated treatment system. The objective of this study is therefore to evaluate the potential for electricity production from electrocoagulation sludge in the context of the implementation of a microbial fuel cell.

Thus, we are going to present the process of treatment of effluents by electrocoagulation which allowed the production of sludge. Then we will present the method of microbiological analysis as well as the process of formation of the electroactive biofilm. We will discuss the operating principle of a microbial fuel cell as well as the operating parameters to be optimized. Finally, we will present the different results obtained with a discussion focused on the power generated by the system.

2 An Overview of the Recovery of Electrocoagulation Sludge

The physic-chemical and morphological characteristics of electrocoagulation sludge depend on the type of electrode used and the nature of the treated effluent.

Sharma, P. et al. [6] worked on sludge from an electrocoagulation process on distillery effluents with stainless steel electrodes. These sludges were valued as an addition in building materials. The optimal percentage of sludges that could replace cement with a marginal modification of the physicochemical properties found was 7.5.

Tezcan Un, U. et al. [7] used electrocoagulation sludge from chromium VI effluents in the production of inorganic pigments.

Sludge from effluent treatment containing TiO2-based nanoparticles has been considered as a catalyst for the activation of peroxymonosulfate (PMS) to degrade ciprofloxacin (CIP) as an emerging pollutant [8]. Treatment with titanium-based electrodes yielded sludge which was incinerated at 600 °C to produce a functional TiO2 photocatalyst. X-ray diffraction analysis revealed that the TiO2 produced under optimal electrocoagulation conditions was predominantly anatase in structure. The specific surface area of the synthesized TiO2 photocatalyst was higher than that of commercially available and widely used Degussa P-25 TiO2 [9]. The iron sludge generated by an electrocoagulation process was used for the degradation of phenol by the photo-Fenton process. Phenol degradation efficiencies were 100%, 71.3, and 51% at initial phenol concentrations of 50 mg/L, 100 mg/L, and 150 mg/L, respectively [10].

Valorisation as a dye adsorbent has also been the subject of studies [11]. Over the past ten years, we have not noted any work on the energy recovery of electrocoagulation sludge.

3 Materials and Methods

3.1 The Electrocoagulation Process

The treated effluent comes from a treatment plant. The electrocoagulation cell consists of an assembly with three electrodes (1.9 cm × 6.6 cm) immersed in the effluent with an inter-electrode distance of 2 cm. One of the electrodes is made of stainless steel serving as the cathode and the other two made of aluminum serving as the anode are connected to a galvanostat using the connection wires. A direct current of 0.66 A, i.e. a current density of 250 A/m^2, is imposed in 2 L of waste water for a period of 1 h. The experiment is repeated several times to obtain a certain amount of sludge. At the end of each experiment, three phases are observed: the lightest sludge is above, the heaviest sludge below and the treated water in the middle. Floating sludge is collected using a spatula. Then the water is decanted to recover the sludge that is at the bottom (Fig. 1).

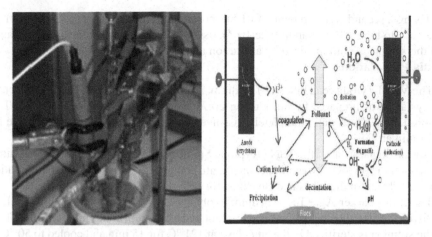

Fig. 1. Electrocoagulation cell and principle of operation

3.2 Microbiological Analysis of Sludge

The microbiological study will consist of identifying and counting the presence of microorganisms, more particularly coliforms, staphylococcus aureus and sulphite-reducing clostridium.

The identification of the microorganisms is done by preparing the EPT (Buffered Peptone Water) for the dilutions and the media where the colonies appear. The operating parameters are optimized by varying: the sample volume of 100 mL; the initial concentration from 5 to 100 mg/L; the current density from 100 to 300 A/m^2 (for an electro-active surface of 14 cm^2, the current is varied from 0.1 to 0.4 A); the initial pH of 3 to 9 (by addition of NaOH and HCl solutions at 0.1 N); the initial conductivity of 0.9 to 4.27 (by addition of a mass of NaCl ranging from 0.1 to 1 g/L); the inter-electrode distance (ied) of 0.25 to 1.5 cm.

Dye concentration was spectroscopically determined using the Beer-Lambert law (Absorbance $= \varepsilon \times \ell \times C$) applied at 592 nm, where ε is the molar absorptivity, ℓ is the solution thickness and C the CV concentration. The absorbance are measured by a spectrophotometer SPECORD 250 PLUS.

Preparing for the EPT

EPT (Buffered Peptone Water) is used for dilutions. The solution is prepared by 10 g of EPT in 500 mL of distilled water and distributed in tubes (9 mL for each tube) then sterilized in an autoclave at 121 °C for 15 min.

Diluting Method

The method of successive decimal dilution is done by aseptic sampling of 1 mL of the stock solution (sludge) using a sterile graduated pipette fitted with a suction bulb. This sample is transferred into the first tube (9 mL of EPT) which will be marked 10^{-1}, the pipette must not penetrate the 9 mL of diluent.

Using a second sterile pipette of 01 ml, proceed in the same way (withdrawal from tube 10^{-1} to tube 10^{-2} ... up to tube 10^{-9}), using a new sterile pipette for each sample and the sample is homogenized by aspiration and discharge three times.

Media Preparation

- The VRBL (violet read bile agar) medium, also called "violet red neutral bile lactose crystal", was prepared by introducing 20.75 g into 500 mL of distilled water. This solution is stirred until completely dissolved and then sterilized in an autoclave for 15 min at 121 °C.
- For the preparation of the TSN (Tryptone Sulfite Neomycin) medium, 20 g are introduced into 500 mL of water then boiled until completely dissolved. Then the solution is distributed in the tubes and sterilized for 15 min at 121 °C in an autoclave.
- The Baird Parker Agar Base medium is obtained by dissolving 30 g in 475 mL of distilled water, then left to soak and brought to the boil with continuous stirring. Then, the solution is sterilized in the autoclave at 121 °C for 15 min and cooled to 50 °C to finally add 25 mL of the vial of egg yolk with potassium tellurite.

For the TSN medium, 0.1 mL of each dilution is poured into a tube containing the medium solution. Afterwards these tubes will be incubated at 44 °C for 24 h. And the other two media (VRBL and Baird Parker) will be well mixed to have a homogeneous solution and the Baird Parker medium is distributed in the Petri dishes because it undergoes surface seeding while the VRBL will undergo deep culture.

Surface Culture
For this method, 0.1 mL of each dilution is deposited on the surface of the agar medium (pre-poured dish) then spread using a spreading rake which is passed over the surface of the agar while turn the box. This method is used for Baird Parker Agar Base medium and is incubated at 37 °C for 24 or 48 h.

Deep Cultivation
Unlike the previous culture, 0.1 mL of each dilution is placed then 10 to 15 mL of agar medium (40 to 45 °C) is poured into the dish and mixed evenly with the inoculum. The dishes are then cooled and incubated. This technique is used for the VRBL medium and the incubation is done at 44 °C in 24 h. In this case the colonies can develop on the surface or in depth.

The counting method
The appearance of colonies in the cultured medium attests to the presence of the bacteria sought in the sample.

These bacteria are determined by the following relationship:

$$\text{Number of bacteria} = \frac{\text{Number of colonies}}{\text{volume introduced} * \text{dilution}} * \frac{M}{z} \tag{3}$$

Volume introduced: 1 mL.

The number of colonies of a dilution represents the total number of colonies on the two dishes or tubes of this dilution divided by 2. The dilution chosen represents the least diluted of the media where the colonies have grown and for each dilution two dishes or tubes are seeded.

3.3 Biofilm Preparation

The biofilm is obtained by introducing carbon tissue 1 cm wide into a solution containing sludge from electrocoagulation stored in an oven at 44 °C for 3 to 4 days. These sludges from electrocoagulation have been enriched with shredded banana envelopes and acetate to increase the proliferation of microorganisms. The latter will be deposited on the surface of the carbon tissues thus constituting the biofilms (Fig. 2).

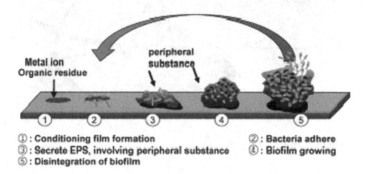

① : Conditioning film formation   ② : Bacteria adhere
③ : Secrete EPS, involving peripheral substance   ④ : Biofilm growing
⑤ : Disintegration of biofilm

Fig. 2. Biofilm formation

3.4 Design of the MFC

The cell designed in this study is entirely microbial. The sludge from electrocoagulation is introduced into the two compartments of the cell. The previously prepared biofilm is immersed in each compartment then these electrodes are connected by a connecting wire to establish a potential difference between the anode and the cathode. A voltmeter and an ammeter were used to measure voltage and current respectively.

Indeed, in the anode compartment 150 mL of sludge are introduced and 75 mL in the cathode to a height of 8.2 cm. To increase the conductivity of the compartment considered as the cathode, NaCl was added. The addition of the substrate (acetate or glucose) in the anode allows the multiplication of microorganisms.

The measurement of current and voltage was done within one day. To maintain the multiplication of microorganisms, the addition of 2 g of substrate was done as soon as there was a decrease in the amount of energy (Fig. 3).

Fig. 3. Microbial fuel cell

3.5 MFC Characterization

The Power
To better visualize the optimal operating point for the use of the battery, the voltage-intensity product is calculated in order to obtain the power output.

$$P = U * I \tag{4}$$

U: the voltage of the battery, I: the intensity of the battery,
The power can be expressed per unit of projected area of electrode (anode or cathode), which gives a surface density of power expressed in mW/m^2.

$$d = 1 - \frac{P}{S} \tag{5}$$

S: surface of the electrode.
Polarization Curves

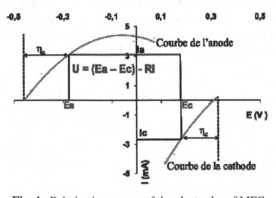

Fig. 4. Polarization curves of the electrodes of MFC

The polarization curves at the anode and at the cathode make it possible to correlate the functioning of the PCM to the kinetics of the electrodes. The current flowing through the MFC is plotted at low scanning speed as a function of the potential of each electrode measured with respect to a reference electrode (Fig. 4). The shape of the polarization curve varies according to the electrode materials and the inter-electrode distance.

For each resistor when the system reaches a pseudo-stationary state (state which is generally established after a few minutes depending on the system and the value of the resistor used), the potential and current values are recorded. This can be done using a potentiostat or simply by charging the battery through external electrical resistors of different values.

Faradic Yield

The faradic yield (R) of a PCM depends on the microorganisms responsible for the oxidation, the nature of the organic carbon serving as fuel and all the alternative reactions that consume this organic carbon [12]. Processes such as aerobic and anaerobic respiration, biomass growth or the formation of reaction intermediates from fermentation can reduce the faradic yield [13].

It can be defined by the following relationship:

$$R(\%) = \frac{Q}{Q_t} * 100 \tag{6}$$

where: Q is the total amount of electricity transferred to the anode

$$Q = \int_0^t idt \tag{7}$$

Q_t is the amount of electricity available in the substrate.

$$Q_t = \frac{nFCV}{M_i} \tag{8}$$

$$R = \frac{M_i \int_0^t idt}{nFCV} \tag{9}$$

In the case of effluent treatment, the available organic matter is measured in terms of chemical oxygen demand (COD) and the faradic yield is calculated from the COD removed:

$$R = \frac{M_i \int_0^t idt}{nFV\Delta(DCO)} \tag{10}$$

With M_i: molar mass of the substrate (g/mol).
n: number of electrons exchanged during the reaction (mol e-/mol).
F: Faraday's constant (C/mol e-).
V: volume of effluent involved (L).
Δ(COD): variation in COD entering and leaving the reactor (g/L).

In the case of effluent treatment, $M_i = 32$ g/mol of O_2, and therefore Δ(COD):) is expressed in g equivalent O_2/L [2].

4 Results and Discussion

4.1 Effluent Treatment by Electrocoagulation

Treatment by electrocoagulation of wastewater allowed a COD reduction from 1193 to 116 mg/L, i.e. a rate of 90.27%. As for the turbidity, it varies from 130 to 37 NTU leading to a reduction in the MES, but also a reduction in parameters such as the aluminum content. The pH went from 7.92 to 9.45 (Fig. 5).

Indeed, the decrease in turbidity is because the complex formed during the process adsorbs the suspended solids which separate from the effluent by flocculation or settling depending on the size of the flocs. This decrease is accompanied by a reduction COD and dissolved oxygen. The evolution of the pH is due to the reaction at the cathode which releases hydroxides in solution [14] (Table 1).

Fig. 5. Electrocoagulation reactor before and after treatment

Table 1. Physico-chemical parameters of wastewater before and after electrocoagulation

Settings	before treatment	after treatment
Conductivité (mS/cm)	2,081	1,493
DCO (mg/L)	1193	116
Teneur en aluminium (mg/L)	1	0,05
Température (°C)	25	21
Oxygène dissout (mg/L)	6,9	1,7
pH	7,92	9,45
Turbidité (NTU)	130	37

4.2 Sludge Analysis

This part of the study consists in determining the micro-organisms present in the sludge. Three species are targeted, namely coliforms, sulphite-reducing clostridium, and staphylococcus aureus. These species have shown their effectiveness for the implementation of microbial stack in previous studies [15] (Table 2).

Table 2. Micro-organisms counted in the sludge.

N(UFC/mL)	Sample		
	Sludge from electrocoagulation	Sludge + sodium acetate (MFC 1)	Sludge + glucose (MFC 2)
coliforms	92000	150	19
sulphite-reducing clostridium	10000	1000	13000
staphylococcus aureus	0	1	2

The microbiological analysis of sludge from electrocoagulation shows the presence of sulphite-reducing coliforms and clostridium and the absence of staphylococcus aureus (92000 CFU/mL for coliforms and 10000 CFU/mL for sulphite-reducing clostridium). These coliforms are more present in sludge than in wastewater (78500 CFU/mL). This can be explained by the fact that the organic matter is concentrated in the sludge compared to the wastewater, thus making its degradation easier and faster.

The sludge after addition of substrate (acetate or glucose) revealed the presence of the three species. In fact, the sludge with acetate contains 150 coliforms, 1000 sulphite-reducing clostridium and 1 staphylococcus aureus, while those with glucose reveal 19 coliforms, 13000 sulphite-reducing clostridium and 2 staphylococcus aureus.

The microbial population of coliforms and sulfito-reducing Clostridium underwent a considerable decrease in the first pile compared to the sludge from electrocoagulation. This decrease is due to the unfavorable environmental conditions caused by the addition of acetate.

The same trend is noted for the coliform species at the level of the second MFC, on the other hand the microbial population of sulphite-reducing clostridium increases. This is consistent with the microbiological results obtained by Xin et al. (2019) as part of the study on the overview of microbial community profiles associated with the production of electrical energy in MFCs [16]. It is therefore noted that the glucose used is more favorable to the growth of clostridia than acetate. The staphylococcus aureus which was absent in the sludge appear in stacks 1 and 2 in small quantities (1 for the first MFC and 2 for the second MFC). Acetate and glucose are favorable to the growth of staphylococcus aureus but glucose remains more effective.

The microorganisms are represented in colonies as shown in the following Fig. 6.

Fig. 6. Micro-organisms present on the surface (A: coliforms, B: sulfito-reducing clostridium)

4.3 MFC Settings

4.3.1 Evolution of Current as a Function of Time

To assess the efficiency of the battery designed previously with acetate or glucose as substrates, the evolution of the intensity of the current as a function of time was studied (Fig. 7).

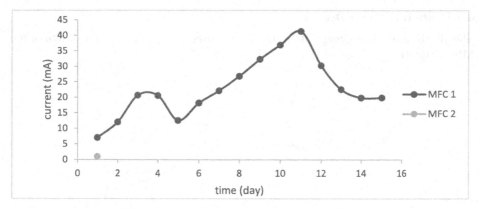

Fig. 7. Variation of current as a function of time

The acetate based MFC (MFC 1) has a current intensity that evolves sinusoidally from 0.033 to 0.102 mA and reaches its maximum on the eleventh day for a value of 0.102 mA while for the MFC with glucose (MFC 2), the values vary between 0.042 and 0.095 mA and its maximum is reached on the sixth day with an intensity of 0.095 mA.

This variation confirms the oxidation of organic matter by bacteria followed by saturation. The addition of acetate or glucose constitutes a contribution of substrate which increases the productivity of the micro-organisms.

4.3.2 Evolution of Voltage as a Function of Time

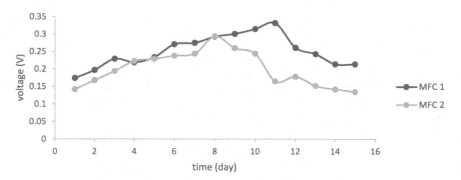

Fig. 8. Variation of voltage as a function of time

This monitoring makes it possible to characterize the speed of transfer of electrons from the biofilm to the anode. For MFC 1, the voltage varies between 0.174 and 0.332 mV and reaches its maximum on the eleventh day while that of MFC 2 varies from 0.135 to 0.294 mV and its maximum is reached on the eighth day. It is noted that the bacteria are more electroactive in the presence of acetate than in the presence of glucose. Also, the life of the MFC1 is longer. Indeed, acetate is more conducive to the development of electrophilic microorganisms than glucose [17] (Fig. 8).

4.3.3 Study of Power Density

The sludge from electrocoagulation treatment is used as inoculum for the design of the MFC (Fig. 9).

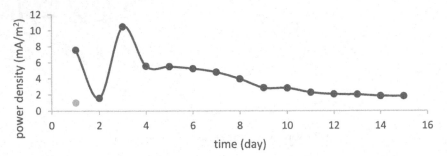

Fig. 9. Variation of power density as a function of time for MFC without substrate

The power density of the MFC varies between 1.6 and 10.4 mW/m^2. From the third day, the power density reaches its maximum (10.4 mW/m^2) then a gradual decrease in the following days was observed.

This development confirms the presence of electroactive microorganisms in the electrocoagulation sludge without adding substrate. Electron transfer is optimum on the third day of operation. Beyond that, there is a saturation which results in a decrease in density.

Based on the observation that the life of the battery is three days, the addition of substrate was made according to this frequency (Fig. 10).

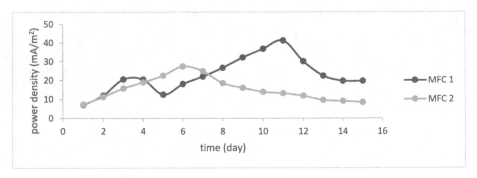

Fig. 10. Variation of power density as a function of time for MFC with substrate

The power density in the MFC 1 varies between 7 and 41 mW/m^2. From the first three days, a gradual increase in power density was observed from 7 to 20 mW/m^2 with the introduction of 2 g of acetate at the anode on the first day. After observing a decrease in power density from the fifth day, 2 g of acetate are added to the same compartment at three-day intervals. On the eleventh day, the density reaches its maximum (41 mW/m^2) and decreases in the following days regardless of the addition of acetate.

The increase in power density is due to a multiplication of microorganisms after addition of acetate while its decrease is caused by a drop in the microbial population. The latter can be explained by the fact that the microorganisms have reached their threshold, which is why they can no longer consume the substrate. Then the energy produced decreases more and more because the electro-active micro-organisms are no longer productive.

In MFC 2 an increase in power density is observed until the sixth day (27 mW/m^2) then a decrease until the end of the experiment with the gradual addition of glucose at 3-day intervals. This result confirms the greater sensitivity of bacteria to acetate.

5 Conclusion

The objective of this study was to show a possible adaptation to climate change through the oxidation of microorganisms present in an environment by bacteria, to produce electricity. Similarly, it was a question of showing the possibility of using sludge from electrocoagulation as fuel in the design of a microbial fuel cell.

These aluminum hydroxide sludges are considered chemical waste because they adsorb the pollutants present in the effluent.

The microbiological study of sludge has shown the presence of certain species such as coliforms and sulphite-reducing clostridium described in the literature as being electrophilic in wastewater.

MFCs based on these sludges have shown their efficiency for energy production. Their performance has been improved by using acetate as a substrate. MFCs therefore appear to be an effective method for the recovery of sludge from electrocoagulation.

The generated power strongly depends on the quality of the biofilm. The formation of the biofilm is conditioned by the electrode materials and the type of effluent which was used for the formation of the sludge. Limits to the development of the MFC could therefore be associated with its lifetime in the case of continuous operation. It is therefore necessary to optimize the operating parameters in order to create an environment favorable to the development of electroactive microorganisms and to the maintenance of electroactivity without the addition of chemical substrates. Parameters such as the nature of the biofilm formed, the mechanisms of electron transfer within the bacterium and from the biofilm to the anode, the electrode materials, and the configuration of the MFC. Can be optimized to improve the power supplied and the lifetime of the MFC.

In perspective, an experimental plan based on a 7-factor HADAMARD matrix will be rolled out to optimize the operation.

References

1. Cercado Quezada, B.: Traitement de déchets issus de l'industrie agro-alimentaire par pile à combustible microbienne, p. 9 (2009)
2. Ketep, F.S.: Piles à combustible microbiennes pour la production d'électricité couplée au traitement des eaux de l'industrie papetière THÈSE Pour obtenir le grade de DOCTEUR DE L'UNIVERSITÉ DE GRENOBLE, p. 47 (2012)

3. Slate, A.J., Whitehead, K.A., Brownson, D.A., Banks, C.E.: Microbial fuel cells: an overview of current technology. Renew. Sustain. Energy Rev. **101**, 60–81 (2019)
4. Philippon, T.: Développement et étude des bio-cathodes dénitrifiantes dans le contexte de la dépollution des zones humides, these de doctorat de l'universite de rennes 1, pp. 29–35 (2021)
5. Flimban, S.G.A., Ismail, I.M.I., Kim, T., Oh, S.-E.: Review overview of recent advancements in the microbial fuel cell from fundamentals to applications. Energies **12**, 1–20 (2019)
6. Sharma, P., Joshi, H.: Utilization of electrocoagulation-treated spent wash sludge in making building blocks. Int. J. Environ. Sci. Technol. **13**, 349–358 (2016)
7. Tezcan Un, U., Onpeker, S.E., Ozel, E.: The treatment of chromium containing wastewater using electrocoagulation and the production of ceramic pigments from the resulting sludge. J. Environ. Manag. **200**, 196–203 (2017)
8. Ghanbari, F., Zirrahi, F., Olfati, D., Gohari, F., Hassani, A.: TiO2 nanoparticles removal by electrocoagulation using iron electrodes: catalytic activity of electrochemical sludge for the degradation of emerging pollutant. J. Mol. Liq. **310**, 113217 (2020)
9. Shon, H.K., et al.: Preparation of titanium dioxide nanoparticles from electrocoagulated sludge using sacrificial titanium electrodes. Environ. Sci. Technol. **44**, 5553–5557 (2010)
10. Samy, M., Alalm, M.G., Mossad, M.: Utilization of iron sludge resulted from electro-coagulation in heterogeneous Phot-Fenton process. Water Pract. Technol. **15**, 1228–1237 (2020)
11. Yilmaz, A.E., Fil, B.A., Bayar, S., Karcioglu Karakas, Z.: A new adsorbent for fluoride removal: the utilization of sludge waste from electrocoagulation as adsorbent. Glob. NEST J. **17**, 186–197 (2015)
12. Nevin, K.P., Woodard, T.L., Franks, A.E., Summers, Z.M., Lovley, D.R.: Microbial electrosynthesis: feeding microbes electricity to convert carbon dioxide and water to multicarbon extracellular organic compounds. MBio **1**(2) (2010)
13. Huang, L., Logan, B.E.: Electricity generation and treatment of paper recycling wastewater using a microbial fuel cell. Appl. Microbiol. Biotechnol. **80**(2), 349–355 (2008)
14. Mbacké, M.K., et al.: Electrocoagulation process applied on pollutants treatment-experimental optimization and fundamental investigation of the crystal violet dye removal. J. Environ. Chem. Eng. **4**(4), 4001–4011 (2016)
15. Cao, Y., et al.: Electricigens in the anode of microbial fuel cells: pure cultures versus mixed communities. Microb. Cell Factor **18**(1), 1–14 (2019). https://doi.org/10.1186/s12934-019-1087-z
16. Xin, X., Hong, J., Liu, Y.: Insights into microbial community profiles associated with electric energy production in microbial fuel cells fed with food waste hydrolysate. Sci. Total. Environ. **670**, 50–58 (2019)
17. Haddour, N., et al.: Rapport de soutenance de projet d'étude. PE n 88: Pile à combustible microbienne. Ecole centrate de Lyon (2015)

AMETHYST: Advanced Microbial Eradication Through High-Intensity Yielding Sterilization Technology - A Multipurpose Decontamination Chamber Using 405 nm HINS Light

Amar Seeam(✉) 🆔

Middlesex University, Uniciti, Flic-en-Flac, Mauritius
a.seeam@mdx.ac.mu

Abstract. This paper presents the design and concept of a multipurpose decontamination chamber named AMETHYST (Advanced Microbial Eradication Through High-intensity Yielding Sterilization Technology), which serves as a cabinet for object decontamination and, with its outward-opening doors, can also effectively decontaminate an entire room. The development of this chamber is driven by the need for efficient and versatile decontamination solutions, particularly in response to the COVID-19 pandemic. The focus of this paper is to discuss various UV light techniques considered during the design process and the ultimate selection of 405 nm High Intensity Narrow Spectrum (HINS) light as the preferred wavelength. The proposed concept offers a flexible, cost-effective, and sustainable solution for achieving high levels of decontamination in both object and room environments.

Keywords: 405 nm · Decontamination · Experimental Validation

1 Introduction

The recent COVID-19 pandemic has brought to light the significance of hygiene and decontamination in public health, particularly in underserved areas where access to basic sanitation and healthcare services is limited.

2 Importance of Decontamination Chambers in Underserved Areas

The significance of hygiene and decontamination in preventing the spread of infectious diseases has been emphasized during the COVID-19 pandemic, especially in underserved regions. In these areas, access to safe water, sanitation, and hygiene (WASH) services is often limited. The integration of decontamination chambers for the disinfection of spaces and items can be instrumental in these settings.

A. Seeam et al. (Eds.): InterSol 2023, LNICST 541, pp. 233–247, 2024.
https://doi.org/10.1007/978-3-031-51849-2_16

- **Reducing Cross-Contamination:** Decontamination chambers can mitigate the risk of cross-contamination in healthcare facilities by disinfecting medical equipment, personal protective equipment, and other items before they are transported from one area to another.
- **Enhanced Cleaning Protocols:** Complementing traditional cleaning methods, decontamination chambers ensure that microorganisms are effectively eliminated.
- **Safety and Efficiency:** The automation of decontamination chambers, often utilizing light technologies or vaporized hydrogen peroxide, offers both safety and efficiency.
- **Public Confidence:** Visible decontamination efforts, such as decontamination chambers, can bolster public confidence in the safety of public spaces.
- **Adaptability:** Decontamination chambers can be adapted for various settings and purposes.
- **Resource Conservation:** In resource-limited settings, decontaminating personal protective equipment is critical for resource conservation.
- **Preventing Future Outbreaks:** By ensuring spaces and items are decontaminated, chambers can contain the current pandemic and prevent future outbreaks.

It is imperative that decontamination chambers be integrated as part of a broader public health strategy, coupled with improvements in WASH services. These measures should be reinforced by education and behavior change campaigns to underscore the importance of hygiene and decontamination in preventing the spread of infectious diseases.

2.1   The Use of 405 nm Light in Decontamination Chambers

Traditional decontamination chambers often employ ultraviolet C (UV-C) light for disinfection. While effective, UV-C light can be harmful to humans and materials, posing a risk of skin burns and eye injuries. Moreover, repeated exposure to UV-C light can lead to the degradation of materials such as plastics.

An alternative and safer approach is the use of 405 nm light for decontamination. This wavelength, which is in the visible spectrum, has been shown to be effective in inactivating a wide range of microorganisms, including bacteria and viruses. The advantages of using 405 nm light include:

- **Safety:** Unlike UV-C light, 405 nm light is safe for human exposure and does not cause harm to the skin or eyes.
- **Material Compatibility:** 405 nm light does not degrade materials such as plastics and textiles, which makes it suitable for decontaminating a wider range of items.
- **Effectiveness:** Studies have shown that 405 nm light can effectively inactivate microorganisms through a different mechanism than UV-C, and is particularly effective against bacteria, including antibiotic-resistant strains.

- **Continuous Decontamination:** Because 405 nm light is safe for human exposure, it can be used for continuous decontamination in occupied spaces, whereas UV-C light can only be used when spaces are unoccupied.

The use of 405 nm light in decontamination chambers provides a safer and often more effective alternative to traditional UV-C light, making it particularly valuable in settings such as healthcare facilities, schools, and public transportation, where safety and material compatibility are paramount.

2.2 Background and Motivation

Studies have shown that 405 nm light can effectively inactivate microorganisms and coronaviruses. Examples include [1–5]. Based on this there is a strong motivation to further develop innovative decontamination chambers using the 405 nm wavelength, which is much safer to use in occupied spaces than the more common UV-C light, with the only penalty being that it takes more time for treatment.

2.3 Research Objectives

The main objectives of this research are to design and evaluate a multipurpose decontamination chamber using 405 nm UV light, focusing on its efficacy in eradicating microbial contaminants on objects and room surfaces.

2.4 Significance of the Study

This study is significant as it offers a new and innovative approach to decontamination that is flexible, cost-effective, and environmentally friendly. It also addresses a critical public health issue.

3 Background

3.1 Decontamination Methods and Challenges

Decontamination is essential in ensuring the cleanliness and safety of environments, particularly in healthcare settings. However, traditional decontamination methods have faced numerous challenges that have highlighted the need for more efficient and effective solutions.

Traditional Decontamination Methods. Traditional decontamination methods primarily involve the use of chemical disinfectants and manual cleaning. Chemical disinfectants, such as hydrogen peroxide, peracetic acid, and hypochlorous acid, are often used to clean surfaces. Additionally, some approaches involve coating surfaces with antimicrobial agents like copper or silver to create self-disinfecting surfaces.

Challenges with Traditional Methods. One of the significant challenges with traditional methods is the suboptimal cleaning and disinfection practices in hospitals. This is often due to various personnel issues and failure to follow the manufacturer's recommendations for disinfectant use. Additionally, some disinfectants lack antimicrobial activity against healthcare-associated pathogens, affecting the efficacy of disinfection practices.

Moreover, manual cleaning is labor-intensive and can be inconsistent, leading to areas being inadequately decontaminated. The human factor in manual cleaning also introduces the possibility of error, and the cleaning process itself can sometimes contribute to the spread of contaminants.

405 nm Light for Decontamination. 405 nm visible light, which is in the range of violet-blue visible light (380–500 nm), has been shown to have germicidal properties and is considered as an alternative to germicidal ultraviolet C (UVC) irradiation for disinfection, especially in environments occupied by humans. The 405 nm light has demonstrated the ability to reduce bacteria, surgical site infections, and inactivate certain viruses. This is believed to be due to the absorption of light by photosensitizers such as porphyrins, which leads to the release of reactive oxygen species (ROS). ROS are known to cause damage to essential biomolecules such as proteins, lipids, and nucleic acids in bacteria, fungi, and viruses, and can also lead to the loss of cell membrane permeability through lipid oxidation.

Although 405 nm light is less germicidal than UVC, it has been shown to have the potential to inactivate pathogenic bacteria such as Listeria spp. and Clostridium spp., as well as fungal species such as Saccharomyces spp. and Candida spp. Furthermore, 405 nm light has been shown to inactivate viruses such as feline calcivirus (FCV), viral hemorrhagic septicemia virus (VHSV), and murine norovirus-1, especially when used in conjunction with media suspensions containing photosensitizers.

In a specific study [6], it was shown that 405 nm light could inactivate SARS-CoV-2 and influenza A H1N1 viruses without the use of photosensitizers, making it directly relevant to clinical environments. The study employed a commercially available visible light disinfection system that ensured the irradiance used was safe and practically achievable in a clinical setting. The study supports the potential use of 405 nm light as a tool for continuous decontamination of respiratory pathogens such as SARS-CoV-2 and influenza A viruses.

3.2   Comparative Analysis Table

Table 1 provides a comparative analysis of three different decontamination methods: AMETHYST, UV Disinfectant Lights, and Traditional Cleaning Methods. It evaluates them across multiple criteria such as their primary goal, mechanism, safety, effectiveness, and areas of application to offer a comprehensive view of their relative advantages and drawbacks.

Table 1. Comparative Analysis Table

Feature	AMETHYST	UV Disinfectant Lights	Traditional Cleaning Methods
Primary Goal	Multipurpose Decontamination	Surface and Air Decontamination	Surface Cleaning
Mechanism	405 nm HINS Light	UV-C Light	Chemical Disinfectants
Human Safety	High	Low (risk of skin and eye damage)	Varies (depends on chemicals)
Material Safety	High (No material degradation)	Low (degrades materials)	Medium (chemical residues)
Effectiveness	High	High	Medium to High
Time Required	More Time Required	Faster	Labor-Intensive, Varies
Areas of Application	Objects and Rooms	Unoccupied Spaces	Surfaces

3.3 Strengths and Weaknesses

3.3.1 AMETHYST

Strengths: Highly effective, safe for humans, versatile, enhances public confidence.

Weaknesses: Takes more time for treatment, relatively new technology.

3.3.2 UV Disinfectant Lights

Strengths: Fast, effective against a broad range of microorganisms.

Weaknesses: Harmful to humans, degrades materials, specific use-cases.

3.3.3 Traditional Cleaning Methods

Strengths: Proven effectiveness, widely available.

Weaknesses: Labor-intensive, chemical residues, inconsistent cleaning, doesn't boost public confidence.

3.4 Underserved Areas

In underserved areas, the challenges of decontamination are often exacerbated. Limited resources and infrastructure mean that access to effective decontamination agents and equipment is restricted. Additionally, there is often a lack of trained personnel to carry out decontamination procedures effectively. The combination of these factors makes infection control in underserved areas particularly challenging. Table 2 summarise some potential solutions.

Table 2. Comparative Analysis of Decontamination Solutions

Solution	Technology	Scope	Suitability for Underserved Areas
CERTEK CMDC	Chemical Decontamination	N95 Masks	High Mobility
She et al. UV-C System	UV-C Light	Surfaces	Low Cost, High Flexibility
Biosept Home UV-C	UV-C Light	Hospital Surfaces	Portable, Non-Toxic
Lifx Clean	HEV Blue Light	Air & Surfaces	Dual-Purpose, Safe

3.5 Other Solutions for Underserved Areas

The CERTEK Mobile Decontamination Chamber (CMDC) presents an innovative approach, particularly advantageous for underserved areas. The CMDC is a transportable decontamination chamber manufactured in one-trip shipping containers. It is capable of decontaminating thousands of N95 compatible masks in one cycle. The chamber is equipped with double doors, LED lighting, and an electrical panel. These mobile decontamination chambers are especially beneficial in areas with limited decontamination infrastructure, as they can be easily transported and deployed [7].

She et al. explore the use of UV-C light as a disinfectant for bacteria and viruses, aiming to develop a cost-effective and portable solution particularly advantageous for low-resource settings. The authors design and validate a lightweight UV-C disinfection system, constructed from readily available components such as a plastic bin and a standard UV-C light bulb. The interior of the system is coated with reflective chrome paint to intensify the UV-C exposure. The efficacy of the system is validated using Bacillus cereus, a gram-positive bacteria known for its resilience to harsh conditions including UV exposure. Analytical calculations and experimental validations suggest that a 3-minute exposure can achieve a UV-C dose exceeding 500 mJ/cm^2, which is well beyond the guidelines for bacterial and viral decontamination. The model they provide also allows for rapid adaptation of the system design to accommodate different light sources or exposure times. This solution is particularly relevant for disaster relief scenarios or healthcare systems in underserved areas where access to large, commercial decontamination systems is limited [8].

The study by Tamires dos Santos and Lívia Furquim de Castro shows that the Biosept Home UV-C device effectively decontaminates hospital surfaces using UV-C light. Notably, its portable nature makes it an advantageous solution for underserved areas that may lack comprehensive decontamination infrastructure. In testing, the device demonstrated complete bacterial inactivation and reduced microbial colonies on hospital surfaces. The Biosept Home UV-C offers a promising, portable, and non-toxic alternative for ensuring hospital cleanliness in resource-limited settings [9].

The Lifx Clean is a smart lightbulb that has been developed to not only provide lighting but also kill bacteria in its vicinity. The bulb utilizes high-energy visible (HEV) blue light of around 405 nm wavelength.

For underserved areas, this technology offers a dual-purpose solution. The Lifx Clean provides both lighting and a degree of microbial disinfection, all integrated into a single household device. Its safety profile makes it more user-friendly compared to other disinfecting technologies like UV light, which can be harmful if used improperly. Though not a complete solution for all types of pathogens, in resource-limited settings where multi-functional devices can be particularly beneficial, Lifx Clean presents a viable option for enhancing cleanliness [10].

4   Design and Development of AMETHYST

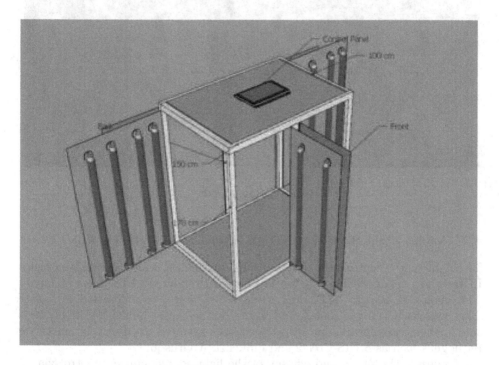

Fig. 1. Initial design

The primary design, as depicted in Fig. 1, conceptualizes the doors as capable of opening outwards entirely, thus ensuring every corner of the room is covered. In essence, the doors offer a seamless, all-encompassing coverage. When closed any items inside the chamber will be disinfected thoroughly.

4.1   System Overview and Components

The AMETHYST system utilizes high-intensity violet light, specifically at a wavelength of approximately 405 nm, to effectively eradicate microbial contaminants. The working principle involves the use of high-power light-emitting diodes

(LEDs) that emit violet light. These LEDs are strategically placed within the decontamination chamber to ensure uniform coverage of the targeted area and within the chamber (Fig. 2 shows room disinfection mode).

Fig. 2. Room mode

4.2   Violet Light Source and High-Intensity LED Technology

The light source comprises multiple disinfection lights, which use high-intensity LEDs sourced from Nichia - the world's largest supplier of LEDs based in Japan. The choice of 405 nm LEDs was made after careful consideration of safety. This wavelength is particularly advantageous because, unlike UV light, it is safe for human exposure, and it has been demonstrated to effectively inactivate pathogens such as SARS-CoV-2 and influenza A virus [6].

To ensure the safety and efficacy of the light source, current control via an LED driver is employed, which maintains the intensity within safety thresholds of a maximum of $10W/m^2$. A lens system is also used based on the distance between the fixture and the disinfection target, as well as the size of the target. This ensures that the light is distributed effectively for disinfection purposes. One of the drawbacks of using 405 nm LEDs for disinfection is the extended duration required for effective decontamination, which can be up to 8 h. However, the ability to use this light source safely in the presence of people is a significant advantage. Additionally, Bluetooth control is being integrated into the system for automation purposes. The light strips, each contain 12 disinfection LEDs and have a dedicated LED driver. A single power supply is used to drive all the strips (Fig. 3).

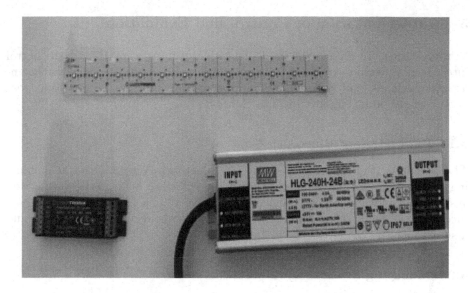

Fig. 3. Strip driver and power supply

4.3   Chamber Design for Efficient Light Distribution

The prototype is meticulously designed to maximize the efficiency of light distribution for disinfection purposes. The doors of the chamber are constructed in a way that allows for full disinfection coverage in a room when the disinfection lights are affixed. When the doors are open, the lights face outward, providing disinfection to the room. When the doors are closed, the lights face inward, disinfecting any items stored within the chamber. This dual-functionality ensures comprehensive decontamination.

The chamber is also designed with flexibility and convenience in mind. It is equipped with wheels, allowing it to be easily moved around a room or facility. This mobility is particularly advantageous for ensuring that all areas of a room can be effectively disinfected. Additionally, the chamber can be fitted with trays, allowing items to be stacked within it during the disinfection process. This is particularly useful for efficiently disinfecting a large number of items at once.

The chamber is equipped with six LED 405 nm strips on each side of the door, ensuring that a large area can be covered by the disinfection light. This is essential for ensuring the efficacy of the disinfection process, particularly given the extended duration required for disinfection with 405 nm light.

Given the safety of 405 nm light for human exposure, and the comprehensive and efficient design of the chamber, it is anticipated that the prototype will be particularly useful in quarantine facilities and other environments where rigorous disinfection is required without compromising human safety.

5   Implementation of Control and Evaluation

In this section, we discuss the implementation of integrating Bluetooth control into the disinfection system of our prototype and evaluate its efficacy in managing scheduling and streamlining the disinfection process. The multipurpose nature of the doors employed is also elaborated on.

5.1   Integration of Bluetooth Control

The prototype features the integration of Bluetooth control aimed at enhancing automation and providing users with the ability to manage the disinfection system remotely via a smart device. To achieve this, a Bluetooth module was incorporated, facilitating communication between the disinfection chamber and a smartphone or tablet.

5.2   Managing Scheduling

The Bluetooth control allows users to manage the scheduling of disinfection processes. This feature is particularly crucial given the extended duration required for disinfection by the 405 nm high-intensity narrow-spectrum light, which can take up to 8 h. The scheduling capability enables users to set the disinfection process during times when the room or facility is not in use, ensuring that the disinfection process does not hinder regular activities.

Furthermore, the system allows for the setting up of recurring schedules, which could prove especially beneficial in institutional settings like hospitals, where it could be programmed to commence disinfection automatically at the end of visiting hours daily.

5.3   Multipurpose Doors

The prototype was meticulously designed to maximize disinfection efficiency. The doors are constructed such that when disinfection lights are affixed, they provide full disinfection coverage within a room when open, and when closed (Fig. 4), they deliver maximum disinfection to any items stored within. Moreover, they have been installed with wheels to facilitate mobility within the room. The doors are thus not only a structural element but also serve a critical function in the disinfection process.

5.4   User Interface and Ease of Use

The Bluetooth control system includes a user-friendly interface on the smartphone or tablet, designed to be intuitive for ease of use. It offers features such as turning the disinfection lights on and off, setting schedules, and monitoring the status of the disinfection process.

5.5   Evaluating Efficacy

In the testing phase, the reliability and responsiveness of the Bluetooth control was evaluated. It was observed that the system promptly responded to commands from the smart device, and the scheduling feature accurately followed the user-set schedules.

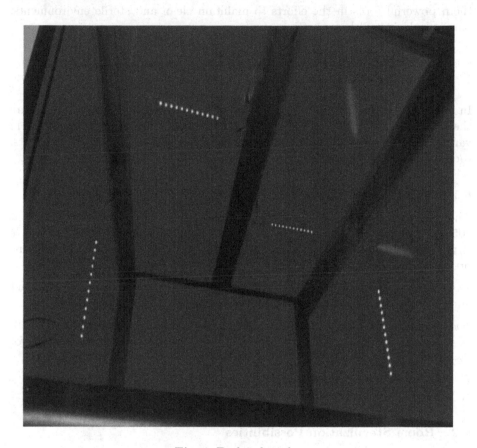

Fig. 4. Enclosed mode

5.6   Discussion

The integration of Bluetooth control and the multipurpose design of the doors in the prototype represent significant advancements in the field of violet light disinfection. The ability to remotely control and schedule the disinfection process enhances convenience and ensures systematic and consistent disinfection, crucial in settings such as hospitals.

While the current design shows promising results, there are areas for potential improvement. Future iterations could include more sensors for real-time feedback on the disinfection process, or integration with facility management systems for further streamlined operations.

In conclusion, the integration of Bluetooth control and the multipurpose nature of the doors in our prototype have proven to be valuable additions to the disinfection system. Their ease of use and reliability in scheduling and managing the disinfection process, as well as their role in efficient light distribution, make them powerful tools in the efforts to maintain clean and sterile environments, particularly in healthcare settings.

6   Practical Applications and Implementation Considerations

In this section, the practical applications of the prototype for disinfection, and the considerations that need to be taken into account for its implementation in various scenarios are discussed. This includes the decontamination of objects, room sterilization, and applications in environmental and healthcare settings.

6.1   Object Decontamination Scenarios

The prototype's design, which employs high-intensity narrow-spectrum light at 405 nm, makes it well-suited for decontaminating objects. In scenarios where it is essential to ensure the sterility of tools, equipment, or other objects, the prototype can be effectively used. For instance:

Laboratories: The prototype can be used to decontaminate laboratory equipment and tools, preventing cross-contamination during sensitive experiments.

Food Industry: In food processing and handling facilities, ensuring the cleanliness of utensils and surfaces is crucial. The prototype can serve as a tool for disinfecting items and surfaces.

Educational Institutions: For educational institutions, especially those with science labs, the prototype can be used to sterilize lab equipment.

6.2   Room Sterilization Possibilities

The mobility and design of the prototype make it versatile enough to be employed in room sterilization. By placing it in a room and engaging its disinfection lights, it can disinfect surfaces and air:

Hospital Rooms: One of the most critical applications could be in hospitals, where preventing the spread of infections is paramount. The prototype could be used to regularly sterilize patient rooms, operation theaters, and isolation wards.

Offices and Workspaces: To maintain a healthy work environment, the prototype could be used to disinfect offices, especially areas with high human traffic such as meeting rooms.

Public Transport: Vehicles such as buses, trains, and airplanes could be sterilized using the prototype to ensure passenger safety.

7   Conclusion

In the final section, the elements of the AMETHYST System are drawn together, summarizing its features and the findings from its deployment. The potential for further advancements and practical implementations in various settings, particularly in underserved areas, is also discussed.

7.1   Summary of AMETHYST System and Findings

The AMETHYST System is a prototype developed to offer a multipurpose, efficient, and safe method for decontamination and sterilization. The key features of this system include:

Multipurpose Doors: The design of the system incorporates doors that serve dual purposes. When open, the doors ensure full disinfection coverage in a room, and when closed, they provide maximum disinfection to any items stored within. This innovative use of space makes the system versatile and highly functional.

High-intensity 405 nm Light: The system employs 405 nm light, which is just beyond the UV range. This high-intensity narrow-spectrum light is known for its germicidal properties while being safer than UV-C light. The choice of this wavelength was made after careful consideration of safety aspects.

Wireless Control: Through the integration of Bluetooth technology, the AMETHYST System can be controlled wirelessly. This allows for automation and ease of use, particularly in settings where manual control is not feasible.

Mobility: The system is designed with mobility in mind, with wheels installed for easy movement around a room or facility. This feature increases its applicability across different scenarios.

Safety and Efficiency: Although the 405 nm light takes longer for disinfection compared to UV-C, it can be used safely in the presence of people, making it suitable for various environments including healthcare settings.

The findings indicate that the AMETHYST System is effective in inactivating pathogens and can be used in various settings, including those with sensitive populations. It offers a balance between safety, efficiency, and versatility.

7.2   Potential for Advancements and Practical Implementation

Applications in Underserved Areas: The mobility and safety features of the AMETHYST System make it particularly suitable for underserved areas where healthcare infrastructure is limited. Its ability to be used safely in the presence of people makes it ideal for community clinics, schools, and other public spaces in resource-limited settings.

Integration with Sensors: Future versions of the AMETHYST System could integrate sensors to detect the level of contamination or the presence of specific pathogens. This would enable more targeted and efficient disinfection processes.

Remote Monitoring and Control: Incorporating IoT technologies could allow for remote monitoring and control of the system, which could be particularly useful in large facilities or in scenarios where the system is deployed in remote areas.

Alternative Power Sources: To increase the applicability in areas with limited or unreliable electricity, the system could be adapted to run on alternative power sources such as solar energy.

Customizable Configurations: Allowing for customizable configurations in terms of light intensity, number of LEDs, and control options could make the system adaptable to specific needs in various settings.

In conclusion, the AMETHYST System represents a significant advancement in decontamination and sterilization technologies. With its multipurpose design, safety features, and wireless control, it holds promise for wide-ranging applications, especially in underserved areas. Further innovations and adaptations can enhance its capabilities and broaden its impact in contributing to public health and safety.

Acknowledgment. The author would like to thank the Mauritius Innovation and Research Council (MRIC) and the IEEE Mauritius Section for funding support. Furthermore, credit goes to Jannish Purmaissur for 3D design work, Divesh Roopowa for assisting with the prototyping of the enclosure and Barlen Maureemoothoo for assistance in Electrical wiring of the light strips.

References

1. Maclean, M., Macgregor, S., Anderson, J., Woolsey, G.: The role of oxygen in the visible-light inactivation of staphylococcus aureus. J. Photochem. Photobiol. B: Biol. **92**(3), 180–184 (2008)
2. Vatter, P., Hoenes, K., Hessling, M.: Photoinactivation of the coronavirus surrogate phi6 by visible light. Photochem. Photobiol. **97**(1), 122–125 (2021)
3. Enwemeka, C.S., Bumah, V.V., Mokili, J.L.: Pulsed blue light inactivates two strains of human coronavirus. J. Photochem. Photobiol. B: Biol. **222**, 112282 (2021)
4. Lau, B., Becher, D., Hessling, M.: High intensity violet light (405 nm) inactivates coronaviruses in phosphate buffered saline (PBS) and on surfaces. In: Photonics, vol. 8, no. 10, p. 414. MDPI (2021)
5. Sinclair, L.G., Ilieva, Z., Morris, G., Anderson, J.G., MacGregor, S.J., Maclean, M.: Viricidal efficacy of a 405-nm environmental decontamination system for inactivation of bacteriophage Phi6: surrogate for SARS-CoV-2. Photochem. Photobiol. (2023)
6. Rathnasinghe, R., Jangra, S., Miorin, L., Schotsaert, M., Yahnke, C., García-Sastre, A.: The virucidal effects of 405 nm visible light on SARS-CoV-2 and influenza a virus. Sci. Rep. **11**(1), 19470 (2021)
7. CERTEK. Decontamination chamber (2023). https://www.certek-usa.com/decontamination-chamber.html. Accessed 30 June 2023
8. She, R.C., Chen, D., Pak, P., Armani, D.K., Schubert, A., Armani, A.M.: Lightweight UV-C disinfection system. Biomed. Opt. Express **11**(8), 4326–4332 (2020)

9. Dos Santos, T., de Castro, L.F.: Evaluation of a portable ultraviolet C (UV-C) device for hospital surface decontamination. Photodiagn. Photodyn. Ther. **33**, 102161 (2021)

10. Porter, J.: Lifx's bacteria-killing smart bulb works, but here's the small print—theverge.com. https://www.theverge.com/2021/3/3/22308944/lifx-clean-germacidal-smart-light-bulb-bacteria-killing-sanitation-high-energy-visible-405nm. Accessed 09 Sept 2023

Digital Learning and Social Adoption

Covid-19 Contact Tracing Application Adoption: A Technology Readiness Model Perspective

Adesola Tolulope Olaegbe and Muhammad Z. I. Lallmahomed$^{(\boxtimes)}$

Middlesex University, Flic En Flacq, Mauritius
z.lallmahomed@mdx.ac.mu

Abstract. In late December 2019, there was an unforeseen outbreak of Coronavirus (COVID-19), which resulted in a global pandemic that claimed millions of lives. To allow individuals to travel freely and the economy to recover, government officials needed to be able to swiftly detect potential COVID-19 situations and track prospective encounters. There are numerous methods for doing contact tracing, one of them is to use contact tracking application. The COVID-19 contact tracing application allows for the tracking of people who encounter individuals who have COVID-19, regardless of where they are. The purpose of the research was to investigate the adoption of contact tracking applications through the theory of technology readiness in Nigeria. A cross-sectional survey was carried out using a non-probability sampling technique. Online questionnaires were sent via social media and email, with a total of 145 individuals taking part in the study. The data collected were analyzed using partial least squares (PLS) utilizing the SmartPLS-3 software to test the hypothesis generated by the research model presented in the study. The results obtained from the data collection and analysis revealed that six of the presented hypotheses were supported. Innovativeness was found to be strongly related to perceived usefulness while discomfort has a negative effect on perceived ease of use and usefulness. Implications of those findings are further discussed.

Keywords: Contact Tracing Application · COVID-19 · Technology Adoption · Readiness

1 Introduction

In late 2019, the first case of Coronavirus (COVID-19) identified and reported was in Wuhan, China. The continuous spread of virus resulted in severe acute respiratory syndrome-Coronavirus 2 (SARS-CoV-2), has led to a global pandemic. There are currently 186,164,398 confirmed cases, 170,302,144 recoveries and a total of 4,022,211 deaths worldwide as of July 8th, 2021 [1]. Some of the preventive measures implemented by countries in response to combating the spread of the virus includes the strict use of face mask, social distancing, self-isolation measures and imposing strict lockdowns [2]. However, the strict lockdowns significantly affect the economic sector as it leads to businesses shutting down and workers losing their jobs, leaving them unable

© ICST Institute for Computer Sciences, Social Informatics and Telecommunications Engineering 2024
Published by Springer Nature Switzerland AG 2024. All Rights Reserved
A. Seeam et al. (Eds.): InterSol 2023, LNICST 541, pp. 251–263, 2024.
https://doi.org/10.1007/978-3-031-51849-2_17

to fend for themselves and family. Research has shown that a crucial way in which the spread of the virus can be reduced is identify people who may have encountered a confirmed case of the COVID-19, this can be done by contact tracing [3].

Contact tracing is a "process of identifying and providing supported quarantine to individuals who have been in contact with people who are infected with SARS-CoV-2 and can be used to find a source of infection by identifying settings or events where infection may have occurred, allowing for targeted public health and social measures" [4]. The manual method of contact tracing involves health workers conducting interviews with infected patients to identify people they may have encounter. The process may be effective, but it comes with its limitation ranging from [a] large number of well-trained health workers to conduct manual interview, [b] inability to identify every single person who have encounter the infected person [5]. Due to the several limitations in the manual process of contact tracing, several countries have found ways of adopting technological solutions to the process of combating the spread of COVID-19 by using contact tracing applications. These applications are dependent on the use of smartphones as it involves the use of proximity tracking tools to trace people who have come in close range with an infected person [6]. Other technologies such as characteristics tracking tools which are based on self-reported signs and symptoms are being adopted to help combat the spread of COVID-19 [7].

Several advantages to adopting COVID-19 contact tracing application include enhancing the traditional method of contact tracing, efficiency, a wide reach and helping to combat the spread of the virus. However, the effectiveness of these application is based on how willing people are to adopting them. Individuals have a lot of concerns when it comes to adopting contact tracing application, this ranges from safety, effectiveness, and privacy issues [8]. Hence, the aim of this research is to investigate the factors that would predict and inhibit the adoption of COVID-19 contact tracing application using the Technology Readiness Model as base framework. We asked the following questions: RQ1: What factors predict the adoption of contact tracing application? RQ2: What factors inhibit the adoption of contract tracing application?

2   Literature Review

Contact tracing is a procedure that involves identifying people who may have encountered an infected person while the person was an active carrier of a disease. This is a time-tested procedure initiated to monitor and control historical outbreaks like Tuberculosis, Lassa fever, Ebola, measles, and HIV [9]. According to the WHO (World Health Organization), contact tracing involves these three steps:

1. Contact Identification: "This requires the infected person recalling activities and roles of persons in-volved". 2. Listing Contacts: "This requires calling the names of potentially infected contacts". 3. Contact Follow-Up: "This requires monitoring any symptoms connected to the viral infection". The usual method of contact tracing involves manually carrying out interviews to trace people who must have met and infected individual. During the pandemic technological solutions are being put in place to enhance the manual method of contact tracing by enhancing contact tracing applications [9]. These applications solely depend on been installed on smartphones and rely on either global

positioning systems (GPS), Wireless Transmitter (Wi-Fi) or Bluetooth connection. The contact tracing application function on a framework which involves smartphones logging close contact with other smartphones running the same application [6].

2.1 Architecture

There are two types of contact tracing application centralized and decentralized.

- Centralized Architecture: Smartphones share anonymous user IDs with a central server, which uses the database to do contact tracking, risk analysis, and alert messaging to users. Detections are executed on centralized server with all information of individuals been transferred to the server.
- Decentralized Architecture: In place of a centralized server, smartphones perform contact tracing and alerting by downloading the contact database directly from the server. The smartphone performances as the local server and only transfers the information of infected people to a centralized server, contact matching is done locally with information been fetched occasionally from the server [10] (Fig. 1).

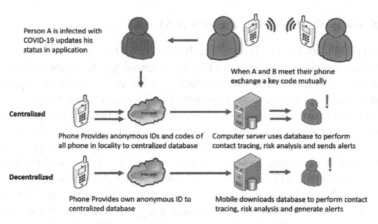

Fig. 1. Contact Tracing Architecture [10]

2.2 Adoption Theories

Adoption theories are used to highlight significant elements that encourage people to participate in specific behaviors [11]. It is used to investigate people and the decisions they make while accepting or declining a development [12]. There is no exact concept for understanding the behavioral shift that occurs when a person adopts a technology. Nevertheless, numerous adoption models from various areas have emerged throughout the years. For this research which is technology based the adoption theories explored include Diffusion of Innovation [13], Theory of Reasoned Actions [14], Technology Acceptance Model [15], Extensions of the Technology Acceptance Model [16], Technology Readiness [17] and Technology Readiness and Acceptance Model [18]. We further review the base model used in this study in the next section.

2.3 Technology Readiness

Parasuraman [17] refers to Technology Readiness (TR) as *"people's propensity to embrace and use new technologies"*. Relaying on people's sentiments, principles, and perceptions towards technological products and services, it can be considered as state of mind determined by predictors and inhibitors when an individual tries to adopt new innovations [17, 19]; Based on this the Technology Readiness Index (TRI) was established to measure the use of technology instead of the capability of use. Technology Readiness is measured using four dimensions, optimism, innovativeness, discomfort, and insecurity. It is known that optimism and innovativeness are the positive predictors and discomfort, and insecurity are the negative inhibitors [20].

- Optimism: "A positive view of technology and a belief that it offers people increased control, flexibility, and efficiency in their lives."
- Innovativeness: "A tendency to be a technology pioneer and thought leader."
- Discomfort: "A perceived lack of control over technology and a feeling of being overwhelmed by it."
- Insecurity: "Distrust of technology and skepticism about its ability to work properly."

2.4 Technology Readiness and Acceptance Model

Lin et al. [18] introduces the Technology Readiness and Acceptance Model (TRAM) by integrating Technology Readiness (TR) and Technology Acceptance Model (TAM) components into a single framework. According to Lin et al. [18] technology readiness (TR) is an originator of both perceived usefulness and perceived ease of use, both of which impact customers proclivity to use e-services. He states that the integrated approach transfers the emphasis from service systems to customers suggesting that it is obvious that the models are connected since TAM assesses a system (system-specific) and TR measures broad technological views (individual-specific). When combining Technology Readiness Index (TRI) and Technology Acceptance Model (TAM), there are several ways in which it can be done. It could be done by examining the aggregate TRI dimension on the TAM construct of perceived usefulness and perceived ease of use [21]. It was discovered by Lin and Chang [22] that the aggregated TRI dimensions had a direct influence on the TAM usage intention construct. The alternative method is to examine the impact of the four TRI dimensions separately, hypothesizing that the dimensions of optimism and innovativeness have a positive influence on TAM constructs, while the remaining dimensions of discomfort and insecurity have a negative effect on TAM constructs [23, 24] (Fig. 2).

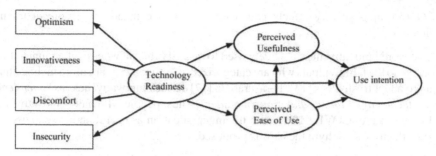

Fig. 2. Technology Readiness and Acceptance Model [18]

2.5 Research Model and Hypothesis Development

The research model (see Fig. 3) for this study was developed based on the previous adoption theories explained above. The research model integrates TAM [25] and TRI [26] to investigate the predictors and inhibitors of adopting COVID-19 contact tracing application. Figure 3 illustrates the research model used for this research.

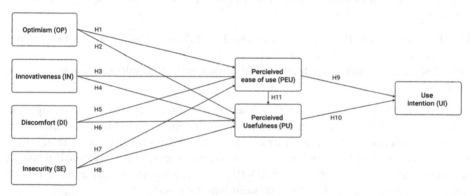

Fig. 3. Research Model

2.6 Hypothesis Development

Parasuraman [17] classifies optimism and innovativeness to be facilitators of technology in Technology Readiness theory. He defines optimism as "*a positive view of technology and a belief that it offers people increased control, flexibility, and efficiency in their lives.*" Individuals who are optimistic about adopting new technology are less likely to pay attention to the negative aspect of innovation. They perceive adopting new technology to improve their lives through efficiency, flexibility, and improvement in controls. Thus, people who are optimistic about innovation are likely to adopt COVID-19 contact tracing application as useful and easy to use. As a result, the following hypothesis was proposed:

H1. Optimism positively affects perceived usefulness in adopting contact tracing application.

H2. Optimism positively affects perceived ease of use in adopting contact tracing application.

The word innovativeness is widely used to quantify the "newness" of an innovation, according to [27]. Individuals who are categorized as "innovative" are more inclined than others to adopt fresh ideas [13]. Parasuraman [17] defines Innovativeness as "*a tendency to be a technology pioneer and thought leader*". Thus, people who have innovativeness are likely to adopt COVID-19 contact tracing application as useful and easy to use. As a result, the following hypothesis was proposed:

H3. Innovativeness positively affects perceived usefulness in adopting contact tracing application.
H4. Innovativeness positively affects perceived ease of use in adopting contact tracing application.

Discomfort is defined as "a feeling of being overwhelmed by technology and a perceived lack of control over it" [17]. Mukherjee and Hoyer [30] feel that complicated features on technology products have a negative impact on product assessment. Thus, individuals who feel a form of discomfort are less likely to adopt COVID-19 contact tracing application as useful and easy to use. As a result, the following hypothesis was proposed:

H5. Discomfort negatively affects perceived usefulness in adopting contact tracing application.
H6. Discomfort negatively affects perceived ease of use in adopting contact tracing application

According to the Parasuraman [17] Insecurity "implies a distrust of technology and doubt about its ability to perform properly". When it comes to adopting new technology, a high level of uncertainty creates a sense of danger, which is proven to have a detrimental influence on perceived ease of use and perceived usefulness. Thus, individuals who feel insecure is less likely to embrace COVID-19 contact tracing application as a helpful and simple. As a result, the following hypothesis was proposed:

H7. Insecurity negatively affects perceived usefulness in adopting contact tracing application.
H8. Insecurity negatively affects perceived ease of use in adopting contact tracing application.

According to the basic TAM model, researchers have been exploring the effect of Perceived usefulness (PU) and Perceived ease of use (PEU) on Use Intention (UI). Reports show that PU and PEU positively impact use intention [25]. However, there have been few research on the intention to adopt COVID-19 contact tracing application. As a result, the following hypothesis was proposed:

H9: Perceived ease of use has a positive influence on intention to adopt contact tracing application.
H10: Perceived usefulness has a positive influence on intention to adopt contact tracing application.

The relationship between perceived ease of use and perceived usefulness has been studied by researchers. Both are thought to be linked. In the context of adopting COVID-19 contact tracing application, a user who deems COVID-19 contact tracing application easy to use would develop a disposition to see them as useful. As a result, the following hypothesis was proposed:

H11: Perceived ease of use has a positive influence on perceived usefulness in adopting contact tracing application.

3 Methodology

To evaluate the derived hypothesis, a cross-sectional survey approach was used in this study. The questionnaire was distributed through the mail and social media in order to optimize response rate and achieve scalability. The questionnaire was created using Google Forms because it not only provides functions to limit what the respondent can answer while also ensuring that the participant is enter the correct data, but it also provides a clear and appealing visual layout, which is important for reliability, validity, and response rate [28]. For this research the non-probability sample was utilized. Non-probability sampling comprises non-random selection based on convenience or other criteria, allowing for more convenient data collection. Using a probability sample is not feasible as a list of all members of the population will be needed in order to draw randomly the desired sample. Using the convenience sampling, the participants for this research were chosen from the general populace since the Nigerian population is too huge to analyze, therefore convenience sampling is a quick, cost-effective, and convenient way to get a sample. The survey utilized for this study was conducted in November 2021. It was circulated via email and social media for people in Nigeria to fill out the online questionnaire. For research using quantitative analysis it is important to select the appropriate data analysis method. The data for this research was evaluated using PLS-SEM (Partial Least Squares - Structural Equation Modelling) and SmartPLS 3.0. SmartPLS 3.0 is a computer program that calculates and evaluates research data and conceptual models [29].

4 Analysis

The questionnaire used for this research was distributed to 200 participants, and a total of 145 were returned, producing a 72.5% response rate. A total of 145 participants data were analyzed after data screening and cleaning. According to the data, males made up 57.9% of the participants, while females made up 42.1%. The majority of the participants were between the ages of 23 and 27 and 28 and 32, according to the statistics. According to the data analysis, 41.4% of the participants were okay with sharing their location on their device, while 58.6% seem to not be okay with the idea sharing their location on their device. Furthermore, 75.8% of participants said they had never used a contact tracing application, while 24.2% said they had used a form of contact tracing application (Table 1).

Internal reliability was measured using composite reliability and are above the recommended 0.70 value [31]. Convergent and discriminant validity were examined using

Table 1. Descriptive Analysis

Description	Options	Frequency	Percentage
Gender	Male	84	57.9
	Female	61	42.1
Age	18–22	22	15.1
	23–27	45	31.0
	28–32	30	20.7
	33–37	24	16.6
	38–42	14	9.7
	43 and above	10	6.9
Education	Diploma or below	38	26.2
	Bachelors	67	46.2
	Masters	25	17.2
	Doctorate	15	10.4
Location Sharing	Yes	60	41.4
	No	85	58.6
Used Contract Tracing Before	Yes	35	24.2
	No	110	75.8

SmartPLS Version 3.0 [32]. Factor loadings are above 0.6 as recommended by [33]. The average extracted variance (AVE) are above 0.5 [34]. Discriminant validity has been established by the square root of the AVE which is greater than the correlations among all the construct (from 0.73 to 0.93). Based on the above criteria, perceived product risk was culled from further analysis.

5 Discussions

Based on the literature review, the research proposed eleven hypotheses. The results shows that six of the proposed hypotheses were supported and proved useful in predicting intentions of adopting COVID-19 contact tracing application while four of the hypotheses were not supported. According to the analysis, H4, H5, H6, H8, H9, and H10 were supported, however H1, H2, H3, H7 and H11 were not supported. Table 2 provides an overview of the hypothesis testing results. Contrary to previous studies [40, 41, 43, 46], the results indicate that both optimism and innovativeness are not significantly related to perceived ease of use.

As technology readiness in influenced by people's personalities and demographics [21] and given the context of Covid-19, this may have adversely affected the positive attitude that our respondents had with regards to the benefits of contact tracing application. As high optimists are very familiar with technology and are unlikely to focus on adverse events [41], the Covid-19 pandemic may have stifled the optimism of our

Table 2. Hypotheses Test

	Hypothesis	Path (β)	T-Value	P-Value	Supported
H1	OP -> PEU	0.03	0.38	n.s	No
H2	OP -> PU	−0.11	1.92	n.s	No
H3	IN -> PEU	−0.09	1.084	n.s	No
H4	IN -> PU	0.28	3.180	$P < 0.001$***	Yes
H5	DI -> PEU	−0.72	10.29	$P < 0.001$***	Yes
H6	DI -> PU	−0.28	2.662	$P < 0.01$**	Yes
H7	SE -> PEU	−0.01	1.58	n.s	No
H8	SE -> PU	−0.36	5.73	$P < 0.001$***	Yes
H9	PEU -> UI	0.35	3.24	$P < 0.001$***	Yes
H10	PU -> UI	0.21	2.24	$P < 0.05$*	Yes
H11	PEU -> PU	0.17	1.55	n.s	No

Note: n.s = non-significant; * $p < 0.05$, ** $p < 0.01$, *** $p < 0.001$ (Using a single line test and bootstrapping with 1,0000 subsample). OP: Optimism, IN: Innovativeness, SE: Insecurity, DI: Discomfort, PU: Perceived Usefulness, PEU: Perceived Ease of Use, UI: Usage Intention

respondents. Moreover, the lack of optimism suggests that the respondents believe that they will not have better control, flexibility and confidence when using contact tracing application [21].

In line with Nugroho and Fajr [43], the result shows that innovativeness is strongly related to perceived usefulness while being non-significant with perceived ease of use. The results demonstrate that innovative individuals are more likely to perceive contact tracing application as being useful rather than being easy to use. Walczuch et al. [24] contend that innovative individuals are familiar with technology and expect technology to meet their demands, hence, the positive relationship with PU. Innovativeness generally measures the degree that individuals perceive themselves as being at the forefront of technology adoption [23]. Innovative people are generally more open to new ideas [35]. It has been demonstrated that an individual's level of creative mindset is a critical factor in his or her acceptance of new technology [36].

Consistent with previous studies [41, 42], the findings also indicate that discomfort has a strong negative significant relationship with both perceived usefulness and perceived ease of use. Insecurity has a strong negative significant relationship with perceived usefulness. Discomfort deals with the fear and concerns that individuals have with regards to the contact tracing application. Therefore, individuals with high level of discomfort towards technology are more likely to perceive adopting COVID-19 contact tracing application as difficult to use and not useful [41].

Individuals lack of trust may contribute towards them feeling insecure towards adopting contact tracing application. Contact tracing app will not only require users to display their location as well as places where they have been recently. Lack of trust has been an important inhibitor to technology adoption [44, 47, 49]. Research defined trust as the willingness to be vulnerable to others and expecting positive intentions towards ones Interest [48].

Other reasons include privacy concerns. Studies involving privacy have shown that privacy risks have a negative effect on use intentions [40, 51]. Harboth and Pape [51] argue that privacy is one of the main reason for the lack of adoption of contact tracing application as individuals were apprehensive about government surveillance [52], leakage of data to third parties [53], exposure of social interactions and secondary data use [54]. These findings have significant implications for Governments trying to use technology to better track and safeguard the population. Governments should work towards alleviating concerns related to insecurity and discomfort with the technology through appropriate training, concerted awareness campaigns. To further alleviate such concerns, the legal implications of such a technology should be looked into. Finally, obtaining a critical mass of users in the first instance could further increase the adoption of the service [55]. Based on TAM model, H9 and H11 were supported. Based on the TAM and numerous studies, the two main predictors of acceptance, perceived useful and ease of use have significant relationship with usage intention. Hypothesis H11 was not supported. It is widely acknowledged that perceived ease of use (PEU) contributes to perceived usefulness (PU) [37, 38]. This is based on the theoretical argument that some user-friendly technologies could be perceived as useful, but not all useful technologies are user-friendly [23]. Overall, the model used predicts 53% in PU and 49% in PEU and 24% of BI.

6 Limitations

To begin, this study was done with a limited sample size from a big population in Nigeria, and the findings obtained cannot properly establish the general community's desire to fully use contact tracing application. Individual opinions change over time, and the findings of this study reflect individual feelings during the time of the crisis. Therefore, further study should be done in the future to obtain more accurate data. Finally, this research depended on quantitative data collecting and analysis. Several academic researchers have emphasized the need of integrating qualitative analysis while studying technology adoption to provide extra insights [39]. Merging qualitative and quantitative approaches in a mixed-method design can further lead to better understanding of adoption of contact tracing apps.

7 Conclusion

The spread of COVID-19 has resulted in a pandemic, with millions of people affected and thousands of deaths globally. Many governments' have put in place strict confinement measures has a way to delay spread of disease and allowed health-care institutions to care for the infected. Various techniques for tracking have been proposed. As a result, contact tracing application has been proposed in a bid to de-escalation the spread of the virus while increasing population safety. The use of contact tracing technology has shown to be useful in countries like South Korea, who have been able to adopt the use of the technology and have been able to maintain the spread of the virus while reactivating its economy due to the use of contact tracing technologies. The research results suggest that the intention to use tracing applications is driven by its perceived usefulness and perceived ease of use. Innovativeness was found to positively influence perceived usefulness while discomfort and insecurity negatively affect usefulness. The findings also demonstrate that discomfort reduces ease of use. This data can be useful to developers that utilize geolocation, as well as governments who must decide whether to use it and what privacy issues it entails. These findings have significant implications for Governments trying to use technology to better track and safeguard the population. Governments should work towards alleviating concerns related to insecurity and discomfort with the technology through appropriate training, concerted awareness campaigns. To further alleviate such concerns, the legal implications of such a technology should be looked into. Finally, obtaining a critical mass of users in the first instance could further increase the adoption of the service. This research backs up the idea that users will be willing to adopt a contact tracing application if they trust it and appreciate its functionality and ease of use, and that privacy concerns are taken into consideration.

References

1. Hopkins, J.: Coronavirus Resource Center (2021). https://coronavirus.jhu.edu/map.html. Accessed 07 Aug 2021
2. Ferguson, N., Laydon, D., Nedjati Gilani, G., et al.: Report 9: Impact of Non-Pharmaceutical Interventions (NPIs) to Reduce COVID19 Mortality and Healthcare Demand, Imperial College London (2020)
3. Sun, K., Viboud, C.: Impact of Contact Tracing on SARS-CoV-2 Transmission. Lancet Infect Dis (2020)
4. WHO. Contact tracing in the context of COVID-19. https://www.who.int/publications/i/item/contact-tracing-in-the-context-of-covid-19. Accessed 9 July 2021
5. Alsdurf, H., et al.: COVID white paper. arXiv preprint arXiv:2005.08502 (2020)
6. Ahmed, N., et al.: A survey of COVID-19 contact tracing apps. IEEE Access (2020). https://doi.org/10.1109/ACCESS
7. Kleinman, R.A., Merkel, C.: Digital contact tracing for COVID-19. CMAJ: Can. Med. Assoc. Journal1/4Journal de L'Association Medicale Canadienne **192**(24), E653–E656 (2020)
8. Vaughan, A.: The problems with contact-tracing apps. New Sci. (2020)
9. Eames, K.T.D., Keeling, M.J.: Contact tracing and disease control. Proceed. Roy. Soc. Lond. Ser. B **270**(1533), 2565–2571 (2003)
10. Shahroz, M., et al.: COVID-19 digital contact tracing applications and techniques: a review post initial deployments. Transp. Eng. **5**, 100072 (2021)
11. Lallmahomed, M.Z.I., Ab. Rahim, N.Z., Ibrahim, R., Rahman, A.A.: A preliminary classification of usage measures in information system acceptance: a Q-sort approach. Int. J. Technol. Diffus. **2**(4), 25–47 (2011)
12. Straub, E.T.: Understanding technology adoption: theory and future directions for informal learning'. Rev. Educ. Res. **79**(2), 625–649 (2009)
13. Rogers, E.: Diffusion of Innovations. Free Press, New York (1983)
14. Fishbein, M., Ajzen, I.: Belief, Attitude, Intention and Behaviour: An Introduction to Theory and Research. Addison-Wesley, Reading (1975)
15. Davis, F.D.: Technology acceptance model for empirically testing new end-user information systems: theory and results. Doctoral dissertation. Sloan School of Management, Institute of Technology: Massachusetts (1986)

16. Venkatesh, V., David, F.: A theoretical extension of the technology acceptance model: four longitudinal field studies. Manag. Sci. **46**, 186–204 (2000)
17. Parasuraman, A.: Technology readiness index (TRI): a multiple-item scale to measure readiness to embrace new technologies. J. Serv. Res. **2**(4), 307–320 (2000)
18. Lin, C., Sher, H., Wang, Y.: Consumer adoption of e-service: integrating technology readiness with the technology acceptance model. In: Technology Management: A Unifying Discipline for Melting the Boundaries, pp. 483–488 (2005)
19. Roy, S.K., Balaji, M.S., Quazi, A., Quaddus, M.: Predictors of customer acceptance of and resistance to smart technologies in the retail sector. J. Retail. Consum. Serv. **42**, 147–160 (2018)
20. Parasuraman, A., Colby, C.L.: Techno-Ready Marketing: How and Why Your Customers Adopt Technology, vol. 224. Free Press, New York (2001)
21. Lin, C., Shih, H., Sher, P.: Integrating technology readiness into technology acceptance: the TRAM model. Psychol. Mark. **24**(7), 641–657 (2007)
22. Lin, J., Chang, H.: The role of technology readiness in self-service technology acceptance. Manag. Serv. Qual. Int. J. **21**(4), 424–444 (2011)
23. Godoe, P., Johansen, T.S.: Understanding adoption of new technologies: technology readiness and technology acceptance as an integrated concept. J. Eur. Psychol. Stud. **3**(1), 38–52 (2012)
24. Walczuch, R., Lemmink, J., Streukens, S.: The effect of service employees' technology readiness on technology acceptance. Inf. Manag. **44**, 206–215 (2007)
25. Davis, F.D., Bagozzi, R.P., Warshaw, P.R.: User acceptance of computer technology: a comparison of two theoretical models. Manag. Sci. **35**(8), 982–1003 (1989)
26. Parasuraman, A., Colby, C.L.: An updated and streamlined technology readiness index: TRI 2.0. J. Serv. Res. **18**(1), 59–74 (2015)
27. Garcia, R., Calantone, R.: A critical look at technological innovation typology and innovativeness terminology: a literature review. J. Prod. Innov. Manag. Int. Publ. Prod. Dev. Manag. Assoc. **19**(2), 110–132 (2002)
28. Saunders, M., Lewis, P., Thornhill, A.: Research Methods for Business Students, 7th edn. Pearson Education, Nueva York (2016)
29. Hair, J.F., Black, W.C., Babin, B.J., Anderson, R.E., Tatham, R.L.: Multivariate Data Analysis. Prentice Hall, Upper Saddle River (1998)
30. Mukherjee, A., Hoyer, W.D.: The effect of novel attributes on product evaluation. J. Consum. Res. **28**(3), 462–472 (2001)
31. Straub, D., Boudreau, M.C., Gefen, D.: Validation guidelines for IS positivist research. Commun. Assoc. Inf. Syst. **13**(1), 380–427 (2004)
32. Ringle, C.M., Wende, S., Becker, J.M.: SmartPLS 3. Oststeinbek: SmartPLS (2020)
33. Hair, J.F., Bush, R.P., Ortinau, D.J.: Marketing Research: Within a Changing Information Environment. McGraw-Hill/Irwin, New York (2003)
34. Fornell, C., Larcker, D.: Structural equation models with unobservable variables and measurement error. J. Mark. Res. **18**(1), 39–50 (1981)
35. Kwang, N.A., Rodrigues, D.: A Big-Five Personality profile of the adaptor and innovator. J. Creative Behav. **36**(4), 254–268 (2002)
36. Brancheau, J.C., Wetherbe, J.C.: The adoption of spreadsheet software: testing innovation diffusion theory in the context of end-user computing. Inf. Syst. Res. **1**(2), 115–143 (1990)
37. Schepers, J., Wetzels, M.: A meta-analysis of the technology acceptance model: investigating subjective norm and moderation effects. Inf. Manag. **44**(1), 90–103 (2007)
38. Venkatesh, V.: Determinants of perceived ease of use: integrating control, intrinsic motivation, and emotion into the technology acceptance model. Inf. Syst. Res. **11**(4), 342–365 (2000)
39. Vogelsang, K., Steinhüser, M., Hoppe, U.: A qualitative approach to examine technology acceptance (2013)

40. Rahmat, T.E., Raza, S., Zahid, H., Abbas, J., Sobri, F.A.M., Sidiki, S.N.: Nexus between integrating technology readiness 2.0 index and students' e-library services adoption amid the COVID-19 challenges: implications based on the theory of planned behavior. J. Educ. Health Promot. **11** (2022)
41. Alharbi, A., Osama, S.: Technology readiness and cryptocurrency adoption: PLS-SEM and deep learning neural network analysis. IEEE Access **9** (2021)
42. Chiu, W., Cho, H.: The role of technology readiness in individuals' intention to use health and fitness applications: a comparison between users and non-users. Asia Pac. J. Mark. Logist. **33**(3), 807–825 (2021)
43. Nugroho, M.A., Fajar, A.: Effects of technology readiness towards acceptance of mandatory web-based attendance system. Procedia Comput. Sci. **124**, 319–328 (2017)
44. Long, M.A.: Understanding non-adopters' intention to use internet pharmacy: revisiting the roles of trustworthiness, perceived risk and consumer traits. J. Eng. Technol. Manag. **59** (2021)
45. Wang, X., Wong, Y.D., Chen, T., Yuen, K.F.: Adoption of shopper-facing technologies under social distancing: a conceptualisation and an interplay between task-technology fit and technology trust. Comput. Hum. Behav. **124** (2021)
46. Flavián, C., Pérez-Rueda, A., Belanche, D., Casaló, L.V.: Intention to use analytical artificial intelligence (AI) in services–the effect of technology readiness and awareness. J. Serv. Manag. **33**(2), 293–320 (2022)
47. Abu-Shanab, E.: E-government familiarity influence on Jordanians' perceptions. Telematics Inform. **34**(1), 103–113 (2017)
48. Abu-Shanab, E.: Antecedents of trust in e-government services: an empirical test in Jordan. Transforming Gov. People Process Policy **8**(4), 480–499 (2014)
49. Lallmahomed, M.Z., Lallmahomed, N., Lallmahomed, G.M.: Factors influencing the adoption of e-Government services in Mauritius. Telematics Inform. **34**(4), 57–72 (2017)
50. Krasnova, H., Spiekermann, S., Koroleva, K., Hildebrand, T.: Online social networks: why we disclose. J. Inf. Technol. **25**(2), 109–125 (2010)
51. Harborth, D., Pape, S.: A privacy calculus model for contact tracing apps: analyzing the use behavior of the German corona-warn-app with a longitudinal user study. Comput. Secur. (2023)
52. O'Callaghan, M.E., et al.: A national survey of attitudes to COVID-19 digital contact tracing in the republic of Ireland. Ir. J. Med. Sci. (2020)
53. Altmann, S., Milsom, L., Zillessen, H., Blasone, R., at al.: Acceptability of app-based contact tracing for COVID-19: cross-country survey study. JMIR mHealth uHealth **8**(8) (2020)
54. Bonner, M., Naous, D., Legner, C., Wagner, J.: The (lacking) user adoption of COVID-19 contact tracing apps–insights from Switzerland and Germany. In: Proceedings of the 15th Pre-ICIS Workshop on Information Security and Privacy, vol. 1 (2020)
55. Van Slyke, C., Ilie, V., Lou, H., Stafford, T.: Perceived critical mass and the adoption of a communication technology. Eur. J. Inf. Syst. **16**(3), 270–283 (2007)

Secondary School Teachers' Adoption of e-learning Platforms in Post Covid-19: A Unified Theory of Acceptance and Use of Technology (UTAUT) Perspective

Rakshay Verma Ramhith and Muhammad Z. I. Lallmahomed[✉]

Middlesex University, Flic-en-Flac, Mauritius
rr678@live.mdx.ac.uk, z.lallmahomed@mdx.ac.mu

Abstract. Following the Covid-19 pandemic, there have been disruptions in the everyday running of educational institutions specially in secondary schools in Mauritius. In order to minimize the disruptions caused, the learning was shifted to an online system and the use of e-learning platforms was introduced. Given the limited number of studies on e-learning adoption by teachers in secondary schools after the Covid 19 pandemic and the more negative responses to e-learning in secondary schools in Mauritius than positive ones, this study sets out to investigate the adoption predictors of e-learning using the UTAUT through a qualitative lens. It seeks out to better understand the experience of secondary teachers using e-learning plaftforms. In total, 18 secondary school teachers were interviewed and the data were analyzed using NVivo software. Data collected were coded and the codes were gathered under themes and sub-themes through Thematic Analysis. One new theme 'accessibility' emerged in addition to the existing five themes from the UTAUT model. The importance UTAUT predictors and behavioral intention was reiterated. Moreover, accessibility has the potential of easing the adoption of e-learning platforms. The main recommendations for the education sector are to provide managerial support in terms of facilities, continuous training, incentives and to adopt a blended approach where e-learning is used as a support to existing teaching methods so that teachers are always technology-ready to switch to exclusive online teaching at short notice should the need arise.

Keywords: eLearning Adoption · Mauritius · UTAUT · Qualitative · Covid19

1 Introduction

In 2019, a deadly virus named the Coronavirus (Covid-19) was discovered in Wuhan, China and within a short period of time it caused the death of thousands of people in China [1]. The virus then spread around the world in 2020 where it infected and killed many more people [1]. Different governments around the world took immediate actions to stop the spread of the deadly virus. They restricted the movement of people and even closed businesses and schools [2]. This caused major disruptions in the everyday running

© ICST Institute for Computer Sciences, Social Informatics and Telecommunications Engineering 2024
Published by Springer Nature Switzerland AG 2024. All Rights Reserved
A. Seeam et al. (Eds.): InterSol 2023, LNICST 541, pp. 264–277, 2024.
https://doi.org/10.1007/978-3-031-51849-2_18

of educational institutions specially in secondary schools. Teachers and students were unable to attend their educational institutions and therefore, could not continue with their normal academic sessions. In order to minimize the disruptions caused, the learning was shifted to an online system and the use of e-learning platforms was introduced [2]. The disruption caused by the Covid 19 virus in the education sector has affected both students and teachers worldwide. Educational institutions have been forced to use and implement online teaching or e-learning systems due to the breakdown in traditional teaching methods caused by the Coronavirus.

In Mauritius, the Government has implemented a series of policies with regards to online teaching and e-learning. They have also provided guidelines for teachers to follow [3]. The implementation of e-learning has changed the way teaching is done. In post covid 19 times, e-learning is being favored instead of face-to-face teaching. The increase in the number of students and teachers using e-learning platforms, has simultaneously increased the use of the internet. This has prompted the Mauritian government to improve the existing network of infrastructures and to implement more e-services. Since the covid 19 outbreak, the use of e-learning platforms has become more and more popular amongst students and teachers specially at the secondary level. Teachers in secondary schools have been preferring the use of e-learning platforms even post covid 19 [4].

Teachers' adoption of e-learning platforms is considered as one of the main factors responsible for successful implementation of e-learning platforms for teaching. There are many studies and models [5–7] that have shown that e-learning has been positively received in the education sector. Studies have discussed about the adoption of e-learning in the education sector by secondary school teachers but only a limited number have focused on its adoption by teachers in secondary schools after the Covid 19 pandemic. Depp and Jeste [8] argued that there have been more negative responses to elearning in secondary schools in Mauritius than positive ones. He stated that this was mainly because of lack of connectivity amongst students and teachers, low level of IT literacy among teachers and a general lack of quality in the contents of courses being delivered through e-learning [8]. The adoption of e-learning platforms by secondary school teachers is an area that has been subjected to limited investigations in recent studies. In this paper we are going to investigate the influence of acceptance predictors on e-learning platforms adoption by secondary school teachers in one secondary school in Mauritius through the use of the Unified Theory of Acceptance and Use of Technology (UTAUT). This study aims to provide clues for easing the implementation of e-learning platform again in the future in other situations for the benefit of students and teachers.

Hence we ask the following question:

Q. How do adoption predictors influence the acceptance of e-learning by secondary school teachers in Mauritius?

2 Literature Review

2.1 E-Learning

Although the term's beginnings are unknown, it is believed that e-learning most likely occurred in the 1980s, around the same time as other online learning delivery methods [9]. Andrews & Haythornthwaite [10] define e-learning as a technology-enhanced learning opportunities, including online and flexible learning, as well as the use of ICT as a tool for group and individual communication and delivery, all serving to support students and enhance learning management. E-learning also includes audio, text, images, and videos. Today's e-learning does not require any specialized hardware or networking. All that is required to access e-learning apps is Internet access and a computer that can run a Web browser [11].

Information Technology has taken up more importance in our daily life during the 21st century and this translates to education also [12]. Information and communication technology (ICT) has become widely employed in education over the past ten years, and as network technologies have proliferated, e-learning techniques have undergone significant change [13]. A classroom with computer terminals connected and where students could listen to recorded lessons of a particular course was developed by the University of Illinois during the 1960's [12]. In the 1990's the internet started to grow, and this gave rise to many distance learning schools with the first online high school being opened in 1994 [12]. Online learning has been growing rapidly in recent years with more students enrolling in online courses provided by educational institutions [13].

Online learning or e-learning has many advantages. E-learning improves the relationship between students and teachers through synchronous and asynchronous communication technologies [13]. E-learning has reduced the hassle in travel and other expenses associated with traditional learning [14]. Teachers and students no longer need to travel by bus or car to school. The time spent in travelling can be used in making longer classes where students and teachers have more interaction [14]. This in turn improves the learning process and increases the enthusiasm, proficiency, intellectual effectiveness and encourages different learning styles [15]. Furthermore, e-learning gives more opportunities to teachers in making their classes more interactive and to increase the engagement levels of their students. When learning becomes more interactive, it changes the focal point to a more active and learner centered approach instead of a passive teacher centered one [15]. Increased interactivity helps students to be more interested in classes and allows them to have more specific practice [15]. The teaching materials provided through e-learning can be easily retrieved from everywhere and at any time [16]. E-learning homogenizes the content and delivery of courses. It prevents situations where teachers explain the same topic to different classes of the same course but there are variations in the way the subject matter is explained [15].

E-learning has many advantages, but it also has its disadvantages. One major disadvantage is that teachers are not able to give practical exercises to students in order for them to apply the theoretical knowledge they have acquired [14]. There are subjects where practical need to be done in school laboratories but with e-learning this cannot be done [14]. In subjects like Biology and Chemistry there are many practical experiments that have to be carried out for better understanding of students but with e-learning it is difficult to do so [16]. Teachers have often complained that they do not have much control through e-learning. They cannot control what the student is doing when they have online classes since they are not physically present to overlook on the educational process [16]. Furthermore, it is very difficult for teachers to make sure that students are actually learning specially when they are given homework. Students may copy and paste answers from the internet without any understanding of the questions [16]. There is the risk of students cheating during online assessments. They may try to work in groups through the use of other applications to find the answers or they may try to look for answers on the net [16]. This can result in students having bad attitudes towards education or their teachers and in a breach of educational values [16].

2.2 Adoption Theories

Important elements that drive people to engage in particular behaviors are described by adoption theories. An adoption theory is employed to look at people and the decisions they make while embracing or rejecting innovation [17]. There have been many adoption models which have emerged during the past years. The Technology Acceptance Model (TAM), Theory of Reasoned Action (TRA), Theory of Planned Behavior (TPB) and Unified Theory of Acceptance and Use of Technology (UTAUT), are the most popular theories [18].

Theory of Reasoned Action (TRA)
According to Taherdoost [44], TRA was established in 1975 by Fishbein and Ajzen where it was initially used in sociology and psychology. In recent years it has become an important aspect in the investigation of behavior patterns when individuals use Information Technology (IT). The National Institute of Mental Health (NIMH) found that there were 8 variables for an individual to engage in a specific behavior. The researchers at the NIMH agreed that only 3 variables were significant in yielding behavior [19] namely:"1. The person has formed a strong positive intention (or made a commitment) to perform the behavior. 2. There are no environmental constraints that make it impossible for the behavior to occur. 3. The person has the skills necessary to perform the behavior" [19]. The Theory of Reasoned Action specifies that behavioral intention is a function of two determinants: a personal factor termed "attitude toward behavior", and a person's perception of social pressures termed "subjective norm" [20]. Attitude refers to the person's own performance of the behavior, rather than his or her performance in general [21]. Subjective norm is a function of a set of beliefs termed normative beliefs. According to Ajzen and Madden [22], normative beliefs "are concerned with the likelihood that important referent individuals or groups would approve or disapprove of performing the behavior". According to the Theory of Reasoned Action, to obtain an estimate of a subjective norm, each normative belief of an individual is first multiplied by motivation to comply with the referent and the cross-product is summed for all salient referents [20].

Technology Acceptance Model (TAM)
According to the Technology Acceptance Model (TAM), user attitudes regarding technological features such as perceived usefulness and perceived ease of use determine behavior intention [23]. The TAM is built on the idea that a user's own ideas, attitudes, and intentions can be used to explain technology acceptance and use. This idea is based on the notion of reasoned action [24]. Numerous studies [25–27] demonstrate that TAM has undergone substantial modification and extension and has demonstrated strength in the adoption of management information systems, information systems, and information technologies. According to Marangunić & Granić [28], a lot of studies have discovered

statistically significant results for the strong influence of perceived utility on behavioral intention to utilize a particular technology. Strong evidence is provided to support TAM as a model for predicting user behaviors in adopting an innovation. A brief, multiple item questionnaire is commonly used to measure the TAM factors [24].

Although TAM has shown success, this paradigm has some flaws. One of TAM's most notable flaws is its inability to identify the factors that influence its independent variables (perceived utility and perceived ease-of-use) [29]. TAM's concentration on information systems that have been implemented in voluntary environments, with little regard for mandatory-use situations, is another flaw. Additionally, rather than from under-developed nations like Uganda, studies employing TAM as their theoretical foundation have primarily been conducted from rich nations like Northern America. Assuming that adoption models or theories for information technology will work equally effectively in various cultural contexts without adjustments would be a grave error. Despite the fact that TAM has been used to explain why students are adopting technology-enhanced learning, extended models like UTAUT and UTAUT2 have shown how social and physical context, as well as consumer judgment, play a part in how students use educational technology [23].

Unified Theory of the Acceptance and Use of Technology (UTAUT)

One of the most recognized and developed areas of information systems (IS) study is on how individuals accept and use information technology (IT) [30]. The idea that one must first use a technology before one can obtain desired outcomes, including an increase in employee productivity and task or job performance in businesses, is also supported by studies on technology adoption by groups and organizations. The Unified Theory of the Acceptance and Use of Technology (UTAUT and UTAUT2), which boosted the explanatory power of earlier technology acceptance models, was created by [30] after empirically comparing and condensing the acceptance literature [23]. Venkatesh, et al. [30] combined these theories around ten years ago to create the Unified Theory of the Acceptance and Use of Technology (UTAUT). Specifically in organisational contexts, UTAUT identifies four key factors performance expectancy, effort expectancy, social influence, and facilitating conditions—as well as four moderators—age, gender, experience, and voluntariness. Performance expectancy can be defined as the extent to which a person thinks that utilizing the system will enable him or her to advance in a career. [31] Effort expectancy can be defined as the perceived ease of use of a system. Social Influence is the extent to which a user believes that influential people consider using technology to be important. Facilitating conditions is the extent to which a person assumes that the system's technological and organizational foundations are in place to facilitate use of the system. These factors are related to predicting behavioral intention to use a technology and actual technology use. UTAUT postulates that performance expectancy, effort expectancy, and social influence have an impact on behavioral intention to use a technology whereas social intent and facilitating circumstances affect technology use [30].

UTAUT based research has flourished even if some believe it has reached its limits in terms of describing individual technology acceptance and use decisions in businesses. Research has specifically used UTAUT to explore a range of technologies in organisational and non-organisational settings, combined it with other theories, or utilized it as is. The propagation and distribution of new ITs, such as enterprise systems, collaboration technology in knowledge-intensive firms, mobile Internet for consumers, agile IS, e-government for citizens, and health IS in the healthcare industry, in organizations and society have contributed to the continued growth of UTAUT-based research [32]. Nearly every part of society has been affected by IT, and many people utilize it in a variety of settings [32]. Routinely assessing the accomplishments of the current studies based on UTAUT can highlight the value of UTAUT and the limits of earlier studies based on UTAUT which one might then utilize to create a new framework for the adoption and use of technology with a view to identifying intriguing areas for future research [30].

2.3 Chosen Underlying Theory

Amongst the different theories discussed above, the Unified Theory of the Acceptance and Use of Technology (UTAUT) has been chosen for this study. It will help in understanding secondary school teacher's approach and purpose in using e-learning platforms after the Covid-19 pandemic. The UTAUT model will likewise help to understand how secondary school teachers have implemented e-learning platforms in their classes. UTAUT was initially developed to better comprehend the elements that affect employees' adoption of and utilization of information technology. However, it has been used in a number of research in an educational setting. In this area, UTAUT has been utilized in technologies including web 2.0, e-learning, computer-based assessment, and mobile learning and also in different countries worldwide [33]. UTAUT synthesizes eight theoretical concepts from psychology and sociological theories that have been utilized in the literature to describe the intention to utilize a technology. TRA and TAM are models that focus more on human behavior in a broad sense whereas UTAUT is more specific in measuring technology acceptance [34]. UTAUT has a better approach to the use of factors such as performance expectancy, effort expectancy, and social influence [35].

3 Methodology

3.1 Data Collection

In this study, a qualitative research method is being used. In order to gather data and acquire understanding of ideas, attitudes, experiences, processes, behaviors, or forecasts [36], a semi structured interviews was carried out. Semi-structured interviews allow the in-depth examination of the use of e-learning platforms by secondary school teachers. The interviews were carried out online and through the phone due to the covid-19 situation which was prevailing in the country at that moment in time where sanitary precautions were taken. Through online phone interviews respondents have been characterized as laid-back and eager to speak freely and openly. Rich, colorful, detailed, and good quality data can be collected with telephone interviews [37]. A pre-test interview was carried out in order to identify mistakes, make sure that questions are in keeping with the main objectives of the study and identify any issues which can be amended before collecting data from the main participants [38] by reviewing the framing of some of the questions. The pre-test was carried out with a limited number of participants (4 teachers). Based on their feedback, interview questions were restructured/rephrased and even merged to allow for simplicity. A few unwarranted mistakes regarding grammar or typing were identified and corrected.

The interviews were carried out online and individually through the phone due to the Covid-19 which was prevailing in the country at that moment in time where sanitary precautions were still being taken. Different sessions of about 30 to 45 min were set up with each respondent at a time that was convenient for both the interviewer and the interviewee. Twenty (20) teachers were contacted for the interview. Eighteen (18) of them responded favorably. Prior to embarking on the interview, the participants were formally invited and were informed of the purpose of the study/project, why they were chosen, free decision to participate and quit at any time, possible risks, data protection and confidentiality clause, the hereafter of the results from this re-search study and the need for consent. Answers to the interview questions were noted down and recorded in the Qualtrics through a link provided. The questions were open ended so as to allow the respondent to expand as much as possible and not be influenced by the interviewer [39]. Through the use of open-ended questions, it is possible to learn from people's spontaneous reactions, avoiding any potential bias that could arise from offering people answers [39].

The data which was collected through interviews was transcribed and analyzed thoroughly so as to gain a comprehensive understanding about research topic. NVivo software was used to perform the analysis. After this process, patterns were identified in the data collected and were categorized into main themes through Thematic Analysis (TA). Thematic analysis (TA), a commonly applied qualitative technique, focuses on the content of participants' remarks by "finding, analyzing and reporting patterns (themes) within data" [40]. A key ability in conducting qualitative data analysis is recognizing recurrent and significant themes, which are found when data are methodically analyzed to uncover trends in order to provide an insightful description of a phenomenon [41]. The main advantage of thematic analysis is that it is an effective technique for data analysis that enables researchers to summarize, highlight, and understand a variety of data sets. Furthermore, it is very accessible to less experienced researchers because there are published descriptions and examples of its use [42].

4   Findings and Discussion

4.1   Performance Expectancy

There were some questions related to how teacher's approach to teaching has changed since the use of e-learning. Most of the respondents have stated that there was a change in their teaching approach. A vast majority of them have said that their teaching has shifted from traditional blackboards to the inclusion of more visual aids through the use of e-learning platforms.

One of the respondents can be quoted as saying: "I had to make more use of visual aids while teaching compared to traditional method. It was more fun, and students enjoyed more!" Another respondent working with science students said: "It has changed my approach towards teaching of science as students are more interested by the tools used and the videos on practical experiments and animations are lively and interactive with visual aids." Some teachers also stated that e-learning platforms have shifted their approach from content based to skill based where students are much more involved in the classes. They added that e-learning has helped students to develop more skills. One teacher said: "The focus of my approach to teaching changed from content-based to skill-based. Through flipped learning, I have been able to switch from teacher-led to student-led lesson, allowing students to develop holistically. For instance, as they are guided through their learning experience, they also develop their self-management skill, communication skill research skill etc."

The interviews have shown that most of the teachers used e-learning alongside traditional teaching to improve the engagement levels in their classes and to help them in the teaching process. The use of a blended approach has had a significantly positive impact on the performance of teachers. There were also more questions asked about how and why e-learning is beneficial to teachers and also about how do teachers perceive that e-learning is beneficial to their teaching. The results from the interviews have shown that there was a significant number of respondents that have said that e-learning was not completely beneficial to them. It saves them time in travelling and they have some level of comfort as they carry out their classes at home, but they added that it will be more beneficial if it is used as an addition to existing teaching methods rather than using it on its own.

One teacher stated that: "E-learning in my opinion cannot be used to wholly replace teaching at school. It can however be used for students who cannot attend school for a long period of time or to catch up with lessons missed." Another teacher has agreed that e-learning has improved performance but had some reservations: "Yes, to some extent as we are in the comfort of our house, no time wasted traveling. If students had been regular and all resources provided, it would have been an excellent way to continue teaching and learning process." On the other hand, some of the teachers have agreed that e-learning can be beneficial to them. A teacher in the English department stated "Yes! I can be more creative and innovative with my teaching! Makes the subject more interesting." A teacher in the science department stated: "Yes, it benefits as it's a new way of teaching with the young generations. Teaching of science is more interesting as it involves more practical experiments through videos, animations. Prior notes, concept maps, video lessons can be forwarded to students".

A vast majority of the teachers that have been asked about the effectiveness of their teaching using e-learning have stated that it has helped to make their day-to-day teaching more effective. One teacher in the English department said it was subject dependent: "I think it depends on the subject. Being an English teacher, it was beneficial in the sense that we could share some resources with students to facilitate understanding."

Another teacher added: "Yes, we are having different methods of teaching I would say for my subject having a simulative lab or a 3D program would be really helpful." However, a teacher in the mathematics department stated: "E-learning is not completely effective. Class teaching where the teacher and students are in the same environment is more effective". This shows that not all teachers that were interviewed were convinced that e-learning would be more effective for their teaching."

4.2 Effort Expectancy

The teachers were asked questions about how they would describe the usability of e-learning systems for teaching. Majority of the respondents answered that they found the use of e-learning platforms for teaching to be quite easy and that the interface was user friendly. There were also some respondents who said that it would have been more effective if it was integrated with the traditional teaching methods and that more encouragement was needed to boost its use.

A teacher stated: "It can be used as a support to help the learning process and not the only means to teach."

Another teacher supplemented: "Though it can be user friendly, but it cannot replace face to face teaching. Long hours on screen make students tired and bored."

A teacher stated: "It is very useful in a blended classroom, where a mixture of online and face to face teaching takes place."

One teacher agreed: "It can be used as a support to help the learning process and not the only means to teach."

A teacher from the physics department stated: "There is much to be done to promote it! More encouragement to adapt to new methods."

There were some respondents who were of a different view. They said that they did not find the e-learning platforms to be very useful for teaching.

One response was: "It is not very effective as students gets tired being for a long time on screen."

4.3 Facilitating Conditions

The interviewees were asked about what more they thought should be done so that e-learning can be easily used in teaching. There was near unanimity among the respondents who stated that they would like to receive more training on how to use the e-learning platforms for teaching pointing to the fact that they were inadequately trained. They also added that there should be adequate online support so that any issues that might arise can be resolved quickly. Some of the teachers have also suggested that an online portal should be developed where all the course materials and resources are provided to students and teachers.

Another teacher stated: "Train teachers so that we make optimum use of the tool. Provide quick online support in case of troubleshoot".

Some were in favor of blended method. One teacher elaborated: "More training should be provided and there should be access to internet in classes. A blended method of teaching should be used in classes, traditional teaching and use of videos to project in classes." A teacher in the biology department stated: "Full-fledged training workshops should be given to educators on online teaching. Online support to be provided for any troubleshooting. Relevant materials to be put on an education online portal for access by students and teachers."

Another teacher in the same department expressed the following: "Developing online portal where students and teachers can easily access relevant materials (worksheets, videos, simulations) for conducive learning".

They were also asked about how their school has helped or provided support to them for the implementation of e-learning in their classes. Most of the teachers have said that they have received limited support from the school highlighting the need of more involvement of management side for an enabling environment. Many respondents pointed out that they had to use their own devices for classes and that they were not compensated for their internet usage even though they had to use own internet connections. They also stated that the support from the school was limited to providing the contact details of the students and contacting them if they have been irregular to classes. A teacher stated: "Teachers had to manage with their own devices and Internet connection at home. We had to submit weekly reports on the conduct of online classes. Schools were however calling students who were not attending the online classes." Another teacher concurred: "Not much was done. They said they will refund us if we are paying packages of students, but nothing was done. We used our own mobiles, computers, or laptops." One teacher confirmed: "Not much support has been provided to educators. Our own devices and Internet connections were used. Students contact details have been provided to all educators. Students who have been irregular were contacted by the school for immediate action." One teacher added: "We had a platform but there were many issues with it! Both students and educators had connection problems".

4.4 Social Influence

The respondents were asked about how their colleagues perceived the use of e-learning platforms for teaching. Most of the respondents answered that their colleagues had mixed feelings about the use of e-learning for teaching. They stated that the younger teachers were more at ease with the e-learning platforms while the older ones had a tough time. Some teachers enjoyed the experience while others found it difficult to give feedback on the work students handed in.

One teacher stated: "Many colleagues would not like to revert back to online classes." A teacher in the biology department stated: "Many were reluctant or at a loss as they were not tech-savvy. Some enjoyed the experience as they were able to cover aspects and complete their syllabus. However, giving feedback was not easy and correction was tiring as we had to read on the screen and used tools, we are not familiar with."

Another teacher stated: "Some had difficulties coping with the use of technologies. Some enjoyed it." A teacher added: "Mixed feeling of colleagues. The younger colleagues were more at ease with it. The less young had difficulty mastering this technique. But e-learning is a good support to keep the work going."

4.5 Behavioral Intention

The interviewees were asked whether they intend to adopt e-learning in their everyday teaching. Most of the respondents testified that they would not use e-learning platforms in their day-to-day classes as they preferred face to face classes. They argued that traditional teaching methods allow teachers to better assess the performance and level of understanding of students.

A teacher stated: "Not really, a lot of preparatory work has to be done to make it really effective. And also, students tend to lose focus mostly during afternoon sessions."

Another teacher added: "I prefer the face-to-face classes as I can see the students and gauge their level of performance and understanding."

On the other hand, there were some teachers who said that they would use e-learning in their classes but would be in favor of a blended approach where e-learning is used as a support to existing teaching methods. A teacher stated: "I would rather go for a blended method Face to face as well as online teaching. "Another teacher added: "Mixed with face to face, online teaching helps to reinforce understanding. If proper incentives such as allowance for internet connection, allowance for compensating family/social life disturbance etc. are provided, the educators will be encouraged to use online teaching."

4.6   New Construct - Accessibility

The interviewees were asked about what they would improve or add to the e-learning approach. Most of the respondents stated that they like the platform to be more accessible. They added that if tablets and internet access was provided to all students and teachers, it would help making e-learning platforms more accessible. Some of the teachers also said that it would be better if there could be resources provided online and more training was provided as the training they received were of a short duration and mainly as a matter of expediency mainly to familiarize with e-learning platforms.

For improving accessibility, one teacher suggested: "Providing access of internet and tablet to all students. A monitor to check attendance so that teachers do not waste time doing it."

Another teacher from the science department added: "A lighter version so that it is accessible to everyone no matter the data usage. Online resources could have been already uploaded on the platform such as textbook, notes, videos, charts, explanation, anything that can facilitate teaching and learning." A teacher from the French department stated: "More training in terms of psychological approach for students! Having an ongoing of blended method for teaching both online and face to face sessions."

A teacher from the biology department expanded further: "Internet access and tablet facilities provided to all students. Online resources made available and uploaded on the platform."

The study shows that the teachers have some personal benefits from the use of e-learning platforms. The most common personal benefit was that it saves them a lot of time as they don't have to travel to school, and they can teach in the comfort of their own house. They would rather use that time to better prepare for the classes which they have for the day. The second most common benefit was that the available resources could be shared with students for either classwork or homework. However, it was also found that almost all of the teachers agreed that they would use a blended approach to teaching where they combine the use of traditional teaching methods with e-learning methods. It was observed that most teachers were more willing to use e-learning platforms as they were user friendly. This made it easy for them to navigate through the system as they were carrying out their classes. However, it was found that many teachers noticed high fatigue levels in students after spending long hours behind the screen. The teachers almost unanimously agreed that there was a lack of training on how to use the e-learning platforms for teaching and that there was not much online support to resolve issues that arise. They suggested that if an online portal was developed and the appropriate resources provided, they would be more encouraged to use e-learning platforms fully. Another finding was that there was not enough support from the school management to facilitate the use of e-learning platforms. Many of the teachers complained that the management limited themselves to providing contact details of students and contacting them when needed.

5 Limitations

The research could have been further expanded to teachers from all over Mauritius and from different types of secondary schools are interviewed as secondary schools that are private grant-aided, private fee paying and state owned could also be investigated separately as three distinct groups being given that the infrastructure and management may be different. A second limitation of this study would be that a qualitative research methodology was used. Using this methodology allowed for only a limited number of teachers to be interviewed for data collection. A quantitative research methodology could be used either as an alternative or alongside the current methodology. This would allow for more teachers to be interviewed and for a greater sample to be selected. The results obtained could be used to have a better analysis of the factors which influence the adoption of e-learning amongst secondary school teachers post Covid-19.

6 Conclusions

This study has investigated the secondary school teachers' adoption of e-learning platforms post Covid-19 through the use of the Unified Theory of Acceptance and Use of Technology (UTAUT) model. E-learning platforms have been in use long before the pandemic, but their use was limited mostly to students. During the Covid 19 pandemic, e-learning platforms have become an integral part of secondary schooling and is still being used in classes post Covid-19. An analysis of the different responses was carried out using the NVivo software. Qualtrics and Momentive tools were used for data collection through interviews. Through this study's analysis and data collection methods, the importance of the five existing factors namely, Performance Expectancy, Effort Expectancy, Facilitating Conditions, Behavioral Intention and Social Influence in promoting the adoption of e-learning post Covid 19 by secondary school teachers were validated. It showed that the above-mentioned factors are crucial in the acceptance of new technology. However, only five factors do not suffice to determine the adoption of e-learning. One additional factor, accessibility, has been identified to be combined to the existing UTAUT model so that there is a more accurate approach. These can provide valuable clues with regards to remedial measures to be proposed for improving the implementation and adoption of e-learning platform by secondary school teachers. It emerged that there was a lack of accessibility to e-learning facilities and even access to the internet. The school did not provide facilities to make the use of e-learning more accessible. It can be argued that if more managerial support was provided and accessibility was eased, it would have helped greatly in the adoption of e-learning platforms by teachers. The main recommendations for the education sec-tor are to provide managerial support in terms of facilities, continuous training, incentives and to adopt a blended approach where e-learning is used as a support to existing teaching methods so that the teachers are always technology-ready to switch on to exclusive online teaching at short notice, should the need arise such as during the acute phase of an epidemic or a natural calamity.

References

1. WHO, Homepage. https://apps.who.int/iris/bitstream/handle/10665/332197/WHO-2019-nCoV-FAQ-Virus_origin-2020.1-eng.pdf. Accessed 30 June 2022
2. UNESCO, UNESCO. https://www.unesco.org/en/covid-19. Accessed 30 June 2022
3. Govmu.org. https://education.govmu.org/Pages/Main/Online-Platforms.aspx. Accessed 30 June 2022
4. Alhumaid, K., et al.: COVID-19 & e-learning: Perceptions & attitudes of teachers towards E-learning acceptance in the developing countries. Multicult. Educ. **6**(2), 100–115 (2020)
5. Elfaki, N., Abdulraheem, I., Abdulrahim, R.: Impact of e-learning vs traditional learning on student's performance and attitude. Int. J. Med. Res. Health Sci. **10**(8), 76–82 (2019)
6. Harandi, S.R.: Effects of e-learning on students' motivation. Procedia Soc. Behav. Sci. **181**, 423–430 (2015)
7. Cidral, W., Oliveira, T., Di Felice, M., Aparicio, M.E.: E-learning success determinants: Brazilian empirical study. Comput. Educ. **122**(1), 273–290 (2018)
8. Depp, C., Jeste, D.: Definitions and predictors of successful aging: a comprehensive review of larger quantitative studies. Am. J. Geriatr. Psychiatry **14**(1), 6–20 (2006)
9. Moore, J., Dickson-Deane, C., Galyen, K.: E-Learning, online learning, and distance learning environments: are they the same? Internet High. Educ. **14**(2), 129–135 (2011)
10. Andrews, R., Haythornthwaite, C.: The Sage Handbook of E-Learning Research. Sage, California (2007)
11. Piotrowski, M.: What is An E-learning Platform? IGI Global, Pennsylvania (2010)
12. Agarwal, H., Pandey, G.: Impact of E-learning in education. Int. J. Sci. Res. (IJSR) **2**(12), 146–147 (2013)
13. Wei, H., Chou, C.: Online learning performance and satisfaction: do perceptions and readiness matter? Dist. Educ. **41**(1), 48–69 (2020)
14. Maatuk, A., et al.: The COVID-19 pandemic and E-learning: challenges and opportunities from the perspective of students and instructors. J. Comput. High. Educ. **34**(1), 21–38 (2022)
15. Jethro, O., Grace, A., Thomas, A.: E-learning and its effects on teaching and learning in a global age. Int. J. Acad. Res. Bus. Soc. Sci. **2**(1), 203 (2012)
16. Alhomos, M., et al.: Financial obstacles and disadvantages of E-learning from the viewpoint of Dammam teachers. Indian J. Forensic Med. Toxicol. **15**(4), 1815 (2021)
17. Zhang, L., et al.: E-learning adoption intention and its key influence factors based on innovation adoption theory. Math. Comput. Model. **51**(11–12), 1428–1432 (2010)
18. Oliveira, T., Martins, M.: Literature review of information technology adoption models at firm level. Electr. J. Inf. Syst. Eval. **14**(1), 110–121 (2011)
19. Fishbein, M., Ajzen, I.: Predicting and Changing Behavior: The Reasoned Action Approach. Psychology press, New York (2011)
20. Yousafzai, S., Foxall, G., Pallister, J.: Explaining internet banking behavior: theory of reasoned action, theo-ry of planned behavior, or technology acceptance model? J. Appl. Soc. Psychol. **40**(5), 1172–1202 (2010)
21. Ajzen, I., Fishbein, M.: A Bayesian analysis of attribution processes. Psychol. Bull. **82**(2), 261 (1975)

22. Ajzen, I., Madden, T.J.: Prediction of goal-directed behavior: attitudes, intentions, and perceived behavioral control. J. Exp. Soc. Psychol. **22**(5), 453–474 (1986)
23. Mehta, A., Morris, N., Swinnerton, B., Homer, M.: The influence of values on E-learning adoption. Comput. Educ. **141**, 103617 (2019)
24. Turner, M., et al.: Does the technology acceptance model predict actual use? A systematic literature review. Inf. Softw. Technol. **52**(5), 463–479 (2010)
25. Mao, E., Palvia, P.: Testing an extended model of IT acceptance in the Chinese cultural context. Database **37**(2&3), 20–32 (2006)
26. Abbad, M.M., Morris, D., De Nahlik, C.: Looking under the bonnet: factors affecting student adoption of e-learning systems in Jordan. Int. Rev. Res. Open Distrib. Learn. **10**(2) (2009)
27. Maleko Munguatosha, G., Birevu Muyinda, P., Thaddeus Lubega, J.: A social networked learning adoption model for higher education institutions in developing countries. On Horizon **19**(4), 307–320 (2011)
28. Marangunić, N., Granić, A.: Technology acceptance model: a literature review from 1986 to 2013. Univ. Access Inf. Soc. **14**, 81–95 (2015)
29. Kimwise, A.: Adoption of e-learning technologies in education institutions/organizations: a literature review. Asian J. Educ. Res. **5**(4), 63–71 (2017)
30. Venkatesh, V., Thong, J.Y.L., Xu, X.: Unified theory of acceptance and use of technology. J. Assoc. Inf. Syst. **17**(5), 328–376 (2016)
31. Chang, A.: UTAUT and UTAUT 2: a review and agenda for future research. Winners **13**(2), 10–114 (2012)
32. Williams, M., Rana, N., Dwivedi, Y.: The unified theory of acceptance and use of technology (UTAUT): a literature review. J. Enterp. Inf. Manag. **28**(3), 444–445 (2015)
33. Escobar-Rodríguez, T., Carvajal-Trujillo, E., Monge-Lozano, P.: Factors that influence the perceived ad-vantages and relevance of Facebook as a learning tool: an extension of the UTAUT. Australas. J. Educ. Technol. **30**(2) (2014)
34. Rahman, M.M., Lesch, M.F., Horrey, W.J., Strawderman, L.: Assessing the utility of TAM, TPB, and UTAUT for advanced driver assistance systems. Accid. Anal. Prev. **108**, 361–373 (2017)
35. AbuShanab, E., Pearson, J.: Internet banking in Jordan: the unified theory of acceptance and use of technology (UTAUT) perspective. J. Syst. Inf. Technol. **9**(1), 78–97 (2007)
36. Rowley, J.: Conducting research interviews. Manag. Res. Rev. **35**(3/4), 260–271 (2012)
37. Novick, G.: Is there a bias against telephone interviews in qualitative research? Res. Nurs. Health **31**(4), 391–398 (2008)
38. Mikuska, E.: The importance of piloting or pre-testing semi-structured interviews and narratives. SAGE Research Methods Cases (2017)
39. Reja, U., Manfreda, K., Hlebec, V., Vehovar, V., Open-ended vs. close-ended questions in web questionnaires. Dev. Appl. Stat. **19**(1), 159–177 (2003)
40. Bennett, D., Barrett, A., Helmich, E.: How to analyse qualitative data in different ways. Clin. Teach. **16**(1), 7–12 (2019)
41. Noble, H., Smith, J.: Qualitative data analysis: a practical example. Evid Based Nurs **17**(1), 2–3 (2014)
42. Kiger, M., Varpio, L.: Thematic analysis of qualitative data: AMEE Guide No. 131. Med. Teacher **42**(8), 846–854 (2020)

Prof Pi: Using Whatsapp Bots and GPT-4 for Tutoring Mathematics in Underserved Areas

Laurie Butgereit[1(✉)] and Herman Martinus[2]

[1] Nelson Mandela University, Gqeberha, South Africa
laurie.butgereit@gmail.com
[2] Long Llama Studio, Cape Town, South Africa
herman@longllamastudio.com

Abstract. Mathematics education is often a prerequisite for studying certain subjects further at tertiary institutions. Mathematics education is a type of gate keeper for further education. In underserved areas, pupils often need more help with mathematics than it is possible to provide. This could be due to financial reasons (lack of budget in the education system), geographical reasons (pupils living in extremely rural areas), or temporary health restrictions (as seen during the COVID lockdowns when schools were closed in many countries). Prior research by the authors showed that *Prof Pi*, a Whatsapp Bot linked to OpenAI's GPT-4 large language model, could tutor mathematics at university level in the Arabic language. While that prior educational research was being conducted, violent unrest rocked the area where the university was located and many people started to leave the area. Sad as this was, it provided an opportunity for the researchers to observe *Prof Pi* operating in an underserved area.

Keywords: Whatsapp · bots · GPT-4 · tutoring · mathematics

1 Introduction

In January each year, the South African Department of Basic Education releases the results of the end of year examinations for the previous academic year for secondary schools. Technically, the examinations are called the *National Senior Certificate* but colloquially they are known as the *matric*. Pupils who had finished Grade 12 just before the Christmas break had spent a nervous holiday season worrying about their *matric* results.

In many ways, however, the various adults involved in education in South Africa such as parents, teachers, school administrators, government officials, and politicians worry about the results of the examinations just as much as the pupils themselves.

With respect to this paper, the examination subject of most interest is the mathematics examination results. South Africa offers two different mathematics examinations for the Grade 12 pupils: Mathematics and Mathematical Literacy. A good result on the Mathematics examination (also called Technical Mathematics) is a pre-requirement to studying more technical subjects at a tertiary level such as physics and computer science.

© ICST Institute for Computer Sciences, Social Informatics and Telecommunications Engineering 2024
Published by Springer Nature Switzerland AG 2024. All Rights Reserved
A. Seeam et al. (Eds.): InterSol 2023, LNICST 541, pp. 278–289, 2024.
https://doi.org/10.1007/978-3-031-51849-2_19

According to the report issued by the Department of Basic Education, a total of 725,146 pupils wrote the examinations at the end of the 2022 academic year. Of those 725,146 pupils, 269,734 wrote the Mathematics examination. And of those 269,734 pupils, only 148,346 (55%) passed the examination with at least a 30% pass mark. This was, sadly, a decrease from the previous year [1].

One could argue that the calculation of the percentage of pupils who passed (55%) should be calculated as a percentage of all of the pupils who wrote the exams and not just the number of pupils who wrote the Mathematics exams. Others prefer to argue that the calculation of the percentage of pupils who passed should be calculated as a percentage of all the pupils who started school back at Grade 0 or Grade 1 twelve or thirteen years prior to this examination. This paper does not touch those arguments.

This paper is not to bemoan the results of these examinations. It is to ask the question of whether or not there are innovative multi-disciplinary ways to help with mathematics education – especially in underserved areas.

Specifically this paper looks at how advances in social media platforms merged with recent advances in language modeling can be used in helping pupils who might need extra tutoring but live in underserved areas where tutors are not available.

This paper describes an artifact called *Prof Pi* which can be used to tutor mathematics in areas where human tutors are not available. These underserved areas could be caused by economic reasons such as lack of finances to pay tutors, physical reasons such a rural areas, or temporary health measures such as happened in 2019 and 2020 during the hard lockdowns imposed by politicians around the world due to the COVID outbreaks.

Section 2 of this paper provides a literature review and specifically looks at prior research done by the authors in mathematics tutoring. Section 3 describes a number of issues or challenges with face-to-face tutoring situations where tutors and pupils meet in-real-life. Section 4 discusses the ethical issues surround this specific project. Section 5 describes the research methodology used for producing this prototype. Section 6 provides a description of the prototype and its components. Section 6 also provides sample dialogs which could happen between a pupil and *Prof Pi*. During the period of time this paper was being written, unrest broke out in Khartoum, Sudan, and *Prof Pi* was deployed to assist university level students with their mathematics problems using Arabic language. Information on that can be found in Sect. 7. Concluding remarks and future work is found in Sect. 8.

2 Previous Research in Distance Education and Remote Tutoring

Remote tutoring is a subset of distance education. Distance education has a very long and rich history. One could actually even argue that distance education is documented in Biblical times referring to Paul's letters to the distant churches.

Rolling through time quickly, however, postal courses in the United States [2] and Britain [3] sent printed materials to students. These students were often in underserved areas where they could not attend face-to-face courses. Radio courses and television courses emerged in the first half of the twentieth century again often targeting students in underserved areas.

These three modes of communication, however, postal, radio, and television, were mostly uni-directional: information was sent from the teacher or tutor to the student or pupil. As the Internet matured, lessons could become bi-directional allowing the student and pupil to actively take part in these remote lessons.

In the underserved world (also often called the *developing world*), the use of cell phones enabled pupils and students to reach chat rooms and mobile websites to assist with their education.

The authors have previously worked on a mathematics tutoring project using text based chat systems. That project, *Dr Math*, is well reported in the literature [4, 5]. Dr Math linked human tutors to pupils using internet technologies. Extensive work was done to handle the potential problems documented in Sub-Sect. 3.2 following.

3   Issues with Face-to-Face Tutoring and Remote Tutoring

There are a number of issues present in face-to-face tutoring and remote tutoring which need to be discussed.

For the scope of this section, the expression *face-to-face tutoring* refers to when a tutor and a pupil meet physically in order to discuss their academic issues. These issues will be discussed in Sub-Sect. 3.1. The expression *remote tutoring* refers to a situation where a real human tutor and a real human pupil communicate using internet technologies such as tele-conferencing or text chat facilities. These issues are discussed in Sub-Sect. 3.2.

3.1   Issues with Face-to-Face Tutoring

In any situation where children meet up with adults, care must be taken to protect the children from any harm perpetrated by the adult. And, care must be taken to protect the adult from any harm to the adult caused by false allegations by a child. Both of these are difficult challenges.

Perhaps the easiest to target is protecting the children from the adult. This is often facilitated by requiring police checks of the adults ensuring they do not have a history of harming children. Other strategies include having unannounced visits by supervisors to check in on the interactions between the adults and children.

Protecting the adult from false allegations by a child is more problematic but the risk can be mitigated by having rules in place which never allow an adult and child alone together in an enclosed area and to always ensure that there are more than one adult and more than one child at each interaction.

In underserved areas, however, many of the attempts to protect the participants are expensive in manpower and can not actually be implemented because of lack of such manpower.

3.2   Issues with Remote Tutoring

In the situation of remote tutoring, there are also a number of concerns. Three of these concerns include 1) the remote tutoring platform being used to exchange unacceptable photographs or conversation (such as pornographic images) 2) the remote tutoring platform being used to facilitate face-to-face meetings between the participants and 3) the remote tutoring platform being used to facilitate the sale of illicit items such as drugs.

There are a number of ways to mitigate these problems depending on whether the remote tutoring is working over chat facilities or tele-conferencing facilities. But both require some sort of keyword recognition and human monitoring.

In the case of underserved areas, both of these can be hard and expensive to implement in terms of manpower.

4   Ethics

This project was to evaluate *Prof Pi*, a Whatsapp Bot linked to the GPT-4 API configured to act as a mathematics tutor, and determine if it was suitable for use in underserved areas. For the scope of this paper, *Prof Pi* was never presented to actual pupils. No minor children or any human subjects were used for the scope of this paper. As such, no ethics approval for this research paper was required. Prior educational research with *Prof Pi* in an underserved area during times of violent unrest which is discussed in Sect. 7 did have an ethics approval by the university involved.

Having said that, the Dr Math project mentioned above in Sect. 2 did have an ethics approval. In many of the publications about Dr Math, conversations were published in papers and in data bundles. Many of those conversations were used as test data in this *Prof Pi* project.

5   Research Methodology

At the beginning of the original development of the *Prof Pi* artifact, it was not known whether or not it would be possible to configure GPT-4 and Whatsapp to work together to provide tutoring services in mathematics. Because of this, Design Science Research methodology was used to guide this project.

Design Science Research is an iterative approach to solving real world problems. Design Science Research involves three inter-woven cycles: 1) A relevance cycle which ensures that a real world problem is being tackled 2) A rigor cycle which ensures that scientific rigor is used in attempting to solve this real world problem and 3) a design cycle which binds everything together [6]. Hevner illustrates these three inter-woven cycles as in Fig. 1.

In attempting to solve a real world problem, followers of Design Science Research must create artifacts. These artifacts embody new knowledge. There are a number of types of artifacts which can be created by Design Science Research. These include constructs, models, frameworks, architectures, design principles, methods, and instantiations [7].

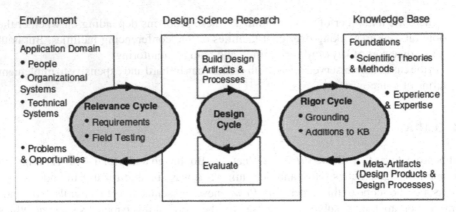

Fig. 1. The three cycles of Design Science Research

6 *Prof Pi* Description

Prof Pi is a Whatsapp bot designed to assist students with their mathematics homework using GPT-4. It offers a powerful and accessible solution for learners seeking guidance and support. This bot operates within the popular messaging platform, Whatsapp, allowing students to interact with it in a familiar environment. By leveraging GPT-4's advanced natural language understanding and generation capabilities, the bot can comprehend and respond to a wide range of mathematical inquiries, ranging from basic arithmetic to more complex concepts. This intuitive interaction makes the learning experience engaging, effective, and enjoyable for students, while also providing instantaneous feedback and personalised assistance.

The integration of GPT-4 into a Whatsapp bot for mathematics tutoring is particularly beneficial and cool because it merges the advanced capabilities of a state-of-the-art AI model with the convenience of a widely-used messaging platform. Students can easily access the bot on their devices, making it an ideal tool for remote learning or on-the-go support. Furthermore, GPT-4's proficiency in natural language processing allows the bot to understand and respond to complex mathematical problems in a conversational manner, simulating the experience of interacting with a human tutor. This innovative approach to math tutoring has the potential to transform the way students learn and engage with mathematical concepts, making education more accessible, significantly more inexpensive and enjoyable for learners of all levels.

One of the most important features of *Prof Pi* is that it is configured to be a Socratic tutor and it does not just provide students with the exact answers to the questions. *Prof Pi* engages the student in dialog so that the student solves his own question and, therby, learns something. If students just want answers, they can access the GPT-4 API directly using OpenAI's chatGPT website. *Prof Pi*, on the other hand, is a tutor to guide the students into solving their own problems.

Sub-Sect. 6.1 describes the overall architecture of the artifact. Sub-Sect. 6.2 provides a brief description of how Whatsapp bots actually work. Sub-Sect. 6.3 provides a description of GPT-4 and some of the configuration problems which needed to be solved.

Sub-Sect. 6.4 provides some sample chat dialogs with the authors to demonstrate how *Prof Pi* works.

6.1 Overall Architecture

The architecture of the system for assisting students with their mathematics homework can be broadly divided into three main components: the Whatsapp interface, the backend server, and the GPT-4 API integration. This can be seen in Fig. 2.

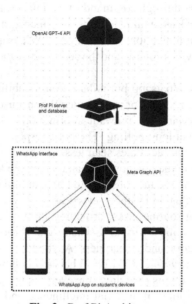

Fig. 2. Prof Pi Architecture

The Whatsapp interface facilitates user interactions, allowing students to communicate with the bot using natural language or mathematical notation. The backend server processes incoming messages, manages user sessions, and orchestrates the communication between the Whatsapp/Meta platform and the GPT-4 API. Lastly, the GPT-4 API integration enables the bot to access the powerful natural language understanding and generation capabilities of the GPT-4 model, allowing it to generate meaningful and contextually relevant responses to students' inquiries.

When a student sends a message or question to the Whatsapp bot, the Whatsapp/Meta platform forwards the message to the *Prof Pi* backend server. The server then processes the message and prepares it for submission to the GPT-4 API. This may involve tokenisation, formatting, or incorporating relevant context from previous interactions. Once the message is processed, the server sends a request to the GPT-4 API, which generates an appropriate response based on its understanding of the context and the mathematical query. The *Prof Pi* backend server receives the response from the GPT-4 API, processes it if necessary, and sends it back to the student via the Whatsapp platform.

The platform is built in such a way that the identity of the student is never received nor stored on the server. The only identifying information is a cell number of the student. The bot is also programmed to filter and delete all attempts to provide personal information. This protects the identities of the students.

6.2 Whatsapp Bots Description

Whatsapp bots are specialised software applications that run within the Whatsapp/Meta messaging platform, automating tasks and providing a wide range of services to users. Bots can interact with users through commands, text, images, and other media, enabling them to perform actions such as sending notifications, managing groups, retrieving information, or facilitating communication. In recent years, Whatsapp bots have gained popularity due to their versatility, ease of use, and the convenience they offer to both developers and end-users.

The functionality of a Whatsapp bot is based on its ability to receive and process user inputs in the form of messages or commands. When a user interacts with a bot, the Whatsapp/Meta server forwards the relevant information to the bot's designated webhook URL or retrieves it via long polling. The bot's response can then be sent back to the user via Whatsapp, which facilitates seamless communication within the platform.

Whatsapp bots have emerged as powerful and adaptable tools without the need for downloading apps. Their low data consumption and minimal hardware requirements make them particularly valuable in underserved areas where access to resources may be limited. By automating routine tasks, providing instant access to information, and facilitating communication, these virtual assistants can greatly improve the user experience for students, educators, and researchers. As the technology continues to evolve, it is likely that the range of applications for Whatsapp bots will only expand, offering increasingly innovative solutions to address the ever-changing needs of the educational landscape. With the integration of artificial intelligence and machine learning, Whatsapp bots hold the potential to revolutionise the way we approach teaching, learning, and research.

6.3 GPT-4 Description

GPT-4, or Generative Pre-trained Transformer 4, is an advanced multi-modal language model developed by OpenAI, which has garnered significant attention due to its remarkable natural language understanding and generation capabilities [8]. Built on the transformer architecture, GPT-4 is pre-trained on a massive corpus of text data, enabling it to generate contextually relevant and coherent responses to a wide range of language-related tasks. With 175 billion parameters, GPT-4 has demonstrated a high level of proficiency in various applications, such as machine translation, summarisation, question-answering, and even tasks that require logical reasoning.

The underlying strength of GPT-4 lies in its self-attention mechanism and unsupervised learning approach, which allow the model to capture complex patterns and relationships within the input data. During the pre-training phase, GPT-4 learns to predict the next word in a sentence based on the context provided by previous words, resulting in a robust understanding of syntax, semantics, and even nuanced language constructs. This extensive knowledge base enables GPT-4 to generate contextually appropriate responses when prompted with user-generated text or questions, making it a versatile tool for various applications.

In the context of mathematics mentoring, GPT-4's ability to understand and generate natural language makes it a promising candidate for providing guidance, explanations, and problem-solving assistance to students. Its proficiency in recognising and processing mathematical notation, coupled with its capacity for logical reasoning, allows GPT-4 to address a diverse range of mathematical topics, spanning from basic arithmetic to advanced concepts. Moreover, its capacity to generate human-like responses enables GPT-4 to engage with students in a more interactive and intuitive manner, potentially fostering a more effective and engaging learning experience.

6.4 Sample Dialogs

This section provides some examples of how the prototype could operate in a tutoring environment for mathematics. The conversations are presented as text taken from the log files. To save space, they are not presented as images from the cell phone screen. There are five examples with one example each in algebra, geometry, trigonometry, calculus, and a story problem.

In the following sample algebra question, the pupil converses with *Prof Pi* as if *Prof Pi* were a human being using expressions such as "umm", and "oh right, my bad."

```
Student: hey, i need help with this question, its asking me to solve 2x - 6 = 10?
Prof Pi: Hi there! Sure, I can help. First, can you try isolating the term with the
variable (x) by performing the same operation on both sides of the equation?
Student: ok so i add 6 to both sides, i get 2x = 16
Prof Pi: Great job! Now, what should you do next to find the value of x?
Student: umm i think i should add 2 to both sides
Prof Pi: Almost! Remember, we want to isolate x by itself. Which operation
should you use to do that?
Student: oh right, my bad, i should divide both sides by 2
Prof Pi: That's correct! Go ahead and divide both sides by 2 to find the value of
x.
Student: cool, so x = 8
Prof Pi: Well done! You've found the correct value for x. Keep practicing, and
you'll continue to improve!
```

Geometry is problematic in a text based system. This prototype did not react to images forcing the pupil to describe the geometry problem in detail.

Student: I'm having difficulty with this geometry problem. It says: In a parallelogram ABCD, angle A is 35 degrees. Find the measure of angle C.

Prof Pi: Hi there! I'm happy to help. Since this is a parallelogram, do you recall the relationship between the opposite angles in a parallelogram?

Student: Yes, the opposite angles are equal.

Prof Pi: That's correct! Knowing that, can you determine the measure of angle C based on the given information about angle A?

Student: I think I've got it. Since angle A is 35 degrees and angle C is opposite to angle A, angle C should be 70 degrees.

Prof Pi: Almost there! Remember, opposite angles in a parallelogram are equal. Can you reconsider the measure of angle C based on this property?

Student: Oh, my mistake! Since angle A is 35 degrees and angle C is opposite to angle A, angle C should also be 35 degrees.

Prof Pi: Excellent! You've correctly found the measure of angle C in the parallelogram. Keep up the good work!

The following example deals in Trigonometry

Student: yo, got this trig thing, idk how to do it: sin x = 0.5, find x

Prof Pi: Hey there! No worries. First, which trig function helps us find the angle when we know the sine value?

Student: umm cosine?

Prof Pi: Almost! It's actually the inverse of another trig function. Can you recall which one it is?

Student: oh right, inverse sine?

Prof Pi: That's correct! Now, use the inverse sine function to find the angle x.

Student: so like x = sin(0.5)

Prof Pi: Close, but remember, we need to use the inverse sine function. Can you try again?

Student: oh, so x = sin^-1(0.5)

Prof Pi: Exactly! Can you calculate the angle now?

Student: x is 60 degrees

Prof Pi: Not quite. Double-check your calculation and make sure you're using the inverse sine function correctly.

Student: My bad, x is 30 degrees

Prof Pi: Great job! You found the correct angle. Keep practicing, and you'll get the hang of trigonometry!

The following conversation deals with Calculus:

Student: Prof Pi, I have calculus problem. Find derivative of f(x) = x^3 + 2x^2 - 5x + 3. Please give me answer.

Prof Pi: I'd be happy to help you, but my goal is to guide you towards the answer. First, do you remember the power rule for finding derivatives?

Student: Yes, I remember. It is nx^(n-1) for x^n.

Prof Pi: That's right! Now, apply the power rule to each term of the function separately.

Student: Ok, so for x^3, it is 3x^2, right?

Prof Pi: Exactly! Now, can you apply the power rule to the remaining terms?

Student: For 2x^2, it is 4x. For -5x, it is -5. For 3, I'm not sure.

Prof Pi: Good progress! Remember, what's the derivative of a constant?

Student: Oh, I see. Derivative of constant is 0.

Prof Pi: Correct! Now, can you combine the derivatives of each term to find the derivative of the whole function?

Student: Yes, so f'(x) = 3x^2 + 4x - 5.

Prof Pi: Well done! You've successfully found the derivative of the function. Keep up the good work!

The following conversation deals with a story problem:

Student: Hey Prof Pi, my teachr gave me this story problm, and I'm stuck. Can u help? It says: "Emma has 3 times as many red aplles as gren apples. If she has a totl of 20 aplles, how many gren aplles does she have?"

Prof Pi: Of course! Let's work through this together. First, let's use a variable to represent the number of green apples Emma has. What do you think would be a good variable to use?

Student: Um, how bout "g" for gren aplles?

Prof Pi: That's a good choice! Now, since Emma has 3 times as many red apples as green apples, can you write an expression for the number of red apples using "g"?

Student: I think red aplles is 3g, right?

Prof Pi: Yes, that's correct! We know that the total number of apples is 20. Can you create an equation using the expressions for green and red apples?

Student: So, I guess it's g + 3g = 20?

Prof Pi: Yes, you're on the right track! Now, can you simplify the equation and solve for "g"?

Student: Umm, 4g is equal to 20, so g = 4?Prof Pi: Almost there! Double-check your calculations, and remember to divide both sides of the equation to solve for "g."

Student: Oh, I see, I messed up. So 4g = 20, and if I divide by 4, g = 5.

Prof Pi: Wonderful! You've found that Emma has 5 green apples. Keep practicing, and you'll get better at solving story problems!

7 Example Use in Khartoum, Sudan

During April, 2023, the authors of this paper were beginning an educational research project in Khartoum, Sudan, at a Sudanese university. Because of GPT-4's multi-lingual capabilities, the goal of that research project was to judge the effectiveness of tutoring university level students in mathematics using the Arabic language [9].

Fig. 3. *Prof Pi* chatting in Arabic

However, in April, 2023, unrest broken out in Khartoum [10] and many universities closed their campuses and students studied from home. Many people fled Khartoum. As sad as the unrest was, this created an opportunity of testing *Prof Pi* in an underserved area during difficult circumstances.

A sample of one of those mathematics conversation can be seen in Fig. 3.

8 Conclusion and Going Forward

Design Science Research was used to generate an artifact to demonstrate if Whatsapp Bots could be linked to GPT-4 to assist pupils with their mathematics homework. Previous research by the authors showed that human-to-human interaction facilitated by the internet could also provide facilities where tutors could help pupils with their mathematics homework. However, when dealing with human-to-human tutoring in previous research, there were always potential issues when linking adults together with children. The safety and security of all parties needed to be ensured.

This project attempts to remove the human tutor from process. Only the GPT-4 API responds to the pupil. No adults are put in contact with the pupils thereby removing any potential danger points.

In addition, while experimenting with this prototype, the authors were extremely happy with the GPT-4 language model. The conversation was very friendly and human like. Slang words such as "cool" and filler words such as "umm" were understood by the language model.

The most difficult part of the project, in fact, was to reign in the power of the GPT-4 language model so that it didn't just answer the question completely. The goal was to only partially answer any question so that the pupil could learn along the way. With this it was very successful.

Going forward, the researchers need to 1) obtain full ethics approval in order to try this language model out with actual primary and/or secondary school pupils and 2) perhaps experiment with images.

References

1. Motshekga, A.: National Senior Certificate Examination Report 2022, Department of Basic Education. https://www.education.gov.za/LinkClick.aspx?fileticket=iS3yg-9HcbU%3d&tabid=92&portalid=0&mid=4359
2. Nasseh, B.: A brief history of distance education. Adult Educ. News **1**(1), 1–14 (1997)
3. Bower, B.L., Hardy, K.P.: From correspondence to cyberspace: changes and challenges in distance education. New Dir. Commun. Coll. **2004**(128), 5–12 (2004)
4. Botha, A., Butgereit, L.: From MXit to Dr Math. In: Berge, Z., Muilenburg, L., (eds.) Handbook of Mobile Learning, pp. 603–616. Taylor & Francis, New York (2013)
5. Botha, A., Butgereit, L.: Dr math: a mobiled scaffolding environment. Int. J. Mob. Blended Learn. **4**(2), 15–29 (2012)
6. Hevner, A.R.: The three cycle view of design science research. Scand. J. Inf. Syst. **19**(2), 87–92 (2007)
7. Vaisnavi, V., Kuechler, W.: Design science research in information systems (2013). http://www.desrist.org/design-research-in-information-systems/
8. GPT-3 powers the next generation of apps. https://openai.com/blog/gpt-3-apps
9. Butgereit, L., Martinus, H., Abugosseisa, M.M.: Prof Pi: tutoring mathematics in Arabic language using GPT-4 and Whatsapp. In: Presented at the International Conference on Intelligent Engineering Systems 2023, Nairobi, Kenya (2023)
10. Ibrahim, A., Siddiqui, U.: Sudan unrest live news: fighting rages as air raids hit Khartoum. AlJazeera Website (2023). https://www.aljazeera.com/news/liveblog/2023/4/16/sudan-unrest-live-news-dozens-dead-as-fighting-enters-second-day

VITAL: Virtual Interactive Telegram Assisted Law Clinic

Preetila Seeam[1] and Amar Seeam[2]($\boxtimes$)

[1] University of Mauritius, Moka, Mauritius
`p.seeam@uom.ac.mu`
[2] Middlesex University Mauritius, Flic En Flac, Mauritius
`a.seeam@mdx.ac.mu`

Abstract. This paper introduces VITAL: Virtual Interactive Telegram Assisted Law clinic, an innovative approach to legal education facilitated by the integration of Artificial Intelligence (AI). The manuscript deliberates on the potential advantages, obstacles, and applications of incorporating AI into legal education. VITAL aims to harness the power of AI to enrich the legal learning experience, providing tangible, experiential education through a virtual clinic utilizing chatbots via the widely-adopted Telegram messaging platform. This initiative brings a revolution in legal education, ensuring accessibility, flexibility, and continual evolution of knowledge imparted to students.

Keywords: Artificial Intelligence · Legal Education · Virtual Learning · Law Clinic

1 Introduction

Legal education has traditionally been centered around case law, statutory interpretation, and Socratic dialogue. However, with the advancements in technology, particularly AI, there is a potential to reshape the learning experience in legal education. AI can be integrated into virtual learning environments to simulate real-life legal scenarios, provide adaptive learning experiences, and enhance students' analytical and critical thinking skills. This paper introduces VITAL (Virtual Interactive Telegram Assisted Law clinic), an innovative project that aims to integrate AI into a virtual clinic for legal education using chatbots.

Chatbots, powered by AI and natural language processing (NLP) technologies, have increasingly become a prevalent tool in various industries. This research investigates the development and implementation of a Chatbot Law Clinic, which aims to provide accessible legal assistance to those in need. The primary aim of this research is to develop an a virtual Interactive Law clinic specifically tailored for Mauritius and hosted on the Telegram platform, ensuring its accessibility to the entire Mauritian population. VITAL will serve as a valuable resource for employees, trade unions, human resource professionals, and employers alike, providing a platform for them to ask questions and obtain legal advice without the need for consulting an actual lawyer.

© ICST Institute for Computer Sciences, Social Informatics and Telecommunications Engineering 2024
Published by Springer Nature Switzerland AG 2024. All Rights Reserved
A. Seeam et al. (Eds.): InterSol 2023, LNICST 541, pp. 290–310, 2024.
https://doi.org/10.1007/978-3-031-51849-2_20

The proposed platform combines the features of an expert system and a chatbot, simulating human conversation to enable users to interact with the system and receive reliable answers to their legal inquiries. By leveraging the widely adopted and user-friendly Telegram platform, VITAL ensures ease of access and continuous availability, which is particularly crucial in the event of future lockdowns due to public health concerns.

At its core, VITAL is a learning-centric system that continually expands its knowledge base through ongoing interactions with users. As the system engages with users, it can identify and track the most common issues faced by different sectors of society, allowing it to provide more targeted assistance. Additionally, VITAL is designed to communicate complex legal concepts in a manner that is easily understandable to the general public.

This research aims to provide an accessible, convenient, and effective legal resource for the people of Mauritius, while simultaneously contributing to the broader understanding of how artificial intelligence can be applied to improve access to legal services.

In underserved areas, access to legal education and resources is often limited due to various factors such as geographical constraints, lack of financial means, and scarcity of educational institutions. The proposed platform addresses these issues by offering a virtual platform where students and legal practitioners can engage in interactive learning experiences without the need for physical presence.

Furthermore, the AI component in VITAL can be programmed to understand and analyze various legal frameworks and jurisdictions. This is especially beneficial for underserved areas that may have distinct legal systems, as the AI can be customized to provide relevant and localized legal content.

Moreover, the system can serve as a bridge between legal experts and the community in underserved areas. Through the platform, legal professionals can offer pro bono services, conduct webinars, and provide mentorship to aspiring legal practitioners in remote areas.

1.1 Beneficiaries

Although VITAL is designed to benefit everyone in Mauritius, it specifically targets individuals who face difficulties in accessing legal aid. A vast amount of knowledge and information is embedded within the laws and acts of Mauritius. However, retrieving relevant information on a specific issue requires not only an understanding of the law but also a deep appreciation for what to look for.

Considering these factors, the primary objective of this proposal is to digitalize these laws and acts, transforming them into an easily accessible, interactive chatbot. This chatbot will incorporate elements of artificial intelligence to assist and guide users towards finding solutions to their legal concerns, both during the COVID-19 crisis and beyond. Our concept makes use of the Telegram Instant Messaging platform (Fig. 1), an alternative to the popular WhatsApp messaging system, that usefully has free to use APIs for conversational agents. A similar concept was successfully implemented through Telegram for a Tourism chatbot, by the authors in [1].

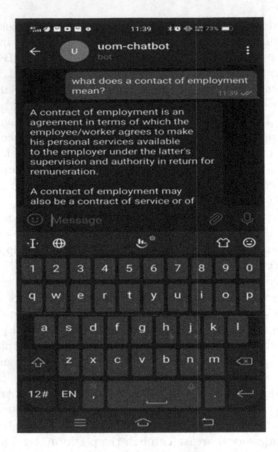

Fig. 1. Telegram bot

1.2   Target Groups

VITAL aims to address the needs of the following target groups, who may experience greater challenges in obtaining legal assistance:

- Low-income individuals who cannot afford traditional legal services
- People living in remote or underserved areas with limited access to legal professionals
- Individuals with disabilities or language barriers that make it difficult for them to navigate the legal system
- Non-profit organizations and community groups that require legal guidance but lack the resources to hire legal counsel

The paper is divided as follows. The subsequent section, Sect. 2, presents a literature review focusing on the use of Artificial Intelligence in education, and specifically its innovative application in legal education. Section 3 delves into the methodology used in the development of VITAL, explaining the AI technologies and strategies employed. Section 4 discusses implementation and testing processes of VITAL Finally, Sect. 5 and 6 concludes the paper with discussion and offers recommendations for future research and development in the field of AI-enhanced legal education.

2   Literature Review

Chatbots are becoming increasingly popular in the educational domain as they have the potential to provide personalized learning experiences to students. The research shows that chatbots can improve educational outcomes by offering timely and constructive feedback to students, guiding them through complex tasks, and encouraging them to engage in active learning.

One of the benefits of chatbots is their ability to personalize the learning experience for students. By using data analytics and machine learning algorithms, chatbots can analyze students' learning patterns and preferences to provide tailored feedback and guidance. This personalization can help to improve students' motivation and engagement with the learning process, leading to better learning outcomes.

Another advantage of chatbots is their ability to scaffold learning. Chatbots can provide step-by-step guidance and support to students as they work through a task, helping them to break down complex problems into smaller, more manageable parts. This scaffolding can help students to build their confidence and competence in the subject matter, ultimately leading to improved learning outcomes.

Chatbots can also engage students in conversation, creating a more interactive and dynamic learning experience. By simulating natural language conversations, chatbots can encourage students to ask questions, explore ideas, and engage in critical thinking. This engagement can help students to develop their communication and collaboration skills, which are essential for success in today's workforce.

However, challenges remain in terms of chatbot design, deployment, and evaluation. Chatbots must be carefully designed to ensure that they are effective and user-friendly. They must also be integrated seamlessly into the educational environment, and their impact on learning outcomes must be evaluated rigorously. Furthermore, chatbots must be continually updated and improved to reflect changing student needs and preferences.

2.1   AI in Education

The integration of AI into educational systems has been gaining momentum and has the potential to reshape the learning experience in various ways. For example, chatbots hold great potential to revolutionize the field of education. For example, [2] demonstrates that they can improve educational outcomes, although research is still nascent. The use of chatbots extends beyond education to healthcare, offering 24/7 access to information and assistance, automating routine tasks, and reducing costs [3]. Concerns persist, however, regarding data privacy, security, and lack of standardization. AI-chatbots have shown promise in enhancing student learning, offering immediate feedback and engaging students [4]. The advent of AI, particularly chatbots like ChatGPT, in the educational sphere does not come without its set of disruptions and challenges. While chatbots offer immediate feedback and active engagement, thus enhancing student learning as suggested by [4], they also introduce new dynamics that educators and administrators must navigate. One such issue is the potential for overuse or misuse by students, which can divert attention away from structured learning experiences and potentially dilute the educational content. An intriguing finding from this multifaceted study is the promise and challenges of using ChatGPT in educational settings. While the tool shows potential, early adopters express safety concerns and highlight the need for specific guidelines. The study, titled 'What if the devil is my guardian angel: ChatGPT as a case study of using chatbots in education,' contributes to both theoretical and practical discussions surrounding the role of chatbots in educational settings. It offers key insights into curriculum development and ethical considerations specific to chatbot use, while also acknowledging limitations such as its emphasis on early adopters and the absence of quantitative data [5].

In another systematic literature review on chatbots in education, the researchers identified three main pedagogical roles of chatbots—supporting learning, assisting, and mentoring—along with four main objectives for their implementation. However, they highlighted challenges in aligning evaluations with these objectives, exploring chatbots' mentoring potential, and leveraging their adaptive capabilities. The study concludes that while chatbots hold promise in education, more research is needed to align technological advancements with educational needs [6]. In [7] a systematic review on the development of emotionally intelligent chatbots is explored, highlighting techniques for emotional response generation and popular datasets like Weibo and Twitter. The review uses both automatic and human evaluations for performance metrics but acknowledges limitations due to time constraints and the nascent state of the field. The work by [8] examines the growing role of AI chatbots in education, made possible by advancements in natural language processing and understanding. The paper reviews methodologies and tools for chatbot design, focusing on language-related challenges, especially in implementing English and Arabic interfaces. A use case involving the Hubert.ai chatbot, used for gathering student feedback on a machine learning course, is also presented to illustrate the educational benefits of chatbots. In the paper by [9] a further systematic literature review using a multi-perspective framework is conducted, to examine the role of chatbots in education, especially in large-scale learning scenarios. Despite the increasing presence of chatbots in various sectors, their systematic study in educational settings has been lacking. Drawing from 1405 articles across different fields, the study narrows down to 80 relevant papers for in-depth analysis. The findings indicate that chatbots are still in the early stages of adoption in education, and their effectiveness varies depending on several factors. The work by [10] investigates the burgeoning role of chatbots in the educational process. Despite the long-standing recognition of conversation as a key element in learning and teaching, the paper argues that chatbots are still in the early phases of their educational utility. However, they do offer substantial benefits. For example, voice chatbots enable more direct and focused interaction with the learning material, enhancing the user experience by eliminating the need for traditional computer navigation. Chatbots also foster a sense of engagement and self-expression among students, and are capable of collecting emotional data to respond to specific situations like elevated student anxiety. This is especially useful in large-scale educational settings such as universities or MOOCs, where chatbots can provide personalized support at a fraction of the cost of human resources. In a comprehensive study by [11], the authors sought to fill a research gap by investigating the use of artificial intelligence (AI) chatbots in educational settings from an educational technology perspective. Utilizing bibliometric and citation network analyses, the study identified emerging trends and applications post-COVID-19. The research revealed that chatbots are increasingly applied in language education, educational services like information counseling and automated grading, as well as in healthcare education and medical training. Despite these advances, the study highlighted several limitations, including a focus on English-language publications and limitations in the authors' technological expertise. Nevertheless, the study offers an extended framework for future applications of AI chatbots in education, emphasizing the need for a holistic approach that considers technological integration.

Notably, AI chatbots have proven effective in teaching foreign languages, particularly in enhancing conversational skills [12]. Furthermore, the use of chatbots as AI conversational partners in language learning tasks shows promising results. They provided scaffolding and support for learners, while engaging them in conversation [13]. Yet, it is critical to address the accessibility of chatbots and students' privacy concerns [9]. Their effectiveness in providing educational advice and supporting students' studies is supported by [14].

Teachers have demonstrated generally positive attitudes towards chatbots in education, acknowledging their utility in providing content, fostering student engagement, and aiding administrative tasks. However, concerns about students' over-reliance on them and their inability to replace human interaction persist [15]. Additionally, while chatbots have the potential to improve communication in education, the risk of disseminating misinformation or interfering with research processes necessitates caution [16]. Chatbots have been increasingly recognized for their potential role in formal education as they offer the ability to deliver educational content, assess student understanding, and provide feedback [17]. Their role as a digital learning tool can increase student engagement in online learning by providing a personalized experience and reducing feelings of isolation [18]. They have been effectively utilized in various higher education tasks, such as delivering information, helping with administrative tasks, offering personalized academic advising, and improving student engagement and retention [19].

Despite their potential, the use of AI chatbots in higher education does come with its challenges. While they can provide personalized support, they are not a panacea and must be used in conjunction with other tools and resources [20]. In flipped learning environments, chatbots can effectively aid in learning content, assessment, and feedback, thus creating a more engaging environment [21]. Exploring the possibilities further, a framework for implementing AI-integrated chatbots in educational settings has been proposed, offering personalized and adaptive learning experiences [22].

In terms of content and language integrated learning (CLIL), chatbots have been proven effective for teaching new vocabulary and concepts [23]. Their application as virtual teaching assistants has also shown improvement in student performance and engagement [24]. Students generally perceive chatbots positively, appreciating their potential as learning tools, but they also point out certain design issues, including the need for natural language understanding and the ability to learn from user interactions [25]. Lastly, [26] found that in Higher Education Institutions, the adoption of chatbots for administrative inquiries is significantly influenced by their design, interactivity, and ethical considerations. These factors collectively build trust among students, thereby increasing the likelihood of chatbot adoption.

2.2 AI in Legal Services and Education

In legal education, AI can be used to create simulations of court proceedings, facilitate legal research through natural language processing, provide instant feedback on legal arguments, and much more. It can also be used to simulate client interactions, which are crucial in training future lawyers. However, research on the integration of AI in legal education is still in nascent stages and there is a need for more empirical studies and practical applications. In the AI and legal field, the authors previously worked on an expert system designed to assist the Mauritian population with inquiries related to labor and employment law. The expert system made use of Machine Learning, Speech Recognition/Synthesis and Natural Language Processing techniques to converse with users through a web interface, and was an early version of a similar chatbot demonstrated in this paper, with a custom interface, minus the learning capabilities and management abilities. [27]

Whilst these directions are promising, the integration of artificial intelligence (AI) into legal services, especially through the use of chatbots, has raised important legal and ethical questions. Legal chatbots have been identified as potentially capable of improving access to justice, offering services faster and cheaper than traditional lawyers, and being particularly beneficial to those who cannot afford legal representation [28]. However, it has also been pointed out that the current lack of regulatory frameworks for chatbots may result in potential issues related to fraud, privacy, and discrimination [29].

Concerning the broader legal status of AI, there seems to be a global lack of specific AI-related legislation. Different countries show varied approaches towards AI regulation, some taking a more proactive stance while others are more hands-off [30]. Interestingly, there is a trend to perceive AI as a tool rather than a legal entity, leading to laws primarily focused on its applications and not on AI itself [30].

The transition from automation to autonomous technology, like self-driving cars, has sparked discussions about legal and ethical responsibility [31]. This raises issues such as who should bear responsibility in case of an accident. Intellectual property rights in disrupted digital learning environments have also been brought to the forefront, emphasizing the need to consider issues around the ownership, licensing, unauthorized use, and protection of digital content [32].

Meanwhile, the advent of "ethical chatbots" based on principles of beneficence, non-maleficence, autonomy, and justice has been proposed as a viable solution to socio-legal issues [33]. AI's ability to model human behavior accurately, as demonstrated with Siri, reinforces the potential of AI as a valuable tool in understanding human behavior [34].

Chatbots also hold promise in disseminating legal information to specific demographic groups. For example, a chatbot framework was successful in simplifying legal rights for children, leading to positive user feedback [35]. Concerning criminal justice, AI systems have the potential to enhance the accuracy of risk assessments, potentially leading to more just outcomes [36]. However, it's important to ensure that these systems don't inadvertently target marginalized groups, highlighting the need for greater transparency and accountability in AI development and use [36].

The conversation around the ethical and legal implications of AI extends into healthcare, where AI-assisted suicide has been a topic of complex debate, weighing its potential benefits and risks. Furthermore, the development of "robot lawyers," AI-based programs capable of understanding natural language to provide legal information and advice, represents an exciting frontier in AI's role within legal services [37].

AI's application is also stretching to law libraries, where it is being harnessed to increase efficiency and accuracy in tasks like legal research, document management, and contract analysis. This usage is projected to grow in the future as demonstrated by [38]. For example, [39] showed that chatbots could be effective in teaching students about complex concepts such as Brooks Law, leading to an improved understanding in comparison to traditional methods.

AI's potential in the legal sector, providing assistance to lawyers and clients alike, is underscored by [40]. A prototype AI system was developed and tested with a group of lawyers, showing significant assistance in legal research and drafting documents. The development of an AI chatbot for Indonesian law on electronic transactions was also examined in [41]. This chatbot was designed to assist users in finding answers to legal questions and provide advice, demonstrating an accurate and effective tool in the legal context. The application of AI-integrated chatbots in e-learning shows promise in creating a more tailored learning experience for students. As indicated by [42], such chatbots can track students' progress, provide feedback, and offer personalized assistance, thus potentially enhancing the e-learning experience.

Perceptions toward the integration of intelligent agents and AI in everyday life are generally positive, though concerns about privacy and security persist, as discussed by [43]. The issue of consumer accessibility to legal services is highlighted in [44]. Many consumers reportedly lack awareness about their legal rights and struggle to access legal services, indicating the need for more readily available legal aid options. People's trust in AI increases when it is presented in a human-like manner and is perceived as an expert, according to [45]. This suggests that the effective use of AI in various fields may depend on how it is represented and communicated.

2.3 Comparative Analysis

Table 1 offers a comparative analysis of chatbots in the fields of Education and Legal Services, breaking down each sector's benefits, challenges, research gaps, notable applications, and user perceptions, summarising the state of the art, central to VITAL's direction.

Table 1. Comparative Analysis of Chatbots in Education and Legal Services

Criteria	Chatbots in Education	Chatbots in Legal Services
General Benefits	Personalized learning, Scaffolding, Student engagement, Timely feedback	Access to justice, Legal advice, Cost efficiency, Speed
Challenges	Design, Deployment, Evaluation, NLP Capabilities	Regulatory frameworks, Data privacy, Fraud and discrimination risks
Research Gaps	Specificity in design	Need for empirical studies, Practical applications, Accessibility to consumers
Notable Applications	Teaching foreign languages, Flipped learning environments, Academic advising	Legal research, Simulations of court proceedings, Document management
User Perceptions	Generally positive but concerns about reliance and design issues	Positive if human-like and perceived as an expert

3 Development of VITAL

VITAL is an innovative project designed to provide users with easy access to information about Mauritian Law. The development of this platform involved the exploration and implementation of two distinct versions, each leveraging different technologies and frameworks to achieve their goals.

The first version of the VITAL employed a combination of TensorFlow, Flask, and MariaDB to create a Telegram bot capable of answering questions about Mauritian Law. This version was characterized by a Flask-based website for law faculty members to manage the training data and a TensorFlow AI model to generate appropriate responses based on user input.

While the first version was successfully developed and tested, it faced several challenges in terms of ease of use and maintainability, prompting the exploration of an alternative solution. This led to the development of the second version of VITAL, which utilized the Rasa X framework. Rasa X provided a more streamlined and user-friendly approach to data management, model training, and deployment, simplifying the overall process and allowing for the seamless addition of new features.

This section will provide a detailed account of the implementation and testing processes for both versions of VITAL, highlighting the challenges faced and the solutions applied to overcome them.

3.1   Steps and Technologies for TensorFlow/Flask Version

The development of the VITAL involved several steps and the integration of various technologies, architectures, and programming languages. The key components of the system include a Telegram bot, a Flask-based website, a TensorFlow AI model, and a MariaDB database (Fig. 2).

1. **Telegram Bot:** Implemented using the Python programming language, the Telegram bot is designed to interact with users and respond to their questions about Mauritian Law. It utilizes TensorFlow to determine appropriate responses based on user input.
2. **Flask-based Website:** The website, built with Flask and MariaDB, serves as a platform for law faculty members to add entries that will be used to train and update the AI model. This ensures that the chatbot has accurate and up-to-date information about Mauritian Law.
3. **TensorFlow AI Model:** The AI model, powered by TensorFlow, is responsible for processing user input and generating responses. It is trained using the data provided by law faculty members through the Flask-based website.
4. **MariaDB Database:** A MariaDB database is used to store intents, patterns, responses, and user interaction logs. This database serves as a central repository for the system's data and is accessed by both the Telegram bot and the Flask-based website. A PHPmyAdmin interface allows direct admin access to the database tables and manipulation in SQL if needed.
5. **System Architecture:** The architecture of the system involves several components, including Nginx as a web server, Certbot for SSL certificate management, and Docker containers for running the different services. These components work together to provide a seamless and secure user experience.

6. **Training the AI Model:** The AI model is trained using a gradient descent algorithm, as detailed in the associated research paper. The training process is initiated by the maintainer through the Flask-based website, which triggers the `train.py` script to update the TensorFlow model based on the latest data in the MariaDB database.

By combining these technologies and following the outlined steps, the Chatbot Law Clinic has been successfully developed to provide accurate and efficient responses to users' questions about Mauritian Law.

3.2   Steps and Technologies for Rasa X

The creation of VITAL incorporated a range of technologies, architectures, and programming languages. The primary components of the system are a Telegram bot and a Rasa X server. The primary components are shown in Fig. 3

1. **Telegram Bot:** Developed using the Python programming language, the Telegram bot is designed to engage with users and provide answers to their questions about Mauritian Law. It leverages the Rasa X framework to decide on appropriate responses based on user input.
2. **Rasa X Server:** Rasa X is an open-source conversational AI framework that replaces the need for TensorFlow, MariaDB, and the Flask-based website. It serves as a platform for law faculty members to add, edit, and manage the training data used to enhance the AI model. Additionally, Rasa X facilitates model training and deployment, streamlining the entire process.
3. **Rasa AI Model:** The AI model, powered by the Rasa framework, is responsible for processing user input and generating responses. It is trained using the data provided by law faculty members through the Rasa X interface.
   Intents: Intents are the core building blocks of the Rasa AI model. They represent the purpose or goal behind a user's input, such as asking a question, requesting information, or performing an action. The model is trained to recognize and extract intents from user inputs by utilizing natural language understanding (NLU) techniques. By accurately identifying intents, the AI model can respond appropriately to user queries and maintain a smooth conversational flow.
   Stories: Stories in Rasa are sample dialogues that represent real-world conversational sequences between a user and the AI model. These stories are used during the training process to teach the model how to handle various conversational scenarios. Each story consists of a series of alternating user inputs (with associated intents and entities) and chatbot responses (with associated actions). By learning from these stories, the AI model becomes proficient at predicting the most suitable actions to take based on the user's input and conversational context.
   Dialogue Management: Dialogue management is a crucial component of the Rasa AI model that determines how the chatbot should respond to user inputs by selecting the most appropriate action. Rasa's dialogue management system

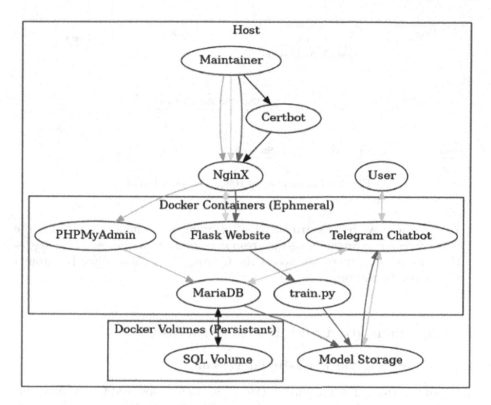

Figure 1: The different processes involved in this project

- Orange lines represent the PHPMyAdmin route to edit the SQL tables
- Cyan lines represent typical maintainer interaction with updating the model via the website
- Green lines represent user interaction with the telegram bot
- Red lines represent triggering the model to train

Fig. 2. Flask based solution (Color figure online)

uses a machine learning-based approach, specifically the Rasa Core, which is responsible for predicting the next action to take based on the conversational history and context. This approach allows the AI model to dynamically adapt to user inputs and maintain a coherent and context-aware conversation, rather than following a static, pre-defined decision tree.

4. **System Architecture:** The architecture of the system includes several components, such as Nginx as a web server, Certbot for SSL certificate management, and Docker containers for running the different services. These components collaborate to offer a secure and seamless user experience.

5. **Training the AI Model:** The AI model is trained using Rasa's built-in machine learning algorithms. The training process is initiated by the maintainer through the Rasa X interface, which triggers the model training and updates it based on the most recent data.

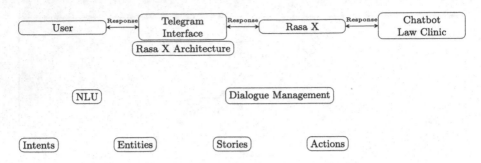

Fig. 3. Components of Rasa X based chatbot

6. **Integration with Telegram:** The Telegram bot communicates with the Rasa X server to provide real-time responses to users' inquiries. This integration ensures that users can access the Chatbot Law Clinic directly through the Telegram platform.

4   Implementation and Testing Processes

4.1   TensorFlow and Flask-Based Version

Implementation. The implementation of the TensorFlow and Flask-based version of VITAL involved several challenges. The first challenge was the development of the Flask-based website, which required constant updates and new functionality to manage and process the data provided by law faculty members. This made the website difficult to use and maintain, as additional features had to be integrated into the system regularly.

Another challenge was the integration of TensorFlow and MariaDB to train the AI model using the data stored in the database. This required careful management of data formats and synchronization between the components to ensure that the AI model was trained correctly and able to provide accurate responses.

Testing. The testing process for the TensorFlow and Flask-based version involved verifying the functionality of the various components and their integration. This included testing the Telegram bot's ability to handle user input, the AI model's capacity to generate appropriate responses, and the Flask-based website's effectiveness in managing the data used to train the model (Fig. 4).

Despite these challenges, the TensorFlow and Flask-based version of VITAL was successfully developed and tested. However, the difficulties faced during implementation and maintenance prompted the exploration of alternative solutions, such as the Rasa X framework.

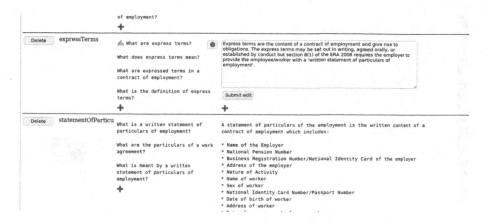

Fig. 4. Flask interface

4.2   Rasa X Version

Implementation. The implementation of VITAL using the Rasa X framework aimed to address the challenges encountered with the TensorFlow and Flask-based version. Rasa X provides a more streamlined approach to data management, allowing the law faculty members to add, edit, and manage the training data directly through the Rasa X interface (Fig. 5).

One of the key benefits of Rasa X is its ease of use, which enabled the team to add new features seamlessly, such as custom scripts for alerting physical operators at the law clinic when new queries required their attention. This resulted in a more efficient and user-friendly system, with improved functionality compared to the previous version (Fig. 6).

Testing. The testing process for the Rasa X version involved verifying the functionality of the Telegram bot and its integration with the Rasa X server. This included testing the bot's ability to handle user input, the AI model's capacity to generate appropriate responses, and the Rasa X server's effectiveness in managing the data used to train the model.

Additionally, the testing process focused on evaluating the new features added through the Rasa X framework, such as custom scripts for alerting physical operators when new queries were received. This helped ensure that VITAL was able to effectively address user inquiries while also providing a seamless experience for the operators managing the system.

In conclusion, the Rasa X version of the Chatbot Law Clinic addressed the challenges faced during the implementation and testing of the TensorFlow and Flask-based version. The Rasa X framework simplified data management and allowed for the seamless addition of new features, resulting in a more efficient and user-friendly system.

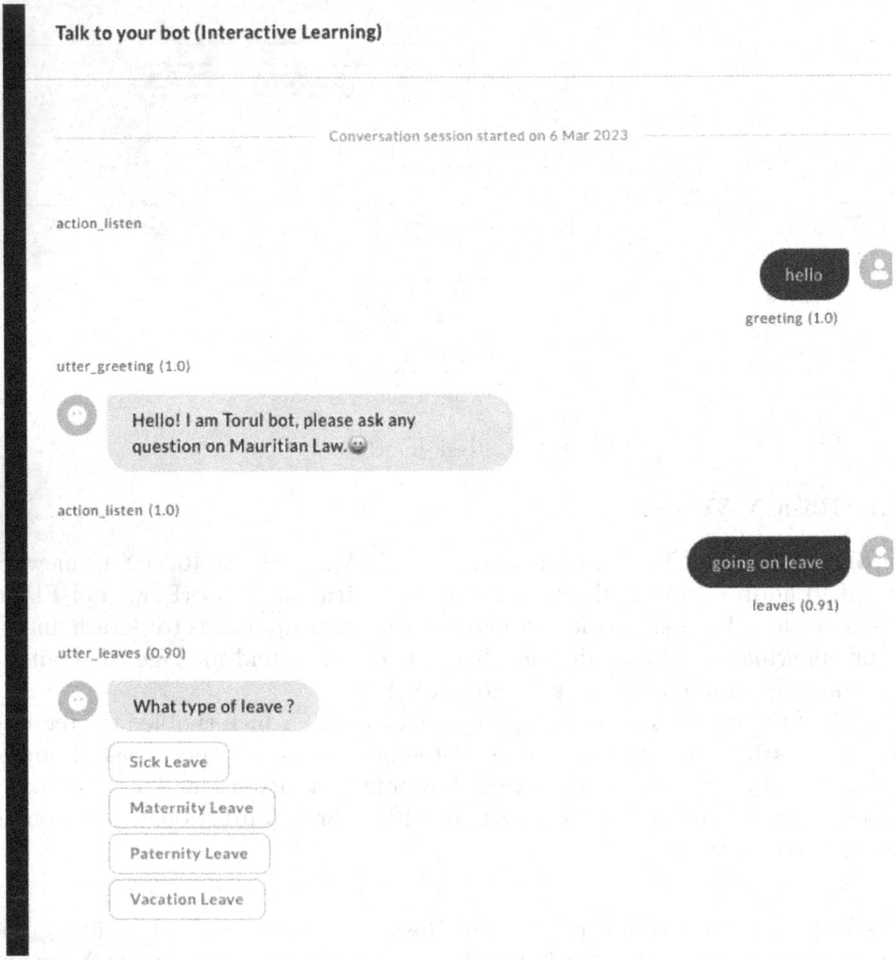

Talk to your bot (Interactive Learning)

Conversation session started on 6 Mar 2023

action_listen

hello

greeting (1.0)

utter_greeting (1.0)

Hello! I am Torul bot, please ask any
question on Mauritian Law.😊

action_listen (1.0)

going on leave

leaves (0.91)

utter_leaves (0.90)

What type of leave ?

Sick Leave

Maternity Leave

Paternity Leave

Vacation Leave

Fig. 5. Rasa X interface allows Telegram to provide the user with options to follow up on query

5   Discussion

The integration of Rasa X and Telegram in the form of the VITAL platform holds the potential to significantly impact the legal profession. This section delves into how this innovation might augment or disrupt conventional legal services, while also considering its benefits and potential challenges beyond education.

5.1   Continuous Learning and Adaptation

Rasa X's inherent capabilities, such as continuous learning from user interactions and expert input, allow VITAL to evolve over time. This results in improved

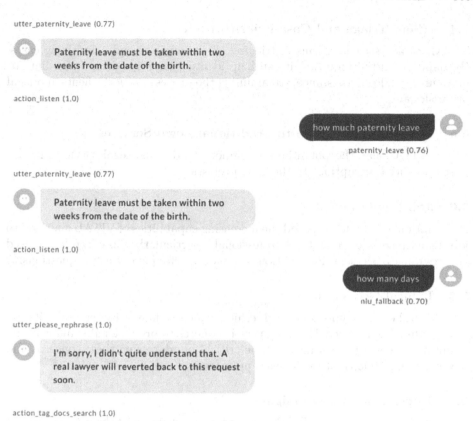

utter_paternity_leave (0.77)

Paternity leave must be taken within two
weeks from the date of the birth.

action_listen (1.0)

how much paternity leave

paternity_leave (0.76)

utter_paternity_leave (0.77)

Paternity leave must be taken within two
weeks from the date of the birth.

action_listen (1.0)

how many days

nlu_fallback (0.70)

utter_please_rephrase (1.0)

I'm sorry, I didn't quite understand that. A
real lawyer will reverted back to this request
soon.

action_tag_docs_search (1.0)

Fig. 6. Rasa X allows follow-up and email notification for queries it cannot comprehend

performance and more precise responses, making it a perpetually developing
resource for both individuals seeking legal information and legal professionals
who contribute to the system's refinement.

5.2 Accessibility and Affordability

With the user-friendly and widely adopted Telegram as its platform, VITAL
can democratize legal consultation, providing easy access to legal information,
especially for those who may not have the resources to engage a legal professional.

5.3 Efficiency

By automating routine tasks, such as answering frequently asked questions or
providing legal advice, VITAL enhances the efficiency of legal professionals,
enabling them to concentrate on more complex cases.

5.4   Client Triage and Case Prioritization

VITAL could assist law firms in triaging client inquiries and prioritizing cases. By handling initial inquiries, it can help identify cases requiring immediate or more in-depth legal assistance, streamlining the process for both clients and legal professionals.

5.5   Potential Disruption to Traditional Legal Services

While VITAL has the potential to augment traditional legal services, it also poses potential disruptions to the legal profession.

5.6   Job Displacement

Automation of routine tasks and the increasing capabilities of VITAL may lead to job displacement for some legal professionals, particularly those in roles focused on providing basic legal information or answering frequently asked questions.

5.7   Ethical Concerns

As VITAL becomes more advanced, ethical concerns may arise regarding its use in providing legal advice. Ensuring that it adheres to professional standards and maintains client confidentiality will be critical in addressing these concerns and maintaining public trust in the legal profession.

5.8   Regulation and Oversight

The rapid advancement of VITAL may outpace the ability of the legal profession to regulate and oversee its use. Establishing appropriate regulations and guidelines to ensure the responsible and ethical use of such platforms in the legal field will be crucial in mitigating potential disruptions.

5.9   Quality Control and Liability

As VITAL increasingly provides legal advice, questions of quality control and liability may arise. Ensuring the accuracy and reliability of advice generated by VITAL will be essential in maintaining the reputation of the legal profession and addressing potential liability issues. Extensions via Rasa X programmability can assist in this.

6   Conclusions

The innovative integration of Rasa X and Telegram serves as a seminal advancement in the development of VITAL, offering particularly valuable features for virtual law clinics. The transition from our initial custom solution to the Rasa X platform has equipped us with advanced capabilities for chatbot development and customization. One notable feature is the human-in-the-loop notifications for unanswered queries, facilitating the chatbot's continuous learning and improvement. In addition, the integration with Telegram, a user-friendly and widely adopted messaging platform, enhances the system's overall accessibility.

6.1   Key Advantages

The integration of Rasa X and Telegram offers several distinct advantages:

- **Open-Source Framework:** Enables unrestricted customization, thereby fostering innovation.
- **Scalability:** Well-suited for accommodating an increasing user base.
- **Advanced NLU (Natural Language Understanding):** Facilitates more accurate and human-like conversational interactions.
- **User Reach:** Telegram's widespread adoption ensures a broader user base.
- **Privacy and Security:** Telegram's robust security measures enhance system reliability.

6.2   Comparison with Existing Solutions

Compared to existing chatbot solutions, the integration of Rasa X and Telegram brings unique benefits that make it a preferred choice for VITAL. These include:

- Extensive customization capabilities
- Cost-effectiveness due to the open-source nature of the platforms
- A greater reach facilitated by integration with the widely-used Telegram platform

6.3   Limitations and Future Research

Although our integration has proven to be a powerful tool for delivering legal services, there are some limitations. It should be noted that at the time of this research, more advanced conversational models like ChatGPT were not utilized. The adoption of such models could be a fruitful avenue for future work, potentially adding further sophistication and naturalness to the conversational interactions.

6.4   Implications for Future Work

As the field of conversational AI continues to evolve, the introduction of more advanced technologies provides an exciting opportunity for the further enhancement of VITAL's capabilities. The integration of Rasa X and Telegram sets a strong foundation upon which future iterations can be built, thereby continuously improving the legal services available to the Mauritian population.

6.5   Future Work

This study has laid the foundation for many promising directions for future research and development. Below, we discuss potential paths to explore:

- **Expanded Language Support:** Currently, the chatbot is designed to communicate primarily in English. As Mauritius is a multilingual country, expanding the chatbot's capabilities to understand and communicate in other local languages such as French and Mauritian Creole could greatly enhance its accessibility and effectiveness.

- **Improved Knowledge Base:** Continuous efforts should be made to expand and update the chatbot's legal knowledge base. This could involve adding more legal categories, integrating new legal regulations, and refining the chatbot's understanding of legal terminologies.
- **Advanced NLP Techniques:** Leveraging more advanced natural language processing techniques could help improve the chatbot's understanding of complex legal questions and provide more accurate and contextually appropriate responses.
- **User Experience Enhancements:** Future work could focus on improving the user interface and making the chatbot more interactive. This could include adding multimedia support, offering predictive text suggestions, or incorporating a voice recognition system.
- **Integration with Other Platforms:** While Telegram offers many advantages, considering integration with other popular messaging platforms like WhatsApp and Facebook Messenger could further expand the chatbot's reach.
- **Evaluation and Feedback Mechanisms:** Implementing an evaluation mechanism for users to rate and provide feedback on the chatbot's responses would help identify areas of improvement and guide future enhancements.

Through these potential avenues of exploration, we hope to continue evolving VITAL, ultimately creating an even more effective, accessible, and comprehensive legal aid resource.

References

1. Chiong, P.S.S.C., Seeam, P., Seeam, A.: Development of a smart tourism information chatbot for Mauritius. In: International Conference on Intelligent and Innovative Computing Applications, pp. 122–130 (2022)
2. Okonkwo, C.W., Ade-Ibijola, A.: Chatbots applications in education: a systematic review. Comput. Educ.: Artifi. Intell. **2**, 100033 (2021)
3. Hammad, R., Bahja, M.: Opportunities and challenges in educational chatbots. In: Trends, Applications, and Challenges of Chatbot Technology, pp. 119–136. IGI Global (2023)
4. Sandu, N., Gide, E.: Adoption of AI-chatbots to enhance student learning experience in higher education in India. In: 2019 18th International Conference on Information Technology Based Higher Education and Training (ITHET). IEEE (2019)
5. Tlili, A., et al.: What if the devil is my guardian angel: ChatGPT as a case study of using chatbots in education. Smart Learn. Environ. **10**, 15 (2023)
6. Wollny, S., Schneider, J., Di Mitri, D., Weidlich, J., Rittberger, M., Drachsler, H.: Are we there yet? - a systematic literature review on chatbots in education. Front. Artif. Intell. **4**, 654924 (2021)
7. Bilquise, G., Ibrahim, S., Shaalan, K.: Emotionally intelligent chatbots: a systematic literature review. Hum. Behav. Emerg. Technol. **2022**, 1–23 (2022)
8. Aleedy, M., Atwell, E., Meshoul, S.: Using AI chatbots in education: recent advances challenges and use case. In: Pandit, M., Gaur, M.K., Rana, P.S., Tiwari, A. (eds.) Artificial Intelligence and Sustainable Computing. Algorithms for Intelligent Systems, pp. 661–675. Springer, Singapore (2022). https://doi.org/10.1007/978-981-19-1653-3_50

9. Winkler, R., Soellner, M.: Unleashing the potential of chatbots in education: a state-of-the-art analysis. Acad. Manag. Proc. **2018**(1), 15903 (2018)
10. Dimitriadis, G.: Evolution in education: chatbots. Homo Virtualis **3**(1), 47 (2020)
11. Lin, Y., Yu, Z.: A bibliometric analysis of artificial intelligence chatbots in educational contexts. Interact. Technol. Smart Educ. (2023)
12. Azuma, J.: Applying TTS technology to foreign language teaching. In: Handbook of Research on Computer-Enhanced Language Acquisition and Learning, pp. 497–506. IGI Global (2008)
13. Belda-Medina, J., Calvo-Ferrer, J.R.: Using chatbots as AI conversational partners in language learning. Appl. Sci. **12**(17), 8427 (2022)
14. Clarizia, F., Colace, F., Lombardi, M., Pascale, F., Santaniello, D.: Chatbot: an education support system for student. In: Castiglione, A., Pop, F., Ficco, M., Palmieri, F. (eds.) CSS 2018. LNCS, vol. 11161, pp. 291–302. Springer, Cham (2018). https://doi.org/10.1007/978-3-030-01689-0_23
15. Terzieva, V., Todorova, K., Kademova-Katzarova, P., Andreev, R.: Teachers' attitudes towards technology rich education in Bulgaria. In: EDULEARN proceedings. IATED (2016)
16. Kooli, C.: Chatbots in education and research: a critical examination of ethical implications and solutions. Sustainability **15**(7), 5614 (2023)
17. Molnar, G., Szuts, Z.: The role of chatbots in formal education. In: 2018 IEEE 16th International Symposium on Intelligent Systems and Informatics (SISY). IEEE (2018)
18. Vanichvasin, P.: Chatbot development as a digital learning tool to increase students' research knowledge. Int. Educ. Stud. **14**(2), 44 (2021)
19. Corral, J.: Artificially intelligent chatbots for health professions education. In: Digital Innovations in Healthcare Education and Training, pp. 127–135. Elsevier (2021)
20. Yang, S., Evans, C.: Opportunities and challenges in using AI chatbots in higher education. In: Proceedings of the 2019 3rd International Conference on Education and E-Learning. ACM (2019)
21. Baskara, F.R.: Chatbots and flipped learning: enhancing student engagement and learning outcomes through personalised support and collaboration. IJORER: Int. J. Recent Educ. Res. **4**(2), 223–238 (2023)
22. Debnath, B., Agarwal, A.: A framework to implement AI-integrated chatbot in educational institutes. J. Student Res. (2020)
23. Mageira, K., Pittou, D., Papasalouros, A., Kotis, K., Zangogianni, P., Daradoumis, A.: Educational AI chatbots for content and language integrated learning. Appl. Sci. **12**(7), 3239 (2022)
24. Belgaumwala, N.: Chatbot: a virtual medical assistant. Int. J. Res. Appl. Sci. Eng. Technol. **7**(6), 1042–1050 (2019)
25. Bell, S., Wood, C., Sarkar, A.: Perceptions of chatbots in therapy. In: Extended Abstracts of the 2019 CHI Conference on Human Factors in Computing Systems. ACM (2019)
26. Rahim, N.I.M., Iahad, N.A., Yusof, A.F., Al-Sharafi, M.A.: AI-based chatbots adoption model for higher-education institutions: a hybrid PLS-SEM-neural network modelling approach. Sustainability **14**(19), 12726 (2022)
27. Seeam, P., Teckchandani, N., Booneyad, H., Torul, V., Seeam, A.: Employment law expert system. In: 2018 International Conference on Intelligent and Innovative Computing Applications (ICONIC), pp. 1–6. IEEE (2018)
28. Queudot, M., Charton, É., Meurs, M.-J.: Improving access to justice with legal chatbots. Stats **3**(3), 356–375 (2020)

29. Tkachenko, T., Neupokoeva, L., Shestakova, A., Shestakov, I.: Chat-bot Digi-talChiefBot. Technical report (2022)
30. Atabekov, A., Yastrebov, O.: Legal status of artificial intelligence across countries: legislation on the move. Eur. Res. Stud. J. XXI **4**, 773–782 (2018)
31. Nersessian, D., Mancha, R.: From automation to autonomy: legal and ethical responsibility gaps in artificial intelligence innovation. SSRN Electron. J. (2020)
32. Mockus, M., Vėgėlytė, E.: Legal issues of intellectual property rights in disrupted technologies era: chatbots and conversational computing platforms. In: Jusletter-IT (2020)
33. Ng, J., Haller, E., Murray, A.: The ethical chatbot: a viable solution to socio-legal issues. Altern. Law J. **47**(4), 308–313 (2022)
34. Bessant, J.: What experts say about artificial intelligence. In: The Great Transformation, pp. 156–182. Routledge (2018)
35. Raskar, A.D., Dongare, A.S., Inamdar, A.S., Kamble, R.B., Patil, P.L., Balshetwar, D.S.V.: Chatbot for children assistance. Int. J. Res. Appl. Sci. Eng. Technol. **10**(3), 1307–1310 (2022)
36. Završnik, A.: Criminal justice, artificial intelligence systems, and human rights. ERA Forum **20**(4), 567–583 (2020)
37. Xu, N., Wang, K.-J.: Adopting robot lawyer? the extending artificial intelligence robot lawyer technology acceptance model for legal industry by an exploratory study. J. Manage. Organ. **27**(5), 867–885 (2019)
38. Craigle, V.: Law libraries embracing AI. SSRN Electron. J. (2019)
39. Martinez, M.A.Q., Ramírez, A.F.A., Arias, S.T.C., Vazquez, M.Y.L.: Teaching Brooks law based on fuzzy cognitive maps and chatbots. In: Ahram, T.Z., Karwowski, W., Kalra, J. (eds.) AHFE 2021. LNNS, vol. 271, pp. 251–258. Springer, Cham (2021). https://doi.org/10.1007/978-3-030-80624-8_32
40. Mowbray, A., Chung, P., Greenleaf, G.: Utilising AI in the legal assistance sector—testing a role for legal information institutes. SSRN Electron. J. (2019)
41. Firdaus, V.A.H., Saputra, P.Y., Suprianto, D.: Intelligence chatbot for Indonesian law on electronic information and transaction. In: IOP Conference Series: Materials Science and Engineering, vol. 830, no. 2, p. 022089 (2020)
42. Senthilkumar, M., Chowdhary, C.L.: An AI-based chatbot using deep learning. Intell. Syst., 231–242 (2019)
43. Singh, S.K., Kumar Srivastava, P.A., Tamrakar, P.S.: Universal artificial intelligence for intelligent agents: an approach to super intelligent agents. IOSR J. Comput. Eng. **12**(6), 43–48 (2013)
44. Navas, S.: The provision of legal services to consumers using LawTech tools: from "service" to "legal product". Open J. Soc. Sci. **07**(11), 79–103 (2019)
45. Fang, C., Wilkenfeld, J.N., Navick, N., Gibbs, J.L.: AI am here to represent you: understanding how institutional logics shape attitudes toward intelligent technologies in legal work. Manage. Commun. Q., 089331892311582 (2023)

Networking Technology for Social Impact

Assessing Data Protection Perspectives Among the Residents of Rumphi and Karonga in Northern Malawi Regarding the Use of Unmanned Aerial Vehicles (Drones) for Humanitarian Intervention

Rogers Alunge[✉]

Faculty of Geo-Information Sciences and Earth Observation (ITC), University of Twente, Enschede, The Netherlands
alungerogers@yahoo.com

Abstract. Drones are used by humanitarian actors to collect data which could be classified as personally identifiable information (PII) and demographically identifiable information (DII). Though said to optimise intervention, they raise significant data protection challenges. An example is transparency: how effectively are community residents informed about the data drones collect of them and their community? How may this awareness affect their desire to consent, engage related group/community data protection rights, or to allow the data collector circumvent these rights to guarantee their faster access to aid.

This paper is based on two case studies: the Northern Malawi districts of Rhumpi and Karonga, earmarked as flood-risk areas and whose residents had witnessed humanitarian drone flights. The research uses qualitative analysis of focus group discussions with selected inhabitants on a series of data protection questions relating to drones. The results show that participants were mostly unaware of the high-resolution images drones take of them and their communities; their consent would hardly be valid because of their vulnerable situation, and they preferred extensive sharing of their data to attract external aid rather than engage any DII rights. This prompted the conclusion that guaranteeing responsible drone data collection and processing in humanitarian settings would rest entirely on the humanitarian organisation, with comparably little or no engagement by the local residents.

Keywords: Humanitarian intervention · data protection · transparency · drones · personally identifiable information · demographically identifiable information · Malawi

© ICST Institute for Computer Sciences, Social Informatics and Telecommunications Engineering 2024
Published by Springer Nature Switzerland AG 2024. All Rights Reserved
A. Seeam et al. (Eds.): InterSol 2023, LNICST 541, pp. 313–336, 2024.
https://doi.org/10.1007/978-3-031-51849-2_21

1 Introduction: Unmanned Aerial Vehicles (UAVs or Drones) in Humanitarian Action

Unmanned Aerial Vehicles (UAVs, otherwise called drones) are aircrafts without a human on board [1] which are controlled remotely, and can be equipped with different sensors that could capture and record visual and audio data for monitoring and mapping operations [2]. Originally, drones were primarily used by military organisations for surveillance and reconnaissance purposes in the 1950s [3, 4]. In recent decades however, they have been increasingly used by civilian sectors for a vast array of activities ranging from logistics, supply chain management [5, 6], agricultural surveys and monitoring [7] aerial imaging, mapping, town planning, or aerial cargo services [8]. Irrespective of their applications, the general motivation behind the use of drones is their ability to increase the speed and flexibility of supply chain, data collection and communication processes, while enhancing precision and cost efficiency. As noted by Jumbert & Sandvik, government actors (first responders like firefighters, search-and-rescue crews, and police), civil society actors (environmentalists, conservationists, cultural-heritage advocates, human-rights activists), the press (especially the so-called "citizen drone" journalists and enthusiasts) as well as the agriculture, mining and maritime industries are all exploring opportunities and possibilities offered by drone technology to attain their objectives, enhance work effectiveness and increase productivity [3]. Drones could be equipped with sophisticated devices to observe and track ground movements with high resolution images, move at alternating altitudes, relay information at very high speed and transport supplies, offering easier and faster data collection processes and enhancing decision-making.

Drones are also increasingly used by humanitarian actors (hence the term "humanitarian drones" [9]) for locating survivors and assessing infrastructure damages following a disaster, and monitoring population movements. They are also useful in conducting needs assessments to determine where, and how many people are in need and what their needs are, and building better short-term strategies for handling humanitarian logistics and distributing relief [10]. Due to their possible remote sensing abilities and rapid spatial information collection, drones have also been widely used in emergency surveying [11], and in case of disasters, they can go deep into specific locations, which reduces danger and security-related issues for accompanying human rescue teams. Significantly, they are equally used for disaster prevention, as they can collect aerial data of an area which can be processed to determine or measure the impact of some predicted disaster, an example being the objectives of the UNICEF Malawi drone corridor[1].

Sophisticated equipment like high-resolution cameras can be attached to a drone to generate clear, high-resolution aerial photographs [12] of a community through which

---

[1] In June 2017, the Government of Malawi and UNICEF launched a 40km-radius air corridor at the Kasungu Aerodrome in Central Malawi to as a base to test drones for various humanitarian purposes including flood modelling. Aerial images would be captured and run through AI image recognition and flood modelling software to predict flood impact and identify areas which will be most affected, aiming to better inform emergency preparedness through early warning. Retrieved from https://www.arm.com/blogs/blueprint/arm-unicef-malawi. Accessed 26/03/2023.

individuals, groups of persons or a community can be identified by the entity which deployed the drone. For this reason among others, notwithstanding their lauded contributions to humanitarian intervention, an important amount of literature attests to the important data protection/privacy and ethical challenges involved with the deployment of drones in humanitarian contexts (so-called humanitarian drones [9]). However, there has not been so much research yet on data protection from the perspective of the data subject i.e. examining the perceptions which people in vulnerable situations may have regarding their privacy and data protection in relation to the use of drones in their towns or community. As contribution towards bridging this gap, this paper examines data protection and/or privacy-related perspectives which persons in vulnerable situations may have regarding humanitarian drones. It investigates their awareness of the data about them collected by means of drone technology (principle of transparency of collection and/or processing), how their awareness may reflect on their readiness or willingness to consent to the data collection, and also discusses the idea of a community rather than individualistic approach to data protection.

The chosen case study areas are the Northern Malawi districts of Rumphi and Karonga, both internationally earmarked as flood-risk areas and tagged by UNICEF Malawi for an impact-based flood-modelling survey using drones. I organised focus group discussions (FGDs) with the locals who witnessed the flying drones, to find out the extent to which they are aware of what data about them and/or their community can or are actually being collected by the drones, and how this awareness could impact their consent to such data collection or processing. Also, I sought to establish whether they may wish to exercise group/community data rights over the processing of aerial, high-resolution images collected on their community, and finally how willing they are to allow the drone-processing organisation to waive aside its data protection responsibilities towards them and their data if that would guarantee faster accessibility to external aid. In this light, the following section briefly presents the subject matter of data protection: personally identifiable information (PII) and demographically identifiable information (DII), and briefly discusses the data protection principle of transparency and its importance in (humanitarian) data collection processes. Section 3 then gives a general presentation of the research project, Sect. 4 presents our methodology and data collection tools i.e. the FGDs, and Sect. 5 discusses the participants' responses gathered from the FGDs. Finally, Sect. 6 presents a general conclusion to the paper.

2 PII, DII and Processing Transparency Regarding Humanitarian Drones

As noted by Weitzberg et al., humanitarian actors increasingly rely on data and technology for humanitarian response [13], with humanitarian drones actively involved in the collection and processing of vast amounts of data. A lot of this data is personally identifiable information (PII) and demographically identifiable information (PII) – a distinction of these follows below. As Kuner et al. importantly observe here, what is of interest in the case of drones as regards data collection and processing is not the use of the drones *per se,* but rather the different technologies they are or could be equipped with, such as high-resolution cameras and microphones, thermal imaging equipment, sensors or devices capable of intercepting wireless communications [14]. It follows that the PII or DII a drone collects or can collect will depend on the data collection devices fitted to it.

2.1 Personally Identifiable Information (PII)

PII is any data that directly or indirectly identifies, or can be used to identify an individual. It includes, but is not limited to the person's name, address, identity number, gender, age or date of birth, financial account numbers, image or location [15] The collection of PII, also known as personal data [16], is crucial for the provision of humanitarian assistance where there is need to determine and identify persons in need e.g. to give out food or cash coupons, or administer medical aid. As pointed out by the World Food Programme (WFP), loss, theft or misuse of personal data may cause harm to the people needing assistance[2]. An individual whose personal data is unduly disclosed may be subjected to very serious abusive behaviours, particularly in armed conflict settings and other highly volatile socio-political situations such as dictatorships or ethnically motivated conflicts. As drones are (always) equipped with cameras, sensors and even with devices capable of intercepting communications, they are very likely to capture PII or communications about individuals. For instance, a political opposition leader fleeing his country and hosted in a refugee camp may be identified from aerial, high-resolution images of the camp and pursued by government officials of his/her country if they get access to those images. Also, when the drone is equipped with two or more multidimensional cameras, it will not only collect data about the target, but also about other persons within the field of view of the drone (like images of people within the confines of their compound). These and related situations raise protection concerns which demand careful and responsible handling of PII by humanitarian drone operators.

2.2 Demographically Identifiable Information (DII)

DII, also known as "group data", has been defined as either individual and/or aggregated data points that allow inferences to be drawn that enable the classification, identification, and/or tracking of both named and/or unnamed individuals, groups of individuals, and/or multiple groups of individuals according to ethnicity, economic class, religion, gender, age, health condition, location, occupation. It can include PII, geographic and geospatial data, environmental data, survey data, and/or any other data set that can – either in isolation or in combination – enable the classification, identification, and/or tracking of a specific demographic categorization constructed by those collecting, aggregating, and/or cross-corroborating the data [17]. In other words, these are data which would not single out an individual from a group, but could rather single out or differentiate a group of persons from within a bigger group of people, or differentiate a community from other (similar) communities. DII would also include (especially in rural, less developed sectors) data like high resolution images of a community depicting data like housing structures, monuments, shrines, agricultural and agropastoral patterns, religious practices, dress codes of the people which (when combined with other available datasets) can

---
[2] Ibid.

enable the identification or recognition of that community from other communities. And like PII, DII could be used to target and harm an identified group of people. A case in point is the Harvard's Signal Program on Human Security and Technology, which operated a project analysing satellite and other spatial data to identify areas most affected during the 2011 conflict in Sudan. The researchers later discovered that their analyses of these data were being hacked and used by hostile actors on the ground to better target their enemies [18].

However, while PII has conveniently been protected under contemporary data protection regulation, there currently is no legal regime *rationae materiae* protecting DII. Current privacy and data protection regulatory frameworks are individualistic, triggered only when the information of a distinct, identified or identifiable individual is processed [19], and as van der Sloot [20] rightfully argues, they do not provide a satisfactory response to risks affecting individuals which arise from processed data relating to groups of individuals[3]. UNICEF for example expressly states in its Policy on Data Protection that the Policy does **not** apply to "...data that can identify a group, demographic or community, but not an individual."[4] Even the World Food Programme defined "personal data" without including data which identifies or which could identify a group of people[5]. Other internationally influential data protection regimes like the 2018 EU General Data Protection Regulation or 2014 African Convention on Cybersecurity and Data Protection also strictly apply to data relating to individuals with no reference to group or community data.

It should be mentioned however, that though contemporary data protection regimes are individualistic, and their data collection and processing principles were conceived to apply (only) to PII, it appears reasonable that DII can be largely covered by these principles. It would obviously be tricky to determine how to enforce rights like the right of access, rectification, or deletion of DII especially as members of the same group or community may feel differently about or could be differently affected by the same dataset. But principles like those requiring a data collector to have a specific, pre-set and limited purpose for processing (purpose limitation), determined period to store the collected data (storage limitation), to collect just what data is needed (data minimisation), taking appropriate measures to secure data collected (security of processing), or having a lawful ground for collecting that data, can all seemingly and conveniently be applied to DII. This observation was echoed by Kuner et al. [15] in their discussion about the use of drones in humanitarian interventions, where they examined the idea of "consent

---

[3] This is even more so considering that the concept of a "group", especially in the age of Big Data analytics, is a vastly dynamic concept with practically unlimited variables, and groups are digitally created by cross-referencing large amounts of data which results in these groups not being structured. And one individual could be the subject of many groups e.g. one individual can belong to the categories "men over 30 who own a car in Kenya" "medical doctors who are married in Kenya", "Manchester United FC football fans below 40 in Africa". See Kammourieh, Lanah, Thomas Baar, Jos Berens, Emmanuel Letouzé, Julia Manske, John Palmer, David Sangokoya, and Patrick Vinck. "Group privacy in the age of big data." *Group privacy: New challenges of data technologies* (2017): 37–66.

[4] Paragraph 8, UNICEF POLICY ON PERSONAL DATA PROTECTION, Document Number: POLICY/DFAM/2020/001. Effective Date: 15 July 2020.

[5] World Food Programme Guide to Personal Data Protection and Privacy (supra).

of the community" or the "consent of authorities" as a plausible alternative to individual consent offered by contemporary data protection regimes. This could involve, for example, obtaining consent only from representatives of a group of vulnerable individuals and not the individuals themselves. The following discussions would therefore examine the FGD results in Annex I below in line with established data protection principles of processing, the implementation of which remains the responsibility of the processing organisation.

2.3   The Data Protection Principle of Transparency

Data protection is here understood as those set of rules and safeguards to be observed when processing (personal) data in order to protect the fundamental rights and freedoms of individuals from any eventual violation [21]. Drones and their applications entail the collection, processing, recording, organisation and storing, of PII. This means their deployment over civilian settlements triggers data protection (and privacy) concerns [22]. Drones have especially offered increased capacity for domestic surveillance through high-definition cameras, real-time video streams, their ability of massive geographical sweep, heat and motion sensors, automated text and facial recognition technologies.[6] Moreover, their small size and ability to fly very high makes them likely to operate undetected, which could raise some issues as regards (the fundamental data protection principle of) transparency.

The principle of transparency in (personal) data protection requires that at least a minimum amount of information concerning the processing be provided to the individual whose data is being collected [14]. Typically, the specifics of the information to give the individual will depend on the legal basis and reason for which the data is being collected, but should generally include the nature of the data, the purposes for which it is collected, how long it shall be stored, whether it shall be transferred to third parties, and any rights which they may have in relation to this processing (e.g. access to their PII, correction or deletion; right to object to or to restrict processing) [23]. This information should be provided before the data is collected, is generally received orally or in writing and communicated directly to the individuals, should be easy to understand, expressed in clear and plain language. However, where this is not possible, the organisation should consider providing information by other means like radio communications, online adverts, flyers, posters displayed in a place and form that can easily be accessed (public spaces, markets, places of worship and/or the organizations' offices), radio communication, or discussion with representatives of the community [14]. Kuner et al. observe that with regard to drones, it would generally, for practical reasons, be difficult to inform everyone in the targeted area individually, which is why the ideal practice will be to use media campaigns targeting the local inhabitants, and actively involving the leaders of the target community, all before the drones are deployed (especially in non-emergency situations, as was the case with the UNICEF Malawi flood modelling activity in Northern Malawi). They also suggest that while flying the drones, the organisation could affix their marks

---

[6] Petition to the Federal Aviation Administration: Drones and Privacy (Washington, D.C.: Electronic Privacy Information Center, 2012), https://epic.org/wp-content/uploads/privacy/drones/FAA-553e-Petition-03-08-12.pdf Accessed 12/3/2023.

or signs on them [or to the extent possible, attach a flag bearing their logo on them] to fulfil transparency and information obligations. [14].

2.4 Importance of Transparency in Community Data Collection

Absence of sufficient communication and information circulation about a DII collection and processing activity in a community could lead to the data collector missing out on important data responsibility measures; a case in point being the collection of data which might be regarded as sensitive within a specific community. Concepts of what information should be considered sensitive or private may vary between cultures, age groups, interest groups and other demographics [24]. For example, traditional shrines or traditional cults are usually sacred to a community and may be accessed only by designated members of the community, which implies data relating to them could be considered sensitive by the community residents. They may not want details of what happens within these sacred settings to be known out of the community, hence they may react negatively to the generation and collection of aerial, high-resolution images depicting these settings.

This in turn impacts on other data protection perceptions which data subjects may have about the data collection, as awareness of exactly what data about them and their community is collected, as well as with whom it can be shared, will certainly be significant in guiding their decision whether to grant permission to the data collector to proceed. It therefore follows that if local residents are made aware in considerable detail of the high-resolution images which drones can take of their community, objects of their community which can come under the drone radar, as well as who will or could have access to these images, this might trigger their (data protection) sensitivities regarding this collection. Gevaert for example, during her research on the use of drones for town planning purposes in Rwanda and Tanzania, established that many residents expressed privacy-related worries regarding the capacity of the drones to take very high resolution and detailed images of their compounds and living environment [25]. Similarly, besides inquiring into their levels of drone awareness, this paper also seeks to find out whether comparable data protection worries will be voiced by the residents of Rumphi and Karonga when they are made aware of the high-resolution images of them and their community being (or capable of being) taken and collected by humanitarian drones.

3 Methodology

3.1 Fieldwork (in Collaboration with UNICEF and DODMA Malawi)

The research was qualitative: focus group discussions (FGDs) [26] with residents of the chosen case study districts who have witnessed drone activity in their community. To achieve this, I worked closely with UNICEF Malawi which had planned an impact-based flood modelling exercise using drones in Northern Malawi in November 2022, which included Rumphi and Karonga. I also enlisted the help of field officers of the Department of Disaster Management (DODMA) of Malawi in Rumphi and Karonga, who helped find volunteer participants for the FGDs (see Sect. 3.2 below). According to our plans, UNICEF Malawi would go to these areas and carry out their flood-modelling exercise, and I come a day later to meet volunteer residents (who witnessed the drones flying overhead) and have group discussions with them on their data protection/privacy perceptions with regard to the drones they saw. The plan went well for Rumphi, but by the time I got to Karonga, the flood modelling activity had not started yet. So in order to attain our survey target, I enlisted the support of a private drone pilot, who flew a drone over the settlement, took high-resolution pictures of the people and their community which I used as the display image during the discussions. Then with the aid of the present DODMA officials, I selected 21 volunteer participants for the FGD from the (curious) onlookers, following the criteria elaborated in Sect. 3.2 below. I estimated that this would not jeopardize the results of the research as the most important factors for the discussions (i.e. residents of a disaster-risk community having witnessed drone activity) were met with this arrangement (Table 1).

Table 1. Summary of the organisation and planning of the FGDs

Casestudy district (villages visited)	Number of participants	Number of FGD sessions	Notable issues
Rumphi (Mlowe, Mzoto Chisokwo, Rumphi Boma)	21 (12 men, 9 women)	3 (7 participants per session)	No specific issues: UNICEF Malawi agents had been on site and flown their drones; participants had witnessed drone activity by the time I arrived
Karonga (Karonga Boma)	21 (11 men, 10 women)	3 (7 participants per session)	The flood-modelling had not begun yet, so a private pilot was hired to fly a drone over the community, and selected participants from the onlookers with the aid of DODMA officials

3.2 The Participants

As mentioned above, DODMA Malawi assisted in selecting participants for the FGDs. They helped select a total of 42 adults who had witnessed the drones flying overhead, 21 from each casestudy district and ensuring an even representation of men and women. I had a total of 6 discussion sessions (3 per casestudy district), with 7 participants per session. And to keep the discussions open and minimise power imbalances within the discussion groups, DODMA ensured that participants in each session were of about the same social class; traditional authorities were excluded from the discussions (see Table 3).

3.3 The FGDs

The discussions were triggered by a series of prepared questions aimed at investigating the participants' knowledge about the data processing abilities of drone technology. This was meant to induce discussions with the participants on any privacy or data protection concerns they may have regarding drone activity in their communities. I was assisted by a translator charged with translating the questions to Chitumbuka (the language commonly spoken in Northern Malawi) and posing them to the participants. We both then listened to their replies which the translator rendered back to me in English. He equally acted as moderator of the discussions. At the start of each FGD session, a prepared consent statement translated to Chitumbuka was read and explained to the participants by the translator. They were required to raise their hand if they still consented to contribute to the study, hence attesting to their valid and unequivocal consent to participate in the discussion. The entire discussions were recorded using an advanced portable audio recorder system. Below are the questions guiding the FGDs (Table 2).

Table 2. The FGD questions

Residents' first impressions on drone technology:	- What were your (first) impressions when you saw the drones fly? - Have you seen other drone flights? - Have you seen a picture taken by a drone before? - Do you think these drones (can) take clear, detailed pictures of your village, farms, houses, children?
Residents' individual opinions about drone image processing	- [Showing them an aerial drone image of a community] What do you see in this image (can they identify, roads, farms, private compounds)? - What are your impressions/opinions of these images? - What do you personally feel about these pictures, seeing that they can show details of your houses, farms and entire community? - Is there anything in this picture you may not like other people in the village or elsewhere to see (e.g. roofless toilets, waste disposal?) - Generally, with who may you not want such images of your property or community to be shared (maybe state land/town planning officials)?

(continued)

Table 2. (*continued*)

Residents' awareness of processing	- Were you aware the UAV flights you witnessed would take place? If yes, how were you informed? By who? - Were you aware or informed that the flying UAVs will be taking clear, detailed images of your community? - Do you know the person or organisation flying the UAV? Did they come and present themselves to you? - Did anyone tell you whether and why it is necessary to take these UAV pictures of you and your community?
Residents' opinions about informed consent for drone data processing	- Do you think you should be informed first before the flying of a UAV over your community to take such pictures? - Would you like to be personally able to grant or refuse permission for these images to be taken and/or shared with others? - In your opinion, should an authority be empowered to give permission on behalf of the entire community for these images to be taken? If yes, who do you think should have that authority? And why?
Residents' awareness of their data protection rights with regard to drone data processes	- Do you feel you may have any individual rights on these images? - Do you think as a community, you all as a group can have rights (besides monetary rights) on these images? - Are you aware of any specific information-related rights (besides monetary rights) you may have on these images? - Has anyone mentioned anything to you about any rights you may have regarding these images of you or your community?

(*continued*)

Table 2. (*continued*)

Residents' opinions of the benefits of UAV data processing	- In what situations do you think UAVs (can) really help or are necessary (maybe medical and relocation assistance in case of floods)? - Would you mind that these detailed UAV images of your property and community is shared with government and other parties, so they help you better during flood crisis, without caring much about your rights around these images? - Do you think humanitarian organisations or government could still help you effectively without the need for these UAV images and activity? - After the above discussions, what is your general opinion about UAV activity? Do you think it a positive or negative development for your community?

3.4   Envisaged Ethical Risks and Corresponding Mitigation Strategies.

Several potential ethical risks were identified which could be encountered during the organisation and progress of the discussions and adopted corresponding mitigation strategies as illustrated in Table 3 below.

Table 3. Potential ethical risks and mitigation strategies

Envisaged potential ethical risks	Mitigation strategies
Getting informed consent from the participants	Consent statement was translated from to Chitumbuka, read out and detailly explained to the participants by our translator at the start of each session
Limited participation	**Rumphi**: DODMA officials helped select one participant per household in each village visited **Karonga**: This was difficult to ensure as I had to select participants from among curious onlookers of our drone launch on the spot
Perception of power imbalance between the researcher and participants	I had a simple, layman appearance, and bore no logo or sign suggesting I am a government official or from any position of authority

(*continued*)

Table 3. (*continued*)

Envisaged potential ethical risks	Mitigation strategies
Intimidation by influential participants	I expressly excluded chiefs and traditional rulers from participating Also, selected participants were visibly of about the same social status [27]
Risk of political/religious opinions expressed during the discussion:	Interpreter was instructed and did well to moderate the discussion and guide the participants against emitting opinions with any political undertones
Risk of (physical and emotional) harm/security issues:	Discussions were moderated to prevent participants' disclosure of any sensitive information about their personal lives or those of other members of the community
Anonymity, confidentiality, and information security	FGD records were immediately transferred using VPN connection to and stored in the password-protected virtual drive of the University of Twente, with Bitlocker encryption installed. The records were then transcribed into text for in-depth analysis, and are currently stored in accordance with the University of Twente research data policies

3.5 Methodology Employed

This research relied on the relatively new Micro-Interlocutor Analysis methodology, proposed by Onwuegbuzie et al. [28]. This method was preferred principally for two main reasons. First because its collection phase is designed to have the opinion of every participant recorded, which is important especially in situations where a participant is silent, introvert or shy. It aims to include all voices, even those less heard during the group discussions. Secondly, the method proves efficient to record the main stance and positions of participants without absolutely needing to transcribe or understand the micro details of their declarations. This is crucial for our research due to the language barrier: I was interacting with the participants through a translator (doing simultaneous and summary oral renditions between Chitumbuka and English). And considering the differences in vocabulary as well as cultural differences in languages (especially regarding technology vocabulary), it would have been unfeasible to have granular details of the conversation orally translated in real time and recorded in English. In this case, it was essential to obtain just the position or opinion of each participant regarding specific questions discussed.

4   Findings Retrieved from the FGDs

After six discussion sessions lasting between 1.5–2 h each, the following findings were arrived at.[7]

4.1   Analysis: Discussion and Analysis of the FGD Results

Several interesting takes could be drawn from the FGDs. Before delving deeper in our analysis regarding data protection and data responsibility, it can be observed from the above table that drone technology is predominantly new to the locals of Rumphi and Karonga, with 88% of participants having never seen a drone fly before the FGDs took place. Notwithstanding, they were much more fascinated and curious than wary of the technology, with only 12% of participants admitting to a feeling of fear at the sight of the drones. There was also an overwhelmingly positive recognition of the advantages of the technology as a tool for community progress and development, with 98% of participants acknowledging drones were overall a positive development for their community.

A strong manifestation of community interests over individual interests could also be noted when discussing the issue of sensitive data with the participants. Illustratively, after being presented with some high-resolution UAV pictures of their community, 90% of the participants asserted that they did not find any unfavourable factors (not even open latrines) which should be considered sensitive enough to not be seen by third parties. These participants were also of the opinion that having images like open latrines or naked children playing shared to third parties would bring shame to the owner of the compound or parents respectively, which would act as a deterrent and coerce them to put roofs over the latrines or take better care of their children. Also, 93% estimated that the images could be shared with a wide range of third parties with no restrictions, even if the images showed details of their households behind a fence which would normally not be visible to their neighbours. They affirmed that to them, fences are built for security reasons (to prevent their livestock escaping or trespassers from getting in) rather than to protect their privacy; i.e. they do not mind the neighbours or a third party knowing details of their private residences behind the confines of their fences through drone aerial images.

Finally, a generally positive impression was noted among the participants regarding the deployment of UAVs for flood-related surveys in their communities, with 98% of them asserting that the abilities of drones to collect such pictures and share them in real time with government officials humanitarian actors makes them very necessary and indispensable for their progressive development. There also were no significant ethical worries or objections to the capacities of UAV technology, with only 4% of participants raising concerns about the possibility of drones capturing data like images of naked children or convicted prisoners (where the drone flies low enough to capture facial imagery), which they considered sensitive. Some specific observations are however worthy to be discussed in more detail, which is attempted below.

---

[7] For the full FGD results, please see ANNEX 1 below.

4.2   The Participants' Desire to Be Informed of UAV Data Processing

In line with the principle of transparency, the discussions revealed in the first place that the total 100% the participants expressed the wish to be informed of drone activities over their communities in advance, in line with the fundamental data protection principle of transparency as well as their right to information of processing. In Rumphi however, where UNICEF Malawi had already flown the drones by the time of our discussion, only 7 of the 21 participants attested to have been informed by traditional authorities who arrived to their homes to inform them about a flood modelling activity which will involve drones. The other 14 specified that while they were informed of a forthcoming flood-mapping exercise, they were not made aware that it will involve machines flying in the sky, taking overhead pictures of the community. One participant even mentioned that at the sight of the drone over his farm, he thought they were doing an aerial survey to sell of his land, which caused some panic.

Further, all 14 participants, after I showed them a sample of drone aerial shots, said they were not aware of the capacities of the drones to take clear, high-resolution pictures of their community, nor that they had the capacity to zoom in and possibly identify individuals. They were not also informed why such pictures are necessary, who they ae or might be shared with, how long it will be stored, which organisation was in charge of the project (the identity of the data controller), nor were they provided with any details on how to contact the organisation in the event of any complaints. Also, they were not made aware of any rights they may have towards any data collected by the drones. Moreover, during the data collection process, the drone pilots did not bear any organisation logos, and 5 of the participants attested to having approached them for identification, and were informed they were there on behalf of UNICEF Malawi.

From the above it can be concluded that UNICEF Malawi, as the data processing organisation, did try to comply with the transparency principle to inform the residents about the data collection process, using door-to-door communications in Rumphi. Notwithstanding, some essential information about the processing was not communicated to the residents. As pointed out by Kuner et al., the medium of information used to inform individuals about the collection or processing of their data, as well as the information considered essential to be communicated to crisis-affected individuals in a humanitarian context are determined on a case-by-case basis [31]. Considering that drones typically process data over a wide surface area, it will be unfeasible to determine exactly which individuals may come under their radar, and hence impracticable to inform people of the locality individually. UNICEF Malawi, by engaging with traditional rulers to inform households, can be said to have used a reasonable medium of communication. Also, with the direct target of this exercise being DII and not individuals, information like who the data will be shared with or how long it will be stored would probably not be essential for the residents in this context. However, knowing who oversees the project and being aware that clear, high-resolution pictures are being taken would probably be information which should have been duly communicated to the residents for transparency purposes.

4.3 The Participants' Desire to Consent to UAV Data Processing

Consent is an age-old concept in legal relations and a basic, well-known pre-condition for contractual engagements between individuals and legal entities. In relation to data protection, it basically is any freely given, specific and informed indication of a data subject's agreement to allow the processing of their PII[8]. While probably the most popular legal ground for processing PII, consent may, however, not always be sufficient especially within a humanitarian context.

As Kuner et al. [14] observe, given the vulnerability of most beneficiaries and the nature of humanitarian emergencies, humanitarian organisations will generally not be able to rely on consent for most of their data processing. As consent in data protection is generally required to be freely given,[9] with the data subject presented with a clear choice to give or withhold it, there could always be situations where making such a choice available to data subjects (and hence making their consent valid) is impracticable. Kuner et al. advance several typical humanitarian situations where an organisation will hardly be in a position to validly and sufficiently inform data subjects about their processing operations in order for their consent to be considered freely given. These included cases where processing operation is of a very large scale and will involve data of a large number of people; where the data subjects are particularly vulnerable (e.g. children, elderly or disabled persons) at the time of giving consent; where they have no real choice to refuse consent due to a situation of need and vulnerability, including a lack of alternative to the specific assistance being offered; or where new technologies are involved, characterized by complex data flows and multiple stakeholders, including data processors and sub-data processors in multiple jurisdictions [15]. It is also interesting to note that while requiring data subjects to be informed of processing to ensure they know what they are consenting to, contemporary data protection regimes do not require an indication from the data subject that they understand the information provided to them by the data controller [29]. This makes it difficult for a processing organisation to get reliable evidence that data subjects effectively understand and appreciate the risks and benefits of a processing operation sufficiently enough to consider their consent valid.

As observed in the FGD results table above, consenting to data collection seemed highly valued among the participants, with 88% wishing their permission could be sought before UAV images of their community are taken and processed. Further, 86% preferred that such consent should not be taken on their behalf (by a traditional authority) but they should be actively involved. However, similar situations as those cited above by Kuner et al. could be equally observed. First, as gathered from my collaboration with UNICEF Malawi, the drones were mapped to cover a very wide scale of territory occupied by thousands of residents among whom there inevitably were elderly people and children. Also, the people had not been proposed alternatives for flood modelling over their communities other than drones; and the drones are relatively new technologies involving data

---

[8] Art.2(h) Data Protection Directive: European Parliament and the Council of the European Union, Directive 95/46/EC of the European Parliament and of the Council of 24 October 1995 on the protection of individuals with regard to the processing of personal data and on the free movement of such data [1995] OJ L281/31 (23.11.1995).

[9] Article 2, Malawi Data Protection Bill 2021; Annex 1 Paragraph 5, UNICEF Policy on Personal Data Protection, July 2020; Recital 32 EU GDPR.

flows between two or more stakeholders (UNICEF engaged an undisclosed third-party processor to fly the drones and collect the data on their behalf in Rumphi). It could equally be observed that the participants had a low level of data literacy and had never been sensitized or triggered on the possibility of UAV-collected or generated PII or DII being misused in ways which could negatively affect them in the short or long run. Concepts like digital surveillance, online tracking and tracing, data breaches or algorithmic bias were completely foreign and unknown to them. Moreover, 76% of the participants said they will not mind the non-consideration of their rights by humanitarian organisations provided the collection and processing of their data grants them access to external aid; a point further confirming the influence of their vulnerability on any consent they might give for processing. These point to the conclusion that though most of the FGD participants voiced their desire to be able to provide their consent for UAV data processing within their communities, their vulnerable position makes such consent a less solid basis for the data processing organisation to rely on. Kuner et al. observe that in such a case, other legal bases might be more appropriate[10].

4.4 Group Data Protection and Community Rights Over UAV-Processed DII

As already discussed above, data protection is intrinsically individualistic, with current data protection frameworks limited in their scope of application to protecting identified or identifiable individuals (PII), and essentially excluding groups of people (DII). So in essence, DII or community data, as long as it cannot be linked to a specific, identified or identifiable individual, will not fall under the scope of current data protection law. As Van der Sloot observes, this status quo tends to inhibit the protective intention of data protection, because nowadays most people are not profiled as individuals but, instead, as a member of a specific (digital) group or community. Organisations no longer tend to gather data about a specific person, but rather an 'undefined number of people during an undefined period of time without a pre-established reason' [20]. These data are then processed on a group or aggregated level through the use of statistical correlations to make targeted decisions; a tendency which has often been criticised for yielding biased or discriminatory results on individuals who get algorithmically classified under such groups but may not actually have the traits for which they were made part of the group [30]. The result is thus that the 'individual' element is mostly lost in the process.

In this light, with data protection having originated from the need to protect the individual's right to privacy in the information age [31, 32], there have been discussions on alternative means of conceiving privacy as a concept which preserves the autonomy of the individual by equally preserving his/her relationship with their immediate surroundings. Proponents of a so-called 'relational autonomy' in particular, argue that people's identities, needs, interests – and indeed autonomy – are always also shaped by their

---

[10] Besides consent, Kuner et al. set out five other legal basis which organisations could rely on to process (personal) data of vulnerable or crisis-affected people: where processing is necessary for the vital interest of the person (e.g. to save the person's life); processing is necessary for important grounds of public interest; processing is necessary for the organisation's legitimate interest; for the performance of a contract to which the organisation is subject; or for compliance with a legal obligation.

relations to others [33]. And as Reviglio & Alunge observe, the view that the individual self is considered constrained by social factors (relational autonomy) and the realization that people are not always in control of information regarding them (especially in the big data era) necessitate the consideration of top-to-bottom norms which emphasize the dignity of humanity as a community or group over the dignity of individuals [34]. It follows therefore that data relating to a community or group through which specific individuals of that community or group may not be identified, but which processing could lead to decisions affecting them, should be covered as practicably as possible by data protection.

Relatedly, during the FGDs in Rumphi and Karonga, a sense of community action towards DII could be observed among the participants. When asked whether they feel they could have any individual claims or rights over the UAV images, 52% of the participants answered in the affirmative. On the other hand, 55% asserted that they believed the entire community as a unit could benefit from community rights on the images, which could probably be engaged and enforced via the traditional chiefs or community leaders if need be. This view was prompted by their observation that because the images depicted their way of life and habits to considerable accuracy, and could influence decisions by the government or UNICEF Malawi affecting them, it was only plausible that they could be given the opportunity to have a say on how the images are processed. Notwithstanding, it is important to point out that these were more of abstract opinions than strong positions which they wished to have implemented, as they were silent and manifested no interest towards discovering any data-related rights they may have as regards the aerial images of their communities. They evidently preferred to trust the government or humanitarian organisations to use the DII diligently and for the best interest of their community. In essence, they were much more interested in getting large scale visibility to attract external aid; and much less vocal about (DII) rights. This further points to the conclusion that the burden of guaranteeing data protection compliance to drone-processed DII relating to the Rumphi and Karonga communities would eventually rest almost entirely on the data controller organisations, with minimal participation expected from the residents.

5 Conclusion

The last few decades have witnessed a progressively important and significant employment of drone technology in humanitarian interventions, and this, it seems, would remain on an increase in the coming years. The advantages offered by drones to reach and collect data from hard-to-access or dangerous areas, cover vastly wide territorial scopes, enable direct communications and data transmissions between humanitarian actors, transport medical and other supplies at much faster rates and at much less costs make them an ideal and arguably indispensable tool for humanitarian action. Still, they are usually equipped with additional technology like remote sensors, high-resolution cameras or even communication interceptors which, though serving the purpose of precise and accurate data collection, pose significant privacy and data protection challenges. Drones have already been originally used and established by military organisations as highly proficient tools for intelligence spying and infiltration during warfare, a fact which is almost inevitably bound to raise concerns regarding surveillance, privacy and data protection whenever they are deployed over inhabited communities.

One of such data protection concerns is transparency of processing: with data protection requiring data subjects to be informed in considerable detail about the processing of their data, it follows that individuals whose data are being processed by drones should at least be made aware of the nature of the data being collected, how that data can be used and why it is collected. Further awareness of the exact nature of the data collected or which could be collected would further inform their decision to consent to this collection (for example, if some of such data is deemed sensitive by their standards), as well as influence any informational rights or claims they may feel they have towards such data. To satisfy the requirement of transparency and hence valid consent as regards drone data processing, a prior, important consideration should be to find out what the residents of the target communities actually know about the processing abilities of drones.

This was the objective of this research carried out, as chosen case study areas, in the Northern Malawi districts of Rumphi and Karonga, both internationally earmarked as flood-risk zones. Both districts were also part of a vast territory to be covered by an impact-based, flood-modelling exercise organised by UNICEF Malawi Malawi, and our intended research targets were 21 residents from each of these districts (total of 42 residents) who had witnessed the drones flying over their community. By the time of our visit, UNICEF Malawi had carried out the exercise in Rumphi but suspended their progress before getting to Karonga, which led us to improvise into hiring a private drone pilot to fly a drone over the community, take some high-resolution pictures and select some research targets from the onlookers. And to ensure engagement from the research targets, this research opted for focus group discussions (FGDs - Khan et al.) as data collection tool, based on the Micro-Interlocutor Analysis methodology proposed by Onwuegbuzie et al.

From the results of the FGDs, it was observed first of all that a large majority of the participants were seeing a drone for the first time (with the UNICEF Malawi flood-modelling in Rumphi and our private drone in Karonga), and were mostly fascinated by it. In Rumphi, they admitted that they were unaware of the high-resolution images of their communities which drones can take; which led to the conclusion that UNICEF Malawi, as data processing organisation, did not adequately inform the locals of their processing operation, hence they did not effectively guarantee the data processing principle of transparency. Also, while most of the participants wished they could provide consent for such high-resolution images to be taken of them and/or their community by drones, the paper concluded that such consent (most certainly through a traditional ruler) would hardly be valid as a ground for collecting and/or processing aerial image data of their community, given their vulnerable position as persons in crisis. And finally, the discussions revealed an albeit slight favourable opinion towards a feeling of community data rights, with a slight majority of the participants believing the nature of the drone images of their community could reasonably warrant some related collective community right or claim. However, they manifested no real interest in knowing more about these community rights on drone images of their settlements. Rather, a significant 76% of them preferring to have drone data of their community shared to as many third parties as possible to attract external aid, and appeared less bothered about any eventual violations of their (DII) community rights.

The above prompts the conclusion that considering certain low levels of data literacy and unawareness of (big) data analytics among people in vulnerable situations, and associated risks like surveillance, algorithmic bias or profiling, protecting PII or DII in humanitarian situations should be the full responsibility of the processing organisation. Not much participation may be expected from the affected individuals who are in (sometimes urgent) need hence vulnerable, or would generally lack the resources to engage with the organisations as regards any rights they may believe they have on data collected about them or their community. This is even more ominous when we consider the idea that humanitarian innovation could be regarded as an inherently 'experimental' process [35] with novel and untested technologies and tools sometimes being deployed to manage crisis. These innovative technologies may also belong to private sector organisations who may be taking advantage of crisis situations to "test" new technologies or products to aid intervention, with the intent of using the feedback to prepare the product for a proper commercial launch. It is worth mentioning here that the 2021 Malawi Data Protection Bill states that personal data can be processed (among other legal bases - and hence no need for consent from the individuals) where such processing is necessary for a 'humanitarian initiative.'[11] A direct interpretation would mean drones could legally be deployed to a community to collect aerial imagery (and without need for consent by the residents) if the collector organisation claims it is doing so for a humanitarian initiative. It would however appear relevant in this context for the Malawi legislator to go further and set the scope of what constitutes a 'humanitarian initiative', specify who can execute it and set other modalities to comply with, in order to prevent abuse of this basis of data processing (and hence avoid humanitarian experimentation) by tech enterprises.

It can therefore be concluded from the above that it is up to organisations to act responsibly and implement data protection-by-design strategies to protect data subjects when deploying drones to these communities e.g. integrating no-fly zones into the drone settings, or ensuring that the technology employed collects just the images needed to attain the objective for collection and/or processing. Another point to consider here for further research and discussion would be to assess the extent to which humanitarian organisations, especially those not subject to national law, invest to comply with their own data protection policies, or otherwise how they can effectively be held accountable for PII or DII processing violations. The conundrum being that though international law does provide for (data processing) principles to which international organisations pledge allegiance, they are not subject to some authority which could, for example, impose sanctions on them for data-related misconducts; like a national data protection authority would do on an organisation subject to national law.

---

[11] Article 18(2)(g), Malawi Data Protection Bill 2021.

ANNEX 1: Full Results of FGDs

FGD QUESTIONS TO PARTICIPANTS	RESPONSES		TOTAL % RESPONSES
	RUMPHI (21 participants. *Pertinent opinions raised by some participants in italics*)	KARONGA (21 participants. *Pertinent opinions raised by some participants in italics*)	
What were your (first) impressions when you saw the drone fly?	15 excited 6 curious	10 excited 6 curious 5 fear	60% Excited 28% Curious 12% Fear
Have you seen other drone flights and where?	16 No 5 yes	21 No	88% No 12% Yes
Have you seen a picture taken by a drone before?	19 No 2 Yes	21 No	95% No 5% Yes
Do you think these drones (can) take clear, detailed pictures of your village, farms, houses, children?	14 yes 7 no *(drones were too far up)*	17 yes (*noticed camera when drone was flying low*) 4 No	74% Yes 26% No
- [Showing them an aerial drone image of their district] What do you see in this example of aerial imagery (can they identify and/or recognise, roads, farms, private compounds)?	21 Can identify objects. *Can also identify richer vs poorer households based on roof material.*	21 Can identify objects. *Can also identify richer vs poorer households based on roof material.*	100% Can identify objects of their community in the aerial images
What are your impressions/opinions of these images?	20 Fascinated, Awed 1 Sceptical: *says they should be informed about purpose of the images*	21 Fascinated	98% Fascinated 2% Sceptical
What do you personally feel about these pictures, seeing that they show details of your houses, farms, and entire community?	19 Positives (*beautiful, touristic pictures; it is good to know what the community looks like*) 2 Worried about zooming ability of the drone and possibility of identifying someone	20 Positives (*the image of my house does not bother me if the image contains other houses of the community*). 1 Worried about purpose for taking the image	93% Positive 7% Express some worries
Is there anything in this picture you may not like other people in the village or elsewhere to see (e.g. roofless toilets, new property, maybe inside a fenced compound)?	20 Nothing about the pictures to hide or is sensitive. [*no police so it contributes to security, community development, flood management, humanitarian intervention. Sharing images of roofless toilets will force owners to put roofs over them to avoid shame. We fence our houses against thieves, not for privacy*] 1 Cites naked children playing as sensitive and should not be	18 Nothing about the pictures to hide or is sensitive. [*Sharing images of roofless toilets will force owners to put roofs over them to avoid shame*] 3 Say prisons could be sensitive [*it's not ok to capture and share identifiable images of high-end criminals like murderers*]	90% Nothing to hide 10% Some data could be sensitive and may not be shared outside the community

	captured		
Generally, with who may you not want such images of your property or community to be shared (maybe state land/town planning officials)?	20 No restrictions: images may be shared widely. [*The wider the shared audience, the more likely we are to receive external aid*] 1 Share widely but first edit out sensitive data like naked children or open toilets.	18 No restrictions: images may be shared widely [*if images depict something shameful it will only deter the person concerned into responsible behaviour*] 3 Share widely, leaving out sensitive data like prisons	**90% No sharing limitations** **10% Some data is sensitive and may not be shared outside the community**
Were you aware the drones flights you witnessed would take place?	7 Yes 14 No [*no one specified that there will be machines flying in the sky and taking pictures*]	[irrelevant]	**67% Yes** **33% No (Rumphi Only)**
If yes, how were you informed? And by who?	Traditional authorities moved door to door	[irrelevant]	**/**
Were you aware or informed that the flying drones will be taking clear, detailed images of your community?	21 No	[irrelevant] *But 21 expressed the wish to be informed beforehand about the details of the images*	**100% No (Rumphi Only)**
Do you know the person or organisation flying the drones?	21 No	irrelevant	**100% No (Rumphi Only)**
Did they come and present themselves to you?	21 No [*5 participants approached the drone pilots and were informed the activity was organised by UNICEF*]	irrelevant	**100% No** **(Rumphi Only)**
- Did anyone tell you whether and why it is necessary to take these drones pictures of you and your community?	21 No	irrelevant	**100% No** **(Rumphi Only)**
Do you think you should be informed first before the flying of a drones over your community to take such pictures?	21 Yes	21 Yes	**100% Yes**
Would you like to be individually able to grant or refuse permission (consent) for these images to be taken and shared with third parties?	18 Yes [*7 of these 18 believed it has to be in consultation with the chief i.e. you have to pass through the chief, then the chief consults them*] 3 Not really [*our government cannot harm us*]	19 YES 2 not really [*once informed, our consent does not need to be sought because it concerns the community*]	**88% Yes** **12% Not Really**

- In your opinion, should an authority be empowered to give permission (consent) on behalf of the entire community for these images to be taken and shared with third parties?	15 NO [*The authority must consult us or at least some key community members*] 5 YES [*provided the images are not sensitive, as is the case with these images*] 1 Neutral	21 NO [Authority must consult us or at least some key members of the community]	86% No 12% Yes 2% Neutral
If yes, who do you think should have that authority? And why?	21 The traditional chief. Because he is closer to the residents.	/	100% Traditional Chief
- Do you feel you may have any individual rights on these images (e.g. how long they keep it, who they share it with), considering they show your compound or farm?	9 Yes 12 No [*The drone images of their community are not so important to warrant individual rights*]	13 Yes 8 No [*The drone images of their community are not so important to warrant individual rights*]	52% Yes 48% No
Do you think as a community, you all as a group can have any rights e.g. how long they keep it, who they share it with, on these images showing your community?	11 yes 10 No [*The drone images of their community are not so important to warrant community rights*]	12 yes 9 No [*The drone images of their community are not so important to warrant community rights*]	55% Yes 45% No
Are you aware of any specific information-related rights you may have on these images?	20 No 1 Yes [*cites their right to access to information in the Constitution of Malawi*]	21 No	98% No 2% Yes
Has anyone mentioned anything to you about any rights you may have regarding these images of you or your community?	21 No	irrelevant	100% No (Rumphi Only)
- Would you mind that these detailed drone images of your property and community is shared with government and other parties so they help you better during (flood) crisis, without caring much about your rights around these images?	21 No, the images can be shared with as many third parties as necessary [*1 participant says they should at least be made aware of whom they intend to share the images with*]	11 No, the images can be shared with as many third parties as necessary. 10 Yes [*if there are any rights available, we still want them to be respected*]	76% No 24% Yes
Do you think humanitarian organisations or government could still help you effectively without the need for these drone images?	21 No [*we think drone pics are necessary, they make it easier to bring us the help needed*].	20 No [*we think drone pics are necessary, they make it easier to bring us the help needed*]. 1 neutral	98% No 2% Neutral
After this discussion, do you think drones are a positive or negative development for your community?	21 Positive [easier survey, faster information processing and communication] *1 participant cites safety concern if drone malfunctions and falls to the ground*]	20 Positive [easier survey, faster information processing and communication] 1 neutral	98% Positive 2% Neutral

References

1. Jones, R.W., Despotou, G.: Unmanned aerial systems and healthcare: possibilities and challenges. In: 2019 14th IEEE Conference on Industrial Electronics and Applications (ICIEA), pp. 189–194. IEEE (2019)
2. Tang, C.S., Veelenturf, L.P.: The strategic role of logistics in the industry 4.0 era. Transp. Res. Part E: Logistics Transp. Rev. **129**, 1–11 (2019)
3. Jumbert, M.G., Sandvik, K.B.: Introduction: what does it take to be good?. In: The Good Drone, pp. 1–25. Routledge (2016)
4. Clarke, R.: Understanding the drone epidemic. Comput. Law Secur. Rev.. Law Secur. Rev. **30**(3), 230–246 (2014)
5. do C. Martins, L., Hirsch, P., Juan, A.A.: Agile optimization of a two-echelon vehicle routing problem with pickup and delivery. Int. Trans. Oper. Res. **28**(1), 201–221 (2021)
6. Haidari, L.A., et al.: The economic and operational value of using drones to transport vaccines. Vaccine **34**(34), 4062–4067 (2016)
7. Bolman, B.: A revolution in agricultural affairs: dronoculture, precision, capital. In: The Good Drone, pp. 129–152. Routledge (2016)
8. Unal, M., Bostanci, E., Sertalp, E.: Distant augmented reality: Bringing a new dimension to user experience using drones. Digit. Appl. Archaeol. Cult. Heritage **17**, e00140 (2020)
9. Wang, N., Christen, M., Hunt, M.: Ethical considerations associated with "humanitarian drones": a scoping literature review. Sci. Eng. Ethics **27**(4), 51 (2021)
10. Lidén, K., Sandvik, K.B.: Poison pill or cure-all: drones and the protection of civilians. In: The Good Drone, pp. 75–98. Routledge (2016)
11. Li, G.Q., Zhou, X.G., Yin, J., Xiao, Q.Y.: An UAV scheduling and planning method for post-disaster survey. Int. Arch. Photogrammetry Remote Sens. Spatial Inf. Sci. **40**, 169–172 (2014)
12. Lei, T., et al.: The application of unmanned aerial vehicle remote sensing for monitoring secondary geological disasters after earthquakes. In: Ninth International Conference on Digital Image Processing (ICDIP 2017), vol. 10420, pp. 736–742. SPIE (2017)
13. Weitzberg, K., Cheesman, M., Martin, A., Schoemaker, E.: Between surveillance and recognition: rethinking digital identity in aid. Big Data Soc. **8**(1), 20539517211006744 (2021)
14. Kuner, C., Marelli, M., Barboza, J.Z., Jasmontaite, L.: Handbook on data protection in humanitarian action. International Committee of the Red Cross (2020)
15. World Food Programme Guide to Personal Data Protection and Privacy (2016)
16. Schwartz, P.M., Solove, D.J.: Defining 'personal data' in the European Union and US. Bloomberg BNA Priv. Secur. Law Rep. **13**(1581), 1–6 (2014)
17. Raymond, N.A.: Beyond "do no harm" and individual consent: reckoning with the emerging ethical challenges of civil society's use of data. Group Priv.: New Challenges Data Technol., 67–82 (2017)
18. Taylor, L.: Safety in numbers? Group privacy and big data analytics in the developing world. In: Taylor, L., Floridi, L., van der Sloot, B. (eds.) Group privacy. Philosophical Studies Series, vol. 126, pp. 13–36. Springer, Cham (2017)
19. Purtova, N.: Health data for common good: defining the boundaries and social dilemmas of data commons. In: Adams, S., Purtova, N., Leenes, R. (eds.) Under Observation: The Interplay Between eHealth and Surveillance. LGTS, vol. 35, pp. 177–210. Springer, Cham (2017). https://doi.org/10.1007/978-3-319-48342-9_10
20. van der Sloot, B.: Do groups have a right to protect their group interest in privacy and should they? Peeling the onion of rights and interests protected under article 8 ECHR. In: Taylor, L., Floridi, L., van der Sloot, B. (eds.) Group privacy. Philosophical Studies Series, vol. 126, pp. 197–224. Springer, Cham (2017). https://doi.org/10.1007/978-3-319-46608-8_11

21. Hustinx, P.: EU data protection law: The review of directive 95/46/EC and the proposed general data protection regulation." Collected courses of the European University Institute's Academy of European Law, 24th Session on European Union Law (2013)
22. Ottavio, M.: Privacy and data protection implications of the civil use of drones European Parliament Brussels (2015)
23. UNICEF Policy on Personal Data Protection (2020). https://www.unicef.org/supply/media/5356/file/Policy-on-personal-data-protection-July2020.pdf. Accessed 27 Mar 2023
24. UN-GGIM, Future trends in geospatial information management: the five to ten year vision, Second Edition, 2015
25. Gevaert, C.: Unmanned aerial vehicle mapping for settlement upgrading (2019)
26. Khan, M.E., Anker, M., Patel, B.C., Barge, S., Sadhwani, H., Kohle, R.: The use of focus groups in social and behavioural research: some methodological issues. World Health Stat. Q. **44**(3), 145–149 (1991)
27. Morgan, D.L.: Focus Groups as Qualitative Research, vol. 16. Sage publications, Thousand Oaks (1996)
28. Onwuegbuzie, A.J., Dickinson, W.B., Leech, N.L., Zoran, A.G.: A qualitative framework for collecting and analyzing data in focus group research. Int J Qual Methods J Qual Methods **8**(3), 1–21 (2009)
29. Solove, D.J.: Murky consent: an approach to the fictions of consent in privacy law. SSRN 4333743 (2023)
30. Dressel, J., Farid, H.: The accuracy, fairness, and limits of predicting recidivism. Sci. Adv. **4**(1), eaao5580 (2018)
31. Solove, D.J.: The Digital Person: Technology and Privacy in the Information Age, vol. 1. NyU Press, New York (2004)
32. De Hert, P., Gutwirth, S.: Data protection in the case law of Strasbourg and Luxemburg: constitutionalisation in action. In: Gutwirth, S., Poullet, Y., De Hert, P., de Terwangne, C., Nouwt, S. (eds.) Reinventing data protection? Springer, Dordrecht (2009). https://doi.org/10.1007/978-1-4020-9498-9_1
33. Dove, E.S., Kelly, S.E., Lucivero, F., Machirori, M., Dheensa, S., Prainsack, B.: Beyond individualism: is there a place for relational autonomy in clinical practice and research? Clin. Ethics **12**(3), 150–165 (2017)
34. Reviglio, U., Alunge, R.: I am datafied because we are datafied: an Ubuntu perspective on (relational) privacy. Philos. Technol. **33**(4), 595–612 (2020)
35. Sandvik, K.B., Jacobsen, K.L., McDonald, S.M.: Do no harm: a taxonomy of the challenges of humanitarian experimentation. Int. Rev. Red Cross **99**(904), 319–344 (2017)

Study of the Rewiring Factor in an Unstructured P2P

Aminata Bagre[1($\boxtimes$)], Moustapha Bikienga[2], and Telesphore Tiendrebeogo[3]

[1] University Joseph KI-ZERBO, Ouagadougou, Burkina Faso
aminbagre@gmail.com
[2] University Norbert ZONGO, Koudougou, Burkina Faso
bmoustaph@yahoo.fr
[3] University NAZI BONI, Bobo-Dioulasso, Burkina Faso

Abstract. Social networking sites allow individuals to communicate and share information. Most of P2P systems assume that all peers cooperate for the benefit of the entire network. However, in practice, there is a significant portion of peers that extract resources from the system without contributing in return. Peer-to-peer applications can benefit from human friendship networks (such as e-mail contacts or instant messaging friend lists). However, these networks are not always available. To this end, we study a protocol, called SLACER (Selfish Link-based Adaptation for Cooperation Excluding Rewiring), that allows peer nodes to create their own friendship networks, through random interactions, producing an artificial social network (ASN) where nodes share high trust with their neighbors. To do so, this paper specifically study P2P networks, which constitute the context for the application of the SLACER protocol; an implementation based on the peersim simulator of the rewiring factor W which represents the possibility of rewiring nodes in a peer network; then our main contribution which is the analysis of simulation results obtained on a larger network size with several values of W; finally we do a performance study by comparative study with SLAC (previous version of SLACER).

Keywords: Cooperation · P2P · Social Networks · Self-Organization · Rewiring

1 Introduction

As long as people have existed, whether in their personal or professional lives, they have come together by interest to form networks. Nowadays, these individuals have the possibility to gather online via the Internet, especially on social networks. In [1] the authors state that peer networks open new perspectives on the way we apprehend distributed computing. Indeed, the entities composing

Supported by organization x.

A. Seeam et al. (Eds.): InterSol 2023, LNICST 541, pp. 337–354, 2024.
https://doi.org/10.1007/978-3-031-51849-2_22

distributed systems are, traditionally, considered as processes having a precisely specified behavior, and thus determined. The emergence of the Internet as a platform for the implementation of these architectures tends to render this hypothesis obsolete, because it brings into play intelligent users who act according to their own strategy. This paper raises the issue of the difficulties of maintaining cooperation and the selfish behavior of peers. In [3] peer-to-peer networks are a beneficial way to offer and share services. In recent years, they have become very popular with the general public and professionals. This is because these systems are inexpensive, fault and disconnection tolerant, easy to use and scale easily (up to several million users). These advantages are due to a strong concept: the decentralization of services. Each user is both customer and provider of a service. Attached is the illustrative Fig. 1 of most important P2P applications.

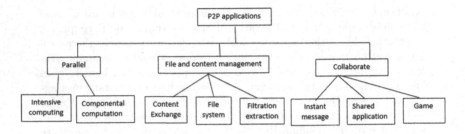

Fig. 1. P2P applications

Selfish behavior of peers [2] is also called "free-riding". Thus "free-ridingis" developing in P2P networks and negatively impacts the robustness and availability of the network. Indeed, some users use files shared by other users without sharing files themselves which would cost them bandwidth. They thus benefit from the advantages of the collective good without paying the cost. Thus, through this free riding behavior, the peers who are among the biggest contributors act as central servers, which could lead to network congestion and instability, problems that the P2P system was supposed to combat. As a result, we see a tragedy of the commons. In [2], this expression (Tragedy of common) illustrates an abusive use of common resources leading eventually to their exhaustion.

Also it is said that in order to answer the various concerns of research works were interested in the question and made it possible to develop protocols of coordination in the peer-to-peer networks.

With the aim of finding elements of answer to the problematic above posed, we leaned on the topic: "Study and simulation of the rewiring factor in an unstructured P2P network." In our review of literature in relation with [2], we saw according to Hales that one of the characteristics of the SLACER protocol is to allow a self-organization of the nodes of the system.

The objective in this document is to make a study then an implementation of the SLACER protocol which will make it possible to obtain cooperative artificial social networks based on the peer-to-peer. The SLACER protocol is a solution proposed by a European project. We will therefore investigate whether the results of the paper are valid for different variations of the rewiring parameter named W and on a wider range of networks. Our paper is structured according to the following plan:

1. First, we present the related work. This part gathers the presentation of the SLAC and SLACER protocol according to our literature reviews. We will also see some concepts and definitions, which will allow us to better understand the rest of the work;
2. In a second step we present and define the simulation environment that would be used for the tests. We present the methodology to be followed to perform the simulation on a larger network size. We discuss random sampling, then the prisoner's dilemma game and the configuration parameters required for the SLACER protocol;
3. In a third step, we present the simulation results obtained for several values of the rewiring factor W as well as the different interpretations;
4. Finally, we present ours contributions and perspectives.

2   Related Work

2.1   SLAC Protocol

In [4] the protocol **SLAC**: (Selfish Link and behavioural Adaptation to produce Cooperation) is an algorithm where each user can, and is in fact encouraged to, act selfishly. In a P2P network there are users who only download files and never share files with others. These users become leeches and drain the resources of the community. These types of users are called free loaders. We show that SLAC allows an unstructured P2P overlay network to evolve to a state where free loaders and attackers are quickly banned without asking any user to behave against their interest.

Unlike free loaders that only reduce network resources, there are also malicious users who launch active DOS attacks against P2P overlay networks. These attacks usually take the form of spreading fake files or overloading the network by flooding with fake requests. they use the flooding mechanism of repeating a message across all networks. A node that initiates the flooding sends the packet to all its direct neighbors, similarly if any network node receives the packet for the first time, it rebroadcasts it to all its neighbors. Thus, from one node to another, the packet floods the network.

SLAC works by taking advantage of a key property of the flooding-based search mechanism used in the unstructured P2P overlay network. In flooding, when a node wants to find a particular piece of data, it sends a search request to all of its neighbors on the P2P overlay network. Its neighbors then in turn forward the search request to their neighbors, and so on. Note that this flooding-based search mechanism allows neighboring nodes to mutually control access to the rest of the network. We present below the Algorithm 1 which represents the SLAC protocol.

Inputs :
        i : node i
        j : node j
        Ui : Utility of node i
        Uj : Utility of node j
        Si : strategy of node i
        Li : Links of node i
Outputs: Operation
Begin:
Compare Ui and Uj
if $Ui <= Uj$ **then**
    Copy Si and Li (*reproduction*)
    Mutate (*with a small strategy*):
    Change *strategy (behaviour)*
    Change *neighborhood (links)*
end if
End

Algorithm 1: SLAC

The algorithm runs continuously in each node. A periodic utility comparison is made between two randomly chosen nodes in the node population. In [2], Utility is a numeric value that each node must calculate on the basis of the particular application domain's specifics. Also the strategy represents the behavior of the nodes at the level of an application. Either by deleting and or creating links to the nodes they know. If the utility of the latter is superior, then copy its strategy and links. Then, perform a mutation with low probability and change your strategy and links.

We try to explain the operation of the SLAC algorithm from Fig. 2.

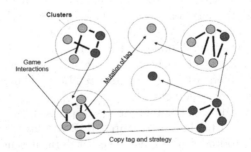

Fig. 2. SLAC operation [11]

In Fig. 2 above, the different circles represent clusters of nodes that are a collection of several nodes that communicate with each other to perform a set of operations. According to [5], tags define social rules of behavior observed in human societies. Each node belonging to a cluster or not, has its own tags. Studied by computational sociology, tags are observable marks (e.g. hairstyle, clothes), which evolve like any other artificial trait and allow to limit interactions between agents with similar tags leading to cooperative altruistic behavior. Thus, we describe our SLAC protocol operation scheme as follows:

- the different nodes in the P2P network move to find cooperative neighbors;
- This perpetual search for cooperation produces a kind of evolution of the network;
- nodes that do not cooperate in the network become isolated.

The results we can have in a duplicate and rewire rule are :

- produce a kind of «cluster selection» between clusters;
- give a functional reason for the temporal structures present in «natural» networks.

In addition the tags can undergo a mutation. According to [5], the mutation of the tags consists in a change of certain features (i.e. certain bits) and the mutation of the strategy, it consists in turning over the strategy bit (from cooperation to defection or vice versa). After the periodic comparison of utilities, whether or not this results in the copying of another node, the node resets its utility to zero.

2.2 SLACER Protocol

In [2] the SLACER algorithm is an extension of the SLAC Algorithm [7] based on the tagging approach from computational sociology that is explained in [6] which has been shown to support high levels of cooperation without the need for central control, reciprocity or other evaluation mechanisms.

Over time, nodes engage in an application task and generate an utility measure U. According to [10], in the SLACER algorithm, each node engaged in a specific application task generates a utility measure called U. Such measures are strictly related to the application domain an can be defined in very different ways according to the application's aims. For example, they could be defined as a function of download speed in a file sharing scenario; as the number of jobs processed in a distributed computing environment; as the latency and ratio of delivered packets in a routing protocol, etc. The higher the value of U, the more the node believes it is working in its target domain.

The authors in [2] state that periodically, each node i compares its performance to that of node j. chosen at random from the population of nodes. The SLACER protocol consists of four steps, which we detail in the algorithm 3, 4, 5, 6 below.

```
Active thread of node i
Inputs :
          Pi : View perimeter of node i
          Ui : Utility of node i
          Uj : Utility of node j
          i : node i
          j : node j
Outputs: Operation
Begin:
do forever
j= GetRandomNode(Pi)
if Uj <= Ui then
   CopyStatePartial(j)
   Mutate (i)
end if
End
```

Algorithm 3: Active thread of node i

```
Function CopyStatePartial of node j
Inputs :
          Ui: Utility of node i
          Uj: Utility of node j
          Si :Strategy of node i
          Sj :Strategy of node j
          Lj :Links of node j
Outputs: Operation
Begin:
Si = Sj
For each Link in Li drop Link with probability W
For each Link in Lj Li.addLink(Link)
End
```

Algorithm 4: Function CopyStatePartial

If utility Ui is less than or equal to that of Uj, node i removes each of its current links to other nodes with high probability W, and copies all the j links and adds a link to j itself. In addition i copies the strategies of j. After the copy operation with low probability M, node i adapts its strategy and then with probability MR adapts its links. The adaptation involves the application of a «mutation» operation. The SLACER algorithm is composed of four parts, mainly divided into two (02) threads and two (02) functions. Indeed, we have :

- an active thread,
- a passive thread,
- a strategy copy function,
- a mutation function where each existing link will be deleted with probability W and, a unique link to a randomly drawn node in the network will be added.

```
Function Mutate of node i
Inputs  :
         Pi: View perimeter of node i
         Si : Strategy of node i
         Sj : Strategy of node j
         Li : Links of node i
         Lj : Links of node j
Outputs: Operation
Li: Links of node i
Si: Strategy of node i
Begin:
Mutate Si with probability M;
Mutate Li with probability MR;
For each Link in Lj drop Link with probability W
i.addLink(SelectRandomNode(Pi))
End
```

Algorithm 5: Function Mutate

```
Passive thread of node j
Inputs  :
         Uj: Utility of node j
         Sj : Strategy of node j
         Lj : Links of node j
Outputs: Operation
Begin:
do forever
Sleep until a request received from node i
Send Uj to node i
Send Lj to node i
Send Sj to node i
End
```

Algorithm 6: Passive thread

The authors of [4] state that SLACER follows the same general approach as SLAC but is more conservative as it maintains old links rather than rewiring all links, it is an adaptation based on selfish links for cooperation outside the rewiring algorithm (SLACER). Assume that peer nodes can change their strategy. Also nodes have the ability to discover other nodes at random from the population set of nodes, compare their performance to those nodes in some way and copy their links and strategies. SLACER implements a simple local adaptation rule: nodes try to use their capabilities to selfishly increase their own performance (or utility) in a greedy environment adaptively by changing their links and strategies. They do this by copying nodes that appear to perform better and making random changes with low probability. The SLACER algorithm runs continuously in each node.

3   Methodology for Implementing the SLACER Protocol

3.1   Definition and Simulation Environment

The peersim simulator environment is released to the public under the GPL open source license. It is written in Java and consists of two simulation engines, a simplified (cycle-based) and an event-driven one. The engines are supported by many simple, extensible and pluggable components, with a flexible configuration mechanism.

In fact, in [9], the main difference between the two models (event-driven, cycle-driven) is the different management of time; in the cycle-driven model, it is given in execution cycles whereas in event-driven mode it is given in units of time. Once the unit of measurement of time (or endtime simulation) has been chosen, consistency is required each time it is necessary to insert or manipulate a time value.

3.2   Random Sampling

In Fig. 2, we assume a function that returns a random node from the entire population of nodes, regardless of the current network topology. This function cannot use the SLACER-managed network itself because it may become partitioned. In our simulations, we used the existing NEWSCAST algorithm [8] to provide this service. NEWSCAST provides exactly this function by maintaining its own scalable and robust random overlay network based on a gossip protocol; in which random gossip neighbors constantly collect their views of the network (the links they have with other nodes). This type of sampling maintains a random, fully connected topology, even under conditions of high node failure and malicious behavior. NEWCAST can be deployed to support SLACER in a modular fashion via a GetRandomNode () function invoked from SLACER.

3.3   The Prisoner's Dilemma Game

In [4], the authors of the paper explain the prisoner's dilemma problem as follows: Assuming that neither player can know in advance which move the other will make and wishes to maximize her own payoff, the dilemma is evident in the ranking of payoffs: $T > R > P > S$ and the constraint that $2R > T + S$. Although both players would prefer T, because its the highest payoff, only one can attain it in a single game. Two players interact by selecting one of the following two choices: Cooperate (C) or Default (D).

According to [1], the authors explain the prisoner's dilemma as follows: «Two suspects in a major crime are held prisoner in separate cells. There is enough evidence to charge each of them with a minor crime, but not enough to charge them with the major crime unless one of them denounces the other (treason). If both inmates remain silent, each will be charged with the lesser crime and will face a one-year prison sentence. If one (and only one) of the two denounces the other, he will be released and will testify against the other who will spend four years in prison. If the two suspects turn each other in, each will face three years in prison.»

Since it is two players, we have four possible outcomes of the game, the players receive specific payoffs. According to [2] both players receive a reward (R) for mutual cooperation and a punishment (P) for mutual defection. However, when individuals choose different moves, the defector receives a temptation payoff (T) and the cooperator receives a sucker payoff (S). T, R, P and S are payoffs ranked from highest to lowest.

This situation can be illustrated by Table 1 which represents a matrix of gains.

Table 1. Prisoner's dilemma game

Player1/Player2	Cooperate	Default
Cooperate	**R/R**	S/T
Default	**T/S**	P/P

Table 1 illustrates a situation in which the players have an interest in cooperating. But, each player has an incentive not to do so (free riding). Furthermore, we let the nodes play probabilistic strategies where their movements were determined by a real value indicating a probability to cooperate (in this case, the mutation involved changing the real value into another one, uniformly selected at random from [0.1]).

3.4   Simulation Indicators

Simulation Cycle: This is the time period during which a node initiates activity at the application level, causing a utility update and executing a Compare Utility call.

Measuring Cooperative Connected Path (CCP): represents the ratio of pairs of nodes connected by paths composed only of cooperative nodes to all possible pairs of nodes in the network. The maximum possible value is obviously 1 [2]. A network does not have to be fully cooperative to reach the maximum value, because it is possible to find other cooperative paths to avoid faulty nodes. We will use Fig. 3 as an illustration. On the other hand, a network cannot reach the maximum value even if it is fully cooperative but also partitioned. Indeed, in this case, there are no paths between the nodes of different partitions of the network.

Giant Connected Component (GCC): It is the largest single connected component. In network theory, a giant component is a connected component of

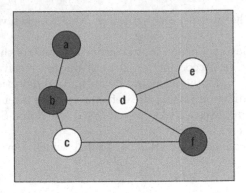

Fig. 3. CCP Measure [2]

a given random graph that contains a finite fraction of the vertices of the entire graph.

Clustering Coefficient (C): The latter is still called clustering coefficient (noted C) for a single node i, is the ratio between the number of current links between its neighbors and the total number of possible links. If Zi is the number of neighbors linked to node i and Yi the number of links between neighbors of node i, with N the total size of the network. The clustering coefficient is represented by the following formula 1:

$$C = \frac{1}{N} \sum_{i \in N} (\frac{2Yi}{Zi(Zi-1)})$$ (1)

The Average Path Length (L): We define L as the shortest possible average path between all pairs of nodes. With d(i,j) the shortest distance between nodes i and j in the network. The average path length is represented by the following formula 2:

$$L = \frac{1}{N} \sum_{i \in N} \sum_{i \neq j} (\frac{d(i,j)}{N-1})$$ (2)

The Average Payoff: The Prisoner's Dilemma application defines the utility value required by SLACER as the average payoff the node received from these game interactions.

3.5   The Configuration Parameters

Figure 4 represent the different parameters to configure on the configuration file to launch the SLACER protocol. The figure shows the SLACER configuration parameters (a) in this part, there are:

```
overlay.size 2000
overlay.maxsize 2000        ──────────────▶  General parameters
overlay.minsize 500


protocol.0 example.newscast.SimpleNewscast
protocol.0.cache 20

protocol.1 slacer.Slacer
#protocol.1.wiresw
#protocol.1.rewireprob 0.1
protocol.1.degree 20
protocol.1.linkable 0
###if defined the reproduction mechanism is probabilistic       Protocol parameters
protocol.1.probabilistic
###probability of originating a query for every node at every cycle
protocol.1.queryprob 0.5
###rate of probabilistic reproduction
protocol.1.reprprob 0.2
###period of deterministic reproduction
protocol.1.period 20
###rate of strategy mutation
protocol.1.mutation 0.005
###rate of tag mutation
protocol.1.tagmutation 0.01
###payoffs - if not defined random values are applied
#protocol.1.penalty 0.002
#protocol.1.sucker 0.001
#protocol.1.temptation 1.9
#protocol.1.reward 1
```

(a)

```
init.0 peersim.dynamics.WireRegularRandom
init.0.protocol 0
init.0.degree 20

init.1 slacer.SlacerInitializer
init.1.protocol 1
###quantity of cooperative nodes
init.1.quantity 0
###drop probability when isolating (difference between SLAC and SLACER)
init.1.isolateprob 0.9
###copy probability when reproducing                              Control parameters
init.1.copyprob 1


observer.0 slacer.SlacerObserver
observer.0.protocol 1
###percentual of satisfied query to stop the simulation - 0 no early stop
observer.0.coopgoal 90

observer.1 slacer.CCPObserver
observer.1.protocol 1
observer.1.period 10
```

(b)

Fig. 4. Parameters of SLACER's configuration (a) Protocol parameters (b) Control parameters

1. General parameters: we define the size of the network;
2. The protocol parameters part: we define the protocols (Newscast and SLACER) then the parameters of the prisoner's dilemma (DP);
3. The control and initialization part used to define the operations that require knowledge and management of the global network, such as initializers (executed at the beginning of the simulation), dynamics (executed periodically during the simulation), and finally observers (executed periodically during the simulation).

4   Simulation Results

The objective here is to analyze the results before proposing solutions to ensure better performance.

Previous work has shown that SLACER takes 90 cycles to reach high cooperation. Compared to the high cooperation simulation cycle, in our case, for W=0.9 it takes 70 cycles to reach high cooperation.

4.1   The Simulation Parameters

In the following simulation, we set the prisoner's dilemma payoffs to:

- T = 1,9
- R = 1
- P = 0,002
- S = 0,001

Therefore, we have set the transfer rates at:

- M = 0,005
- MR = 0,01

Nodes were also allowed a maximum size of 20 neighbors. We ran a simulation with rewiring factor for W = 0.4, W = 0.9, W = 1.

4.2   Simulation Results and Interpretations

In our experiments, we initialized the entire population of nodes over a range of N = 2000 to 100000 nodes. In the initial state, all nodes were in the defection state and we connected them in a random network topology.

1. Simulation cycle

    The presentation focuses on the average number of cycles to achieve high cooperation for different values of W.

    Figures 5 represent the average number of cycles to reach high cooperation for different network sizes.

    Figure 5 bearing the letter (a). The values taken are a function of the rewiring factors W=0.9 (this rewiring factor represents the SLACER algorithm). The network takes 70 simulation cycles to reach high cooperation. In this case we can deduce that the higher the size of the network the faster the cooperation, and SLACER can thus escape a total defection.

    And W = 1 (rewiring factors represents the SLAC Algorithm) for Fig. 5 bearing the letter (b). Cooperation does not begin until cycle 50 and reaches its emergence at cycle 70. Then, as the simulation continues we observe a drop in cooperation. This means that the nodes become isolated afterwards, creating a disconnected network.

    Figures 6 represent the average number of cycles to reach high cooperation for different sizes of the network. The values taken are a function of the rewiring factor W=0.4. At this level, according to the figure, it can be observed that cooperation takes place rapidly and is maintained throughout the cycle.

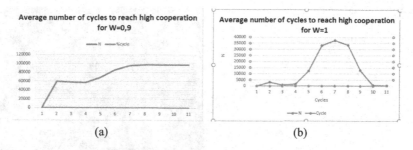

(a)   (b)

Fig. 5. Average number of cycles to reach high cooperation for W = 0,9 and W = 1.
(a) W = 0,9. (b) W = 1.

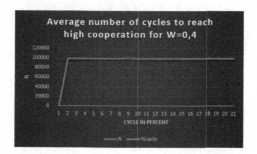

Fig. 6. Average number of cycles to reach high cooperation for W = 0,4.

2. GCC and CCP measurements

We present the GCC and CCP measurements for W = 0.4, W = 0.9 and W = 1.

Figures 7 represent the size of the largest component as a proportion of the network size as well as the cooperative connected path measure for W = 0.4, W = 0.9 (SLACER) and W=1 (SLAC). Each bar shows an average of 10 runs.

For W = 0.4, we observe that almost all nodes inhabit a giant connected component (GCC) which, although containing faulty nodes, provides a cooperative route between the vast majority of its members. The high CCP indicates that the majority of nodes within the GCC are interconnected by cooperative paths.

For W = 0.9, we can see from the figure that almost all nodes inhabit a giant connected component (GCC) that, although containing faulty nodes, provides a cooperative route between the vast majority of its members. The high CCP indicates that the vast majority of nodes within the GCC are connected by cooperative paths. This means that SLACER therefore generates cooperative ASNs (artificial social networks).

However, for W = 1, we observe that at the beginning of the simulation the nodes inhabit a giant connected component (GCC or PGC) which decreases as the simulation continues until it becomes very negligible. This means that

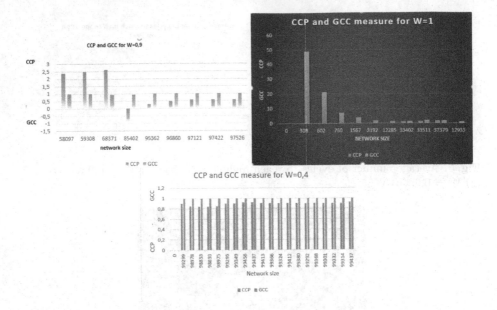

Fig. 7. GCC and CCP measure for W = 0.4, W = 0.9 and W = 1

we had few cooperative routes between the nodes. The level of the PGC being very low means that the vast majority of nodes within the GCC are not connected by cooperative paths. We can therefore say that SLAC provides a network of disconnected nodes.

3. Average length L and clustering coefficient C measurements
   Figure 8 result representing the measure of the clustering coefficient (C) and the average path length (L) for different variations of W.
   Figure 8 with the letter (a) represents the measurement of the clustering coefficient (C) and the average path length (L) for W = 0.4. At this level we can see that while the level of C rises rapidly at the beginning of the simulation and eventually falls and finally remains more or less constant. We can therefore say here that with a W = 0.4, we witness a massive clustering of nodes at the beginning of the simulation and then an isolation of clusters of nodes that are characterized by the decrease of the clustering coefficient C. As for L, it takes more than 70 cycles to reach emergence. This means that within a cluster, the nodes are connected by jumps.
   Figure 8 with the letter (b) for W = 1 following different network sizes. Each point is an average value of 10 cycles of simulations. Each point is an average value of 10 cycles of simulations. We observe that as the simulations evolve, L evolves according to the network while C experiences some variations. This means that there is a clustering of nodes at the beginning of the simulation, however this level of clustering drops for a while causing some nodes to become isolated before gradually recovering. L being high indicates that most nodes are connected by a few hops.

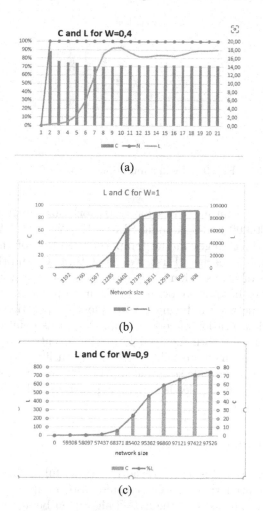

Fig. 8. Average path length L and clustering coefficient C for W = 0,4, W = 0,9 and W = 1. (a) W = 0,4. (b) W = 0,9 (c) W = 1

Figure 8 with the letter (c) represents the measurement of the clustering coefficient (C) and the average path length (L) for W = 0.9 following different network sizes. Each point is an average value of 10 cycles of simulations. We observe that the level of C and L increases progressively with the size of the network. The level of C means that we are witnessing a reorganization of the network into a small world topology. L being high indicates that most of the nodes are connected by hops, so the nodes are connected by short paths.

4. Global simulation This figure below shows a series of runs for a network size ranging from 2000 to 100,000 nodes running W = 0.9

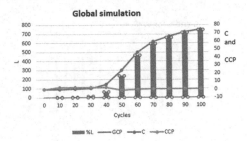

Fig. 9. Global simulation for W = 0,9

Figure 9 shows a runtime series for a network size ranging from the interval 2000 to 100,000 nodes running SLACER (W = 0.9). We can identify a number of distinct stages in the temporal evolution of the network before high cooperation is reached. First, we notice that (C) and (L) increase before the emergence of cooperation. Just after cycle 60, via a random mutation, two linked nodes become cooperative. When cooperation emerges, it spreads over the whole network reducing C to L. Once cooperation emerges, this will lead to a rapid saturation of cooperation. From this point on, we distinguish four stages: random rewiring, seed formation events, defectors will tend to disappear as nodes move to tribes with better utility. However, by defecting and acting selfishly, a node sows the seeds of its own tribe's destruction, as a node's high initial utility leads to it being surrounded by copycat defectors, reducing its gains.

5   Propositions

We believe that SLACER is a step towards very useful artificial social networks. We are also convinced that SLACER could also be applied to more realistic and useful application tasks as the SLAC algorithm being an earlier version of SLACER is applied to a P2P file sharing application and we should follow the same approach. Also we have a specific interest in producing Artificial social networks (ASN) for collective filtering of P2P viruses, spyware and spam. There are also applications that support trust and cooperative interactions between nodes in a P2P search engine.

However, although sophisticated P2P algorithms already exist, they tend to assume that all peers will act cooperatively. This is dangerous because there will always be a need for pre-existing trusted social networks to provide input, yet this is not always available or appropriate.

When dealing with complex applications, involving many types of trust and peer interaction tasks, it would be possible to create multiple instantiations of SLACER each supporting different tasks running simultaneously. In this way, each ASN would be tailored to the particular requirements of the specific task associated with it. This could be likened to the way humans form many networks around the different goals and tasks they have to accomplish in daily life.

6 Conclusion

In our paper, our main contribution lies in the simulations performed for several values of the rewiring factor W in P2P networks in order to analyze the results obtained and compare them to those of the literature. In our simulation scenario, we use a network size between 2000 and 100,000 nodes and the parameters T = 1.9, R = 1, P = 0.002, S = 0.001. We also fixed the mutation rates at M = 0.005, MR = 0.01. Nodes were also allowed to have a maximum size of 20 neighbors. While the author uses a network size between 2000 and 64000. The mutation rates at M = 0.001 and MR = 0.01. All nodes are placed in the defection state, which allows us to see if the SLACER protocol can escape total defection. This allows us to say that SLACER is robust. Previous work has shown that SLACER takes 90 cycles to reach high cooperation. Compared to the high cooperation simulation cycle, in our case, for W = 0.9 it takes 70 cycles to reach high cooperation. In this case we can deduce that the higher the network size the faster the cooperation, and thus SLACER can escape total defection.

In the future, it would be interesting to evaluate SLACER's performance by considering a study of DHT (Distributed Hash Table) systems to improve routing and search performance, as well as collaborative anti-spam or anti-spyware systems.

References

1. Anceaume, E., Gradinariu, M., Ravoaja, A.: Théorie des jeux et systemes de pairs. Publication interne- IRISA (2004)
2. Hales, D., Arteconi, S.: SLACER: a self-organizing protocol for coordination in peer-to-peer networks. J. IEEE Intell. Syst. **21**, 29–35 (2006)
3. Siebert, J., Ciarletta, L., Chevrier, V.: Impact du comportement des utilisateurs dans les réseaux pair-à-pair (P2P): modélisation et simulation multi-agents. In: 16es Journées Francophones des Systèmes Multi-Agents-JFSMA'08, pp. 129–138 (2008)
4. Hales, D., Arteconi, S.: Friends for free: self-organizing artificial social networks for trust and cooperation. arXiv preprint cs/0509037 (2005)
5. Marzolla, M.: Simulating overlay network with Peersim. http://www.moreno. marzolla.name
6. Sueur, C.: Analyse des réseaux sociaux appliquée à l'éthologie et l'écologie. publisher=Éditions Matériologiques (2015)
7. Hales, D.: From selfish nodes to cooperative networks-emergent link-based incentives in peer-to-peer networks. In: Proceedings of the Fourth International Conference on Peer-to-Peer Computing, 2004. Proceedings, pp. 151–158. IEEE (2004)
8. Jelasity, M., Guerraoui, R., Kermarrec, A.-M., van Steen, M.: The peer sampling service: experimental evaluation of unstructured gossip-based implementations. In: Jacobsen, H.-A. (ed.) Middleware 2004. LNCS, vol. 3231, pp. 79–98. Springer, Heidelberg (2004). https://doi.org/10.1007/978-3-540-30229-2_5
9. Montresor, A., Jelasity, M.. PeerSim: a scalable P2P simulator. In: 2009 IEEE Ninth International Conference on Peer-to-Peer Computing, pp. 99–100. IEEE (2009)

10. Hales, D., Arteconi, S., Babaoglu, O.: SLACER: randomness to cooperation in peer-to-peer networks. In: 2005 International Conference on Collaborative Computing: Networking, Applications and Worksharing, p. 5. IEEE (2005)
11. Hales, D., Arteconi, S., Babaoglu, O.: SLAC and SLACER: simple copy and rewire algorithms for trust and cooperation in P2P

Networked Micro-services: Empowering Local Micro-enterprises in a South African Township Through Community Wireless Networks

Ndinelao Iitumba[1]([✉])[iD], Hafeni Mthoko[2][iD], Keegan White[1][iD],
Mapule Madzena[1], Tristan Drummond[1], David Johnson[1][iD],
and Melissa Densmore[1][iD]

[1] University of Cape Town, Cape Town, South Africa
{ITMNDI001,whtkee004}@myuct.ac.za, ndinelaoiitumba@gmail.com,
melissa.densmore@uct.ac.za
[2] NURTUREID8, Windhoek, Namibia
hafeni.mthoko@nurtureID8.com

Abstract. Internet and cloud resources are a growing resource for micro-enterprises. However, small businesses in low-income communities struggle to use these resources due to the cost of access and the perceived cost of producing digital applications. In this paper, we draw on interviews with residents and small business owners from a South African township, towards the design of services to support micro-services through locally-hosted infrastructure. We present design implications for the architecture of these services, discussing the merits of internet-based versus community-based architectures, and present four prototypes to demonstrate possible designs of local centered e-commerce applications. This paper extends insights about local micro-enterprises' feature requirements and no-code local content creation services in remote communities. It also illustrates some factors that hinder the success of e-commerce in remote areas and how CWNs mitigate that. This work aims to contribute to both Sustainable Development Goals (SDG) goal 8, which focuses on promoting economic growth, and goal 11, which aims to build sustainable communities.

Keywords: Human Computer Interaction(HCI) · Community Wireless Networks · User-Centered Design

1 Introduction

The high cost of mobile data and monthly WiFi packages has limited the ability of underserved communities and those at the fringes of networks to harness the potential of the internet in supporting their local businesses. However, framing this issue solely around "Internet access" assumes that local businesses require

A. Seeam et al. (Eds.): InterSol 2023, LNICST 541, pp. 355–378, 2024.
https://doi.org/10.1007/978-3-031-51849-2_23

global internet connectivity for their success. Conversely, many local businesses seek stronger connections within their own communities. Community wireless networks (CWNs) serve as a means to facilitate local connections and community development. CWNs are community-owned mesh wireless networks that allow communities to pool their demand for internet access and share network resources locally [9,11,37]. Community development involves collaborating with individuals within a community to establish sustainable approaches that uplift the community by addressing existing imbalances [1]. In this research, we collaborate with a community to gain a better understanding of how Information Communication Technologies (ICTs) can be leveraged to achieve their goals [26].

Our focus includes empowering individuals within this community by promoting local services and enhancing local business activities [36], an objective shared by our community partners. Local services refer to products and services produced and sold within the community, often considered more affordable and accessible to community members. These services play a pivotal role in empowering communities and contributing to community development. While the creation of platforms that can host and support local services for communities is desirable, it presents a challenge. The design of such platforms needs to account for community constraints and environmental factors [44]. In this research, we delve into the design of a platform suitable for hosting local services, tailored to community users. Unlike non-local platforms such as Takealot (a popular South African e-commerce site), LinkedIn (a professional social networking site), and Spotify (a music-streaming service), which are often inaccessible due to data costs and prerequisites like access to email and credit cards, our community members lack access to the required infrastructure. As such, the question of appropriate architectures for locally hosted alternatives remains unanswered, as does the inquiry into effectively integrating and innovating new platforms designed specifically for CWNs and the operating communities.

This paper presents four case studies of applications developed by the authors to support local services in Ocean View, a low-income community in Cape Town, South Africa, facilitated by the iNethi community wireless network. These case studies focus on designing applications to facilitate the buying and selling of face masks, music sharing, the creation of a business directory, and the establishment of an employment-seeking platform for domestic workers within the Ocean View community. Through the provision of platforms that support and empower local community businesses, this work aims to make a meaningful contribution toward achieving Sustainable Development Goals (SDG), particularly Goal 8, which focuses on promoting economic growth, and Goal 11, which centers on building sustainable communities.

The research and development processes for these case studies involved conducting interviews with various stakeholders, including directors of OVCOMM Dynamic (the cooperative responsible for managing the network), local business owners, domestic workers, community members, CWN users, and musicians in Ocean View. Based on these interviews, the authors created prototypes and evaluated services to meet the participants' needs. This study presents design implications for the architecture of these "local" services, discusses the merits of internet-based versus community-based architectures, and showcases four prototypes to demonstrate potential designs.

This paper is structured as follows: "Background and Related Works" offers a brief overview of the Community Wireless Network (CWN) in Ocean View and the services it provides. The "Methods" section outlines the authors' approach to gathering insights from community members to inform the design of CWNServer services. "Case Study Findings" presents the four case studies, each with its overarching architecture and design rationale, drawn from interviews with directors of OVCOMM Dynamic, local business owners, domestic workers, community members, CWN users, and musicians in Ocean View. The "Discussion" section analyzes the needs identified through the case studies, deliberates on the trade-offs between CWNServer-hosted and cloud-hosted services, and concludes by outlining requirements for services that support micro-enterprises.

2 Background and Related Work

2.1 Ocean View

Ocean View is a small coloured township (peri-urban) community located forty-five kilometers from Cape Town, South Africa. The establishment of Ocean View in the late 1960s to 1970s was a consequence of the Group Areas Act, which granted the apartheid government in South Africa the authority to forcibly relocate people of colour (including mixed-race, Khoi, San, Indian, Chinese, and specifically in Cape Town, descendants of Malay slaves, excluding black Africans) from what were designated as 'white-only communities' [32]. The township was named Ocean View due to its residents' connection to the sea. The majority of Ocean View's residents face bandwidth constraints due to unequal coverage and the high data costs prevailing in South Africa [18,23].

Ocean View Community Wireless Network. The Ocean View community wireless network (OVCWN) is a community-owned mesh wireless network in South Africa. Using the CWN, residents can share access to locally-hosted resources and access the internet at a low cost, leveraging a shared connection [44]. Inethi Network[1] is an edge-hosted cloud platform that supports sharing of content and services within a community. The Inethi Network network deployment in Ocean View demonstrates and presents the benefits of CWNs in low-income/under-served communities. Inethi Network acts as an open-source quasi Internet Service Provider (ISP) that comprises a voucher system, locally-hosted services, and monitoring services that allow the community to set up a micro-ISP and deliver lower-cost Internet access. These services include platforms to deliver educational content, content related to local businesses, local music sharing, and social media platforms such as WhatsApp and Facebook. The OVCWN

---

[1] Project names changed/obfuscated for anonymity.

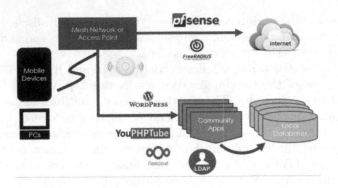

Fig. 1. The Inethi Network Design master plan.

hosts an instance of Inethi Network and presently entails 20 hot spots [14]. The OVCWN network can be accessed by anybody that is within range of any of the WiFi hot spots. Hence, Inethi Network provides an interface that empowers the Ocean View community to leverage wireless communications to increase community digital participation, increase the value of local resources, and bring communities together [33,40]. The network design presented in the Fig. 4 shows that this network provides the Ocean View community with access to the Internet, access to local content, and services via a WiFi mesh network across the community. The Inethi Network provides data backup and remote access by synchronising with a paired instance hosted by Amazon Web Services [21,32]. Members of the community can purchase vouchers that are priced at R20/GB, which makes them at least five times discounted than the lowest cost bulk 1GB voucher available from mobile operators within South Africa [47] (Fig. 1).

2.2   Services in Community Wireless Networks

Currently the primary role of Community wireless Networks (CWNs) is to provide access to the internet by providing a framework for distributing broadband services to under-resourced areas. However, various CWNs, especially wireless user groups (WUGs) have also explored shared access to local resources and services [46]. CWNs can benefit developing communities by minimizing the cost of internet access and improving socio-economic development in these communities through skills and job generation [15,20,22,24,36,39].

Some CWNs offer business services, often specifically adapted for low-income communities, and usually based on open-source software. Furthermore, CWNs assume mobile-first interaction, better catering to typical CWN users [10]. Community members can share files and use these internet services via the CWNs to access information that is available globally; such as access to education and health resources/opportunities. In addition, CWNs also support under-served communities by giving them access to online resources such as educational materials, e-commerce support, marketing, and finding jobs online [6,7].

2.3   Micro-services for Small Businesses in Developing Regions

Micro-services are an approach to software development that structures an application as a collection of small, independent, and loosely coupled services. In a micro-services architecture, each service is responsible for performing a specific business capability and communicates with other services through a well-defined interface [45]. This approach promotes modularity, scalability, and fault tolerance, as each service can be developed, deployed, and maintained independently [27]. Micro-services are often implemented using containerization and orchestration technologies, such as Docker and Kubernetes, which provide a lightweight and flexible way to package, deploy, and manage individual services. While, a micro-enterprise is a small business that employs fewer than 10 people, has an annual turnover of less than ZAR 1 million, and has assets worth less than ZAR 1 million. Micro-enterprises are often sole proprietorships or family-owned businesses that operate informally in the informal economy [2]. The South African government recognizes the importance of micro-enterprises in driving economic growth, reducing poverty, and creating jobs, particularly in disadvantaged communities. As such, it has implemented various policies and initiatives to support the development and growth of micro-enterprises [2,26][?]. Local small businesses have the potential to grow bigger and faster if they use ICTs, internet resources and platform services to become more profitable [35].

3   Methods

For this research, we partnered with a cooperative running a community wireless network for a coloured[2] township. In this study, the authors identified various areas for the development of community-based networked services, based on previous community engagements. Four student co-authors selected an application area each and conducted interviews with community members interested in their respective areas, as identified by the cooperative directors. Subsequently, we developed a prototype based on community engagement and solicited feedback from the same community members regarding the prototypes. The engagements took place between July and August 2020.

The authors acknowledged that the traditional ethnographic method was not ideal for this study due to the Covid-19 Pandemic at the time. As a result, we opted to apply remote ethnography by utilizing digital tools to share low-fidelity prototypes and developed applications with participants before conducting remote interviews via video-conference calls and WhatsApp. Remote ethnography is a research methodology used to study how people interact with technology and how technology impacts their daily lives without physically being present with them [34]. With remote ethnography, researchers can collect data

---

[2] In South Africa, the term 'coloured' specifically refers to a multiracial ethnic group native to Southern Africa that was officially defined by the South African government from 1950 to 1991.

Table of Participants

	Business Directory	Facemask	Music Sharing	Employment
Requirement Interviews	4 entrepreneurs 2 community 6 total	3 seamstresses 2 NGO managers 7 community 12 total	3 musicians 3 researchers 6 total	7 community 7 total
Prototype & App feedback	Same participants as above	3 seamstresses 7 community 10 total	Same participants as above	Same participants as above
Total	6	12	6	7

Fig. 2. The table above presents the number of participants that took part in interviews, prototype feedback, and application testing for each case study.

without being physically present by using digital tools and communication technologies. We modified and extended remote ethnography by screen sharing: To observe how participants interact with the applications, that allowed us to view their screen as they complete tasks, Conducted follow-up interviews: After participants complete the usability test, we followed up with them to ask additional questions about their experience. This provided valuable insights into how participants felt about the applications and identified areas for improvement. By modifying the remote ethnographic methodology to include these approaches, we conducted effective usability testing remotely during COVID-19.

The four applications areas include: 1) a business directory to support advertising of local businesses within the community, 2) a music-sharing service to enable local artists to track interest in their recordings and sell music, 3) cloth face mask production, meeting a new demand in the early days of the pandemic, and 4) an employment resource to help address high rates of unemployment in South Africa.

In the following section we present each of these areas as case studies depicting the community need, the design of a system intended to address that need, and feedback from the participants on these prototypes. Based on these case studies we discuss local networked micro-services, highlighting the key concerns that emerged from our experiences in an initial co-design of the applications for the community wireless network (Fig. 2).

3.1 Participants

The participants of this study were residents of the Ocean View community and other stakeholders: directors of OVComm Dynamic, the Ocean View-based cooperative running a local community wireless network (CWN); and researchers and software developers building Inethi Network, a software and hardware solution used to manage the network services. The participants were selected on criteria that they belong to the Ocean View Community or they use the CWN for internet connection and access to local services. The OVComm directors helped with recruiting participants by providing us with the contact details of some CWN users. Using the snowballing method, we were able to find more participants that were directed to us by our first initial participants. Each case study had specific requirements for participants to be selected for interviews. For the face-mask application, the participants were required to specifically have interest in cloth face masks, or be individuals that make face masks from home and those that benefit from any face mask donations to the community. While for the music-sharing application the participants were required to be musicians/artists within OV, prospective music consumers, and included one of the directors and a researcher who was also a musician. The business directory required participants that were local business owners and local domestic workers that were seeking jobs for the employment-seeking application.

3.2   Initial Community Interviews

We constructed interview questions that were based on current challenges related to buying and selling face-masks, music sharing, the business directory, and employment seeking for domestic workers. We discussed possible solutions and had insightful discussions on the problems with the participants before we started identifying the features of the potential systems/platforms/applications or websites that would best fit as the solution. Through these interviews, we sought to better situate each of the applications in the context of the target users, and to co-ideate approaches to addressing their needs.

3.3   Prototype Development

Based on the key requirements emerging from the community interviews, each student developed a prototype application. These applications were to be viewed not necessarily as a definitive architecture emerging from the engagement, but rather as technical probes to help elucidate specific community needs and other issues surrounding the deployment of services within the community [5,16,42]. Molapo [25] problematizes attempts to co-design ideas when participants do not have experience with the design artefact [25]. Hence, the mutual development of the prototype also serves as a step towards making participants more co-design ready by giving them concrete "sketches" of systems to engage with [13]. Which is essential for developing community ownership and ease sustainability for co-designed services.

3.4   Prototype Feedback

Each student conducted a second set of interviews to present application prototypes to participants for feedback. Application requirements were assessed again after development, and participants were consulted for testing and to identify problems for correction. New participants were recruited if necessary. During the prototype feedback interviews, students presented paper prototypes via online video conference tools like Zoom and Microsoft Teams. Participants provided feedback on the design and functionality of the applications remotely by listening to students demonstrate the prototype drawings online. After explaining the user interface design, participants were asked about their views on application pages, page navigation flow, login methods, electronic payments, and card payments. Feedback was used to improve the user interface designs for the final application prototype.

3.5   Analysis

After the interviews, we analyzed each case study separately using thematic analysis. Students went through each interview transcript looking for themes. Based on the research questions, similar themes regarding changes on the user interface were selected and considered to be implemented on the final applications development. The following themes emerged: the preference of using cell phone numbers for authentication purposes, using cash on delivery over electronic bank card payments, and using a WhatsApp chat bot over mobile applications for domestic employment seeking were selected by participants, each student then developed an application that would use cellphone numbers for that specific case study.

We consolidated prototype feedback in the form of further updates to the applications, the final version of which is presented in this paper. For this paper, the co-authors then shared findings across the case studies, discussing where design decisions converged and diverged. The results in this paper are based on our collective analysis of the four cases.

4   Findings

Together with the community we identified four potential services of interest and worked with community members to receive feedback on prototypes and evaluate how these might be implemented. In this section we present the case study for each application area. Each case study first outlines the need as identified in our initial interviews with key stakeholders. Then we present a proposed architecture for a community-based service designed to meet this need, together with our design rationale. Finally we present community feedback on the proposed systems (Fig. 3).

4.1   Case 1: Mask Making

For this case study we engaged three local seamstresses (people interested in income generation through making masks), two managers of organisations seeking to distribute masks within OV, and seven other OV community members as potential buyers of masks.

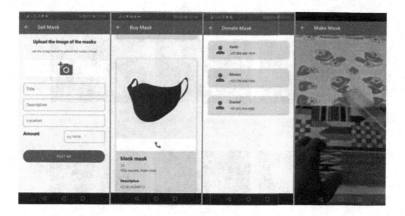

Fig. 3. This figure displays the Face Mask application for selling, buying, donating and learning how to make face masks.

Community Needs. Amid the breakdown of Covid19 in March 2020, wearing face masks became mandatory in public spaces [19]. People started sewing cloth masks as they were reusable as they could be washed many times. While in lockdown, some OV community members started sewing cloth face masks for their families and later saw it as an opportunity to generate income. These community members started selling face masks within the community. Due to the restrictions of the lockdown, it was difficult for community members to both sell and buy face-masks. Hence, the goal of the face mask app was to link potential local face mask producers with buyers, link locals to face mask donors, and share a face mask making video tutorial.

Proposed Architecture. This is a basic client-server service, with a mobile app connecting to a cloud-based server hosted by Firebase. The server is used to store the mask listings.

Users would log in to the mobile app using their cell number and a one-time password (OTP) sent via SMS to verify the number. Upon log in they can view a list of masks for sale or create a sale listing. The app also includes contact information for prospective mask donors and a short video tutorial on how to make a mask. The option for facemask donations was useful because most residents could not buy facemasks and they got their facemasks from church and NGO donations in the OV community. The app does not support direct financial transactions. Instead, listings include the contact information of the seller, allowing potential buyers to contact the sellers directly.

Design Rationale

– **Website vs Mobile App:** The mobile application was designed targeted at the Users (Ocean View Community members and OVCWN users). We

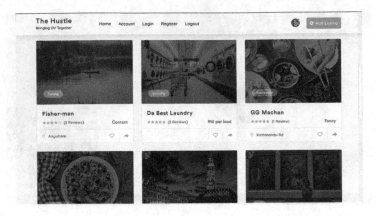

Fig. 4. The figure above presents the business directory platform.

considered developing a website but it was not fit for the users as they did not have access to laptops or tablets to get the best experience from a website. Most users had android smartphones and a mobile application was the ideal platform as they wanted an application to use on their phones.

– **Cloud vs Local Services** The mobile application is connected to a cloud server hosted by Firebase. The app APK(Android Package) was to be placed on the Inethi Network application folders in an executable form for an Android phone. The app traffic would be white-listed to the Internet through the network to be data-free. This way the users could access the app at no cost, although it still required an active internet connection.

– **Login mechanism:** To verify the users we opted to use phone numbers because most of our participants did not make use of email addresses or have access to emails. To ensure that the users entered the correct phone number, they had to verify with the OTP from the Firebase database to complete a user login and registration.

– **Payments:** During the interviews, most users outlined that they are not comfortable with using bank cards to purchase goods online, while others indicated that they hardly ever use cards to purchase local goods/services. They mostly use cash, especially around the community. The mobile application was to cater for online payments but tailors or face mask sellers that participated preferred to receive cash on delivery/pick up.

– **Video Tutorial:** During the interviews, some community members outlined that they can make their face masks if given guidelines because they can reuse old clothes as materials to make their masks at home. One participant said, "I prefer to make my face mask because the ones being sold are too small and uncomfortable because they start getting wet after some minutes". We found several video tutorials and selected one that was simple because it presented making your face mask using tools that one is likely to find in their home (thread, cloth material and scissors). With permission from the video owner, the video tutorial was incorporated directly in the app to make it readily available offline.

User Evaluation. The face mask app was evaluated by potential users from the Ocean View community and OVCWN users. We shared with the users the app apk via Whats app chat and they installed it on their cellphone. This was because all users were on whats app and they preferred to download it from there. Each participant was then given a task to download the app and register/login to the app then make a post as a seller, make a purchase as a buyer, and view the video tutorial. Participants responded positively to the tasks by posting pictures of the face masks that they are selling. Participants were also able to contact sellers using the sellers contact details displayed alongside the face mask image. They could all open the video tutorial and expressed that they would have preferred if the app presented more videos.

4.2   Case 2: Music Sharing

For this case, we interviewed three musicians that make hip-hop music from OV and three researchers from the university that are involved in Community Wireless Networks.

Community Needs. Ocean View has a thriving community of artists, including the presence of a Rastafarian settlement at the edge of the community [21, 38]. Sharing music files without unlimited internet access can be costly especially when uploading music files on YouTube and Sound Cloud. Cloud services such as YouTube and Sound Cloud have a global audience but limited access for community members. Therefore, community members shared music files among each other via Bluetooth and Whats-app. Hence, the goal of the music-sharing application was to create a music sharing platform that allows local musicians to share their music with residents of OV community and people residing outside of OV at low or free internet access.

Proposed Architecture. From the prototype evaluation, the musicians needed to increase their audience beyond OV community, we created two instances of the music sharing website. The first version was for users that would access the website using a wireless access point within the community location. While the second version was hosted on an Amazon Web Services (AWS) server that can be accessed globally by anyone.

Design Rationale

- **Wordpress** We elected to leverage an existing content management platform, Wordpress, because it does not require any coding experience to edit pages and configure plugins. This would make it easier for a resident in OV with no programming knowledge to edit and adapt the website front-end and its features as they see fit.

- **Cloud vs Local Services** Our participants sought a platform that would enable music sharing within the OV community and also aimed at reaching music lovers beyond Ocean View. This was achieved by hosting the website on the local server in OV and synchronising it with an instance of the website on an AWS instance for global access.
- **Login mechanism:** Logins were done by a wordpress plugin. To sign up and login, users need to enter their user name and password that they used to register.
- **Payments:** For both users, the seller and music buyers have to upload their banking details on the web application. The banking details were tested with Postman manually. The Postman tests involved entering incorrect bank details, bank details missing fields and then correct bank details. These were all sent to the API using get requests and the responses for all tests displayed the correct output. This was done to ensure that users enter the correct banking details.
- **The song downloads indicator:** For the users to download the songs, we needed to use the song indicator to query the downloads for a newly uploaded songs, querying the downloads for a song multiple times within a thirty-minute period and querying a song that had been downloaded a known amount of times to allow users to flexibly be able to get the songs.
- **Song Upload and Coupon Generation:** Another purpose of the music sharing website was to promote local content and assist with stimulating the community economy by helping local musicians generate income from producing music. To do this we included an essential e-commerce feature, coupon generation that allows music fans to buy coupons to download music.
- **Social media profiles:** To assist musicians with making money we also included a social media profile feature that allows musicians to market themselves online. The social media platforms also accepted donations to musicians and allowed them to share their contact details for possible collaborations with other musicians. This profiles were very useful for OV based musicians as they played an important role with increasing the music audience.

User Evaluation. The web application technical ability of users was tested by the OVCOMM directors and they managed to upload and download songs. They indicated that the a website feature (help page) pre-populated with detailed explanations of the core functionality of the website would be great and how to make use of these services. One participant brought forward that this was necessary as the average users have not made use of technology beyond WhatsApp messaging. This meant that features of the website could not be assumed to be intuitive. This was corroborated by the other participants. All the artists, outlined that they liked the genre tagging system, the profile page because they can share their details. They also engaged and interpreted the analytics page well as they could track user engagement and a way for users to preview their music. This was really amazing because they presented how enthusiastic they are about the music sharing application.

4.3   Case 3: Business Directory

For this case study we enquired with four local entrepreneurs during the requirement interviews and we were joined by two community members from Ocean View during feedback engagements.

Community Need. While many NGOs in Ocean View have websites, these are primarily outward-facing, aimed towards donors or other people outside the community rather than serving as a resource within the community [31]. Moreover, Ocean View business owners have no access to a local website for their products and services. Hence, the goal of the business directory was to help members of the Ocean View community to connect, to seek services within the community and not just from outside.

Proposed Architecture. This is a Word Press website application connecting to the Inethi Network local Server and AWS Inethi Network cloud server. The base components were built using the following dependencies (Docker→Nginx, MariaDB →Word Press). The web application has a business listing Page and a business portfolio page. The user (OV business owners or NGO) can register and create a business page for their business that will be displayed on the directory. On the business portfolio, each business owner can enter their business name and register under the right category (clothes, food, services etc.). The owner will provide the pricing model of the business, upload pictures of their business, add a phone number, email address, and a location. The name, featured photo, categories, pricing and location are displayed prominently in a tile in the directory User Interface (UI).

- **Website vs Mobile App:** Just like the music sharing web application, a business directory Word Press application was more suitable for Ocean View business owners and prospective customers from the community. This is because the OV business owners have windows laptops and Android cell phones like most community members. A Word Press web application is also more suitable as a community software because local network operators can make changes to the front-end without any programming skills.
- **Cloud vs Local Services:** The business directory web application used both local Inethi Network and cloud AWS servers for the business directory to be accessed by Ocean View community members and people out of Ocean View. This way the users within Ocean View community will access the business directory at no cost through the local server or cloud server because the business directory traffic is white-listed for community members.
- **Login mechanism:** The business owners have to register and sign up with their cellphone number. The users cellphone number was used for verification by receiving an OTP pin to ensure the number is correct and the owner can be contacted to verify the business page.

- **Payments:** Simplicity is favoured by the community in a number of ways, including the opinion that online sales were not favourable for the majority of business owners in OV. Cash was and still is king; the accessibility of cash to all (alongside the physical transaction meaning that business owners are able to build a relationship with their customers) trumps the efficiency of online payments in OV.
- **Business Owner Persona:** The design behind the business owner persona is that the business owner wants the business to be discovered by potential customer who are searching for their product/service, they want space to adequately convey the brand values, and to accurately display relevant information to those viewing the business listing (such as pricing, operational hours, location, etc.)on this space. The business owners also outlined that they have no way of building a rapport amongst the community, and this makes it more difficult to convince new customers of the business'reliability and standard. The business directory solves these problems with its design and features. A user can create a business listing that will be displayed on the directory. This listing contains the following features that can be set by the user at the listing creation and edited at any point thereafter. The business is required to have a name. The business listing can then be categorised in multiple of the available categories. The owner can set the pricing model of the business, upload pictures of the business, add a phone number and email address, and a location. The name, featured photo, categories, pricing and location are displayed prominently in a tile in the directory user interface. Within the listing, a dynamic, large text field can be used to display price lists, the business mission and vision, contact instructions and links to the internet and device apps (e.g. to Facebook pages, the default phone or mail application, or WhatsApp chat).
- **(Potential) Customer Persona:** This second persona of the business directory was designed for the costumers, it aimed to provide solutions for Ocean View residents that are looking for specific products or services within the community. Users (potential customers) without creating an account, can do a simple, multi-variable search across all businesses listed on the business directory. This provides the users with relevant businesses based on location, category, name and any other information added by the business (e.g. slogan). In the search results, they can view the star rating of the business, pricing and structure. After performing a search, the user can select to be notified of new listings within that category using an RSS Feed. Upon tapping a listing, they are then presented with the full details of the listing, options to contact the business full reviews of the business by other users of the business. After transacting with the business, the customer can then leave a review for others to immediately see. The website, using a cookie, can remember your details for future reviews without creating an account if the optional checkbox is selected.

User Evaluation. During the user evaluation phase, participants (local business owners and local customers) tested the web application by completing the following tasks: Registering an account, adding a business listing, searching for their listings by tag, text or location, rating other businesses and viewing or changing one's profile. Participants managed to navigate through the website to complete those tasks. They also stated their own desire to introduce others to the business directory and show them how to use it. They said that having the ability to point their customers towards their listing on the site was a good thing and that being able to be discovered by those searching and browsing on the directory is really exciting because it can boost their business.

4.4 Case 4: Domestic Workers Employment Seeking Channel

For this case study we interviewed and received feed back from seven community members from Ocean View with interests and experience in domestic jobs around Cape Town.

Community Need. The high unemployment rate in South Africa affects the townships and rural areas more especially when it comes to domestic workers due to the lack of online platforms [43]. Most domestic workers from townships do not have emails, Linked-In platforms to submit and seek job applications. Locals miss out on opportunities due to a lack of online platforms and services to interact with potential employers. Amid Covid-19 locals from townships struggled more to find jobs due to the restrictions as communication migrated to online channels [41]. Our goal was to link domestic job seekers with potential employers through a free-data platform that allows job seekers to interact with potential employers.

Proposed Architecture. This is a Whats app chat bot designed using Land bot with an emulated wizard-of-z back end. The features of the WhatsApp bot came from the user requirement interviews with participants(Job seekers from Ocean View Community). Users need to save the what app chat bot number and start interacting with the welcome menu.

The initial start up menu on the whats app bot welcomes the user to the platform and gives the users an option to choose the language they prefer to use and gives the users options on what service they want to use: apply for a job or post a job opportunity, ask frequently asked questions and join domestic workers union. The User data collection feature collects personal information from the user, such as their Name, contact details, address, education background, skills and experience. This information is stored in the whats app bot domain. The data collected is then used to generate a simple CV and cover letter for the users. The CV and cover letter can be viewed by potential employers and community members can use them do apply and seek for jobs.

- **A chatbot vs Mobile app:** A whats app chat bot was designed targeted at the Users (Ocean View Community job seekers or OVCWN users). We were looking at developing a mobile application but participants preferred a Whats app chat bot because most community members with smartphones use whats app and a mobile application will take up extra storage capacity on their devices. We used a Whats app bot because participants expressed that WhatsApp is cheaper for them because they can purchase a WhatsApp ticket (data bundles for WhatsApp) for 7 days. The whats app bot is easily accessible via whats-app app, the users will only need to set is up by saving the Whats app bot number.

- **Cloud vs Local Services** The whats app chat bot is to be assessed via both the Inethi Network server and AWS cloud server so that users can access it via the Inethi Network network.
- **Option for different Language:** Most participants from Ocean View that are interested in finding domestic work opportunities were not good in reading and writing in English. Therefore, they suggested the use of other language options such as Afrikaans and isiXhosa to make it easy for our participants to be a part of the application process sidelined.
- **Features to improve your employ-ability:** While job seekers outlined that they cannot receive individual feedback when their applications are not successful, information on how they can improve their CVs. Features to improve and determine their employ-ability includes how to refine your short description since this is what can attract the employers as well as their skills.
- **Creation of Curriculum Vitae:** Potential domestic work seekers from the community that participated in this research were 45 years old and above, with many having obtained grade 11 which was then known as Standard 9 in the BEE syllabus, they outlined that CV formats were not taught during their days and they still cannot understand how they work and they mostly have to ask their children or grandchildren to help them with the writing of CV. It is for this reason that we had to fill in the need by having an auto-generated CV on the WhatsApp bot platform.
- **Creation of the cover letter:** For the same reason why the creation of the CV had to be filled in, our participants did not know how a cover letter is formatted, they outlined that most of the time if they were to find a job application requesting for a cover letter, they would immediately leave the application and focus on other ones.
- **Frequently asked questions (FAQs):** Frequently asked questions (FAQs) are provided in many sites to help customers, especially if a site does not support a help desk. To answer some of the questions that applicants and employers will post, an FAQ section on the WhatsApp bot was included to help users answer some questions.
- **Terms and conditions:** Before posting a job, a user had to agree to the terms and conditions that were published in the labor laws of domestic workers act of the Republic of South Africa, that way if a scam is reported, a case can be reported to the South African Police Service (SAPS).

User Evaluation. The Whats app chat bot was evaluated by potential users from Ocean View Community and OVCWN network users. We shared with the participants the whats app chat bot number that they should save and text on the whats app application. Most participants could navigate through the chat bot, only one participant said that she had to get her daughter to help her and this was due to the language barrier. She then suggested that language options should be provided on the startup menu in which she mentions Afrikaans is the language she would prefer. Other participants outlined that they will refer fellow community members to the chat bot as they believe that this could help more people. One employee also preferred if they could be any way to verify if the job posted is for real and not some scam wherein people will contact you and tell you to send money for your application to be processed. She further expressed how an agreement on terms and conditions should be included before posting or applying for a job. An employer stated that he would like to know his domestic workers in detail, not just the things written out in the CV but things like the criminal record for safety purposes. After the walk through, participants had questions about when they should get the feedback on their applications, how can they update their CV, and if they want some type of help where they should ask. This was reasonable and important feedback from participants because it touches on having frequently asked questions in our WhatsApp bot.

5   Discussion

5.1   Local vs Cloud-Based Services

In contrast to the general trajectory of the internet towards cloud-based services [32], the Inethi Network platform specifically advocates for "local" services, for which clients can leverage community-hosted resources instead of paying for internet to connect with people outside their community. In this research, we look at networked services, with an eye towards understanding to what extent can we support the OV community business market using cloud-based services that will not require them to pay premiums. In this project, two cases opted to develop WordPress-based services hosted on the Inethi Network, one developed a WhatsApp chatbot, and another developed a dedicated mobile app. Here we discuss the trade-offs between each of these approaches for the communities.

In the case of WordPress-based sites, the service sacrifices availability for ease of updating content. End users are effectively connecting to a local "cloudlet" to access the services, but they can only do so when they are actively connected to the OVCWN network. In the case of the mask app, the designer prioritized availability of content, which was not expected to change frequently. Updates could occur when connected, but users would retain access to that content even when not connected to the CWN. Likewise, by using a WhatsApp chatbot, the employment service compromised on cost of participation in favor of universal access, recognizing that 'social bundles' offering a discounted rate for WhatsApp data can help ameliorate data costs if the service is of sufficient utility. However this comes at the cost of hosting; while the cost of hosting a WordPress site on Inethi Network is an existing sunk cost on the Inethi Network, the cost of running a publicly-hosted chatbot using Landbot is likely to be unaffordable for the community. Thus while no one architecture is necessarily appropriate for every audience or service, the choice of platform and hosting entails tradeoffs in terms of hosting costs, ease of content updates, user data costs, and offline access to resources.

Data Costs vs Availability. If the local people were to sell/promote their local businesses on highly established platforms such as Takealot.com, BidorBuy and Superbalist (all popular South African e-commerce sites), the cost involved will be unsustainable, they have to pay subscription fees to host their products on the platforms, they will need data to monitor their products on the platform and local community members (potential customers) will also need data to access the products on those platforms which is expensive. Moreover, promoting music through traditional media such as radio and television will also require local people to spend airtime while if they need to use modern online platforms like iTunes, and Spotify they have to pay subscription fees to promote their music there. On the other hand, local job seekers cannot use most platforms like LinkedIn, email based applications, and website applications to seek/apply for jobs, as these platforms require the use of data and they are complicated for locals to submit application documents. Africa has already the minimum rates of internet dispersion when compared to other continents and many people cannot afford internet access especially here in South Africa [12,31]. The monthly WiFi packages in South Africa cost around 300 Rands a month for limited WiFi, while mobile data is also not affordable because of high rates as indicated here: R59 for 500MB, R113 for 1 GB, R226 for 2 GB, R452 for 4 GB, R903 for 8 GB. People from townships cannot afford monthly packages or mobile data as most of them, their monthly income is around R 1600 [31]. This means that most people especially those from townships will not be able to access available services as they do not have connectivity means to use these services. This also contributes to township businesses low performance.

The Neo-Colonial Enterprise (or Who Pays and Who Earns). The use of international/ foreign owned applications that facilitate local businesses does not uplift the community much as the communities do not gain full profits from them. Due to the newness of the Inethi Network service platform, three of the case studies depend on external, internet-based services to support their functioning. In the case of the WhatsApp chat-bot - service fees for hosting as currently architect-ed would be unsustainable without donor support. This issue has also been observed with other USSD/SMS and WhatsApp services, where the cost per user is extremely high. Fire-base, as used with the mask-making service, is relatively low cost - but also depends on the user having data, and the number of transactions being hosted. This is feasible, assuming users are within the coverage area of the wireless network. However - this also necessitates paying outside entities (i.e. Fire base/Google and mobile service providers) for services that are essentially local only to the community. The payments mechanism integrated with the music service is also from outside the community - these services typically charge 6–20 percent of the transaction costs. Thus in order to be truly local, to keep these costs within the community, the Inethi Network platform will need to integrate its own payment mechanisms, have more reliable database services, and to increase coverage so that those in the community can access the services without relying on internet access, using the local network.

Platform Familiarity and Critical Mass. WhatsApp is one of the most used smartphone message platforms in the world and more especially here in South Africa [17,29]. The use of mobile applications especially for business purposes are the next easiest, most used, and common platforms for online shopping and service rendering. Mobile apps guarantee and provides an excellent presentation of the products at any time on the application and bring flexibility for both the buyers and the sellers. They provide a common interface for a bespoke service, and if they are well-designed they do not require any training, they can help businesses reach critical mass. Web-based applications are not only best because they are cross platform, Web-based apps (e.g., word-press) are also familiar and easy to access.

Critical mass is the turn point for businesses' when they reach a point in which they no longer require further investments on cash to keep going. Critical mass especially for small start-ups can be reached depending on the number of users on the platform to determine the success of the platform and how valuable the product/service is. How can local businesses reach critical mass if they do not have cloud services to host their local products or if their customers cannot afford to get data to buy? The lack of data and local cloud services has made business exceedingly difficult for locals and has affected their chances of reaching critical mass. Business platforms count on direct and indirect network to charm, attract and maintain customers. Newly launched platforms deployed in communities have difficulties in picking up well as community members are already used to physical buying or selling [4,8]. It's easier to achieve critical mass when the platforms have a pre-existing network structure in case of Ocean View, the participants or users might have already used Inethi Network local content/services before.

However critical mass can be overrated, just because many people use WhatsApp does not mean many people will necessarily connect to a service on WhatsApp. They are willing to chat on WhatsApp or make calls but not join a chat bot. Additionally, websites and mobile applications are severely in use especially for business purposes but people might not be interested in downloading the mobile application and keeping it on their phones, they might just download the app and use it to purchase whatever they want and some might delete it after using it/keep it in obsolete unless they need to keep using it more often depending on their interest in the products/service. The use of well-known applications/ websites interfaces does not guarantee a visit to your website/app. No particular architecture will necessarily solve the problem of gaining an audience.

Our case studies improve the chances of local businesses to reach critical mass as they will not be required to make any payments on hosting their businesses on the cloud. Our applications and website on the Inethi Network server will also contribute to local businesses reaching critical mass as the customers will easy access the businesses without mobile data. This will increase the customers and decrease the expenses of the business owners. Our case study applications aimed to improve the identified challenges local business owners and community members go through which may have been exacerbated by the COVID-19 so we found different means which are cheap and accessible to help the community.

A Hybrid Approach. Social network platforms may remove existing barriers and contribute to improving local business through network creation. Through, the social networks, people connect, keeping instant communication discussing real time news and information while having general fun and enjoyment. Social networks do not only connect people to people around them but connects people at national and global level. A cross tactic approach might improve the participation of community members interest local content and services and draw participants from neighbouring locations. This can work by using a social network platform that is linked to the Inethi Network content were people can cross post as a means of bootstrapping participation. Building a profitable and sustainable community owned connectivity network need a global and local reach to make the content visible and reachable to a great audience. MEs owners from marginalised communities lack advertising expertise, hindering growth to their businesses. MEs products/services can circulate on social platforms and not get attention. Besides that, the competition from foreign brands is so strong weakening the products of MEs in the marketplace.

Managing of Payments. The use of cloud services to host websites/apps for local products /services may possibly lead to the methods of payment to migrate to online/electronic payments. When considering the use of e-commerce, payment systems are needed, we can either opt for payment service. Payment service includes the use of cash deposits, electronic payments such as direct debits/transfers, debit/credit card. These forms of payments can affect MEs negatively if customers are not familiar with them [28], which also depends on the market. For example, some customers will be comfortable buying music with their card but they will not be willing to do the same when buying face masks online. The use of card payments requires the business owner to have a secured online payment system or POS (point of sale) machine connected to bank account which both come with extra charges. This might also be hard to manage because the business owners cannot afford to facilitate those and they require up time connection to work. The use of community payment service such as Person-to-person (P2P) can be more available as an option. Our applications do not manage to have electronic payment services as the buyer needs to collect or get the product from the seller. The business is transacted directly between the buyer and seller using our platforms/ applications an intermediary between the buyer and the seller.

Facilitating Connection. There is a need to re-approach the use of internet in our communities. The availability and use of internet have a profound impact on promoting local products and services. But they are mostly used to encourage people to face outwards and purchase from external markets instead of purchasing local products. The use of internet in local communities has most interactions concentrated between members within the same geographical area which has the potential to boost and promote local products/services [18]. Our applications are hosted on the Inethi Network server which facilitates connection within the OV community which minimises the barrier of internet connection for community members to interact with each other.

No-Code Local Content Creation Services. Creating local content applications can be difficult for community members because software development skills are difficult to acquire [3]. Maintaining applications that require programming skills can be a problem for community members, with applications such as Word press and auto mobile application generators it is easier to edit and make changes to the application interfaces [30]. The business directory and music sharing website applications were developed using Word press to make sure we minimised complexity for community members when they need to make changes because with Word press you can do content management using the widgets and plugins which makes it easy to customize themes. Despite this, word press can be locally hosted on a web server or cloud which is the best option for community wireless networks.

6 Conclusion

The lack of affordable means of Internet access in low-income or bandwidth constrained communities in South Africa has minimised the impact of e-commerce in these areas. This paper identified some of the needs of local businesses in a local township and explored the development of platforms that can support local content in Ocean View community through community wireless networks. Communities at the edges of networks cannot capitalize on the Internet to support their local businesses. This paper uses four case studies of local micro-enterprise needs in a South African township to articulate some of the problems entailed in rolling out services, to both motivate the need for community-based services, and to inform their design. Key to this is the issue of payments: local infrastructure reduces internet access and service hosting costs while enabling a local economy - but has limited applicability until critical mass enables network effects for service adoption. Our next steps are to further develop the OV CWN platform to better support these services, to create a toolkit that will enable community members to easily create their own services, access other community members, and to monetize their work within the community and more broadly.

Whats App bot for domestic employment seeking- One of the suggested future work on the Whats App bot is to extend the system to other languages such as Tshivenda and Xitsonga. Presently, the Whats App bot only has three languages: English, Afrikaans and isiXhosa. While there are 11 official languages in South Africa and should be taken into consideration for the future extension of the WhatsApp bot to other communities.

References

1. Ardle, O.M., Murray, U.: Fit for measure? evaluation in community development. Community Devel. J. **56**(3), 432–448 (2021)
2. Bvuma, S., Marnewick, C.: Sustainable livelihoods of township small, medium and micro enterprises towards growth and development. Sustainability **12**(8), 3149 (2020)
3. Chang, Y.H., Ko, C.B.: A study on the design of low-code and no code platform for mobile application development. Int. J. Adv. Smart Convergence **6**(4), 50–55 (2017)
4. Cho, H.: Theoretical intersections among social influences, beliefs, and intentions in the context of 3G mobile services in Singapore: decomposing perceived critical mass and subjective norms. J. Commun. **61**(2), 283–306 (2011)
5. Densmore, M.: Claim mobile: when to fail a technology. In: Proceedings of the SIGCHI Conference on Human Factors in Computing Systems, pp. 1833–1842 (2012)
6. Efstathiou, E., et al.: Building secure media applications over wireless community networks. In: 13th HP Openview University Association (HPOVUA) Workshop, Nice, France (2006)
7. Elianos, F.A., Plakia, G., Frangoudis, P.A., Polyzos, G.C.: Structure and evolution of a large-scale wireless community network. In: 2009 IEEE International Symposium on a World of Wireless, Mobile and Multimedia Networks & Workshops, pp. 1–6. IEEE (2009)
8. Evans, D.S., Schmalensee, R.: Failure to launch: critical mass in platform businesses. Rev. Netw. Econ. **9**(4) (2010)
9. Farao, J., Burse, M., Mthoko, H., Densmore, M.: Stakeholder relations and ownership of a community wireless network: the case of iNethi. In: Thorn, J.P.R., Gueye, A., Hejnowicz, A.P. (eds.) InterSol 2020. LNICST, vol. 321, pp. 176–191. Springer, Cham (2020). https://doi.org/10.1007/978-3-030-51051-0_13
10. Farooq, U., Carroll, J.M., Kavanaugh, A.: Mobilizing community networks. Center for Human-Computer Interaction, Department of Computer Science, Virginia Polytechnic Institute and State University (Virginia Tech), umocec (2003)
11. Forlano, L.: Codespaces: community wireless networks and the reconfiguration of cities. In: Handbook of Research on Urban Informatics: The Practice and Promise of the Real-time City, pp. 292–309. IGI Global (2009)
12. Formoso, A., Chavula, J., Phokeer, A., Sathiaseelan, A., Tyson, G.: Deep diving into Africa's inter-country latencies. In: IEEE INFOCOM 2018-IEEE Conference on Computer Communications, pp. 2231–2239. IEEE (2018)
13. Greenberg, S., Buxton, B.: Usability evaluation considered harmful (some of the time). In: Proceedings of the SIGCHI Conference on Human Factors in Computing Systems, pp. 111–120 (2008)
14. Hadzic, S., Phokeer, A., Johnson, D.: TownshipNet: a localized hybrid TVWS-WiFi and cloud services network. In: 2016 IEEE International Symposium on Technology and Society (ISTAS), pp. 1–6. IEEE (2016)

15. Hammond, A., Paul, J.: A new model for rural connectivity. World Resources Institute, Development Thought Enterprise, pp. 1–14 (2006)
16. Hutchinson, H., et al.: Technology probes: inspiring design for and with families. In: Proceedings of the SIGCHI Conference on Human Factors in Computing Systems, pp. 17–24 (2003)
17. Jindal, G., Upadhyay, D., Jha, A.: Whatsapp chatbot. Technical report, EasyChair (2020)
18. Johnson, D.L., Pejovic, V., Belding, E.M., van Stam, G.: VillageShare: facilitating content generation and sharing in rural networks. In: Proceedings of the 2nd ACM Symposium on Computing for Development, pp. 1–10 (2012)
19. Kampf, G.: Protective effect of mandatory face masks in the public-relevant variables with likely impact on outcome were not considered. Proc. Natl. Acad. Sci. **117**(44), 27076–27077 (2020)
20. Kozma, R.: Toward an African knowledge network: ICT, rural development and the green revolution. In: Proceedings of the International Conference eLearning Africa 2007, pp. 28–30 (2007)
21. Lorini, M.R., et al.: Localize-it: co-designing a community-owned platform. In: Krauss, K., Turpin, M., Naude, F. (eds.) IDIA 2018. CCIS, vol. 933, pp. 243–257. Springer, Cham (2019). https://doi.org/10.1007/978-3-030-11235-6_16
22. Mandioma, M.: Rural internet connectivity: a deployment in Dwesa-Cwebe, Eastern Cape, South Africa. Ph.D. thesis, University of Fort Hare (2007)
23. Mathur, A., Schlotfeldt, B., Chetty, M.: A mixed-methods study of mobile users' data usage practices in south Africa. In: Proceedings of the 2015 ACM International Joint Conference on Pervasive and Ubiquitous Computing, pp. 1209–1220 (2015)
24. Mattheem, K., Mweemba, G., Pais, A.V., Rijken, M., Van Stam, G.: Bringing connectivity to rural Zambia using a collaborative approach. In: ICTDâAZ07: International Conference on Information and Communication Technologies and Development, Bangalore, India (2007)
25. Molapo, M., Densmore, M., Morie, L.: Apps and skits: enabling new forms of village-to-clinic feedback for rural health education. In: Proceedings of the 7th Annual Symposium on Computing for Development, pp. 1–10 (2016)
26. Naudé, W., Krugell, W.: African economic growth: wrong to rely on small businesses? J. Small Bus. Entrepreneurship **16**(2), 21–44 (2002)
27. Newman, S.: Building Microservices. O'Reilly Media, Inc., Sebastopol (2021)
28. Oakes, L.: Faster payments: managing customer expectations. J. Payments Strategy Syst. **5**(1), 30–37 (2011)
29. O'Hara, K.P., Massimi, M., Harper, R., Rubens, S., Morris, J.: Everyday dwelling with WhatsApp. In: Proceedings of the 17th ACM conference on Computer Supported Cooperative Work & Social Computing, pp. 1131–1143 (2014)
30. Oltrogge, M., et al.: The rise of the citizen developer: Assessing the security impact of online app generators. In: 2018 IEEE Symposium on Security and Privacy (SP), pp. 634–647. IEEE (2018)
31. Phokeer, A., Densmore, M., Johnson, D., Feamster, N.: A first look at mobile internet use in township communities in South Africa. In: Proceedings of the 7th Annual Symposium on Computing for Development, pp. 1–10 (2016)
32. Phokeer, A., et al.: Inethi community network: A first look at local and internet traffic usage. In: Proceedings of the 3rd ACM SIGCAS Conference on Computing and Sustainable Societies, pp. 342–344 (2020)
33. Phokeer, A., Johnson, D., Densmore, M.: Characterisation of mobile data usage in township communities (2016)

34. Pink, S., Horst, H., Postill, J., Hjorth, L., Lewis, T., Tacchi, J.: Digital ethnography: principles and practice. Sage (2015)
35. Qureshi, S., York, A.S.: Information technology adoption by small businesses in minority and ethnic communities. In: Proceedings of the 41st Annual Hawaii International Conference on System Sciences (HICSS 2008), pp. 447–447. IEEE (2008)
36. Rey-Moreno, C., Graaf, M.: Map of the community network initiatives in Africa. L. Belli, Community Connectivity: Building the Internet From Scratch, pp. 149–169 (2016)
37. Saldana, J., et al.: Alternative networks: toward global access to the internet for all. IEEE Commun. Mag. **55**(9), 187–193 (2017)
38. Schoon, A.: Distributing hip-hop in a South African town: from the digital backyard studio to the translocal ghetto internet. In: Proceedings of the First African Conference on Human Computer Interaction, pp. 104–113 (2016)
39. Takavarasha Jr, S., Adams, C., Cilliers, L.: Community networks for addressing affordability of ICT access in African rural areas: a case study of Zenzeleni, Makhosi. In: Affordability Issues Surrounding the Use of ICT for Development and Poverty Reduction, pp. 1–27. IGI Global (2018)
40. Teixeira, R., Demoulin, H.M.: You mess the kitchen, you do the dishes (2020)
41. Visagie, J., Turok, I.: Rural-urban inequalities amplified by COVID-19: evidence from South Africa. Area Develop. Policy **6**(1), 50–62 (2021)
42. Wardle, C.J., Green, M., Mburu, C.W., Densmore, M.: Exploring co-design with breastfeeding mothers. In: Proceedings of the 2018 CHI Conference on Human Factors in Computing Systems, pp. 1–12 (2018)
43. Weir-Smith, G.: An overview of the geographic data of unemployment in South Africa. South Afr. Geogr. J.= Suid-Afrikaanse Geografiese Tydskrif **96**(2), 134–152 (2014)
44. White, K., Johnson, D., Densmore, M., Mthoko, H.: Bootstrapping the development of services for wireless community networks (2021)
45. Wolff, E.: Microservices: Flexible Software Architecture. Addison-Wesley Professional, Boston (2016)
46. Yucel, S.: Smart community wireless platforms. In: Proceedings of the International Conference on Modeling, Simulation and Visualization Methods (MSV), pp. 87–93. The Steering Committee of The World Congress in Computer Science, Computer Engineering and Applied Computing (WorldComp) (2017)
47. van Zyl, A., Johnson, D.L.: iNethi: locked down but not locked out. XRDS: Crossroads, ACM Mag. Stud. **27**(2), 54–57 (2020)

Fundamental Limitations in High Speed and Low Cost Architecture Free Space Optical (FSO) Networks for Rural Populations

Djibril Mbaye, Mamadou Diallo Diouf[✉], Wilfried Albert Duniwangda Kiélem, and Omar Gueye

Thies Polytechnic School (EPT), Labolatory of Information Processing and Intelligence Systems (LTISI), Dakar, Senegal
{mbaye.djibril2,gueye.omar}@ugb.edu.sn, mddiouf@ept.sn
http://www.ept.sn

Abstract. The Free Space Optical (FSO) network system is a technology that uses part of the light spectrum, which is near infrared, to transmit a large amount of information at the speed of light. It offers high bandwidth, low deployment cost, license-free spectrum, and unparalleled security compared to radio communication. The major concern of this technology lies in its transmission channel, which is the atmosphere, because of its many variations in time and space. The objective of this manuscript is to study the limiting factors for high-speed transmission in FSO networks. We offer a complete low-cost FSO network architecture to provide high-speed connections to the rural population. The different blocks of parameters of the architecture of the FSO network are evaluated according to the limiting factor (rain, fog, turbulence, etc.) dominating in the area. In this proposal, we use Optisystem and matlab software to evaluate the maximum range for each factor limiting the FSO channel using the bit error rate and the Q factor indicator.

Keywords: FSO technology · Optisystem · Fog · Rain · Snow · Scintillation

1 Introduction

Nowadays, transmission systems are undergoing a great evolution and affect several sectors of life. In fact, there has been a considerable increase in multimedia services such as the Internet with the arrival of very high-speed television, the increase in the size of digital photos and videos, the need to share and exchange files between Internet users, as well as the arrival of other services such as telemedicine, videoconferencing, video calls, online courses, online shopping, etc. These services promote a great need of high bit rate and high demand for bandwidth. Today, with the decentralization of many activities, the displacement of certain companies to establish themselves in other localities as well as the need to connect the rural population which does not always have access to high-speed services because its geographical position, it is necessary to set up

© ICST Institute for Computer Sciences, Social Informatics and Telecommunications Engineering 2024
Published by Springer Nature Switzerland AG 2024. All Rights Reserved
A. Seeam et al. (Eds.): InterSol 2023, LNICST 541, pp. 379–390, 2024.
https://doi.org/10.1007/978-3-031-51849-2_24

long-range networks capable of ensuring connectivity and the implementation of universal services and accessible to everyone. With the increase in population, the number of subscribers is constantly changing. In addition, the need for services in all essential areas of activity, in particular with real-time communication (voice and data), supervision of transactions with video surveillance, the arrival of the Internet of Things (IOT) with the 5th generation of mobile networks, the need for high-capacity infrastructure is in high demand. Thus, to satisfy this strong demand which continues to grow, the Internet Service Provider (ISP) first proposed a wired network based on copper. This technology does not allow to reach a certain flow rate and a certain range because of the nature of the material. Suppliers have migrated to optical transmission systems with the use of optical fiber as the information transmission medium. It is a technology that has allowed today to acquire a certain number of advantages, in particular with very high speed [1] with a link that can reach several kilometers. With the need for communication while on the move, subscriber's have embraced wireless transmission systems with the adoption of microwave beams as the solution to user mobility. Certainly a technology that has solved the problem of mobility but has a limited flow. Thus, to maintain user mobility with comparable speeds, suppliers have opted for fixed/mobile convergence with a core network based on optical fiber. However, the spectrum of conventional RF type radio wireless signals is increasingly crowded to support various IoT applications. Indeed, the saturation of the radio-electric band due to the extension of existing services and the advent of new services such as the Internet of Things, electromagnetic pollution, the cost and difficulties linked to the deployment of optical fiber as well as the quest for broadband are among other reasons that have led to the new wireless optical communication techniques, the FSO (Free Space Optics) systems. The basic principle of FSO transmission is similar to fiber optic communication except that the modulated data is transmitted through an unguided channel instead of an optical fiber. The interception and detection of the laser beam is difficult, which makes FSO communication better for security. FSO systems are therefore better candidates for enabling populations to access broadband at a lower cost in unreached areas. In this work, we focus on a proposal of a low-cost FSO network architecture that can offer high bit rate and allows the connection of the most remote areas such as the rural population. We offer the characteristics of the transmitter modules, the FSO type transmission channel and the receivers to meet these bandwidth and range needs. The parameters of the different blocks of the FSO network architecture will be evaluated according to the limiting factor (rain, fog, turbulence etc.) dominating in the area.

2   Related Work

The data transmission in free space optical networks is a major subject which interests several telecommunications community. Recently, many scientific works have been done to study the communications in FSO networks. Thereby, in [2] H. Singh and D. P. Chechi evaluate the performance of Free Space Optical (FSO) Communication Link. They give the attenuation caused by the rain, the snow and the fog effects in differents lenghts of transmission. The paper in [3] simulates 30 Gbps ground-to-geostationary satellite-FSO communication link under different atmospheric effects like haze and fog; and under different types of cloud-like stratus, cumulus and cumulonimbus; while doing so, the effect of moderate atmospheric turbulence and intensity scintillation is always considered. The work shows that a 2×2 MIMO system having QPSK modulation with coherent detection and digital signal processing gives an extremely low symbol error rate in almost all weather and all cloud conditions. The work published in [4] are accentuated on the study of the environmental parameters effect like rain, fog, haze, snow, and dust on the performance of optical wireless communications using Opti-system program. This work considers the visibility effect as well as operating wavelengths on atmospheric attenuation in different weather conditions for FSO link. The results obtained by Sangeetha A, Nalini Sharma, and Ipsita Deb in [5] are focused on the evaluation of the MIMO Based FSO Links flexibility. Their simulation results show that by implementing Multiple Input Multiple Output (MIMO) techniques for FSO systems, it is possible to reduce the BER for different range and achieve the accurate transmitted data at the receiver side. The performance improvements vis-a-vis, received power levels, bit error rate (BER), Q-factor and link distance range have been demonstrated in the presence of atmospheric turbulence conditions like haze, fog, clear sky etc. In satellite communication systems, R. Samy and al in [6] give an ergodic capacity analysis in SAG-FSO/SH-FSO/RF transmission. The autors used respectively Gamma-Gamma and Rician distributions to characterize FSO and RF links. They uses numerical examples to highlight the significant potential of the SAG-FSO/SH-FSO/RF Integrated Satcom System over existing solutions. They also explain the capacity gain of the integrated Satcom systems with intensity modulation and direct detection in terms of capacity compared to those which integrate heterodyne detection on all the zenith angles of the satellite. fT. N. Khajwal, A. Mushtaq and S. Kaur, in their proposal in [7], focused on the performance analysis of FSO-SISO and FSO-WDM systems under different atmospheric conditions. They conclude that the transmitting optical power above 9 and 15 dB is required in case of FSO-SISO system for transmission of data without error for Moderate and Heavy fog conditions respectively. But, for FSO-WDM system, they suggested power above 16dB in case of Moderate fog conditions for optimal transmission. In summary, we can conclude that several results on FSO transmission systems have been published. But it should be noted that most works consider a typical value equal to 25 dB/km to represent the losses of the FSO signal due to atmospheric conditions. A large number of FSO network architecture proposals have also been provided by the scientific community. However, the proposed networks are very expensive and do not encourage their deployment in rural areas. This work presents a complete low-cost FSO network architecture, capable to provide high bit rate connections to the rural population. The parameters of the different blocks of the FSO network architecture will be evaluated according to the limiting factor (rain, fog, turbulence etc.) dominating in the area.

3   Free Space Optical System Model

In an FSO system, a laser beam is emitted from the source towards the receiver. The intensity of the beam is concentrated in the direction of the receiver in order to ensure safety and the exchange of a large amount of information. Thus, FSO links require direct visibility (LOS: light of sight) between the two entities wishing to communicate. The Free Space Optical communication system 1 is identical to that of fiber optic transmission. But the only difference is at the channel level where the FSO systems use the atmosphere as the medium for transmitting information. It allows the transmission of a large amount of information at speeds equal to that of optical fiber while benefiting from the opportunities of wireless. This information is first received at the modulator block in electrical form. The modulator as its name suggests performs the modulation step by modifying the signal into another form which will be transmittable by the optical source (usually a laser diode or a light emitting diode). Then the signal is transmitted to the receiver via an FSO (free space) channel. At the reception level, the reverse operation of the transmission is carried out, that is to say that the optical signal will be converted into an electrical signal, then demodulated in order to be able to recover the information [9]. The following Fig. 1 illustrates the block diagram of an optical transmission FSO system. An FSO network is a technology that uses the atmosphere as a medium for transmitting information. Since the atmosphere is a complex, turbulent and time-varying medium, the optical signal transmitted through the medium is affected by the physical properties of the environment. This affects transmission efficiency. These factors are simply related to atmospheric and climatic phenomena such as fog, rain, atmospheric scintillation, etc. In this proposal we will study the impact of these factors through an optisystem model.

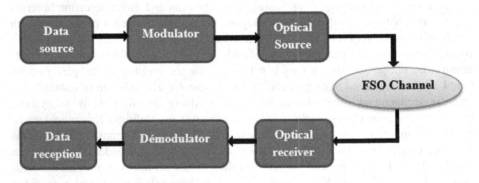

Fig. 1. Transmission schema of an FSO system

4   Free Space Optical Optisystem Model

Our proposal aims to study a low-cost, high-speed architecture for point-to-point communications links in rural areas. We use light to support information through FSO networks. The following Fig. 2 shows our simulation model based on the optisystem software [10]. The transmission block consists of a Pseudo Random Sequence Generator (PRBS) which generates a binary sequence, an NRZ type encoder (Non-Return to Zero) which generates an electrical signal. This electrical signal will modulate the laser with a device external to the source by an external modulation called a Mach Zehnder. A DL(lasser diode) optical source is used to convert the electrical signal into an optical

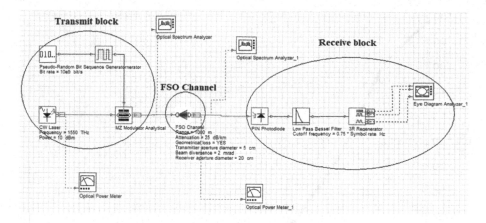

Fig. 2. Transmission schema of an FSO system

signal transmetted to optical channal FSO. The reception bloc is made up of a PIN type photodetector which allows the reverse operation of the optical source. In other words, the photodetector converts the received optical signal to an electrical signal. Low pass filtering is also used to minimize distortion and eliminate some unwanted frequencies. The repeater (3R regenerator) allows reamplification, shaping and resynchronization of the signal in order to compensate for some of the attenuations suffered by the signal during its propagation.

5   Simulation and Results

In this section, we evaluate the fundamental limiting factors in FSO network transmission. These factors are very often related to different atmospheric conditions such as fog, rain, scintillation etc. These different atmospheric conditions are grouped often around a typical value of 25 dB/km by the scientific community. The Table 1 below gives the different simulation parameters used in this proposal. The Fig. 3 above gives the variation of the signal quality obtained on reception as a function of the range of the link.

Table 1. Typical simulation parameters values

similation parameters	Parameters values
Bit rate	10 Gbts
signal pwer	10 dBm
Wavelengh	1550 nm
attetuaton	25 dB/km
Modulation type	External modulation

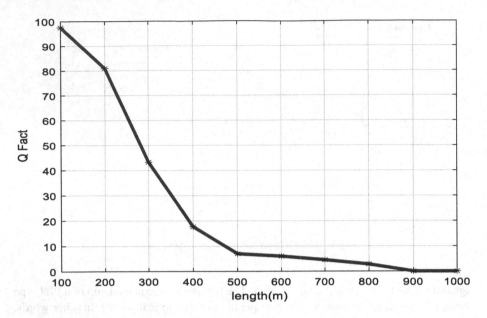

Fig. 3. Performance of FSO links with typical parameter value attenuator (25 dB).

The performance of the link, given by the Fig. 3, is evaluated over a distance ranging from 100 m to 1 km. The results show that, for a range varying from 100 m to 500 m, we observe a very rapid decrease in the quality factor. Beyond 500 m, the variation becomes slow until it reaches its limit value. In addition, the maximum range reached is 520 m with a bit error rate and an acceptable Q-factor (Q-Fact = 6.00028). Beyond this range, the signal obtained is of poor quality with a great Binary Error Rate (BER) and a quality factor less than 6.

In this proposal, a detailed study is carried out on all the limiting propagation factors of the optical signal for a best appreciation of the FSO channel quality impact in an optical transmission in free space link. Indeed, on several articles provided by the experts, the various limiting factors are grouped around a typical value of 25 dB/km. For a best apprication and application of FSO networks in African countries, we have carried out a detailed study on each limiting factor (rain, fog, sparking) to understand its effect on the FSO link. Thus, for each limiting factor, we will use a mathematical model to determine the value of the FSO channel attenuation. Then, we used the Optisystem software to establish the network architecture and perform a series of simulations and visualization of the results. The matlab software is used to determine the evolution of the quality factor, the bit error rate according to the range of the link.

5.1   Rain Limitations in FSO Networks

The rain is one of the factors limiting optical free space transmission. It affects the signal quality in the FSO channel. The losses of the optical signal related to rain are defined by the relation (1) [8]:

$$Att_{rain} = 1,076R^{0,67} \qquad (1)$$

R gives the precipitation rate in (mm/h).

A simulation was carried out for different forms of rain (Drizzle, light, medium and heavy rain). The simulation parameters are grouped in the Table 2 below which gives for each type of rain, the variation of the attenuation according to the rate of precipitation. The Fig. 4 represents the comparison made between the different types of rain on the quality of the FSO link.

Table 2. Attenuation of the different types of rain according to the rate of precipitation

Rain type	R (mm/h)	Attenuation value (dB/km)
Drizzle	0.25	0.42
Light rain	2.5	1.98
Averange rain	12.5	5.84
Heavy rain	25	9.29
storm	100	23.54

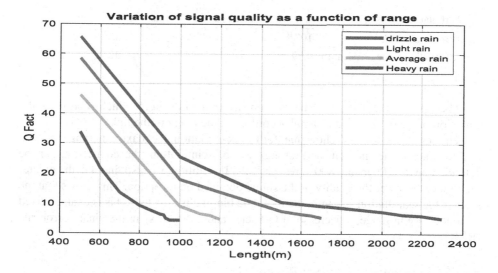

Fig. 4. Comparison of the different forms of rain

For light rain, the connection can be extended up to a range of 2200 m. For light, medium and heavy rain, the maximum range reached is 1650 m, 1150 m and 920 m respectively. For the same range value (for example 500 m), we also observe that, light rain has the greatest performance on reception with a quality factor of 65.699 while heavy rain has the lowest performance compared to the others types of rain. This shows that, for the case of rain, the higher the precipitation rate, the more the link is affected and the more the range is limited.

5.2   The Turbulence Effects in the FSO Network

The scintillation is also one of the factors limiting optical free space transmission. The optical signal losses related to scintillation are defined by the equations (2),(3).

$$Aff_{scin} = 2\sqrt{23,17 \times K^{\frac{7}{6}} \times C_n^2 \times L^{\frac{11}{6}}} \tag{2}$$

where

$$K = \frac{2\pi}{\lambda}, \tag{3}$$

In (2), K gives the wave number, C_n^2 the turbulence intensity and L the distance of the
link between the transmitter and the receiver.

The simulation is done under different conditions, i.e. for the weak, medium and strong scintillation case. The following Table 3 gives for different scintillation strength, the value of the corresponding attenuation.

Table 3. Attenuation of scintillation

Turbulance Intensity	Low Turbulance	Medium Turbulance	High Turbulance
Turbulance value	10^{-16}	10^{-14}	10^{-13}
Attenuation value (1550 nm)	0.39	3.87	12.25

The results obtained are visualized on the following Fig. 5 which represents the variation of the quality of the signal according to the range of the link.

The results in the Fig. 5 show that, for low scintillation, the maximum range reached is 2200 m. For the medium and strong case of scintillation, the connection can be extended up to 1200 m and 800 m respectively. In addition, we also find that the greater the range, the lower the quality of the signal obtained on reception. This shows that the greater the scintillation strength, the more the binding is affected. This is characterized by a decrease in range, a decrease of Q-Factor and an increase in the binary error rate (BER).

5.3   Fog Limitations in FSO Networks

The fog limits also the performance of the free space optical transmission network. In this section we first focus on the tests of the signal FSO quality in clear weather, in light, moderate, thick and then dense fog. The Eqs. (4), (5), (6), (7) explain the optical signal losses due to fog [2]

$$\Gamma_{brouillard} = \frac{3,91}{V} \times \left(\frac{\lambda}{550}\right)^{-q} \tag{4}$$

$$\beta(\lambda) = \frac{1}{L} * 10log_{10}\frac{P_t}{P_r} = \frac{1}{L} * 10log_{10}(e^{\gamma(\lambda)*L}) \tag{5}$$

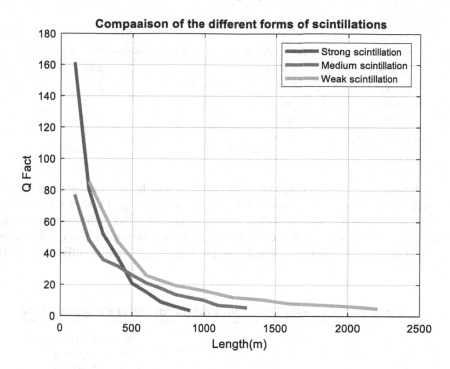

Fig. 5. Comparison of the different forms of scintillation

KRUSE MODEL

$$q = \begin{cases} 11,6 & if \quad V > 50\,km \\ 1,3 & if \quad 6\,km < V < 50\,km \\ 0,585V^{\frac{1}{3}} & if \quad 0\,km < V < 6\,km \end{cases} \tag{6}$$

KIM MODEL

$$q = \begin{cases} 11,6 & if \quad V > 50\,km \\ 1,3 & if \quad 6\,km < V < 50\,km \\ 0,16 * V + 0,34 & if \quad 1\,km < V < 6\,km \\ V - 0,5 & if \quad 0,5\,km < V < 1\,km \\ 0 & V < 0,5\,km \end{cases} \tag{7}$$

V (km) represents the visibility, λ(nm) the wavelength of the radiation, q is the parameter that depend on the particle size.

However, a comparison is made to see the effect of fog on the FSO channel compared to other factors. The following table gives for different types of fog, the corresponding attenuation according to these different parameters given by Table 4 below

.

Table 4. Fog attenuation values

Atmosphetiques conditions	Visibility (meters)	Q visibility parameters	Specific fog loss
clear weather	20.000	1.3	0.01
light fog	770	0.27	3.84
moderate fog	500	0	7.824
thick fog	200	0	19.56
dense fog	50	0	78.24

With parameters values obtained in the Table 4, we obtain an attenuation of 0.22 for clear weather atmospheres conditions, 16.68 for light fog, 33.9792 for moderate fog, 84.948 in thick fog and 339.792 in dense fog atmospheres conditions. The results obtained are displayed in the figure 6 below. It represents the variation in quality of the signal obtained on reception as a function of the range of the link for different types of fog.

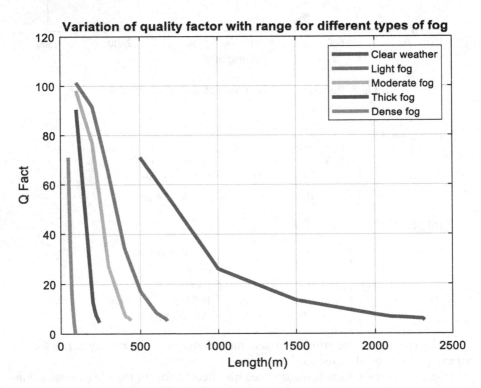

Fig. 6. Comparison of the different forms of fog

The results in the Fig. 6 show that in a clear atmosphere where with no climatic phenomenon (rain, fog, snow, etc.), a FSO link can be extended up to a range of 2310 m.

On the other hand, in the presence of light, moderate, thick or dense fog, the range is limited to 660 m, 430 m, 230 m and 80 m respectively. Which shows that the fog greatly affects the performance of the link. Compared to other factors such as rain, snow, and scintillation, fog gives more degradations in the optical signal. This is justified by the fact that in a situation of heavy rain or strong scintillation, the range is limited to 920 m and 800 m respectively, while in a situation of light fog the maximum range reached is 660 m. This shows that light fog affects the signal more than any other factor present in the atmospheric channel. This means that fog is the main factor limiting optical transmission in free space as confirmed by the simulation results.

6 Conclusion and Futures Works

The main objective of this work is to propose a high-speed point-to-point communications architecture for the most remote areas of operators, such as rural areas. We have proposed a free space optical transmission network based on the FSO. A study of all the factors limiting transmission was carried out with the aim of analyzing and evaluating the performance of the atmospheric channel of the FSO link. The performance of the link is analyzed by evaluating the bit error rate, the quality factor as well as the range of the link in the presence of each phenomenon. However, it should be noted that fog is the major problem of FSO systems among all the limiting factors. Thus, the performance of the link can be improved by considering either MIMO technology, or the implementation of hybrid FSO-RF systems.

References

1. Houngnibo, C.Y.R.: University of Abomey-calavi, Study and modeling for an (Free Space Optics) channel for a MATLAB/Optisystem co-simulation (2018–2019)
2. Singh, H., Chechi, D.P.: Performance evaluation of free space optical (FSO) communication link: effects of rain, snow and fog. In: 2019 6th International Conference on Signal Processing and Integrated Networks (SPIN), pp. 387–390 (2019). https://doi.org/10.1109/SPIN.2019.8711672
3. Bhatt, P., Sedani, B., Kotak, N.:Designing and simulation of 30Gbps FSO communication link under different atmospheric and cloud conditions. Int. J. Eng. Trends Technol. **69**(5), 228–234 (2021). https://doi.org/10.14445/22315381/IJETT-V69I5P229
4. Ali, H.A.E.M., Said, E.S.S.A., Yousef, M.E.: Effect of environmental parameters on the performance of optical wireless communications. Int. J. Optics, **2019**, Article ID 1828275, 12 pages (2019). https://doi.org/10.1155/2019/1828275
5. Sangeetha, A., Sharma, N., Deb, I.: Feasibility evaluation of MIMO based FSO links. J. Commun. **14**(3), 187–194 (2019). https://doi.org/10.12720/jcm.14.3.187-193
6. Samy, R., Yang, H.C., Rakia, T., Alouini, M.S.: Ergodic capacity analysis of satellite communication systems with SAG-FSO/SH-FSO/RF transmission. IEEE Photonics J. **14**(5), 1–9. Art no. 7347909 (2022). https://doi.org/10.1109/JPHOT.2022.3201046
7. Khajwal, T.N., Mushtaq, A., Kaur, S.: Performance analysis of FSO-SISO and FSO-WDM systems under different atmospheric conditions. In: 2020 7th International Conference on Signal Processing and Integrated Networks (SPIN), pp. 312–316 (2020). https://doi.org/10.1109/SPIN48934.2020.9071116

8. Recommandation UIT-R P.1814: Méthode de prévision nécessaire pour la conception de liaisons optiques de terre en espace libre (2007)
9. Ben Ahmed, F., Kanoun, B.: Project report "Analisys of the performance of an optical communication in free space" TUNIS school of communications (2014–2015)
10. https://optiwave.com/optisystem-overview/
11. Ali, H.A.E.M., Dit, E.S.A., Yousef, E.: Effect of environmental parameters on the performance of WOC, 2 Mai (2019)
12. Sangeetha, A., Sharma, N., Deb, I.: Feasibility evaluation of MIMO based FSO link. J. Commun. **14**(3), 187–194 (2019)
13. Da, S., Chakraborty, M.: ASK and PPM modulation based FSO system under varying weather conditions (2016)

F4PW: Fog Computer for Pregnant Women

Amy Sene[1]([⊠]), Ibrahima Niang[1], Alassane Diop[2], and Assane Gueye[1]

[1] Cheikh Anta Diop University, Dakar, Senegal
amy.sene@uadb.edu.sn
[2] Alioune Diop University, Bambey, Senegal

Abstract. Maternal health is very important for healthy and productive populations. Women need access to high quality care during pregnancy. With the significant advance of technology, the use of IoT (Internet of Things) can be a mean to provide a medical quality system. Our paper presents a new architecture called F4PW (Fog for Pregnant Woman). F4PW is inspired from Fog Computing and uses the Wireless Body Area Networks (WBANs). The purpose of this new architecture is to provide an end-to-end real-time remote monitoring to pregnant women during the pregnancy period. Medical applications cannot tolerate high latency and should be reliable at any time. F4PW provides functionality for quickly processing, analyzing and transmission of collected data.

Keywords: Network · Biosensors · Health · F4PW · Fog Computing · WBAN

1 Introduction

Maternal health is paramount for healthy and productive populations. Women need access to high quality care during pregnancy. Unfortunately, most women who are in remote areas and poorer communities struggle to access and to receive adequate care during pregnancy. Some countries fall [13] below the WHO (World Health Organization) standards about the minimal threshold of doctors, midwives and nurses per population. According to the WHO [3], maternal mortality is higher in developing countries, and women living in rural areas or in poorer communities are especially vulnerable. The majority of maternal deaths can be prevented with adequate access to health care before, during, and after pregnancy.

To improve the quality maternal health, and avoid predictable complications during pregnancy we propose a real-time and remote system monitoring during the pregnancy periodical. For this, we have implemented a new communication and computing architecture F4PW (Fog For Pregnant Women). F4PW is based on a 3 layers architecture inspired from Fog Computing which [1] is an extension of the cloud computing paradigm from the core of network to the edge of the network that provides computation, storage, and networking services between end devices and traditional cloud servers. Fog Computing can analyze data collected from IoT devices with minimal overhead in real-time. While the combination of IoT and cloud can solve many challenges; additional challenges are anticipated due to the integration of these two technologies.

A. Seeam et al. (Eds.): InterSol 2023, LNICST 541, pp. 391–402, 2024.
https://doi.org/10.1007/978-3-031-51849-2_25

To collect medical data from pregnant women, F4PW uses the Wireless Body Area Network (WBAN) which [2] is a type of wireless sensor network that requires a number of nodes to be worn on the body or implanted within the human body to collect the vital information from the body. The biosensors are limited resources (such as battery, central processing units (CPUs), memory and storage). Therefore for permanent storage, the generated data must be sent and stored permanently in the cloud (using the Internet), for examination by a staff medical.

Medical applications cannot tolerate high latency and should be reliable at any time. They require [4] real-time monitoring, availability, immediate response and guarantees. Therefor; data collected by the biosensors need to be send in the cloud with very low latency.

Taking account of all these requirements, F4PW permits the analysis of data collected by biosensors and minimizes latency for transmission in the Cloud. To achieve this performance, F4PW determines dynamically the best way with low latency communication and data processing before sending measured data in the Cloud.

F4PW proposal defines measurement frequencies for biosensors. These measurement frequencies indicate the interval time between 2 successive measurements and are adapted according to the state of health of the pregnant woman to be monitored.

This paper is organized as follow. Section 2 offers an analysis of fog computing including fundamental principles, fog computing architecture. A literature review is presented in Sect. 3. Section 4 and 5 give respectively a detailed description and the result performances evaluation of F4PW. Finally, Sect. 6 concludes the paper.

2 Fog Computing

The generated data continues to grow with the proliferation of recent technologies, such as the Internet of Things (IoT) and the Intelligence Artificial. The volume of global real-time data is expected to expand tenfold from 5 to 51 zettabytes [5] between 2018 and 2025, and global data creation is projected to grow to more than 180 zettabytes by 2025. As data is increasingly generated therefore, an essential structure that can effectively process data near IoT, is needed. Fog computing is a layered model for enabling ubiquitous access to a shared continuum of scalable computing resources. The model facilitates the deployment of distributed, latency-aware applications and services.

Fog computing architecture consists of three layers named Cloud layer, Fog layer and the Terminal layer.

- The terminal layer is responsible for extending cloud computing services for the end devices and is located near the end-consumers physical environment. It comprises several IoT-based smart devices, such as mobile phones, sensors, smart vehicles, readers, and smart cards, which devices are used to sense the data to process and transmit the sensed data to the upper layer.
- The fog layer is composed of a large number of distributed fog nodes, where gateways, access points, routers, switches, fog services, and base stations are merged. This layer is located at the network edge.
- The cloud layer comprises several servers and storage devices that offer high-performance computing resources and services to various applications, such as smart

transportation, smart home, and smart factories. It has powerful computing resources to perform extensive computation analysis and provides storage to permanently store a huge amount of data.

3 Related Works

Various research on the use of Iot in Fog Computing has been done.

This paper [6] presents a solution for using Fog Computing in healthcare. To identify the data that required low latency time and prioritize, they used a new layer after the end user, to classify the data according to the application. In addition, they use a Fog Computing Point which receive the traffic collected from the sensors and then validate the traffic to relay in the remote Cloud and the part to process locally. The authors [7] proposed A Multilevel Mobile Fog Computing that offers a multilayer architecture whose processing begins with the lowest level. If the latter is unable to process the data for example for lack of resources, it sends the information back to the upper layer and so on until it reaches the last layer. [8] Proposed a solution for ends users by adopting a 3-layer architecture. Each node is attached to the fog server within its range. For any required information, the end node sends a request to its attached server (that is on second level). The result will be send to the node if the server finds the answers, otherwise it asks the third level that contains all the information. Due to the large number of requests and data received in the cloud, [9] they classifies the requests from ends devices. Thus, a weight is assigned to each type of traffic. This ensures through their forwarding policy the transmission of traffic to the appropriate cloud requests. In [10], after the end layer, it adds an additional module layer. This layer is used to retrieve data from the end devices. After this recovery, the data is grouped according to the types of applications. The GKS (Greedy Knapsack-based Scheduling) algorithm is used for allocating appropriately resources to modules. [11] Proposals a Fog clusters on layer 2. Each fog cluster is composed of several fog nodes. This layer is responsible for recovering data from layer 1 and transferring in cloud. Each fog cluster has a load balancer that allows load balancing between clusters. All load balancers are managed by a main load balancer which ensures load balancing according to the predefined states associated with each cluster. The authors [12] of this article have proposed a solution to improve the monitoring of patients suffering from chronic diseases and requiring remote intensive care by referring to fog computing. For this they adopt an algorithm called TCVC (Tasks Classification and Virtual Machines Categorization). The algorithm allows to classify the tasks in 3 categories (from the most important to the least). Thus each type of task is allocated to a type of VM whose resources are dynamically allocated as needed.

Most of these studies focus on proposals allowing to identify the type of traffic to be processed locally and the part to send to the cloud, which level is used to process a request or attach a node to a server.

Through our proposal we minimize latency while sending all traffic in the cloud by taking into account mobility.

4 F4PW Operation

F4PW is inspired from Fog Computing and provides a regular and real-time monitoring to women during pregnancy. F4PW uses biosensors.

The biosensors are limited resources (such as battery, central processing units (CPUs), memory and storage). Therefore for permanent storage, the generated data must be stored permanently in the cloud and accessible to medical staff.

Real-time processing and event response are essential in Healthcare, data must be immediately available to enable staff medical to make decisions based on evidence. However, the mobility independence and usual living situation for pregnant women must not be affected by this requirement. Similarly, the staff medical must be able to access to measured data regardless of their geographical location. Taking into consideration all these constraints and important factors, we propose a new architecture F4PW inspired from Fog Computing and providing end-to-end services. F4PW is a 3 layers architecture for receiving, analyzing and storing data coming from biosensors worn by pregnant women. F4PW minimizes latency, supports mobility and dynamically adapts according to the mobility of pregnant women and medical staff. Figure 1 depicts the F4PW architecture with the three different layers namely: F4PW-T1, F4PW-T2 and F4PW-T3.

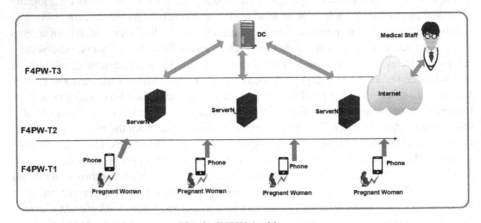

Fig. 1. F4PW Architecture

4.1 F4PW-T1

The F4PW-T1 is the lower layer. F4PW-T1 is composed with different biosensors worn by pregnant women. These biosensors are used to generate and collect healthcare data from the pregnant woman. The phone acts as a gateway between F4PW-T1 and F4PW-T2. Biosensors and the phone communicate through wireless Wi-Fi or Bluetooth.

In order to determine the health status of the pregnant woman, we must have some information. For that, we use blood pressure, blood glucose, temperature, pulse biosensors. The biosensors allow the measurement of health-related physiology. For each, thresholds are defined to classify data (Table 1).

After each measuring data, the following algorithm is used to determine the health status (Fig. 2):

For each state, a measuring periodicity validated by a doctor is predefined. This frequency (F) indicates the interval time between 2 successive measurements. We can

Table 1. Data Classification

Type	Class 1	Class 2	Class 3	Class 4
blood pressure	$7 \leq D \leq 8$ and $12 \leq S \leq 13$	$6 \leq D < 7$ or $13 < S \leq 14$	$5 \leq D < 6$ or $14 < S \leq 15$	$5 < D$ or $S > 15$
blood glucose (G) g/l	$0,7 \leq G \leq 1$	$1 < G \leq 1,1$	$1 < G \leq 1,25$	$G > 1,25$ or $G < 0,7$
Pulse (P) beats/min	$80 \leq P \leq 120$	$120 < P \leq 140$	$140 < P \leq 160$	$P > 160$
Temperature	$37.6° \leq T \leq 38$	$38 < T \leq 39$	$39 < T \leq 40$	$T > 40$

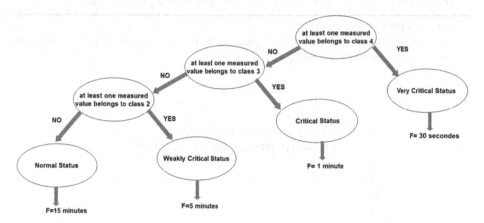

Fig. 2. Algorithm for Health Care Status

see through the algorithm that, more the health status becomes critical, more the higher the frequencies.

4.2 F4PW-T2

The second layer is the F4PW-T2 layer. F4PW-T2 supports collaborations between the F4PW-T1 and F4PW-T3. This layer has the responsibility to receive data generated in FW4P-T1 and their transmission to FW4P-T3. In others words, this layer consisted as the communication between the phone and the F4PW-T3 layers. Health data are delay-sensitive and real-time. To ensure that measured data is delivered to the cloud with very low delay, F4PW minimizes the latency for transmitting data to F4PW-T3.

Through the defined frequency, the phone knows the duration of the next measurement. Therefore just before measurement by biosensors the following steps are performed by the phone:

- The phone needs to look up the network latency with each serverN to determine which offers the low latency connectivity services. This latency refers to the time it takes for data to travel from the phone to a serverN. Obviously latency can depend on geographical distance to the destination. But sometimes it can happen that a remote server offers lower latency than a near server. Hence the importance of determining before each measurement the latency time to reach the different servers. To get this metric the phone sends a ping request to each serverN. The ping result between the phone and each server N is represented by P.

- To obtain the second metric, a same process is executed regularly on each server N to determine the local processing time (Tlp) of the serverN. The execution of this process locally on each server makes possible to have the time it takes by each serverN to process a request. This procedure allows to know, the local performance of the serverN.

At this step, the phone has the required information (latency and local processing time) for each serverN.

In order to identify the optimal serverN, the following algorithm is executed:

- n defined the number of ServerN
- Each ServerN is characterized by 2 parameters P and L where: P is the latency to reach the Server and L is local processing time.

```
Int array[n-1]
Pi= Result ping from phone to ServerN0
Li= Result local processing time of ServerN0
Ti= Pi+Li
Array[0]=Ti
b=0
B=Ti
FOR (i=1 to i=n-1)
        Pi= Result ping from phone to ServerNi
        Li= Result local processing time of ServerNi
        Ti= Pi+Li
        Array[i]=Ti
IF array[i]<B
                B=array[i]
                b=i
        END IF
        END FOR
```

The serverN(i) with the lowest B is considered to be the best. Therefore, the phone sends the data to this server. The same procedure is repeated before each measurement. With this technique, F4PW can independently on the geographical position of the pregnant woman, dynamically determine the server that offers the best performances, unlike to solutions that associate a user to a nearest server. Whereas, a remote server can be more available than a nearest.

This level also allows notifications. Instead to waiting for arrival and analyzing data in the F4PW-T3 level before notifying the medical staff can increase medical intervention times. Notifications are generated according to the health status of the pregnant woman. The phone sends a mail and SMS to medical staff in critical and very critical.

The phone takes into the Biofeedback: that can help to improve the woman's health during pregnancy. Through this layer, the phone has the possibility to generate audio messages in anomaly situations to alert the pregnant woman.

4.3 F4PW-T3

For providing high-availability and improving data accessibility we set up multiple serversN connected to the cloud DC. Therefore, even when a serverN fails, the other serversN continue working and hence the failure has no major consequences. These servers ensure the role of permanent storage and in-depth analysis of all global data. They are accessible to medical staff in charge of patient follow-up. For accessing to serverN, the medical staff uses the same scenario described in F4PW-T2.

We have the same database in all serversN and Cloud DC to ensure data conformity. For this, F4PW uses automatic replication data between databases. The DC is the central element for the automatic replication.

We have a master slave relation between the DC and each ServerN. As shown in the following figure; any change operating in a ServerN is automatically duplicated on to the Cloud DC and after the change is instantly applied from the cloud DC to others serversN (Fig. 3).

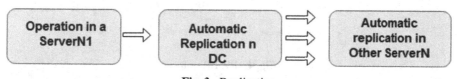

Fig. 3. Replication

Thus, the staff medical handle the same information regardless the serverN they are connected to.

5 Performance Evaluation

In this section, the experimental performance of F4PW is evaluated. To demonstrate the efficiency of F4PW, we have deployed 4 ServerN in dispersed geographical locations. We have also 4 persons distributed geographically as follows:

- PW1 is living in the same geographical area than ServerN1
- PW2 is living in the same geographical area than ServerN2
- PW3 is living in the same geographical area than ServerN3
- PW4 does not live in any of these areas

The following table gives the distance between the ServerN (Table 2).

After several sequences made by each person residing in these different areas, the following results (latency + local processing time), are obtained (Fig. 4, 5, 6 and 7).

Table 2. Distance between ServerN

	ServerN1	ServerN2	ServerN3	ServerN4
PW1	near	53,28 km	230 km	4088 km
PW2	53,28 km	near	260 km	4094 km
PW3	230 km	260 km	near	4285 km
PW4	107 km	54,22 km	274 km	4124 km

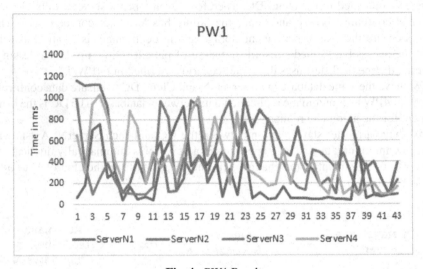

Fig. 4. PW1 Result

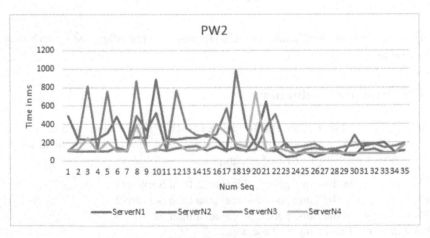

Fig. 5. PW2 Result

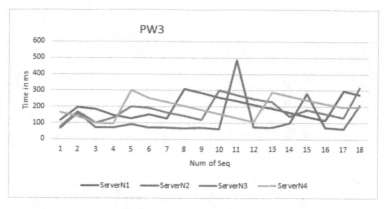

Fig. 6. PW3 Result

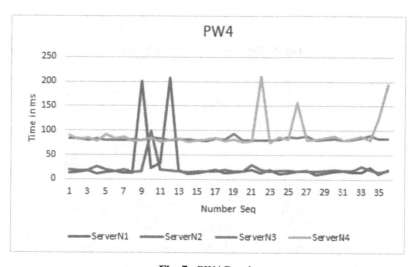

Fig. 7. PW4 Result

An in-depth analysis of these figures confirms that a geographically remote ServerN can offer higher performance than a near ServerN. Hence the importance of determining for each ServerN the B value before each measurement to allow the phone to check on which server it should send the measured data.

The following figures give for each PW the percentage of use per server. If we take the PW3 example, for all his sequences the serverN associated with its area never provided the best performance, which is why he used the other serversN for transmitting data (Fig. 8, 9, 10 and 11).

Through the results, we can see that PW4 which lives in the capital obtains the lowest delta values compared to the others which obtain higher values. These values confirm the significant gap in household connectivity between large cities and rural areas. Thus pregnant women residing in remote areas should not be left out. To address

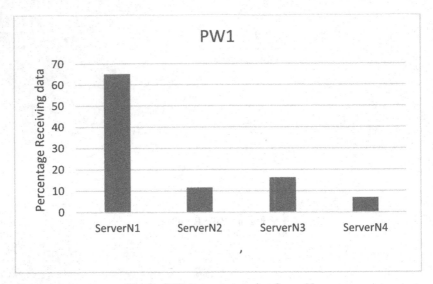

Fig. 8. PW1 Percentage using ServerN

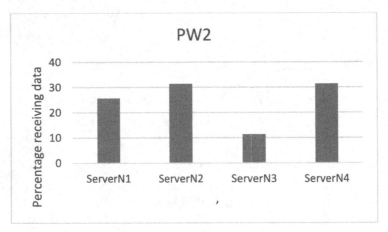

Fig. 9. PW2 Percentage using ServerN

these disparities, F4PW provides a solution which minimizes the time needed to send the data of these pregnant women to the cloud.

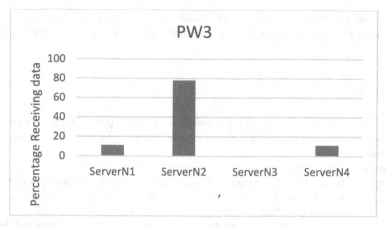

Fig. 10. PW3 Percentage using ServerN

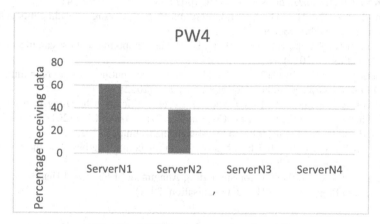

Fig. 11. PW4 Percentage using ServerN

6 Conclusion

The use of Fog Computing in IoT can improve our quality of life especially in healthcare and particularly for pregnant women. In this paper, we proposed a new architecture called F4PW inspired from Fog Computing. The purpose of F4PW is to provide better care for pregnant women especially those residing in rural areas and help achieve health equity. F4PW provides accurate real-time data and facilitates remote monitoring for pregnant women. Low latency is required in healthcare. F4PW provides functionality for quickly processing, analyzing and transmission of data collected from biosensors. The results obtained through our simulation prove that F4PW provides very minimal latency whatever the geographical position of the pregnant woman as well as the medical staff.

The results obtained through our proposal are satisfactory and open many research perspectives. For improvement, we plan in our future work to have a cluster at the third level.

References

1. Yi, S., Li, C., Li, Q.: A survey of fog computing: concepts, applications and issues
2. Pushpan, S., Velusamy, B.: Fuzzy-based dynamic time slot allocation for wireless body area networks (2019)
3. https://www.who.int/news-room/fact-sheets/detail/maternal-mortality
4. Pareek, K., Tiwari, P.K., Bhatnagar, V.: Fog computing in healthcare: a review (2020)
5. Yang, M., Chen, X., Tan, L., Lan, X., Luo, Y.: Listen carefully to experts when you classify data: a generic data classification ontology encoded from regulations (2022)
6. Lee, Y.-H., Lin, F.J.: Enabling IoT/M2M System Scalability with Fog Computing. In: Li, B., Zheng, J., Fang, Y., Yang, M., Yan, Z. (eds.) IoTaaS 2019. LNICSSITE, vol. 316, pp. 489–502. Springer, Cham (2020). https://doi.org/10.1007/978-3-030-44751-9_41
7. Chen, Z., Xiao, N., Han, D.: A multilevel mobile fog computing offloading model based on UAV-assisted and heterogeneous network (2020)
8. Sheltami, T.R., Shahra, E.Q., Shakshuki, E.M.: Fog computing: data streaming services for mobile end-users (2018)
9. Al Masarweh, M., Alwada'n, T., Afandi, W.: Fog computing, cloud computing and IoT environment: advanced broker management system (2022)
10. Dadmehr, R., Nickray, M.: Low-latency and energy-efficient scheduling in fog-based IoT applications. Turkish J. Electr. Eng. Comput. Sci. **27**(2), 1406–1427 (2019)
11. Singh, P., et al.: A fog-cluster based load-balancing technique (2022)
12. Aladwani, T.: Scheduling IoT healthcare tasks in fog computing based on their importance. Procedia Comput. Sci. (2019)
13. Health Workforce Thresholds for Supporting Attainment of Universal Health Coverage. In: The African Region: World Health Organisation (2021)

Author Index

A

Adewale, M. D.   131
Aggrey, E. M.   131
Alunge, Rogers   313
Anne, Sada   151
Awodele, O.   131
Azeta, A.   131

B

Bagre, Aminata   337
Bassioni, Ghada   173
Bassolé, Didier   15
Bekaroo, Girish   3, 33, 66
Bikienga, Moustapha   337
Bini, Kouadio Kra Norbert   205
Boukar, Moussa Mahamat   161
Butgereit, Laurie   278

D

Densmore, Melissa   355
Dieye, Bounama   187
Dimitri Ouattara, Jean Serge   15
Diop, Alassane   391
Diouf, Mamadou Diallo   379
Drummond, Tristan   355

E

Ebem, D. U.   131
El-Shahat, Fathy   173
Faye, Babacar   187

G

Gaye, Amadou Thierno   187
Gueye, Amadou Dahirou   151
Gueye, Assane   391
Gueye, Omar   379

I

Iitumba, Ndinelao   355

J

Johnson, David   355

K

Kane, Cheikhou   218
Kiélem, Wilfried Albert Duniwangda   379
Kissoon, Harshad   3
Kouakou, Malanno   205
Kouamé, Appoh   205

L

Lallmahomed, Muhammad Z. I.   251, 264

M

Madzena, Mapule   355
Mahamat, Assia Aboubakar   161
Malo, Sadouanouan   205
Martinus, Herman   278
Mbacké, Maryam Khadim   218
Mbaye, Djibril   379
Mbaye, Mamadou Lamine   187
Mbengue, Malick   218
Mostafa, Manar   173
Mthoko, Hafeni   355
Muhammed, U. I.   131

N

Nana, Sidwendluian Romaric   15
Niang, Ibrahima   391

O

Ochou, Ochou Germain   205
Oju, J.   131
Okechalu, E. A.   131
Olaegbe, Adesola Tolulope   251
Olayanju, K. A.   131
Oluyide, O. P.   131
Otu, G. A.   131
Owolabi, A. F.   131

Published by Springer Nature Switzerland AG 2024. All Rights Reserved
A. Seeam et al. (Eds.): InterSol 2023, LNICST 541, pp. 403–404, 2024.
https://doi.org/10.1007/978-3-031-51849-2

R
Rago, Deepesh   113
Ramhith, Rakshay Verma   264
Ramsurrun, Visham   48, 81, 99, 113
Riede, Moritz   173

S
Sadien, Yash Krishna   33
Seeam, Amar   48, 81, 99, 113, 233, 290
Seeam, Preetila   290
Seetamonee, Thejmeela   66
Sene, Amy   391
Sharma, Mrinal   81, 99, 113
Sié, Oumarou   15
Soochit, Sarvesh Yugesh   99

Sy, Aby   218

T
Tehia, Kouaho N'Guessan Narcisse   205
Tiendrebeogo, Telesphore   337

U
Ubadike, O. C.   131

V
Veerabudren, Karel   81, 99, 113
Veerapen, Pierre Clarel   48

W
White, Keegan   355

Printed in the United States
by Baker & Taylor Publisher Services

Printed in the United States
by Baker & Taylor Publisher Services